THE PICKERING MASTERS

THE WORKS OF DANIEL DEFOE

General Editors:
W. R. Owens and P. N. Furbank

THE NOVELS OF DANIEL DEFOE

THE NOVELS OF DANIEL DEFOE

General Editors: W. R. Owens and P. N. Furbank

Volume 8:

THE HISTORY AND REMARKABLE LIFE OF THE TRULY HONOURABLE COL. JACQUE (1723)

Edited by
Maurice Hindle

LONDON
PICKERING & CHATTO
2009

Published by Pickering & Chatto (Publishers) Limited
21 Bloomsbury Way, London, WCIA 2TH

Old Post Road, Brookfield, Vermont 05036, USA
www.pickeringchatto.com

BRITISH LIBRARY CATALOGUING IN PUBLICATION DATA

Defoe, Daniel, 1661?–1731
The novels of Daniel Defoe
Part 2, vols. 6–10. – (The works of Daniel Defoe) (The Pickering masters)
1. Defoe, Daniel, 1661?–1731 – Criticism and interpretation 2. Adventure stories, English 3. Adventure stories, English – History and criticism
I. Title II. Owens, W. R. III. Furbank, Philip Nicholas
823.5[F]

ISBN-13: 9781851967537

This publication is printed on acid-free paper that conforms to the American
National Standard for the Permanence of Paper for Printed Library Materials

Typeset by P&C

Printed in Great Britain at the University Press, Cambridge

CONTENTS

INTRODUCTION

Published in late December 1722, the same year that *Moll Flanders* appeared, *Col. Jacque* could in many ways appear to offer the male version of Moll's story, since the two picaresque narratives share a number of features. Both protagonists are born orphaned bastards who become preoccupied with aspirations to gentility, but are embroiled in crime until the providential placing of them on Virginian tobacco plantations sets them on the road to moral reform and prosperity through trade, and settled marriages are finally attained. The prefaces to each work also enjoin us to read them as personal histories of characters whose repentance of their wicked thieving ways should teach us valuable lessons – even if most readers can hardly fail to notice that Moll and Jack end up being far from devout Christian converts. Yet closer inspection shows that the differences between the books and their design and execution are as great as their similarities. *Col. Jacque* certainly has more serious intentions than its exorbitant title-page – seemingly trailing a picaresque frolic in the *Moll Flanders* mould – would seem to suggest.[1]

It may be a way of beginning a discussion of Defoe's novel to ask ourselves why it bears the semi-Frenchified title *Col. Jacque*. The nice story of the naming of the nurse's three orphan boys as 'Captain Jack' (i.e. her own son), 'Major Jack' (the aristocratic love-child) and 'Colonel Jack' (our hero), and of their acrimonious jostling for the premier rank, gives us the ostensible reason for the 'Col.' of the title.[2] But matters are in fact not quite so clear-cut. Indeed the hero finds the whole subject of his name bewildering. When asked what his name is he answers, simply, 'Jack'. 'You have some

---

1   It is unlikely that the title-page – for long the province of the market-conscious bookseller by 1722 – was Defoe's own work; see Rodney M. Baine, 'The Evidence from Defoe's Title Pages', *Studies in Bibliography*, 25 (1972), pp. 185–91.

2   *The History and Remarkable Life of the Truly Honourable Col. Jacque*, below, p. 34. Further references are to this edition, and are given in parentheses in the text.

1

other Name besides *Jack*, han't you', asks the kindly gentleman from the custom house. 'Yes', says Jack, 'They call me, *Col. Jack*'. Why is this, asks the gentleman. Because, says the hero, 'They say my Father's Name was *Col.*' When Jack, as a young man, joins the British army as a common soldier, he shows a remarkable aptitude for arms-drill, and this leads the Sergeant to make waggish play with his name or sobriquet. 'They call you Col.', he says, 'and I believe you will be a Col. or you must be some Colonel's Bastard or you would never handle your Arms as you do at once or twice showing' (pp. 58, 110).

Many years pass. Jack, having been carried against his will to Virginia, rises from the status of slave or prisoner to that of a rich merchant, and he decides to revisit England. However, on nearing the mouth of the English Channel the ship he is travelling in is captured by a French privateer, and he is forced to spend a year or so as a prisoner of war in Bordeaux. As a result, he becomes extremely fluent in French. At last, he is officially exchanged with a French prisoner of war, and is able to pursue his way to England. Any notoriety that he had there has largely died down; nevertheless he thinks it a shrewd move to pass himself off as a Frenchman, frequenting the fashionable French (Calvinist) church,[3] talking French as much as possible and employing a French servant. His name, however, is a problem for his French associates. 'Jack' means nothing to them, so they will either call him 'Monsieur Jacque' or 'Colonel Jacques'. 'Jacques' was the correct French spelling, though sense-wise it was the equivalent, rather, of 'James', but both it and 'Jacque' sounded phonetically like 'Jack'. Thus in England he comes generally to be known as 'Colonel Jacque'. He marries disastrously and, having obtained a divorce, he returns to France. It is 1701, the year of the beginning of the War of the Spanish Succession, and he purchases a company in an Irish regiment, fighting for the French. It suits him admirably, and he tells himself he 'had never till now liv'd the Life of a Gentleman' (p. 188). Moreover, to his great satisfaction, he discovers that he is a brave and enterprising soldier. Indeed his gallantry in defence of Cremona, during the 1701 campaign, comes to the ears of Louis XIV, who sends Jack a 'publick Testimony of his accepting my Service' in the shape of a commission as Lieutenant-Colonel (p. 189). Thus Jack's old nurse's fantasy that he 'should be a Colonel' (p. 34) proves to have been prophetic, and he has become, in all literalness, 'Colonel Jack' – in the French army! The novel's title, *Col. Jacque*, is an ironical reflection of this. It is remarkable how much Defoe, who was always fascinated by names and anonymities, has been able to make of the naming of Jack.

3 See note 330, p. 284 below.

On Becoming a Gentleman

A number of writers have seen *Col. Jacque* as an early example of the *Bildungsroman*, or novel of education.[4] Given the stress Defoe always put on education in his writings, there is no reason to doubt the value he attaches to it in *Col. Jacque*. In the preface he projects education as an antidote to the evils of a society where '*so many unhappy Children ... are every Year Bred up for the Gallows*' who might otherwise have been helped to avoid this fate, had a system of improved '*publick Schools, and Charities*' existed to offer them the '*Blessing, and Advantages of a sober and well govern'd Education*' (p. 31). Defoe explains how the '*miserable Condition*' endured by these unhappy children will be '*abundantly seen in the History of this Man's* [i.e. Jack's] *Childhood*', concluding: '*If he had come into the World with the Advantage of Education, and been well instructed how to improve the generous Principles he had in him, what a Man might he not have been*' (p. 31). Defoe also describes how '*though Circumstances form'd him by Necessity to be a Thief, a strange Rectitude of Principles remain'd with him, and made him early abhor the worst Part of his Trade, and at last wholly leave it off*' (p. 31). The 'strange Rectitude of principles' embedded in his personality that checks Jack in his criminal career finds distinct echoes at several places in his memoir. It is particularly noticeable when he tells us at one point that he had a 'strange kind of uninstructed Conscience' (p. 73) tormenting him for the suffering he felt he was causing merchants whose bills of exchange he and his crony Will had stolen from them. To describe Jack's 'principles' and 'uninstructed conscience' as 'strange' is certainly apt up to a point, for the sources of the responses to the world that go to make up our individual personalities can no doubt be complex and obscure, making them hard to identify. However, given the primary importance played by Jack's 'internal censor' in urging him to resist strongly the norms of his criminal environment – such that he comes to feel set apart from the other thieves among whom he grows up but from whom he learns his trade – it is important to establish and explore the spur to Jack's sense of difference, so persistently does this feature of his consciousness keep erupting throughout the narrative.

---

4 Both Maximillian E. Novak, in *Economics and the Fiction of Daniel Defoe* (Berkeley and Los Angeles, California, 1962), and Samuel Holt Monk, in the Introduction to his edition of *Colonel Jack* (London, 1970), note the pattern of upward mobility in Jack's story, stressing how education assists his social and economic advances.

The spur for Jack to feel different from others arises from a deep personal investment in the conviction that he is a 'gentleman'. He reports at the outset of his narrative how the nurse who brought him up had been given careful instructions by Jack's father:

> that if I liv'd to come to any bigness, capable to understand the meaning of it, she should always take care to bid me *remember, that I was a Gentleman*, and this he said was all the Education he would desire of her for me, for he did not doubt, he said, but that sometime or other the very hint would inspire me with Thoughts suitable to my Birth, and that I would certainly act like a Gentleman, if I believed myself to be so. (p. 33)

We are never quite told what schooling Jack has received, apart from his having learned to read and write before he was ten years old (p. 36). But it is clear that he has internalised his father's expectations of him from the moment he learned about them. Statements and events described in the narrative frequently reveal how the belief in his elevated social origins inspired him with 'Thoughts suitable' to his birth, and this belief often triggers reflections that become important in shaping his actions and behaviour. We can in fact discern from the outset of *Col. Jacque* that Defoe is weaving into the novel at least two kinds of narrative thread: a didactic thread pointing towards the value of education, and a more uncertain thread linked to personal motivation and belief. The latter thread is less certain because however motivated and single-minded an individual may be to achieve his or her goals, it will always to a great degree depend on how he or she responds to the unpredictable challenges of historical contingency as to whether his or her advances are successful or not.

This uncertainty is shown early on, for the idea of Jack's father, that 'all the Education he would desire' for him is in the remembering of his gentle birth, avails Jack little when at the age of ten the 'good Woman' his nurse dies, and he and the other two Jacks are 'turn'd loose to the World' on the streets of Stepney (p. 37). Here, although the principal learning activities of 'the three Jacks' are for running errands, begging and picking pockets, narrator Jack, alluding wryly to his gentlemanly status, recalls how 'the Colonel always held talk with the better Sort ... I was always upon the Inquiry, asking Questions of things done in Publick as well as in Private, particularly, I lov'd to talk with Seamen and Soldiers about the War, and about the great Sea-Fights, or Battles on Shore, that any of them had been in' (p. 39). In this way, reports Jack, though still only about fourteen, he became 'a kind of an Historian', and in many ways this fascination with talk, history, ships and warfare (i.e. 'things done in Publick') serves as a kind of a signal planted by Defoe that Jack's later fortunes in the world could involve him in military and other 'Publick' adventures. But, in the meantime, he has to survive as best he can around Stepney and the City under the tutelage of his companion in thievery, Will.[5]

The first substantial criminal exploit that puts money into Jack's hands, when he goes out on a pickpocketing expedition with his 'new Instructor' to 'the Long Room at the Custom-house' (p. 45) in the City's commercial trading district, is an event with repercussions telling us much about the nature of money, and the way that two segments at least of the 1722 London social order deal with it. Entirely ignorant of how the bills of exchange system works at this stage of his criminal career, Jack nevertheless pockets the £5 share of cash Will gives for helping him steal away a letter case of bills, having changed one of the smaller notes for money. Well, he *would* pocket the money if he could, but, as he says, not only have all his pockets got holes in, and without lodging, drawer or box to put his money in, and knowing no one in the world to help store it for him, he is 'full of Care, for what to do to secure my Money I could not tell, and this held me so long, and was so Vexatious to me the next Day, that I truly sat down and cryed' (p. 48). Money, in fact, puts an end to Jack's previously carefree life. The spectacle of the boys' extreme destitution in the opening pages of the novel has almost the quality of an idyll. The young Jack and the other two Jacks, ragged and filthy as they are, live a tranquil existence, fed by their benevolent neighbours and sleeping cosily on the warm ashes of glasshouse factory floors. It is money which causes Jack's expulsion from this Eden, plunging him into fearful anxieties – not least about how to look after his new-found wealth. It is a variant, beautifully conceived, of Crusoe's troubled relationship to money.[6]

After a sleepless night dreading the money will be stolen by his companions lying in the glasshouse ashes, Jack wanders near Bethnal Green and discovers a hole in a tree where he conceals his bundle of riches, only to find the tree is hollow and the bundle drops out of his reach. Having had money, but now finding himself in a friendless world full of holes where nothing can be held on to or contained, Jack is 'in despair, crying, and roaring like a little Boy that had been whip'd' (p. 50). But presently, moving to the other side of the tree, 'behold the Tree had a great open Place in the Side of it close to the Ground [and] to my inexpressible Joy, there lay my Money', so that soon he has 'hug'd and kissed the dirty Ragg a hundred

5   This character is initially called Robin, clearly in error. See p. 54, and note 91, p. 272 below.

6   On this, see Introduction to *The Life and Strange Surprizing Adventures of Robinson Crusoe*, in *The Novels of Daniel Defoe*, Vol. 1, ed. W. R. Owens, pp. 24–6.

times', and 'run from one End of the Field to the other' in celebration (p. 50). The personal drama conveyed in this scene perhaps bears comparison with the one in which Robinson Crusoe finds the single footprint in the sand, so stunning and affecting is its emotional impact on the reader.

Furthermore, as Lars Hartveit has observed, this 'incident could serve as a fable about the transition from a society without to a society with banking facilities'.[7] The transition in effect plays itself out in the long dialogue that takes place between Jack and the man he will later come to call his 'Benefactor, the clerk, at the custom house' (p. 88). Although advancing quickly in the pickpocket's profession, Jack's conscience at the same time presses on him so much that he resolves the large uncashed bills of exchange stolen by Robin and himself must be returned to their rightful owner. Using his 'natural Talent of Talking' (p. 36), Jack tells the clerk at the custom house that he knows the whereabouts of the bills, has prevented them from being burned, and, having also heard there was a reward for their return, has come to tell his story. And Jack tells the story of his life and dilemmas with such art (or guile) that the clerk and his associates are won over with pity for his plight, especially when, crying, he tells how he is afraid 'they' will rob, cheat or kill him for his money:

> *They*, says he, Who? what sort of Gangs of People art thou with?
>
> I told him they were all Boys, but very wicked Boys, Thieves and Pick-Pockets, *said I*, such as stole this Letter Case, a sad Pack, I can't abide 'em.
>
> Well, *Jack*, said he, what shall be done for thee? will you leave it with me, shall I keep it for you?
>
> *Yes*, said I, with all my Heart, if you please. (p. 61)

It is the episode of the hollow tree and the long passage from which the foregoing is extracted that moved Charles Lamb to say that the beginning of *Col. Jacque* 'is the most affecting picture of a young thief that was ever drawn'. For Lamb, these elements, and 'several similar touches on the sad history of the Colonel, evince a deep knowledge of human nature, and putting out of the question the *romantic* interest of the latter, in my mind very much exceeds Robinson Crusoe'.[8] Passages such as these and responses such as Lamb's suggest that *Col. Jacque* should be acknowledged as including, very much ahead of its time, elements of the novel of sentiment. That genre will have its eighteenth-century flowering in the 1760s–80s, but

---

7 See Lars Hartveit, 'A Chequer-work of Formulae: A Reading of Defoe's *Colonel Jack*', *English Studies*, 63 (1982), pp. 122–33 (at p. 129).

8 Charles Lamb, 'Estimate of De Foe's Secondary Novels' (1829), in *The Works of Charles and Mary Lamb*, ed. E. V. Lucas, Vol. 1, *Miscellaneous Prose 1798–1834* (London, 1903), pp. 523, 524.

then be reconceived by the nineteenth-century master of sentimental fiction (as well as of much else, it goes without saying), Charles Dickens.

There are several important points for us to note in Jack's momentous encounter with the custom house clerk, all revolving around money and the various ways in which money can be understood and used. For the segment of society from which Jack has so far gained his experience in Stepney, money is simply a means of satisfying immediate needs: for food, shelter, some basic clothing. But the gentleman clerk's approach to money is quite different from that of Jack's street society. He regards it, indeed, as a means to purchase commodities – items of consumption – but where there is a surplus, to invest it in business or trade ventures, or the bank. All these options for dealing with money are alien to Jack and his street community. But in meeting the clerk who takes a shine to him and is sympathetic to his dilemmas, Jack has been doubly lucky. For this man is someone who not only undertakes to invest Jack's money for him ('I'll give you a Bill for it, and for the Interest of it, and that you may keep it safe enough', p. 61), in doing so he is giving Jack access to – even if he has yet to discover it – the world of banking and trade. In his becoming befriended by the clerk, it is of great consequence that Jack has achieved a valuable *social* point of access to the powerful order of gentlemen to which he aspires, the new friend who retains his bill of exchange being a key gentlemanly link in the network of London's commercial traders.

It is six years later before Jack, now aged twenty, next meets the clerk. He again seeks to use his 'benefactor' as a banking facility to invest money (gained once more from restoring stolen bills to their owner) prior to his leaving London for Scotland with Captain Jack. In these remaining London years, during which he grows into manhood and has only Will, his 'Master and Tutor in Wickedness' (p. 92), to guide him, Jack lives in an uneasy tension between pursuing criminal activities and feeling conscience-stricken for carrying them out. The most striking example of the way this conscience pierces Jack's essentially kind heart is when he is egged on by Will to rob a nurse and maidservant of their money while these women are walking home to Kentish Town. Such is the effect on his conscience of stealing from people who were already obviously poor, that it comes into his 'Head with a double force, that this was the High Road to the Devil, and that certainly this was not the Life of a Gentleman!' (p. 81). He is already aware that Will's understanding of the word 'gentleman' is 'nothing more or less than a Gentleman Thief, a Villain of a higher Degree than a Pick-pocket'; whereas Jack feels that 'my Gentleman that I had my Eye upon, was another thing quite, tho' I cou'd not really tell how to describe it neither' (p. 78). The matter is forced to an interim resolution both for

Jack's mental dilemmas and for the advance of his moral education when he visits Will in Newgate, since his companion in crime has finally been taken for robbery and murder, and is awaiting execution: 'He said a great many things to warn me of following the steps he had led me; I was far out Jack, said he, when I told you to be a notorious Thief, was to live like a Gentleman' (p. 92). Since Captain Jack had also been involved in the robbery for which Will is to be hanged, he and Jack now decide to travel to Scotland to escape the law, and start a new life. However, before leaving, Jack decides he must 'go to Kentish-Town, and do justice to the poor old Nurse' he had robbed, by returning her money: 'my Heart had reproach'd me many a time with that cruel Action', he confesses to us (p. 94). In his poverty-stricken childhood and youth, as Defoe's preface has stated, Jack's '*Circumstances form'd him by Necessity to be a Thief*' (p. 31). But as Maximillian E. Novak has observed in his valuable essay on the morally complex area of 'necessity' in Defoe's work, Defoe also 'counselled restitution after the dangers of necessity were passed, and Jack feels it is his duty to right the wrong he has committed'.[9]

Jack is therefore now resolved – a word we find him using frequently, since personal 'resolution' is so often needed to help him negotiate his uneasy existence – 'to leave off the wicked Course I was in' (p. 94). He has managed to put thieving well behind him when, some two years later, he becomes a soldier along with Captain Jack in Scotland. Finding he has 'a secret Satisfaction at being now under no Necessity of stealing ... it was an inexpressible ease to my Mind, that I was now in a certain way of Living which was honest, and which I could say, was not unbecoming a Gentleman' (p. 110). So naturally does he take to the military life, that when he learns he is to be shipped out to join his regiment at Flanders, and realises he can avoid this potentially uncomfortable outcome by cashing in his £94 bill in London to buy colours in a new regiment, this idea 'whetted [his] Ambition,' and he 'Dream't of nothing but being a Gentleman Officer, as well as a Gentleman Soldier' (p. 111). Unfortunately, his ambition is destined to remain a dream for a good while longer, when he discovers that the captain of the ship supposedly taking him to London has kidnapped him and his comrades, and is conveying them instead to the Virginia plantations in America to be sold as slaves.

---

9   Maximillian E. Novak, 'The Problem of Necessity in Defoe's Fiction', *Philological Quarterly*, 40 (1961), pp. 513–24 (at p. 520).

From Slavery to Success

At its beginning, this phase of Jack's story seems to show a young man deprived of all opportunity to advance himself in the world. Yet his being taken to America will not only enable him and his irrepressible ingenuity to gain a professional career and some book learning, but his experiences here will also set him on his way to 'acquiring a series of roles in the rest of the book which marks him as the most versatile of all Defoe's narrators'.[10] Sold to a plantation owner for whom he will work out five years of servitude, Jack finds himself trying to make sense of his situation, his conclusion being that he has been 'brought into this miserable Condition of a Slave by some strange directing Power, as a Punishment for the Wickedness of my younger Years' (p. 121). But even if Defoe is hinting that some kind of retribution may be at hand for Jack under his new master – like the Kentish Town woman Jack had so cruelly robbed, he is named Smith – the anxiety does not last long either for Jack or the reader. This is because we are soon made aware of how the unequal power relationship operating between the plantation owner and his servants and slaves has the potential of bestowing rewards on them – and more – should they perform in a satisfactory way as indentured workers. As we shall see, the 'and more' mentioned here is presently to be developed by Jack into what he calls the 'Principle of Gratitude', an approach to people-management which will eventually improve the management relations and economic output of his master's plantations almost to a revolutionary extent. The seeds of the idea seem to be sown in Jack's mind when, after being a year on the plantation, he becomes 'exceedingly mov'd' when hearing the life story told to Mr Smith by a newly arrived transported felon. The career of this teenage pickpocket parallels his own so closely that after the master's careful and close questioning of the boy about his criminal activities, Jack feels 'sure my Master was some extraordinary Man, and that he knew all things that ever I had done in my Life' (p. 123). Jack's admiration intensifies to awe when, instead of using the discovery of this new young slave's life of continuous crime as an excuse to punish him further, Mr Smith *pardons* him, offering him a 'second chance' to start life anew on his plantation.

When his master notices Jack's emotional identification with the other boy's story and calls on him to give an explanation for his tears, Jack is clever enough in the long private dialogue with him that ensues to turn his sorrowful tale – 'the hardest, and most unjust thing that ever came before

---

10   John Richetti, *Defoe's Narratives: Situations and Structures* (Oxford, 1975), p. 166.

you', he tells him (p. 124) – to his own account, being careful to mention that he is the owner of a bill of exchange for £94. Hearing this from the young ragged labourer standing before him whom he knows only as 'Colonel', this story arouses Mr Smith's curiosity and interest so much that, like the custom house clerk before him, he is charmed into a willingness to assist the young man of promise. For, unlike the other slaves and servants, Jack seems also here to have been singled out for consideration by Mr Smith for his 'have' rather than 'have-not' status; and Jack knows this, clearly perceiving that as a man of power and influence, his master will be impressed by his material wealth. Before he knows it, therefore, Jack has been promoted to the rank of overseer and, needing to be suitably clothed for the job, is told by the keeper of the clothing warehouse to 'go in there a Slave, and come out a Gentleman'. Offered such an invitation, it is hardly surprising that we read how he now 'began to hope for something better than ordinary' (p. 127). The fulfilment of this hope comes with his response to the increasing difficulties he faces as overseer in dealing effectively with what the text conveys as the 'Brutallity, and obstinate temper of the Negroes, who cannot be mannag'd by Kindness, and Courtisy, but must be rul'd with a Rod of Iron' (p. 128). Dismayed that his kindly temperament will not allow him to wield such a rod, and hating the physical cruelty of flogging, Jack reaches a crisis point and, when his failure to manage the men successfully results in 'Disorder', this is reported to Mr Smith. However, Jack's unease at the situation does not last long. With a history of social circumstances that have frequently put his powers of survival and inventiveness to the severest of tests, Jack finds he is now able to weigh up carefully such circumstances and turn them both to the economic advantage of the plantation, and to his own advancement.

What dawns on Jack is that the awesome respect and gratitude he came to feel for his own strict but humane master, who has helped set him on the road from slavery to success, could be a means whereby the African slaves might be humanely managed too. He has already noticed that the overseers 'did not take the best Course with them, to make them sensible, either of Mercy, or punishment; and it was Evident to me, that even the worst of those tempers might be brought to a Compliance, without the Lash, or at least without so much of it, as they generally Inflicted' (p. 128). It is at this point, when he has been summoned to explain himself to his master for his poor managerial performance that Jack, through clever forward planning, demonstrates how he has confidently and imaginatively manipulated the situation in order to create the productive opportunity he needs to win over Mr Smith to his new social-psychological ideas of people-management. During a long debate with his master that reveals as much about his powers of persuasion as it does his genius for social engineering, Jack has a quick answer to the objection that 'these Fellows have no Sense of Gratitude', when he says that this is because they are 'never Pardon'd', clinching his point with the rhetorical observation that, 'if they Offend they never know what Mercy is, so what then have they to be Grateful for?' (p. 133). He now spells out in detail how he has successfully tried and tested his 'Principle of Gratitude' upon the recalcitrant slave Mouchat, gaining his utter loyalty and faithfulness in the process, and being able to boast further how other overseers have succeeded in the same way with like offenders:

> Namely, first to put them into the utmost Horror and Apprehensions of the Cruelest Punishment that they had ever heard of, and thereby enhaunce the Value of their Pardon, which was to come as from your self, but not without our great Intercession: Then I was to argue with them, and Work upon their Reason, to make the Mercy that was Shew'd them sink deep into their Minds, and give lasting Impressions; explain the Meaning of Gratitude to them, and the Nature of an Obligation, and the like, as I had done with *Mouchat.* (p. 140)

The reader cannot help feeling that this is a morally very dubious form of trickery. However, it seems that Jack regards the plantation workers much in the same way as he regards himself, as a feeling, reasonable human being with interests to preserve and ambitions to fulfil. So that even when occasionally he comes across an unyielding, resentful servant, 'by talking to them in a plain Reasoning way, I found the Temper of the Roughest of them, would break and soften; the Sense of their own Interest would prevail with them first, or last' (p. 152). No doubt as an inquisitive, thoughtful and adventurous man who sees the value of talk and discussion, and is very good at both, he is able to recognise these qualities in others. To the extent that a character can be represented as championing equality of opportunity in 1722, Defoe seems (in part at least) here to be attempting that representation in the person of Jack. His master, Mr Smith, is impressed by this new approach too, though not without at first being sceptical, wondering how such a system could work, since (he tells Jack) 'you see 'tis against the receiv'd Notion of the whole Country'. Utterly unperturbed by the objection, Jack's answer is a simple one: 'There are it may be Publick and National Mistakes and Errors in Conduct, and this is One' (p. 133).

Richetti regards (what he calls) the 'slave management incident' in *Col. Jacque* as the 'high point' of Jack's career.[11] It is true that Jack himself is

---

11 Richetti, *Defoe's Narratives*, p. 170.

proud to be able to assert that 'the plantations in Maryland' were subsequently 'the better for this Undertaking' – the innovatory 'undertaking' of having Negro workers being 'reason'd into things as well as other people' – and claims that such plantations 'are to this Day less Cruel and Barbarous to their Negroes, than they are in Barbados, and Jamaica' (p. 144). It has been said that one of the 'characteristics of Virginia throughout its history as a slave-employing territory' was the 'relatively benign treatment offered by tobacco planters'.[12] Certainly, that Jack's people-management methods are efficacious both in moral and economic terms[13] comes as a blessing that is more than sufficient for his kindly master, who, in giving him his liberty two years before it is due, and setting him up with his own plantation and house, ensures that Jack has now the possibility of becoming a prosperous and contented planter and merchant in his own right.

Having attained a kind of plateau of success in Virginia, it is significant that Jack self-consciously sees himself as having gone through a series of 'progressive' stages in his life up to this point, this being made clear by the reflection:

> thus I was Set up in the World, and in Short, removed by the degrees that you have heard from a Pick-pocket, to a Kidnapp'd miserable Slave in Virginia; (for Maryland, is Virginia,[14] speaking of them at a distance,) then from a Slave to a Head Officer, and Overseer of Slaves, and from thence to a Master Planter. (p. 146)

We might be reading an interlude of reflection in one of Dickens's first-person autobiographical novels. And the reflections deepen. Jack's London merchant (the clerk) having transformed at Mr Smith's request his £94 into tradeable goods and sent these to him by boat, but the ship and cargo then being lost at sea, Jack becomes even more indebted to his master, who without hesitation makes good the loss by loaning him the money that he says can be repaid through the payments he will in time receive through continuing to manage his patron's plantation. Further deliberation makes Jack glad that his goods have been lost at sea: since they were 'ill gotten Goods' he has merely 'lost what I had stolen' (p. 150), revealing how he has

12 Hugh Thomas, *The Slave Trade: The History of the Atlantic Slave Trade, 1440–1870* (London and Basingstoke, 1997), p. 207.

13 On this point, Maximillian Novak has said that 'not only is Jack's kindness an economic expedient, but it is in these terms that it must be measured', and given Defoe's sustained prioritising of the values and practice of trade in establishing a sound basis for social progress, this seems right. See Novak, *Economics and the Fiction of Daniel Defoe*, p. 91.

14 Maryland was commonly referred to as 'Eastern Virginia' on seventeenth-century maps.

progressed morally as well as in terms of social and economic status. The realisation that his life has changed for the better, and 'that I cou'd live by my own Endeavours', has in it for Jack 'something more than commonly pleasing and agreeable', and his frankness in declaring that such reflections proceeded not from 'any serious Religious reflections' or from 'the uneasiness of Conscience, but from meer Reasonings with myself' (p. 150) shows him to be a far more complexly developed and *secularly* thinking character than any of Defoe's previous first-person narrators, from Crusoe to Moll.

During the following twelve years when Jack prospers as a tobacco planter and trader with a London merchant, his 'good Friend and Benefactor' dies, and we receive more evidence that Jack has acquired further sound secular values, hearing how in particular it was Mr Smith's friendship and social sustenance which had mattered more to him than material support over the years:

> I was grown really Rich, considering my first Circumstances that began, as I may say, with nothing: That is to say, I had nothing of stock, but I had a great Beginning, for I had such a Man's Friendship, and Support in my Beginning, that indeed, I needed no other Stock, and if I had had 500*l*. to have begun with, and not the Assistance, Advice, and Countenance of such a Man, I had not been in a better Condition; but he promised to make a Man of me, and so he did ... (p. 151)

At the same time as counting his blessings for having attained to a better life, Jack has yet been thinking of further possibilities, 'that I might still be born for greater things than these' (p. 150). These thoughts become greatly multiplied when, having the leisure time to read, he not only begins to study ancient and modern European histories, but surges forward in his studies and ambitions when he takes on one of the transported felons – 'a clever Fellow' – as his servant, tutor in Latin, and much else. As well as being a Latin scholar, Jack's tutor is a Christian penitent whose efforts to convert his new student to deep religious belief are largely unsuccessful, except for the moment when he tells Jack that the greatest realisation he has had about himself was not concerning his numerous crimes, 'but the Wonders of that merciful Providence, which when it has Mercy in store for a Man, often brings him into the Briars, into Sorrow and Misery for lesser Sins; that Men may be led to see how they are spar'd from the Punishment due to them, for the greater Guilt which they know lies upon them' (p. 156). This seems to fit in well with Jack's 'Principle of Gratitude', whereby mercy is shown at appropriate times to obtain reasonable and loyal behaviour from a servant; the 'manager' in this case taking the place of Providence, and severe punishments for bad behaviour being replaced with an act of clemency that obliges the evil-doer to accept his situation as providing an opportunity to reform. Perhaps Jack's instinctive grasp of this kind of providential mechanism is the reason for his more enthusiastic response when his tutor introduces him to books of history rather than of religious instruction: for he is a man of action who enjoys a life-challenge, and especially the long-term challenge of becoming a gentleman.

By reading histories to him, and, 'where Books were wanting', by giving him 'Ideas of those things which had not been recorded by our modern Histories,' Jack tells us that his tutor raised in him an 'unquenchable thirst ... after seeing something that was doing in the World, and the more because all the World was at that time engag'd more or less, in the great War wherein the French King might be said to be engag'd with, and against all the Powers of Europe' (p. 161). This enthusiasm for learning more about contemporary historical events in Europe is a distinct echo of how he had listened with rapt attention in his London youth to the talk of 'Seamen and Soldiers about the War, and about the great Sea-fights, or Battles on Shore, that any of them had been in' (p. 39). The difference of course is that Jack is now a man of some substance, comfortably off, and with solid prospects of gaining more prosperity. So, promising and prosperous though his current life may be, it is no great surprise to hear that he now looked on himself 'as one Buried alive, in a remote Part of the World, where I could see nothing at all, and hear but a little of what was seen, and that little, not till at least half a Year after it was done ... and in a Word, the old Reproach often came in my way; Namely, that even this was not yet, the Life of a Gentleman' (p. 161).

Jack of course exaggerates somewhat by stating that he saw himself at this time 'as one Buried alive', for he has clearly made great and spirited advances in his life over the years in Virginia. But having created something of a social and economic revolution on the Virginian plantations, he is characteristically keen to move on and become an active player on the stage of history that is in the making in Europe. Spending three years to build up and secure the future prosperity of his plantations and their sustenance by trade, which includes promoting his tutor to oversee these operations, in order that he may pursue his ambitions unhindered, is obviously a sound approach for Jack to take as he makes his plans to escape to new adventures in Europe. It seems that the involvement in European sea fights and land battles played out in his youthful fantasies and his dreams of becoming a gentleman, are nagging at him so much that he wants as a man of action to participate in the *immediacy* of making these fantasies a reality.

14

But in what way precisely does Jack want to become involved in the scene of European history in the making? There is something obtuse and worrying about the way he communicates his plans to us:

> I now began to Frame my Thoughts for a Voyage to England; resolving then to Act as I should see Cause, but with a secret Resolution, to see more of the World, if possible, and realize those things to my Mind, which I had hitherto only entertain'd remote Ideas of, by the helps of Books. (p. 161)

Why a 'secret' resolution to see more of the world? And why do we fear for him when we realise he seems willing only to 'realize' those things to his 'mind', that he had only entertained remote ideas of in books? His resolution to 'see' rather than be a committed participant in the historical world of Europe suggests that he still feels guilt for his criminal past, feeling he cannot be 'open' about his activities. And with the further suggestion that he expects somehow to receive 'mental' confirmation from the world he is about to explore, of his former impressions of that world as previously imagined from books, one may be forgiven for asking the question: Is there not a touch of the Don Quixote about Jack and his ambitions, as expressed? I think so, and I think Defoe may aim to have us realise how vulnerable and complex this extremely self-possessed Col. Jack character is when it comes to testing himself out in historical places. Although he is very frequently the man of action who learns to adapt in a speedily pragmatic way to the events of his life, Jack is also a *secretive* character burdened by the guilt of his early existence, someone who feels compelled to maintain a radical 'apartness' from those events, even as he seems to participate in them. This apartness from events is matched by Jack's need repeatedly to 'play a part' rather than adopt a consistently open and public identity of his own, particularly in the last part of the novel. Moll Flanders had shown herself to be a pragmatically adept mistress of disguise, but in the final third of *Col. Jacque* Defoe has his ambitious hero attain to new and more flamboyant heights of impersonation and self-invention.

Naming and Identity: Military, Marital and Mercantile Adventures

Having prudently shipped off several vessels loaded with tobacco for England instead of risking all his cargo in one boat, Jack finally sets sail himself in an armed ship with similar cargo aboard, encountering his first adventure when, upon entering the English Channel, his ship is attacked and captured by a French privateer. Mortified at not only being taken prisoner on a French ship but also by seeing his own cargo-laden boat moving off to St Malo manned by Frenchmen, he suffers even greater mortification at being told that an English warship has in turn taken it from the French, and carried it to Portsmouth. Jack's French privateer finally arrives in Bordeaux, but not before giving chase to a richly laden English cargo ship returning from Jamaica, which fights bravely to fend off the attackers, but is finally captured and taken to the French port. Such maritime adventures are not only authentic to the period in which the novel is set – a late seventeenth century when, as Novak has observed, there was little distinction on the high seas 'between privateering and piracy'[15] – but they also set the tone for this last and highly eventful third of the novel, which nears its end in a similarly adventurous fashion, though this time it will be Jack's own privateering exploits which provide the thrills and spills, as he greedily indulges in his own illicit maritime trading around the Spanish Caribbean.

In the meantime he becomes extremely active in the way of having both military and marital adventures, but his initial arrival in Europe as a prisoner of the French offers little scope for his native ingenuity to operate in. However, he does manage to escape a ransom payment to secure his freedom through the aid of fellow merchants in touch with his own merchant friend at London, and is able by their intervention and clever dealing by means of a merchant prisoner exchange, to travel a free man with a French passport via Dunkirk to Ghent, in the Spanish Netherlands. This occurs 'just as the Armies were going to take the field' (p. 169), and we sense that Jack has already auspiciously landed on his feet for a while at least, a position secured among the very class of people with whom he feels most at home – the men of trade. The sense of security conveyed continues when at the invitation of an English officer at Ghent he quarters with him in his tent, 'to live as I would, and either carry Arms, or not, as I saw Occasion' (p. 170). Without an army commission obliging him to fight, it is clear that his resolution 'to see more of the World' really does at this point involve for him a mere 'seeing', his indifference to the cause of either side – even that of the English – being palpable:

> The Prince of Orange had been made King of England, and the English Troops were all on his Side, and I heard a great deal of Swearing and Damming for King William among the Soldiers, but as for Fighting, I observ'd the French Beat them several times ... (p. 170)

---

15 Novak, *Economics and the Fiction of Daniel Defoe*, p. 104.

In fact, Jack counts himself lucky that at the time when the English were surrounded and captured, he was by luck 'stroll'd away that Day to see the Country about, for it was my Delight, to see the strong Towns, and observe the Beauty of their Fortifications; and while I Diverted myself thus, I had the happy Deliverance of not being taken by the French for that time' (p. 170).

Back in London, Jack's enquiries reveal that Captain Jack had grown 'an eminent Highway-man' before he 'made his Exit at the Gallows', while in France Major Jack 'grown famous by the name of Anthony ... had the Honour to be broke upon the Wheel at the Greve in Paris' (p. 171). Jack himself has found a safer – and more enduring – route to prosperity than his 'brothers' had. His material wealth is secure too. The shipped Virginian merchandise having been converted into over £1,000 cash (*c.* £100,000 by today's values), and with 'nothing to do now, but to entirely conceal myself' (p. 170), it is unsurprising to hear him proudly report that 'I was now at the height of my good Fortune,' possessing the 'Reputation of a very considerable Merchant' (p. 171). Interestingly, just at the moment he discloses the necessity of his remaining an anonymous presence in the London of his criminal past, he gives a seemingly simple account of how he had acquired the Frenchified name of Colonel Jacque. But there is more to naming, identity and status in this novel than that, just as there is more than meets the eye to Jack's statement that 'I was infinitely fond of having every Body take me for a Frenchman', during the two years he now spends living as a merchant in London (p. 171). This is because all of Jack's single-minded ambitions for social and commercial success seem to be part of what David Blewett has called Defoe's 'larger preoccupation with the ambiguities of identity and disguise, reality and illusion, and with the irony that gentility itself may be a mode of deception'.[16] On the one hand, ever alert to finding ways of fulfilling his ambition to become a gentleman, but on the other, of never knowing quite what a gentleman really *is*, the fact seems to be that Jack's ability to pass 'for a Foreigner, and a Frenchman' (p. 171) is symptomatic of a character trait that periodically emerges quite clearly: his delight in convincingly acting out a role.

The reason for this seems equally clear, and goes back to the fact that Jack was born in ignorance of his real name and origins, his birthright resting on a mere assurance that he 'was a Gentleman,' and that this knowledge would inspire him 'with Thoughts suitable to [his] Birth' that would supposedly lead him to 'certainly *act* like a Gentleman' (p. 33, emphasis added). Jack has been 'acting' with varying degrees of success all

16   David Blewett, *Defoe's Art of Fiction* (Toronto, 1979), p. 94.

his life, but at many stages of it – until he is expertly schooled in the trade of a Virginian planter – his thoughts, choices and actions in society have often been governed by chance, and the stimulation of a largely self-directed imagination. That self-directed imagination will frequently prove to be an unreliable guide to action – and none more so it seems than when it comes to Jack's improvised fantasies of what a gentleman might be. As Defoe himself explained in a later work, unless a 'born Gentleman' (as Jack arguably is) were 'bred up as a gentleman ought to be, that is, educated in learning and manners suitable to his birth', he could not be considered a 'compleat gentleman'.[17] So long as he relies so much on his self-directed imagination to make his moves, and remains deficient in a proper education,[18] Jack's 'quest for gentility', as Blewett observes, is bound to be 'often ironically misdirected'. Furthermore, it is the fact that Jack is 'capable and ambitious, but also naïve and easily deluded', that accounts in the last third of his memoirs for some of these 'later social, marital, and political misadventures'.[19]

Jack's first marital misadventure occurs as he is preening himself on his successful life as a prosperous merchant in London. Yet he is the first to admit that his succumbing to the charms of 'one of the subtilest Women on Earth' – who no doubt had easily learned of Jack's pride-filled 'Reputation of a very considerable Merchant' – was because he had been 'a meer Boy in the Affair of Love' (p. 172). It will be the first in a series of three disastrous marriages with women who cuckold him one and all. The fourth and happy marriage to 'Moggie' (the only wife, perhaps significantly, whom he ever names) will end with her untimely death, and the fifth – also eventually happy besides being the most interesting and enduring – is a remarriage to this first, morally reformed wife. It is when he is forced into a violent confrontation with his first wife's lover that Jack confesses another aspect of his ignorance of what a gentleman really is: 'tho' I had learn'd a great many good things in France to make me look like a Gentleman; I had forgot the main Article, of learning, how to use a sword, a thing so universally practis'd there' (p. 183). Sore not least from the wounds of a brutal attack upon him instigated by his (now divorced) wife's belligerent lover, but also from the damage she has inflicted on his pocket during three years of financial profligacy, Jack decides to cut his losses and move to

---

17   *The Compleat English Gentleman* ([1728–9]), in *Religious and Didactic Writings of Daniel Defoe* (10 vols, London, 2006–7), Vol. 10, ed. W. R. Owens, p. 23.

18   In his Introduction to *The Compleat English Gentleman*, W. R. Owens states that 'education, for Defoe, is above all what makes a gentleman' (ibid., p. 18).

19   Blewett, *Defoe's Art of Fiction*, p. 99.

France, purchasing a company in an Irish regiment. It is 1701, the year of the beginning of the War of the Spanish Succession, so he has now finally taken sides and will fight for the French. Quickly pleased with his new situation, Jack reports how he was now wont to tell himself that 'I was come to what I was Born to, and that I had never till now liv'd the Life of a Gentleman' (p. 188). Furthermore, once entered into the thick of battle in defence of Cremona during the 1701 Italian campaign, he discovers to his great satisfaction that he is a courageous soldier and enterprising leader of men. His gallantry coming to the ears of Louis XIV, Jack says that the French king not only sent him 'a publick Testimony of his accepting my Service', but that he also received by courier 'a commission for Lieutenant Colonel' (p. 189). (In recalling how he had over a period gained the 'Reputation of a good Officer', he more tellingly confides how other 'particular Posts' he had gained, supplied him with something he 'lik'd much better, and that was a good deal of Money' (p. 189). Before long we come to realise that wealth is in reality Jack's ruling passion.) So does this mean that because the fantasy name given him by his nurse in childhood has now turned into a real military title, Jack has attained his goal of becoming a gentleman? Well, perhaps ... except that Jack has won the rank of colonel in the army of a country about to resume war with his own nation, England's traditional arch-enemy, France! That Defoe should have skewed the plot in this direction is no accident, as I will presently show.

Although the series of military exploits and episodes in Italy which Jack now describes shows that he has been involved in real historical events, it has to be admitted that this is the least interesting section of the novel. In the midst of his detailed narrative, Jack interrupts himself to say that he will now 'hasten on to my own History, for I am not writing a Journal of the Wars' (p. 194). Unfortunately, this is exactly how his memoirs are reading to us at this point, and despite his self-interruption, for some pages more Jack persists with a less-than-involving account of Prince Eugene's campaigns. Significantly, it is only when he is badly wounded in battle and in a rash, drunken moment agrees to marry the daughter of an Italian burgher in whose house he recovers – deciding here that he has had enough of fighting, and has 'a secret Design to quit the War' (p. 199) – that our interest in Jack's story revives. This hiatus has the effect of reminding us of why we are normally such avid page-turners of the memoirs of Defoe's first-person fictional protagonists: what we love is their spontaneous willingness to share with us secret and often shocking confidences that emerge from identities adrift from and at odds with the social norm, a process which makes us feel excitingly (and sometimes uncomfortably) party to their own vividly conveyed sense of radical 'apartness'.

Such apartness is shown not only by the difficulties Jack faces in extricating himself from the war, knowing as he does that 'it was counted so Dishonourable a Thing to quit, when the Army was in the Field' (p. 199). It is also demonstrated in the solution he applies to this problem, an impulsive decision to join the Old (Stuart) Pretender in a French-organised invasion of Scotland, merely designed (as Jack recognises) by Louis XIV 'to give the English a Diversion'. In order to join the Jacobite expedition, he tells how he now 'pretended a great Zeal for this service', making use of the fact that he was 'esteemed as a Man of Consideration, and one that must have a considerable Interest in my own Country'. (He passes as a Frenchman.) The truth of course is that even though he was 'very well received by the Chevalier',[20] and had 'a great deal of Honour paid me ... I had no particular attachment to his Person, or to his Cause, nor indeed did I much consider the Cause, of one Side or other' (pp. 199–200). The 'truly honourable Col. Jacque' of the book's title is thus shown by Jack's apolitical pragmatism and duplicity not only to be an ironic fictional device, but also to be in entire contradiction to Jack's opportunistically 'Frenchified' outlook at this point in his history. For as an actor in the Chevalier's expedition to Scotland, he becomes a blatant traitor to his own country, a point he in effect freely confesses by stating that in their escaping the English fleet, which was 'Superior in force to the French', he had also 'escap'd being hang'd' (p. 200).

His dangerous dallying with Jacobitism deepens later on, simultaneously getting Jack into hot water and enabling Defoe to teach important political lessons. But, in the meantime, finding on his return to Paris that his wife has betrayed him, Jack separates from her after fighting a duel with the marquis her lover. Although his first impulse following this second marital disaster is to return to the safe and easy prosperity of Virginia, he decides that 'to go hither ... was to be bury'd a-live', and instead resolves 'to settle somewhere in England, where I might know every Body, and no Body know me'. Canterbury being an established refuge for the French since the time of Elizabeth I, Jack settles there, calling himself 'an English Man, among the French [Mr Charnock]; and a French Man among the English [Monsieur Charnot]; and on that score was the more perfectly concealed'. Here, he says, he therefore 'liv'd perfectly Incog', making 'no particular Acquaintance, so as to be intimate, and yet I knew every Body, and every Body knew me [and] was well enough receiv'd by all Sorts; but

20 Jack, now a part of the Jacobite cause, explains how committed supporters of the Old Pretender called him 'the new King ... tho' more generally he was called, the Chevalier de St. George' (p. 199).

as I meddled with no Bodies business, so no Body meddl'd with mine; I thought I liv'd pretty well' (pp. 299–300).

It is because Jack lives 'pretty well' in Canterbury that he becomes dissatisfied with being alone, and ends up marrying a widow with 'one of the most beautiful faces upon earth' (p. 210). But he is once more doomed to marital failure. His wife succumbs to drink after several years and takes up with another man, forcing Jack to remove the family from a 'Life of Hellish Excess' (p. 214) to a town near Lancaster, but only after he has beaten her seducer to a pulp – Jack now has no fears of entering into a violent confrontation. Eighteen months later she dies, leaving him 'once more a free Man'. As he comments, one might think he had learned by now 'that Matrimony was not appointed to be a state of Felicity to me' (p. 215), but after a year of discontent with no mother for his children, he meets Margaret – whom he comes to call Moggy – and persuades himself he should find what he wanted 'in an innocent Country Wench', in contrast with his previous wives, the 'two Gentlewomen, and one Citizen', who had 'prov'd all three Whores' (p. 217). Jack is indeed lucky this time. For, despite discovering after Moggy's death some years later that she had 'made a Slip in her younger Days' and got pregnant 'by a Gentleman of a great Estate in the Country who promised her Marriage' (p. 219), she makes him very happy, he remembering her fondly as 'an admirable Family Manager' and 'an excellent Wife' (p. 219). An experienced manager himself, he was not only very appreciative of Moggy's talents in this regard, but also tells us he had 'cause to bless the Memory of my Moggy' for having dissuaded him from joining the Jacobites in the battle at Preston, they having come down from Scotland in 1715 to invade England in the hope of restoring the Catholic Stuarts (p. 220).

Jacobitism now becomes an issue again in the novel, but only after Jack, having lost most of his children to smallpox, decides it is time to return to Virginia, where, being absent for what he calls 'a Ramble of four and Twenty years', he is received by his plantation manager and ex-tutor 'with a transport of joy' (p. 221). Although shaken to find that among his three hundred servants there are two or three transported Jacobites with whom he had become associated at Preston, he is even more shocked to discover his first divorced wife among his plantation workers. Hearing her sorrowful story at length, of how her immoral and criminal existence had resulted in transportation, Jack becomes sympathetic to her case, so much so in fact that her refusal to accept his tutor-manager's offer of marriage due to her feeling that she owes her gratitude and loyalty to Jack *alone*, finally convinces him that she is a true penitent. This change of heart in her has the effect of bringing about some significant changes in Jack's own feelings.

For one thing, her change of heart chimes well with his 'Principle of Gratitude', suggesting that she is likely to turn out a good and appreciative wife
to him. Her story and her heartfelt pleas also affect him so much that the
tears run down his face 'almost as fast as they did on hers' (p. 224); he
finally becoming so moved that he resolves to make her his wife again.
(This is another episode showing *Col. Jacque* to have proto novel-of-senti-
ment leanings.) Another factor weighing heavily in her favour for Jack
must also have been the report he had received from his tutor before her
disclosures: 'I have had a very good Account of your Management' (p.
223). But the most radical change to take place in Jack comes when many
more of the Preston Jacobites arrive in his service, his overwhelming fear
now being that he will be recognised and exposed by them as a previous
Jacobite sympathiser, and lose the position and wealthy station in life he
has spent so much time building up. In what is a crucially important narrative move, Defoe has the desperate and previously secretive Jack confess all
to his wife, allowing her to become his life-guide. This marks a complete
reversal of attitude in a hero who hitherto has been left – as Jack says of
himself – 'to choose his own Fortunes, and be guided by his own short
sighted Measures' (p. 230). In other words, for the first time in his life, Jack
is honest and courageous enough to put his trust in the guidance of another
– a woman at that – declaring that he is deeply glad to have done this, for
'a faithful Counsellor is Life from the Dead, gives courage where the Heart
is sinking, and raises the Mind to a proper use of Means ... it was by her
Direction that I took every Step that follow'd for the extricating my self
out of this Labrinth' (p. 234).

True friend to his cause as she now is, his wife assures him that she can
manage to extricate him from his difficulties. Her two-pronged plan of taking him safely away to the hot baths of Antigua to cure the rheumatic gout
he has pretendedly contracted, while a request that King George pardon
Jack for his Jacobite misdemeanours be sent over to England, more than
meets with his approval:

> This was so generous, and so handsome a Declaration of her Fidelity, and so
> great a Token too of the Goodness of her Judgement, in considering of the
> Things which were before her, and of what my present Circumstances called
> for, that from that time forward, I gave my self chearfully up to her Manage-
> ment, without any Hessitation in the least, and in about ten Days
> Preparation, we embark'd in a large Sloop of my own of about Sixty Ton. (p.
> 236)

Regardless of the turns that now take place in Jack's life and adventures as
he sets off for what will finally become for him hair-raising but highly prof-

itable trading ventures in the Spanish Caribbean, it is not to be underestimated how revolutionary the narrative function of this renewed marital relationship is for him, quietly underpinning as it does the remainder of the story. Always willing to learn from experience, but frequently giving himself up to dangerously impulsive life moves, his now being able to rely on a wife whose 'goodness of judgement' is sound suggests that their relationship is to embody some of the key features required of the 'felicitous' marriage, in which – as Defoe himself wrote elsewhere – the couple 'make each the Object of a reciprocal Choice, and fix all the View of their future Felicity in the Possession of the Person so loved'.[21] This is far from the undifferentiating valuation placed on all of Jack's marriages by John Richetti, for whom they are 'merely entangling problems, puzzles for the resourceful self and opportunities for excursions into various social arrangements hitherto unexplored'.[22] These marriages may indeed in general terms have offered Defoe's hero such opportunities. But it is important to notice how substantially different our assessment of this final part of the novel becomes, once we recognise the powerfully positive valuation Jack himself places on his last and radically renewed marriage.

The final fifty pages of Jack's adventures therefore launch him and us into a stirring finale to the novel, which in some ways returns us to the thrills and spills of his youthful criminal exploits on the streets of London; but this time the dangers are maritime and mainly derive from pirates and the forceful policing of their *de facto* trading monopoly in the Caribbean that the Spanish jealously exercise. The first excitement does indeed erupt on a sea journey when the master of Jack's sloop starts to outrun two pirate ships who are in hot pursuit of them, but are finally chased away by an English man-of-war, allowing them and their cargo to arrive safely at Antigua, where it is sold off. The sloop then making several successful trading runs back and forth to Virginia, its luck finally runs out when pirates strip her of cargo, though when the empty sloop arrives back in Antigua Jack is delighted to find a packet of letters from his wife containing the news from England that King George has issued a general free pardon to Jacobite rebels; this shows that the threat of punishment hanging over him as a traitor is now removed. Interestingly, when he elaborates on how he was now 'sincerely given in to the Interest of King George', Jack's explanation parallels the 'Principle of Gratitude' he had himself laid down for the humane

21   Defoe, *Conjugal Lewdness* (1727), in *Religious and Didactic Writings*, Vol. 5, ed. Liz Bellamy, p. 93.

22   John Richetti, 'The Family, Sex, and Marriage in Defoe's *Moll Flanders* and *Roxana*', *Studies in the Literary Imagination*, 15 (1982), pp. 19–35 (at p. 19).

management of slaves, i.e. that 'to those who graciously give us our lives, when it is their Power to take them away; those Lives are a Debt ever after ... for Gratitude is a Debt that never ceases while the Benefit receiv'd remains' (p. 240). Hence it is through the theme of Jacobitism, against which Defoe tirelessly campaigned throughout his writings, that, as Blewett has argued, he 'extends this concept of the "Principle of Gratitude" to the highest power, the king'. Defoe seems to be suggesting that the act of grace of the Hanoverian king should also be seen as 'part of the proper Christian relationship which governs parents and children, master and servants, rulers and subjects'.[23]

But Defoe has not yet finished with Jack or us in the way of adventures. For, although he has Jack vowing that once returned to Virginia, he 'will never to wander any more' (p. 241), during the voyage home a violent storm blows his sloop on to Cuba, where it is seized and taken into Havana, then the largest Spanish port in the Caribbean. Jack, being fluent in Spanish, manages through his native powers of persuasion and flattery to gain enough liberty and privileges to sell his cargo. As ever eloquent in his impersonating deceits, he tells us how he 'fail'd not to talk up the Gallantry and personal Bravery of his Catholic Majesty on all occasions', discovering that 'any thing went down with them, if it did but praise the King of Spain' (p. 242). He is so successful in gaining the provincial governor's confidence that the latter agrees to allow Jack's sloop to return to Virginia. Alert to the dangers of maritime attack, Jack takes the precautionary measures of sending the boat off under Spanish colours and command, and – showing a careful regard for the benefits of gracious dispensation – renaming it the 'Nuestra Segniora de la Val de Grace'. Having ensured it would be 'loaded back' to Havana with trading cargo, on the sloop's arrival Jack is able to buy his freedom with a ransom, and in turn gets on so well with the Spanish traders he carouses all night with on his boat that he agrees to take both them and some trading goods back to their base near Vera Cruz, on the Mexican coast. Jack's greed now starts to get the better of him. Witnessing the huge profits to be made by illegally trading with the Spanish merchants ashore, north of Vera Cruz, he agrees with one of the onshore merchants to return with goods he will trade with him, computing that he will be able to make 400 per cent profit out of the

---

23   Blewett, *Defoe's Art of Fiction*, p. 101. As Blewett observes, Defoe's own *Family Instructor* (1715, 1718) and his *The Great Law of Subordination Consider'd* (1724) are in the seventeenth- and early eighteenth-century traditions of treatises arguing that society should be organised 'on the basis of a system of mutual duties and obligations between pairs of related groups such as these' (ibid., n. 27).

trip. Jack is aware of the danger of being taken by the Spanish while he trades on their coast, but cannot resist the profits to be made. Arming his sloop with twelve guns against pirates and taking with him his wife to pursue what he calls his 'West-India Project', he eventually becomes very rich, clearing in three months 'five and Twenty Thousand Pounds Sterling in ready Money' (p. 255).[24] Despite being warned by a sensible wife against questing for more riches, Jack now starts dreaming of 'nothing but Millions and Hundred of Thousands; so, contrary to all moderate Measures, I push'd on for another Voyage' (p. 255).

Of course, his luck cannot hold. In what becomes his final West Indian trading jaunt, although managing to escape with some trading goods to his Spanish friends ashore, when the sloop is spotted as a foreign privateer standing off the Mexican coast by Spanish customs officials, it is hotly pursued until the master is forced to run it aground at the mouth of the Mississippi river. Jack is now stranded and out of contact with his wife. But he is saved by being able to stay, in some luxury, with his trusted Spanish merchant friend, who passes him off as 'a Merchant come from old Spain' and 'dress'd like a Spaniard of the better sort', he now takes on the persona of 'Don Ferdinand de Villa Moresa' from Old Castile (p. 259). So, occupying yet another disguise, Jack is for the moment content, and full of admiration for the prodigious trade that makes his new Spanish friends so wealthy: for 'certainly no Men in the World live in such splendour, and wallow in such immense Treasures, as the Merchants of this Place' (p. 259). He just cannot resist the thrill of making money, and especially when he can do it by getting his own back on another in an atmosphere of risk and danger, as he has been able to do in the Spanish Caribbean.[25] We are entertained by his exploits, and, as Novak has commented, it might be expected 'from these events that Defoe's audience would have enjoyed an episode concerning an innocent Virginia merchant who succeeded in tricking the Spanish authorities'.[26]

And then in typical fashion – perhaps one might even say rather like some of the protagonists of Defoe's previous novels – Jack goes on to repeat various routine Christian homilies regarding repentance and providence in the final pages of his memoir. But the conclusion of Jack's tale is

24   Equivalent to about £2.5 million today.

25   This is the burden of Jack's comment that he should by his quasi-illegal trading in the Caribbean 'make my full amends of Jack Spaniard [i.e. the Spanish authorities], for all the injuries he had done me' (p. 248).

26   Novak, *Economics and the Fiction of Daniel Defoe*, p. 124.

unlike those of the previous novels, due to its concentrating so vividly on the processes and benefits of trade. Describing how his Spanish friends, unable to transport him home to Virginia, instead arrange for him to travel as a Spanish merchant in a galleon to Cadiz along with all his treasure, from whence he goes on to London, Jack reports how at this juncture in his adventures he writes to his wife in Virginia, and 'in about five Months more, she came over to me, leaving with full satisfaction the Management of all our Affairs in *Virginia*, in the same faithful Hands as before' (p. 265). Jack therefore concludes his story back in London, where he had started out in life on its streets, penniless; he now has wealth, a faithful wife and merchant friends – and all, it seems, being owed to the providential power of trade.

Despite the relative success of Defoe's novel in its own time, a significant degree of dissatisfaction with it has been expressed by some critics, who are inclined to regard its second half as somewhat of a failure. For example, although Ernest Baker sees the first part of *Col. Jacque* as 'a realistic and sympathetic study of manners and social conditions', for him 'the later career of the hero is a series of aimless and insipid adventures'.[27] Then again, despite being the first critic to identify the importance of the theme of gentility in the story, noting how by its deployment Defoe succeeds 'in making an organic whole of the novel', William H. McBurney is unhappy about its second part, which for him 'lacks the sustained interest and straightforward progression of the rise from orphan to wealthy planter' of the first.[28] Even such indefatigable explorers and admirers of Defoe's work as P. N. Furbank and W. R. Owens, arguing persuasively that what distinguishes the 'mode of construction' of much of Defoe's writing is its 'improvisatory character', are severely disappointed when it comes to the novel's last part. While asserting that 'the improvisatory method, where Defoe's inspiration can sustain it, produces very satisfying fictional form', they find that 'when inspiration fails, as it does half-way through *Colonel Jack*, the result is catastrophic'.[29]

These responses do not really do justice to the final third of the novel. To be sure, once Jack leaves Virginia and the remainder of his memoirs recount what I have called his military, marital and mercantile adventures, the narrative shifts somewhat in its settings, its methods and in its con-

---

27   Ernest Baker, *History of the English Novel* (10 vols, New York, 1950), Vol. 3, p. 206.

28   William H. McBurney, '*Colonel Jacque*: Defoe's Definition of the Complete English Gentleman', *Studies in English Literature 1500–1900*, 2 (1962), pp. 321–36 (at p. 331).

29   P. N. Furbank and W. R. Owens, *The Canonisation of Daniel Defoe* (New Haven, Connecticut, and London, 1988), p. 133.

cerns. However, as I have tried to demonstrate, there is a subtle *pattern* underlying the purpose and structure of the last part of *Col. Jacque* that may not be easy to discern at first reading, given the radical swerve in the pace and texture of the writing at this point. A sweeping shift takes place from Jack's intimate involvement with a relatively small range of individuals, to what may seem like miscellaneous adventures involving a multitude of characters, this shift providing startlingly new and frequent changes of circumstance. These changing circumstances present Jack with the need to make more choices more quickly, repeatedly challenging his capacity to cope and advance in a world he has mostly only read and wondered about, and has yet to experience. In other words, this proto-*Bildungsroman*, this many-sided novel of education,[30] continues to test Jack out, but not necessarily in ways that he (or we) may want it to. By definition therefore we are no longer in the world of the first half of the book, sharing Jack's criminal and other adventures in the streets of London, in the north and Scotland, or spending time with him in the relatively unthreatening domains of the Virginia plantation. Rather, we are flung into a world of intense historical contestation between the European nations, in which Jack's part of chronicling his ambitious attempts at soldiering, marriage and trade is matched only perhaps by Defoe's own ambitious attempts to contain so much experience in so few pages.

Yet to a remarkable degree Defoe succeeds. Although in the wider and more threatening cultural arenas of Europe and the Spanish Caribbean of his times Jack faces a bewildering array of dangerous challenges and choices, he somehow comes through, and triumphs. As a soldier he may never be in danger of becoming the 'truly Honourable Col. Jacque' of the novel's title-page, but, as we noted at the outset, he does become a genuine colonel, ironically while serving under England's enemy Louis XIV, and pragmatically pretending for his own ends to join the Catholic Pretender to England's throne. As trader and merchant, Jack succeeds too, though by putting his hero at such risk in order that he may make great sums of money and dream of gaining untold riches, Defoe is also offering a cautionary tale on the dangers of greed.

However, as I have argued, it is in the arena of Jack's final (re)marriage that the threads of Defoe's themes are drawn together into resolution and resonance so effectively – albeit in a quiet and understated fashion. From his childhood, Jack has always paid attention to people who offer him prac-

---

30 Maximillian Novak has noted how 'in one sense *Colonel Jack* is a novel of education, for the hero has a tremendous drive to learn'; *Economics and the Fiction of Daniel Defoe*, pp. 79–80.

tical help or who inspire him to self-reflection, such as the custom house clerk, and Mr Smith the plantation owner, the person whom he says 'made a man' of him. Yet in so many ways it is the penitent first wife he remarries who makes the successful final phase of Jack's memoir possible. Until he comes face to face with the gratitude she so genuinely expresses for the providential eventuality of ending up on his plantation, at his mercy, Jack has never before experienced anyone being so grateful to him in such a profoundly honest way. This encountering of his own 'Principle of Gratitude' in someone whom he had previously loved, offers a living demonstration of how the principle can apply to his own case, in a situation where he feels himself to be vulnerable and in profound danger. The treasonable move of becoming a Jacobite had been a naive one on Jack's part, but by putting himself in the capable hands of his managerially minded and now unconditionally loving wife, not only is a great burden lifted from his life, it is the first time that trust and a true balance of energies has for him been achieved. *Col. Jacque* may be a novel that relies for its dynamism upon its hero's resourceful pursuit of status, wealth and adventure. But it is frequently the feelings of positive sentiment and trust conveyed in the relationships he develops with characters encountered in this pursuit that give the work its human interest and value; and none more so than when it comes to the partnership with the woman who makes the final phase of his story possible.

THE

HISTORY

And REMARKABLE

LIFE

Of the truly Honourable

Col. *JACQUE,*

COMMONLY CALL'D

Col. *JACK,*

WHO WAS

Born a Gentleman, put 'Prentice to a PICK-POCKET, was Six and Twenty Years a THIEF, and then Kidnapp'd to *VIRGINIA.*

Came back a Merchant, was Five times married to Four *Whores*;[a] went into the *Wars*, behav'd bravely, got Preferment, was made Colonel of a Regiment, came over, and fled with the *Chevalier*, is still abroad[b] compleating a Life of Wonders, and resolves to dye a GENERAL.

LONDON:

Printed, and Sold by J. BROTHERTON, at the *Royal-Exchange*; T. PAYNE, near *Stationers-Hall*; W. MEARS, at the *Lamb*, and A. DODD, at the *Peacock* without *Temple-Bar*; W. CHETWOOD, in *Covent-Garden*; J. GRAVES, in St. *James's-Street*; S. CHAPMAN, in *Pall Mall*, and J. STAGG, at *Westminster-Hall*. MDCCXXIII.
Price Six Shillings.

THE

PREFACE.

Sir,

It is so customary to write Prefaces to all Books of this Kind to introduce them with the more Advantage into the World, that I cannot omit it, tho' on that Account, 'tis thought, this Work needs a Preface *less than any that ever went before it; the pleasant and delightful Part speaks for it self; the useful and instructive Part is so large, and capable of so many Improvements,*[1] *that it would imploy a Book, large as it self, to make Improvements suitable to the vast Variety of the Subject.*

Here's Room for just and copious Observations, on the Blessing, and Advantages of a sober and well govern'd Education, and the Ruin of so many Thousands of Youths of all Kinds, in this Nation, for want of it; also how much publick Schools, and Charities[2] *might be improv'd to prevent the Destruction of so many unhappy Children, as, in this Town, are every Year Bred up for the Gallows.*

The miserable Condition of unhappy Children, many of whose natural Tempers are docible,[3] *and would lead them to learn the best Things rather than the worst, is truly deplorable, and is abundantly seen in the History of this Man's Childhood; where, though Circumstances form'd him by Necessity*[4] *to be a Thief, a strange Rectitude of Principles remain'd with him, and made him early abhor the worst Part of his Trade, and at last wholly leave it off: If he had come into the World with the Advantage of Education, and been well instructed how to improve the generous Principles he had in him, what a Man might he not have been.*

The various Turns of his Fortunes in the World, make a delightful Field for the Reader to wander in; a Garden where he may gather wholesome and medicinal Plants, none noxious or poisonous; where he will see Virtue and the Ways of Wisdom, every where applauded, honoured, encouraged, rewarded; Vice and all Kinds of Wickedness attended with Misery, many Kinds of Infelicities, and at last, Sin and Shame going together, the Persons meeting with Reproof and Reproach, and the Crimes with Abhorrence.

Every wicked Reader will here be encouraged to a Change, and it will appear that the best and only good End of a wicked mispent Life is Repentance; that in this, there is Comfort, Peace, and often times Hope, and that the Penitent shall be return'd like the Prodigal,[5] and his latter End be better than his Beginning.[6]

While these Things, and such as these, are the Ends and Designs of the whole Book, I think, I need not say one Word more as an Apology for any part of the rest, no, nor for the whole; if Discouraging every thing that is Evil, and encouraging every thing that is vertuous and good; I say, If these appear to be the whole Scope and Design of the Publishing this Story, no Objection can lye against it, neither is it of the least Moment to enquire whether the Colonel hath told his own Story true or not; If he has made it a History *or a* Parable, *it will be equally useful, and capable of doing Good; and in that it recommends it self without any other* Introduction.

Your

Humble Servant,

The EDITOR.

THE

LIFE

OF

Col. *JACK*, &c.

SEEING my Life has been such a Checquer Work of Nature,[7] and that I am able now to look back upon it from a safer Distance, than is ordinarily the Fate of the Clan to which I once belong'd; I think my History may find a place in the World, as well as some, who I see are every Day read with pleasure, tho' they have in them nothing so Diverting, or Instructing, as I believe mine will appear to be.

MY original may be as high as any Bodies for ought I know, for my Mother kept very good Company, but that part belongs to her Story, more than to mine; all I know of it, is by oral Tradition thus; my Nurse told me my Mother was a Gentlewoman, that my Father was a Man of Quality, and she (my Nurse) had a good piece of Money given her to take me off his Hands, and deliver him and my Mother from the Importunities that usually attend the Misfortune, of having a Child to keep that should not be seen or heard of.

MY Father it seems gave my Nurse something more than was agreed for at my Mother's request, upon her solemn Promise that she would use me well, and let me be put to School, and charg'd her that if I liv'd to come to any bigness, capable to understand the meaning of it, she should always take care to bid me *remember, that I was a Gentleman*, and this he said was all the Education he would desire of her for me, for he did not doubt, he said, but that sometime or other the very hint would inspire me with Thoughts suitable to my Birth, and that I would certainly act like a Gentleman, if I believed myself to be so.

BUT my Dissasters were not directed to end as soon as they began; 'tis very seldom that the Unfortunate are so but for a Day; as the Great rise by degrees of Greatness to the Pitch of Glory, in which they shine, so the Miserable sink to the depth of their Misery by a continu'd Series of Dissaster, and are long in the Tortures and Agonies of their distress'd Circumstances before a Turn of Fortune, if ever such a thing happens to them, gives them a prospect of Deliverance.

MY Nurse was as honest to the Engagement she had enter'd into, as cou'd be expected from one of her Employment, and particularly as honest as her Circumstances would give her leave to be; for she Bred me up very carefully with her own Son, and with another Son of shame[8] *like me*, who she had taken upon the same Terms.

MY Name was *John*, as she told me, but neither she or I, knew any thing of a Sir-name that belong'd to me; so I was left to call myself Mr. Any-thing, what I pleas'd, as Fortune and better Circumstances should give occasion.

IT happen'd that her own Son (*for she had a little Boy of her own, about One Year older than I*) was call'd *John* too, and about two Year after she took another *Son of Shame*, as I call'd it above, to keep as she did me, and his Name was *John* too.

AS we were all *Johns*, we were all *Jacks*, and soon came to be call'd so, for at that Part of the Town, where we had our Breeding, *viz.* near *Goodman's-fields*,[9] the *Johns* are generally call'd *Jack*; but my Nurse, who may be allow'd to distinguish her own Son a little from the rest, would have him call'd Captain, because forsooth he was the eldest.

I WAS provok'd at having this Boy call'd Captain, and I cried and told my Nurse I would be call'd Captain, for she told me I was a Gentleman, and I would be a Captain, that I would: The good Woman to keep the Peace, told me ay, ay, I was a Gentleman, and therefore I should be above a Captain, for I should be a Colonel, and that was a great deal better than a Captain; for my Dear, *says she*, every Tarpawlin[10] if he gets but to be Lieu-tenant of a Press-Smack[11] is call'd Captain, but Colonels are Soldiers, and none but Gentlemen are ever made Colonels; besides, *says she*, I have known Colonels come to be Lords, and Generals, tho they were Bas—ds[12] at first, and therefore you shall be call'd Colonel.

WELL, I was hush'd indeed with this for the present, but not thoroughly pleas'd, till a little while after I heard her tell her own Boy, that I was a Gentleman, and therefore he must call me Colonel, at which her Boy fell a crying, and he would be call'd Colonel; that Part pleas'd me to the Life, that he should cry to be call'd Colonel, for then I was satisfy'd that it was above a Captain: So universally is Ambition seated in the Minds of Men, that not a Beggar-boy but has his share of it.

SO here was Colonel *Jack*, and Captain *Jack*, as for the third Boy, he was only plain *Jack* for some Years after, till he came to Preferment by the Merit of his Birth, as you shall hear in its Place.

WE were hopeful Boy's all Three of us, and promis'd very early by many repeated Circumstances of our Lives, that we would be all Rogues, and yet I cannot say, if what I have heard of my Nurses Character be true, but the honest Woman did what she cou'd to prevent it.

BEFORE I tell you much more of our Story, it would be very proper to give you something of our several Characters, as I have gather'd them up in my Memory, as far back as I can recover things, either of myself, or my Brother *Jacks*, and they shall be Brief and Impartial.

Capt. JACK, was the eldest of us all, by a whole Year, he was a squat, big, strong made Boy, and promis'd to be stout when grown up to be a Man, but not to be tall. His Temper was sly, sullen, reserv'd, malicious, revengeful; and withal, he was brutish, bloody, and cruel in his Disposition; he was as to manners a meer[13] Boor, or Clown, of a Carman[14] like Breed; sharp as a Street bred Boy must be, but ignorant and unteachable from a Child. He had much the Nature of a Bull Dog, bold and desperate, but not generous[15] at all; all the School-Mistresses we went to, could never make him learn, no, not so much as to make him know his Letters; and as if he was born a Thief, he would steal every thing that came near him, even as soon almost as he could Speak; and that, not from his Mother only, but from any Body else, and from us too that were his Brethren and Companions. He was an original Rogue, for he would do the foulest and most villainous Things, even by his own Inclination; he had no Taste or Sense of being Honest, no, not, I say, to his Brother Rogues; which is what other Thieves make a point of Honour of; I mean that of being Honest to one another.

THE other, that is to say, the youngest of us *Johns*, was called Major *Jack*, by the Accident following; the Lady that had deposited him with our Nurse, had own'd to her that it was a Major of the Guards that was the Father of the Child; but that she was obliged to conceal his Name, and that was enough. So he was at first call'd *John* the *Major*, and afterwards the *Major*, and at last, when we came to rove[16] together, Major *Jack*, according to the rest, for his Name was *John*, as I have observ'd already.

Major JACK was a merry, facetious pleasant Boy, had a good share of Wit, especially *Off-hand-Wit*,[17] as they call it; was full of Jests and good Humour, and as I often said, had some thing of a Gentleman in him; he had a true Manly Courage, fear'd nothing, and could look Death in the Face, without any Hesitation; and yet if he had the Advantage, was the most generous and most compassionate Creature alive; he had native Principles of Gallantry in him, without any thing of the brutal or terrible Part that the Captain had, and in a Word, he wanted nothing but Honesty to have made him an excellent Man; he had learned to read as I had done, and as he talk'd very well, so he wrote good Sense, and very handsome Language, as you will see in the process of his Story.

As for your humble Servant, Colonel *Jack*, he was a poor unhappy tractable Dog, willing enough, and capable too, to learn any thing, if he had had any but the Devil for his School-Master: He set out into the World so early, that when he began to do Evil, he understood nothing of the Wickedness of it, nor what he had to expect for it: I remember very well, that when I was once carried before a Justice, for a Theft which indeed I was not guilty of, and defended my self by Argument, proving the Mistakes of my Accusers, and how they contradicted themselves, the Justice told me it was pitty I had not been better employ'd, for I was certainly better taught; in which however his Worship was mistaken, for I had never been taught any thing, but to be a Thief; except, as I said, to read, and write, and that was all, before I was ten Years old: But I had a natural Talent of Talking, and could say as much to the Purpose as most People that had been taught no more than I.

I pass'd among my Comrades for a bold resolute Boy, and one that durst fight any thing; but I had a different Opinion of my self, and therefore shun'd Fighting as much as I could, tho' sometimes, I ventur'd too, and came off well, being very strong made, and nimble withal. However, I many times brought my self off with my Tongue, where my Hands would not have been sufficient; and this as well after I was a Man, as while I was a Boy.

I was Wary and Dextrous at my Trade, and was not so often catch'd as my Fellow Rogues, I mean while I was a Boy, and never, after I came to be a Man, no, not once for 26 Years, being so old in the Trade, and still unhang'd as you shall hear.

As for my Person, while I was a dirty Glass-Bottle House[18] Boy, sleeping in the Ashes, and dealing always in the Street Dirt, it cannot be expected but that I look'd like what I was, and so we did all; that is to say, like a *Black your Shoes your Honour*, a Beggar Boy, a Black-Guard Boy,[19] or what you please, despicable, and miserable, to the last Degree; and yet I remember, the People would say of me, that Boy has a good Face; if he was wash'd, and well dress'd, he would be a good pretty Boy, do but look what Eyes he has, what a pleasant smiling Countenance, 'tis Pitty! I wonder what the Rogues Father and Mother was, and the like; then they would call me, and ask me my Name; and I would tell them my Name was *Jack*. But what's your Sir Name, Sirrah?[20] says they: I don't know says I: Who is your Father and Mother? I have none, said I. What, and never had you any? said they: No, says I, not that I know of: Then they would shake their Heads, and cry, poor Boy! and 'tis a Pitty! *and the like!* and so let me go. But I lay'd up all these things in my Heart.[21]

I WAS almost 10 Year old, the Captain 11, and the Major about 8, when the good Woman my Nurse died; her Husband was a Seaman, and had been drown'd a little before in the *Gloucester* Frigat, one of the King's Ships which was Cast away going to *Scotland* with the Duke of *York*,[22] in the Time of King *Charles* II. and the honest Woman dying very Poor, the Parish was oblig'd to bury her; when the three young *Jacks* attended her Corps, and I the Colonel, for we all pass'd for her own Children, was Chief Mourner, the Captain who was the eldest Son, going back very sick.

THE good Woman being dead, we, the three *Jacks*, were turn'd loose to the World; as to the Parish providing for us, we did not trouble our selves much about that; we rambl'd about all three together, and the People in *Rosemary-Lane*, and *Ratcliff*,[23] and that Way knowing us pretty well, we got Victuals easily enough, and without much Begging.

FOR my particular Part, I got some Reputation for a mighty civil honest Boy; for if I was sent of an Errand, I always did it punctually and carefully, and made haste again; and if I was trusted with any thing, I never touch'd it to diminish it, but made it a Point of Honour to be punctual to whatever was committed to me, tho' I was as Errant[24] a Thief as any of them in all other Cases.

IN like Case, some of the poorer Shop-Keepers, would often leave me at their Door, to look after their Shops, 'till they went up to Dinner, or 'till they went over the Way to an Ale-House, and the like, and I always did it freely and chearfully, and with the utmost Honesty.

Capt. JACK on the contrary, a surly, ill-look'd, rough Boy, had not a Word in his Mouth that savoured either of good Manners, or good Humour; he wou'd say yes, and no, just as he was ask'd a Question, and that was all, but no Body got any thing from him that was obliging in the least; if he was sent of an Errand he would forget half of it, and it may be go to play, if he met any Boys, and never go at all, or if he went never come back with an Answer; which was such a regardless, disobliging Way, that no Body had a good Word for him, and every Body said he had the very look of a Rogue, and would come to be Hang'd: In a Word he got nothing of any Body for good will, but was as it were oblig'd to turn Thief, for the meer Necessity of Bread to eat; for if he beg'd, he did it with so ill a Tone, rather like bidding Folks give him Victuals, than entreating them, that one Man of whom he had something given, and knew him, told him one Day, Capt. *Jack, says he,* thou art but an awkward, ugly sort of a Beggar now thou art a Boy, I doubt thou wilt be fitter to ask a Man for his Purse,[25] than for a Penny, when thou comest to be a Man.

THE Major was a merry Thoughtless Fellow, always Chearful, whether he had any Victuals or no, he never complain'd, and he recommended himself so well by his good Carriage that the Neighbours lov'd him, and he got Victuals enough one where or other: Thus we all made a shift, tho' we were so little, to keep from starving, and as for Lodging, we lay in the Summertime about the Watch-houses, and on Bulk-heads,[26] and Shop-doors, where we were known; as for a Bed we knew nothing what belong'd to it for many Years after my Nurse died, and in Winter we got into the Ash-holes, and Nealing-Arches[27] in the Glass-house, call'd *Dallows*'s Glass-house, near *Rosemary-Lane,* or at another Glass-house in *Ratcliff-high-way.*

IN this manner we liv'd for some Years, and here we fail'd not to fall among a Gang of naked, ragged Rogues like ourselves, wicked as the Devil cou'd desire to have them be, at so early an Age, and Ripe for all the other Parts of Michief that suited them as they advanc'd in Years.

I remember that one cold Winter Night we were disturb'd in our Rest with a Constable, and his Watch, crying out for one *Wry-Neck*, who it seems had done some Roguery, and requir'd a Hue and Cry of that Kind, and the Watch were inform'd he was to be found among the Beggar-boys under the Nealing-Arches in the Glass-house.

THE alarm being given, we were awaken'd in the Dead of the Night with *come out here*, ye Crew of young Devils, come out and show yourselves; so we were all produc'd, some came out rubbing their Eyes, and scratching their Heads, and others were dragg'd out, and I think there was about Seventeen of us in all, but *Wry-Neck*, as they call'd him, was not among them; it seems this was a good big Boy that us'd to be among the Inhabitants of that Place, and had been concern'd in a Robbery the Night before, in which his Comrade who was taken, who in hopes of escaping Punishment had discover'd him, and inform'd where he usually Harbour'd; but he was aware it seems, and had secur'd himself, at least for that time; so we were allow'd to return to our warm Appartment among the Coal-ashes, where I slept many a cold Winter Night: Nay, I may say, many a Winter, as sound, and as comfortably as ever I did since, tho' in better Lodging.

IN this manner of living, we went on a good while, I believe two Year, and neither did, or meant any Harm: We generally went all Three together; for in short, the Captain for want of Address, and for something disagreeable in him, would have starv'd if we had not kept him with us: As we were always together, we were generally known by the Name of the three *Jacks*; but Col. *Jack* had always the preference upon many Accounts; the Major, as I have said, was Merry and Pleasant, but the Colonel always held talk with the better Sort; I mean, the better Sort of those that would Converse with a Beggar-boy: In this way of Talk, I was always upon the

Inquiry, asking Questions of things done in Publick as well as in Private, particularly, I lov'd to talk with Seamen and Soldiers about the War, and about the great Sea-Fights, or Battles on Shore, that any of them had been in; and as I never forgot any thing they told me, I could soon, that is to say, in a few Years give almost as good an Account of the *Dutch* War,[28] and of the Fights at Sea, the Battles in *Flanders*, the taking of *Maestricht*,[29] and the like, as any of those that had been there, and this made those old Soldiers and Tars[30] love to talk with me too, and to tell me all the Stories they could think of, and that not only of the Wars then going on, but also of the Wars in *Oliver's* time, the Death of King *Charles* the first,[31] and the like.

BY this means, as young as I was, I was a kind of an Historian, and tho' I had read no Books, and never had any Books to read, yet I cou'd give a tollerable Account of what had been done, and of what was then a doing in the World, especially in those things that our own People were concern'd in. I knew the Names of every Ship in the Navy, and who commanded them too, and all this before I was 14 Year old, or but very soon after.

Capt. JACK, in this time fell into bad Company, and went away from us, and it was a good while before we ever heard Tale or Tidings of him, till about half Year, I think or there abouts: I understood he was got among a Gang of Kidnappers, as they were then call'd, being a Sort of wicked Fellows that us'd to Spirit Peoples Children away, that is snatch them up in the Dark, and stopping their Mouths, carry them to such Houses where they had Rogues, ready to receive them, and so carry them on Board Ships bound to *Virginia*, and sell them.

THIS was a Trade that horrid *Jack*, for so I call'd him, when we were grown up, was very fit for, especially the violent Part; for if a little Child got into his Clutches he would stop the Breath of it, instead of stopping its Mouth, and never Trouble his Head with the Childs being almost strangl'd, so he did but keep it from making a Noise. There was it seems some Villainous thing done by this Gang about that time, whether a Child was murther'd among them, or a Child otherwise abus'd; but it seems it was a Child of an eminent Citizen, and the Parent some how or other got a Scent of the thing, so that they recover'd their Child, tho' in a sad Condition, and almost kill'd; I was too young, and it was too long ago for me to remember the whole Story, but they were all taken up, and sent to *Newgate*,[32] and Capt. *Jack* among the rest, tho' he was but young, for he was not then much above 13 Year old.

WHAT punishment was inflicted upon the Rogues of that Gang I cannot tell now, but the Captain being but a lad, was order'd to be three times soundly Whipt at *Bridewell*;[33] my Lord Mayor, or the Recorder telling him, it was done in pitty to him, to keep him from the Gallows, not forgetting to tell him that he had a Hanging look, and bid him have a care on that very Account; so remarkable was the Captain's Countenance, even so young, and which he heard of afterwards on many Occasions: When he was in *Bridewell*, I heard of his Misfortune, and the Major and I went to see him, for this was the first News we heard of what became of him.

THE very Day that we went, he was call'd out to be Corrected, *as they call'd it*, according to his Sentence, and as it was order'd to be done soundly, so indeed they were true to the Sentence, for the Alderman, who was the President of *Bridewell*, and who I think they call'd Sir *William Turner*,[34] held preaching to him about how young he was, and what pitty it was such a Youth should come to be hang'd, and a great deal more, how he should take warning by it, and how wicked a thing it was that they should steal away poor innocent Children, and the like; and all this while the Man with a blue Badge on, lash'd him most unmercifully, for he was not to leave off till Sir *William* knock'd with a little Hammer on the Table.

THE poor Captain stamp'd, and danc'd, and roar'd out like a mad Boy; and I must confess, I was frighted almost to Death; for tho' I could not come near enough, being but a poor Boy, to see how he was handled, yet I saw him afterwards, with his Back all wheal'd with the Lashes, and in several Places bloody, and thought I should have died with the Sight of it; but I grew better acquainted with those Things afterwards.

I DID what I could to comfort the poor Captain, when I got Leave to come to him. But the worst was not over with him, for he was to have two more such Whippings before they had done with him; and indeed they scourg'd him so severely, that they made him Sick of the Kidnapping Trade for a great while; but he fell in among them again, and kept among them as long as that Trade lasted, for it ceased in a few Years afterwards.

THE Major, and I, tho' very Young, had sensible Impressions made upon us, for some time, by the severe Usage of the Captain, and it might be very well said we were corrected as well as he, tho' not concerned in the Crime: But it was within the Year, that the Major, a good Condition'd easy Boy, was wheedled a way, by a couple of young Rogues that frequented the Glass-house Appartments, to take a Walk with them, as they were pleased to call it: The Gentlemen were very well match'd, the Major was about 12 Year old, and the oldest of the Two that led him out, was not above fourteen; the business was to go to *Bartholomew* Fair,[35] and the End of going to *Bartholomew* Fair, was in short, to pick Pockets.

THE Major knew nothing of the Trade, and therefore was to do nothing, but they promised him a Share with them for all that, as if he had been as expert as themselves; so away they went. The two dexterous young Rogues manag'd it so well, that by about 8 a Clock at Night, they came back to our dusty Quarters at the Glass-House, and sitting them down in a Corner, they began to share their Spoil, by the Light of the Glass-House Fire: The Major lug'd out the Goods, for as fast as they made any Purchase,[36] they unloaded themselves and gave all to him, that if they had been taken, nothing might be found about them.

IT was a devilish lucky Day to them, the Devil certainly assisting them to find their Prey, that he might draw in a young Gamester, and encourage him to the Undertaking, who had been made backward before, by the Misfortune of the Captain. The List of their Purchase the first Night, was as follows.

I. A white Handkerchief from a Country Wench, as she was staring up at a *Jackpudding*,[37] there was 3*s.* 6*d.* and a Row of Pins, tyed up in one End of it.

II. A colour'd Handkerchief, out of a young Country Fellow's Pocket as he was buying a *China* Orange.[38]

III. A Ribband Purse[39] with 11*s.* 3*d.* and a Silver Thimble in it, out of a young Woman's Pocket, just as a Fellow offer'd to pick her up.

    N.B. She mist her Purse presently, but not seeing the Thief, charg'd the Man with it, that would have pick'd her up, and cry'd out a Pick-Pocket, and he fell into the Hands of the Mobb, but being known in the Street, he got off with great Difficulty.

IV. A Knife and Fork, that a Couple of Boys had just bought, and were going Home with; the young Rogue that took it, got it within the Minute after the Boy had put it in his Pocket.

V. A little Silver Box, with seven Shillings in it, all in small Silver, 1*d.* 2*d.* 3*d.* 4*d.* Peices.

    N.B. This, it seems a Maid pull'd out of her Pocket, to pay at her going into the Booth to see a Show, and the little Rogue got his Hand in and fetch'd it off, just as she put it up again.

VI. Another Silk Handkerchief, out of a Gentleman's Pocket.

VII. Another.

VIII. A Joynted Baby,[40] and a little Looking-Glass stolen off a Toy Seller's Stall, in the Fair.

ALL this Cargo to be brought Home clear in one Afternoon, or Evening rather, and by only two little Rogues, so young, was it must be confess'd, Extraordinary; and the Major was elevated the next Day to a strange Degree.

HE came very early to me, who lay not far from him, and said to me Colonel *Jack*, I want to speak with you. Well, said I, what do you say? Nay, said he, it is Business of Consequence, I cannot talk here, so we walk'd out: As soon as we were come out into a narrow Lane, by the Glass-House, look here, says he, and pulls out his little Hand almost full of Money.

I WAS surpriz'd at the Sight, when he puts it up again, and bringing his Hand out, here says he, you shall have some of it, and gives me a Six-pence, and a Shillings worth of the small Silver Peices. This was very welcome to me, who, as much as I was of a Gentleman, and as much as I thought of myself upon that Account, never had a Shilling of Money together before, in all my Life, not that I could call my own.

I WAS very earnest then to know how he came by this Wealth, for he had for his Share 7*s*. and 6*d*. in Money, the silver Thimble and a silk Hand-kercher,[41] which was in short an Estate to him, that never had, as I said of myself a Shilling together in his Life.

AND what will you do with it now *Jack* said I? I do, *says he*, the first thing I do, I'll go into Rag-Fair,[42] and buy me a pair of Shoes and Stockings, that's right, *says I*, and so will I too; so away we went together, and we bought each of us a pair of Rag-Fair Stockings in the first Place for 5*d*. not 5*d*. a Pair, but 5*d*. together, and good Stockings they were too, much above our wear I assure you.

WE found it more difficult to fit our selves with Shoes, but at last, having look'd a great while before we cou'd find any good enough for us, we found a Shop very well stor'd, and of these we bought two Pair for Sixteen-pence.

WE put them on immediately to our great Comfort, for we had neither of us had any Stockings to our Legs that had any Feet to them for a long time: I found myself so refresh'd with having a Pair of warm Stockings on, and a Pair of dry Shoes; things, I say, which I had not been acquainted with a great while, that I began to call to mind my being a Gentleman; and now I thought it began to come to pass; when we had thus fitted ourselves, I said, harkye Major *Jack*, you and I never had any Money in our Lives before, and we never had a good Dinner in all our Lives; What if we should go somewhere and get some Victuals, I am very hungry?

So, we will then says the Major, I am a hungry too; so we went to a boiling Cook's[43] in *Rosemary-Lane*, where we treated our selves Nobly, and as I thought with my self we began to live like Gentlemen, for we had Three-penny-worth of boil'd Beef, Two-penny-worth of Pudding, a penny Brick, (as they call it, or Loaf) and a whole Pint of strong Beer, which was seven Pence in all.

N.B. WE had each of us a good mess of charming Beef Broth into the Bargain; and which chear'd my Heart wonderfully, all the while we were at Dinner, the Maid and the Boy in the House every time they pass'd by the open Box[44] where we sat at our Dinner, would look in, and cry, Gentlemen Do ye call? and do ye call Gentlemen? I say this was as good to me as all my Dinner.

NOT the best House-keeper in *Stepney* Parish, not my Lord Mayor of *London*, no, not the greatest Man on Earth could be more happy in their own Imagination, and with less mixture of Grief, or Reflexion, than I was at this new Peice of Felicity, tho' mine was but a small Part of it, for Major *Jack* had an Estate Compar'd to me, as I had an Estate compar'd to what I had before: In a Word, nothing but an utter Ignorance of greater Felicity, which was my Case, could make any Body think himself so exalted as I did, tho' I had no share of this Booty but Eighteen-pence.

THAT Night the Major and I triumph'd in our new Enjoyment, and slept with an undisturb'd Repose in the usual Place, surrounded with the warmth of the Glass-house Fires above, which was a full amends for all the Ashes and Cinders which we roll'd in below.

THOSE who know the Position of the Glass-houses, and the Arches where they Neal[45] the Bottles after they are made, know that those Places where the Ashes are Cast, and where the poor Boys lye, are Caveties in the Brick-work, perfectly close, except at the Entrance, and consequently warm as the Dressing-room of a *Bagnio*;[46] that it is impossible they can feel any Cold there, were it in *Greenland*, or *Nova Zembla*,[47] and that therefore the Boys lye not only safe, but very comfortably, the Ashes excepted, which are no Grievance at all to them.

THE next Day the Major and his Comrades went abroad again, and were still Successful; nor did any Disaster attend them, for I know not how many Months, and by frequent imitation and direction, Major *Jack* became as dexterous a Pick-pocket as any of them, and went on thro' a long variety of Fortunes, too long to enter upon now, because I am hastening to my own Story, which at present is the main thing I have to set down.

THE Major fail'd not to let me see every Day the Effects of his new Prosperity, and was so bountiful, as frequently to throw me a Tester,[48] sometimes a Shilling; and I might perceive that he began to have Cloths on his Back to leave the Ash-hole, having gotten a Society Lodging[49] (of which I may give an Explanation by itself on another Occasion) and which was more, he took upon him to wear a Shirt, which was what neither he, or I had ventur'd to do for three Year before and upward.

BUT I observ'd all this while, that tho' Major *Jack* was so Prosperous and had thriven so well, and notwithstanding he was very kind, and even generous to me, in giving me Money upon many Occasions, yet he never invited me to enter myself into the Society, or to embark with him whereby I might have been made as happy as he, no, nor did he recommend the Employment to me at all.

I WAS not very well pleas'd with his being thus reserv'd to me; I had learn'd from him in General, that the Business was Picking of Pockets, and I fancy'd that tho' the Ingenuity of the Trade consisted very much in slight of Hand, a good Address,[50] and being very Nimble, yet that it was not at all difficult to learn; and especially I thought the Opportunities were so many, the Country People that come to *London*, so foolish, so gaping, and so engag'd in looking about them, that it was a Trade with no great hazard annex'd to it, and might be easily learn'd, if I did but know in general the Manner of it, and how they went about it.

THE subtile Devil never absent from his Business, but ready at all Occasions to encourage his Servants, remov'd all these Difficulties, and brought me into an Intimacy with one of the most exquisite Divers, or Pick-pockets in the Town; and this our Intimacy was of no less a Kind, than that, as I had an Inclination to be as wicked as any of them, he was for taking Care that I should not be disappointed.

HE was above the little Fellows, who went about stealing Trifles, and Baubles in *Bartholomew-Fair*, and run the Risque of being Mobb'd for three or four Shillings; his aim was at higher things, even at no less than considerable Sums of Money, and Bills[51] for more.

HE solicited me earnestly to go and take a Walk with him, as above, adding that after he had shown me my Trade a little, he would let me be as wicked as I would, that is, as he express'd it, that after he had made me capable, I should set up for my self if I pleas'd, and he would only wish me good Luck.

ACCORDINGLY as Major *Jack* went with his Gentleman, only to see the manner, and receive the Purchase, and yet come in for a Share; so he told me if he had Success, I should have my Share as much as if I had been Principal;[52] and this he assured me was a Custom of the Trade, in order to encourage young Beginners, and bring them into the Trade with Courage, for that nothing was to be done if a Man had not the Heart of the Lyon.

I hesitated at the matter a great while, objecting the Hazard, and telling the Story of Captain *Jack* my elder Brother, as I might call him: Well, Colonel, says he, I find you are faint Hearted, and to be faint Hearted, is indeed to be unfit for our Trade, for nothing but a bold Heart can go Thro'-Stitch[53] with this Work; but however, as there is nothing for you to do, so there is no Risque for you to run, in these things the first time, if I am taken says he, you having nothing to do in it, they will let you go free, for it shall easily be made appear that whatever I have done, you had no Hand in it.

UPON those perswasions I ventur'd out with him; but I soon found that my new Friend was a Thief of Quality, and a Pick-pocket above the ordinary Rank, and that aim'd higher abundantly than my Brother *Jack*; he was a bigger Boy than I a great deal; for tho' I was now near 15 Year old, I was not big of my Age, and as to the Nature of the thing, I was perfectly a Stranger to it; I knew indeed what at first I did not, for it was a good while before I understood the thing, as an Offence: I look'd on picking Pockets as a kind of Trade, and thought I was to go Apprentice to it; tis true, this was when I was young in the Society, as well as younger in Years, but even now I understood it to be only a thing, for which if we were catch'd, we run the Risque of being Duck'd or Pump'd,[54] which we call'd Soaking, and then all was over; and we made nothing of having our Raggs wetted a little; but I never understood, till a great while after, that the Crime was Capital,[55] and that we might be sent to *Newgate* for it, till a great Fellow, almost a Man, one of our Society was hang'd for it, and then I was terribly frighted, as you shall hear by and by.

WELL, upon the perswasions of this Lad, I walk'd out with him; a poor innocent Boy, and (as I remember my very Thoughts perfectly well) I had no Evil in my Intentions; I had never stolen any thing in my Life, and if a Goldsmith[56] had left me in his Shop with heaps of Money, strew'd all round me, and bad me look after it, I should not have touch'd it, I was so honest; but the subtile Tempter baited his Hook for me, as I was a Child, in a manner suited to my Childishness, for I never took this picking of Pockets to be dishonesty, but as I have said above, I look'd on it as a kind of Trade, that I was to be bred up to, and so I enter'd upon it, till I became harden'd in it beyond the Power of retreating; and thus I was made a Thief involuntarily, and went on a Length that few Boys do, without coming to the common Period[57] of that kind of Life, I mean to the Transport Ship, or the Gallows.

THE first Day I went Abroad with my new Instructor, he carried me directly into the City, and as we went first to the Waterside, he led me into the long Room at the Custom-house;[58] we were but a Couple of ragg'd Boys at best, but I was much the worse, my Leader had a Hat on, a Shirt, and a Neckcloth; as for me, I had neither of the three, nor had I spoil'd my Manners so much as to have a Hat on my Head since my Nurse died, which was now some Years; his Orders to me were to keep always in sight, and near him, but not close to him, nor to take any notice of him at any time till he came to me; and if any hurly burly happen'd, I should by no means know him, or pretend[59] to have any thing to do with him.

I Observ'd my Orders to a tittle; while he peer'd into every Corner, and had his Eye upon every Body, I kept my Eye directly upon him, but went always at a Distance, and on the other Side of the long Room, looking as it were for Pins, and picking them up on the Dust as I cou'd find them, and then sticking them on my Sleeve, where I had at last gotten 40 or 50 good Pins; but still my Eye was upon my Comrade, who I observ'd was very busy among the Crowds of People that stood at the Board, doing business with the Officers, who pass the Entries, and make the Cocquets,[60] &c.

At length he comes over to me, and stooping as if he would take up a Pin close to me, he put something into my Hand and said, put that up,[61] and follow me down Stairs quickly: He did not run, but shuffl'd along a pace thro' the Crowd, and went down not the great Stairs, which we came in at, but a little narrow Stair-Case at the other End of the Long Room; I follow'd, and he found I did, and so went on, not stopping below as I expected, nor speaking one Word to me, till thro' innumerable narrow Passages, Alley's and Dark ways, we were got up into *Fenchurch-street*, and thro' *Billiter lane* into *Leadenhall-street*, and from thence into *Leadenhall-Market*.

It was not a Meat-Market Day so we had room to sit down upon one of the Butcher's Stalls, and he bad me Lug out;[62] what he had given me, was a little Leather Letter Case, with a *French* Almanack stuck in the inside of it, and a great many Papers in it of several kinds.

We look'd them over, and found there was several valuable Bills in it, such as Bills of *Exchange*, and other Notes, things I did not understand; but among the rest was a Goldsmith's Note, *as he call'd it*, of one Sir *Stephen Evans*[63a] for 300*l.* payable to the Bearer, and at Demand, besides this there was another Note, for 12*l.* 10*s.* being a Goldsmith's Bill too, but I forget the Name; there was a Bill or two also written in *French*, which neither of us understood, but which it seems were things of value, being call'd foreign Bills accepted.[64]

The Rogue my Master knew what belong'd to the Goldsmith's Bills well enough, and I observ'd when he read the Bill of Sir *Stephen*, he said this is too big for me to meddle with, but when he came to the Bill for 12*l.* 10*s.* he said to me, *this will do, come hither* Jack; so away he runs to *Lombard-street*,[65] and I after him huddling the other Papers into the Letter Case; as he went along, he enquir'd the Name out[66] immediately, and went directly to the Shop, put on a good grave Countenance, and had the Money paid him without any Stop or Question ask'd; I stood on the other side the Way looking about the Street, as not at all concern'd with any Body that way, but observ'd that when he presented the Bill he pull'd out the Letter Case, as if he had been a Merchant's Boy, acquainted with Business, and had other Bills about him.

THEY paid him the Money in Gold, and he made hast enough in Telling it over, and came away, passing by me, and going into *Three-King-Court*, on the other Side of the way; then we cross'd back into *Clements-Lane*, made the best of our way to *Cole-Harbour*,[67] at the Water-side, and got a Sculler for a Penny to carry us over the Water to St. *Mary Overs* Stairs,[68] where we Landed, and were safe enough.

HERE he turns to me Col. *Jack*, says he, I believe you are a lucky Boy, this is a good Jobb, we'll go away to St. *George's*-Fields,[69] and Share our Booty; away we went to the Fields, and siting down in the Grass far enough out of the Path, he pull'd out the Money, look here *Jack*, says he, did you ever see the like before in your Life? no, never says I, and added very innocently, *must we have it all?* we have it! says he, who should have it? Why says I, must the Man have none of it again that lost it; he have it again! says he, what d'ye mean by that; Nay, I don't know, says I, why you said just now you would let him have the tother Bill again, that you said was too big for you.

HE Laught at me, you are but a little Boy *says he*, that's true, but I thought you had not been such a Child neither; so he mighty gravely Explain'd the thing to me thus: That the Bill of Sir *Stephen Evans* was a great bill for 300*l.* and if I, *says he*, that am but a poor Lad should venture to go for the Money, they will presently say, how should I come by such a Bill, and that I certainly found it or stole it, so they will stop me *says he*, and take it away from me, and it may be bring me into Trouble for it too; so, *says he*, I did say it was too big for me to meddle with, and that I would let the Man have it again if I could tell how; but for the Money *Jack*, the Money that we have got, I warrant you he should have none of that; besides *says he*, who ever he be that has lost this Letter Case, to be sure, as soon as he miss'd it, he would run to a *Goldsmith* and give notice, that if any body came for the Money, they should be stopp'd, but I am too Old[70] for him there *says he*.

WHY *says I*, and what will you do with the Bill, Will you thro' it away? if you do, somebody else will find it *says I*, and they will go and take the Money: No, no, *says he*, then they will be Stopp'd and Examin'd, as I tell you, I should be: I did not know well what all this meant, so I talk'd no more about that; but we fell to handling the Money, as for me, I had never seen so much together in all my Life, nor did I know what in the World to do with it, and once or twice I was a going to bid him keep it for me, which wou'd have been done like a Child indeed, for to be sure, I had never heard[71] a word more of it, tho' nothing had befallen him.

HOWEVER, as I happen'd to hold my Tongue as to that part, he shar'd the Money very honestly with me, only at the end he told me, that tho' it was true, he promis'd me half, yet as it was the first time, and I had done nothing but look on, so he thought it was very well if I took a little less than he did; so he divided the Money, which was 12*l.* 10*s.* into two exact Parts (*viz.*) 6*l.* 5*s.* in each Part, then he took 1*l.* 5*s.* from my Part, and told me I should give him that for Handsel.[72] Well, *says I,* take it then, for I think you deserve it all; so however, I took up the rest, and what shall I do with this now, *says I,* for I have no where to put it? why have you no Pockets? *says he,* yes *says I,* but they are full of Holes; I have often thought since that, and with some Mirth too, how I had really more Wealth than I knew what to do with, for Lodging I had none, nor any Box or Drawer to hide my Money in, nor had I any Pocket, but such, *as I say,* was full of Holes; I knew no Body in the World, that I cou'd go and desire them to lay it up for me; for being a poor nak'd, ragg'd Boy, they would presently say, I had robb'd some Body, and perhaps lay hold of me, and my Money would be my Crime, *as they say* it often is in foreign Countries: And now as I was full of Wealth, behold! I was full of Care, for what to do to secure my Money I could not tell, and this held me so long, and was so Vexatious to me the next Day, that I truly sat down and cryed.

NOTHING cou'd be more perplexing than this Money was to me all that Night, I carried it in my Hand a good while, for it was in Gold all but 14*s.* and that is to say, it was in four Guineas, and that 14*s.* was more difficult to carry then the four Guineas; at last I sat down and pull'd off one of my Shoes, and put the four Guineas into that, but after I had gone a while, my Shoe hurt me so, I could not go, so I was fain to sit down again, and take it out of my Shoe, and carry it in my Hand, then I found a dirty Linnen Rag in the Street, and I took that up, and wrapt it all together, and carried it in that, a good way. I have often since heard People say, when they have been talking of Money, that they cou'd not get in, I wish I had it in a foul Clout:[73] In truth I had mine in a *foul Clout,* for it was foul according to the Letter of that saying, but it serv'd me till I came to a convenient Place, and then I sat down and wash'd the Cloth in the Kennel,[74] and so then put my Money in again.

WELL, I carried it home with me to my Lodging in the Glass-house, and when I went to go to Sleep, I knew not what to do with it; if I had let any of the black Crew I was with, know of it, I should have been smother'd in the Ashes for it, or robb'd of it, or some Trick or other put upon me for it; so I knew not what to do, but lay with it in my Hand, and my Hand in my

Bosom, but then Sleep went from Eyes: O! the weight of Human Care! I a poor Beggar Boy could not Sleep as soon as I had but a little Money to keep, who before that, cou'd have slept upon a heap of Brick-bats, or Stones, Cinders, or any where, as sound as a rich Man does on his down Bed,[75] and sounder too.

EVERY now and then dropping a sleep, I should Dream that my Money was lost, and start like one frighted; then finding it fast in my Hand, try to go to sleep again, but could not for a long while, then drop and start again; at last a Fancy came into my Head, that if I fell a sleep, I should Dream of the Money, and Talk of it in my sleep, and tell that I had Money, which if I should do, and one of the Rogues should hear me, they would pick it out of my Bosom, and of my hand too without waking me, and after that Thought I could not sleep a wink more; so that I pass'd that Night over in Care and Anxiety enough, and this I may safely say, was the first Nights rest that I lost by the Cares of this Life, and the deceitfulness of Riches.[76]

As soon as it was Day, I got out of the Hole we lay in, and rambled abroad into the Fields, towards *Stepney*, and there I mus'd and consider'd what I should do with this Money, and many a time I wish'd that I had not had it, for after all my ruminating upon it, and what Course I should take with it, or where I should put it, I could not hit upon any one thing, or any possible Method to secure it, and it perplex'd me so, that at last, as I said just now, I sat down and cryed heartily.

WHEN my crying was over, the Case was the same; I had the Money still, and what to do with it I could not tell; at last it came into my Head, that I would look out for some Hole in a Tree, and see to hide it there, till I should have occasion for it: Big with this discovery, as I then thought it, I began to look about me for a Tree; but there were no Trees in the Fields about *Stepney*, or *Mile-End* that look'd fit for my purpose, and if there were any that I began to look narrowly at, the Fields were so full of People, that they would see if I went to hide any thing there, and I thought the People Eyed me as it was, and that two Men in particular follow'd me, to see what I intended to do.

THIS drove me farther off, and I cross'd the Road at *Mile-End*, and in the middle of the Town went down a Lane that goes away to the *Blind Beggars* at *Bednal-Green*;[77] when I came a little way in the Lane, I found a Foot-Path over the Fields, and in those Fields several Trees for my Turn, as I thought; at last one Tree had a little Hole in it, pritty high out of my Reach, and I climb'd up the Tree to get to it, and when I came there, I put my Hand in, and found, (as I thought) a Place very fit, so I placed my Treasure there, and was mighty well satisfy'd with it; but behold, putting my Hand in again to lay it more commodiously, as I thought, of a Suddain it slipp'd away from me, and I found the Tree was hollow, and my little Parcel was fallen in quite out of my Reach, and how far it might go in, I knew not; so that, in a Word, my Money was quite gone, irrecoverably lost, there could be no Room, so much as to Hope ever to see it again for it was a vast great Tree.

As young as I was, I was now sensible what a Fool I was before, that I could not think of Ways to keep my Money, but I must come thus far to throw it into a Hole where I could not reach it; well, I thrust my Hand quite up to my Elbow, but no Bottom was to be found, or any End of the Hole or Cavity; I got a Stick off of the Tree and thrust it in a great Way, but all was one; then I cry'd, nay, I roar'd out, I was in such a Passion, then I got down the Tree again, then up again, and thrust in my Hand again till I scratch'd my Arm and made it bleed, and cry'd all the while most violently: Then I began to think I had not so much as a half Penny of it left for a half Penny Roll, and I was a hungry, and then I cry'd again: Then I came away in despair, crying, and roaring like a little Boy that had been whip'd, then I went back again to the Tree, and up the Tree again, and thus I did several Times.

THE last time I had gotten up the Tree, I happen'd to come down not on the same Side that I went up and came down before, but on the other side of the Tree, and on the other Side of the Bank also; and behold the Tree had a great open Place in the Side of it close to the Ground, as old hollow Trees often have; and looking into the open Place, to my inexpressible Joy, there lay my Money, and my Linnen Rag, all rap'd up just as I had put it into the Hole: For the Tree being hollow all the Way up, there had been some Moss or light Stuff, which I had not Judgement enough to know was not firm, and had given way when it came to drop out of my Hand, and so it had slip'd quite down at once.

I WAS but a Child, and I rejoiced like a Child, for I hollow'd quite[a] out aloud, when I saw it; then I run to it, and snatch'd it up, hug'd and kiss'd the dirty Ragg a hundred Times; then danc'd and jump'd about, run from one[b] End of the Field to the other, and in short, I knew not what, much less do I know now what I did, tho' I shall never forget the Thing, either what a sinking Grief it was to my Heart when I thought I had lost it, or what a Flood of Joy o'er whelm'd me when I had got it again.

WHILE I was in the first Transport of my Joy, as I have said, I run about and knew not what I did; but when that was over, I sat down, open'd the foul Clout the Money was in, look'd at it, told it,[78] found it was all there, and then I fell a crying as savourly[79] as I did before, when I thought I had lost it.

IT would tire the Reader should I dwell on all the little Boyish Tricks that I play'd in the Extacy of my Joy, and Satisfaction, when I had found my Money; so I break off here: Joy is as Extravagant as Grief,[80] and since I have been a Man, I have often thought, that had such a Thing befallen a Man, so to have lost all he had, and not have a bit of Bread to Eat, and then so strangely to find it again, after having given it so effectually over, *I say*, had it been so with a Man, it might have hazarded his using some Violence upon himself.

WELL, I came away with my Money, and having taken Six-pence out of it, before I made it up again, I went to a Chandler's Shop[81] in *Mile-End*, and bought a Half-Penny Roll, and a Half Pennyworth of Cheese, and sat down at the Door after I bought it, and eat it very heartily, and begg'd some Beer to Drink with it, which the good Woman gave me very freely.

AWAY I went then for the Town to see if I could find any of my Companions, and resolv'd I would try no more hollow Trees for my Treasure; as I came along *White-Chapel*, I came by a Broker's Shop,[82] over against the Church, where they sold old Cloaths, for I had nothing on but the worst of Rags; so I stopp'd at the Shop, and stood looking at the Cloaths which hang'd at the Door.

WELL, young Gentleman, says a Man that stood at the Door, you look wishly, do you see any thing you like, and will your Pocket compass a good Coat now, for you look as if you belong'd to the ragged Regiment: I was affronted at the Fellow, what's that to you, *said I*, how ragg'd I am, if I had seen any thing I lik'd, I have Money to pay for it; but I can go where I shan't be Huffed at[83] for looking.

WHILE I said thus, pretty boldly to the Fellow, comes a Woman out, What ail you, *says she?* to the Man, to Bully away our Customers so; a poor Boy's Money is as good as my Lord Mayors; if poor People did not buy old Cloths, what would become of our Business? and then turning to me, come hither Child, *says she*, if thou hast a mind to any thing I have, you shan't be Hector'd by him; the Boy is a pretty Boy, I assure you, *says she*, to another Woman that was by this time come to her, ay, *says the t'other*, so he is, a very well looking Child, if he was clean and well dress'd, and may be as good a Gentleman's Son for any thing we know, as any of those that are well dress'd; come my Dear, *says she*, tell me what is it you wou'd have? she pleas'd me mightily to hear her Talk of my being a Gentleman's Son, and it brought former things to mind, but when she talk'd of my being not Clean, and in Rags, then I cry'd.

SHE press'd me to tell her, if I saw any thing that I wanted, I told her no, all the Cloths I saw there, were too big for me; come Child, *says she*, I have two things here that will fit you, and I am sure you want them both, that is, first a little Hat, and there, *says she, tossing it to me,* I'll give you that for nothing; and here is a good warm Pair of Breeches; I dare say, *says she,* they will fit you, and they are very tite,[84] and good; and, *says she,* if you should ever come to have so much Money, that you don't know what to do with it, here are excellent good Pockets, *says she,* and a little Fob[85] to put your Gold in, or your Watch in, when you get it.

It struck me with a strange kind of Joy, that I should have a Place to put my Money in, and need not go to hide it again in a Hollow-Tree; that I was ready to snatch the Breeches out of her Hands, and wonder'd that I should be such a Fool, never to think of buying me a pair of Breeches before, that I might have a Pocket to put my Money in, and not carry it about two Days together in my Hand, and in my Shoe, and I knew not how; so in a Word, I gave her two Shillings for the Breeches, and went over into the Church-yard[86] and put them on, put my Money into my new Pockets, and was as pleas'd as a Prince is with his Coach and six Horses; I thank'd the good Woman too for the Hat, and told her I would come again when I got more Money, and buy some other things I wanted, and so I came away.

I was but a Boy 'tis true, but I thought my self a Man now I had got a Pocket to put my Money in, and I went directly to find out my Companion, by whose means I got it; but I was frighted out of my Wits when I heard that he was carried to *Bridewell*; I made no Question but it was for the Letter Case, and that I should be carried there too, and then my poor Brother Captain *Jack's* Case came into my Head, and that I should be Whip'd there as cruelly as he was, and I was in such a fright that I knew not what to do.

But in the Afternoon I met him; he had been carried to *Bridewell*, it seems upon that very Affair, but was got out again: The Case was thus, having had such good Luck at the Custom-House the Day before, he takes his Walk thither again, and as he was in the long Room gaping and staring about him, a Fellow lays hold of him, and calls to one of the Clerks, that sat behind, *here,* says he, *is the same young Rogue, that I told you I saw Loitering about t'other Day when the Gentleman lost his Letter Case, and his* Goldsmith's *Bills; I dare say it was he that stole them*; immediately the whole Crowd of People gather'd about the Boy, and Charg'd him point Blank; but he was too well us'd to such things to be frighted into a Confession of what he knew they could not prove, for he had nothing about him belonging to it, nor had any Money, but Six-pence and a few dirty Farthings.

They threatened him, and pull'd, and hall'd[87] him, till they almost pull'd the Cloths off of his Back, and the Commissioners[88] examin'd him; but all was one, he would own nothing, but *said, he* walk'd up thro' the Room only to see the Place both then, and the time before, for he had own'd he was there before; so as there was no proof against him of any Fact,[89] no, nor of any Circumstances relating to the Letter Case, they were forc'd at last to let him go; however, they made a show of carrying him to *Bridewell*, and they did carry him to the Gate, to see if they could make him confess any thing; but he would confess nothing, and they had no *Mittimus*;[90] so they durst not carry him into the House, nor would the People have receiv'd him I suppose, if they had, they having no Warrant for putting him in Prison.

WELL, when they could get nothing out of him they carry'd him into an Ale-house, and there they told him, that the Letter Case had Bills in it of a very great Value, that they would be of no use to the Rogue that had them, but they would be of infinite Damage to the Gentleman, that had lost them, and that he had left word with the Clerk, who the Man that stop'd this Boy had call'd to, and who was there with him, that he would give 30*l.* to any one that would bring them again, and give all the Security that could be desir'd that he would give them no Trouble, whoever it was.

HE was just come from out of their Hands, when I met with him, and so he told me all the Story; *but,* says he, *I would confess nothing, and so I got off and am come away clear.* Well, says I, *and what will you do with the Letter Case, and the Bills, will not you let the poor Man have his Bills again?* No, not, I, *says he,* I won't trust them, what care I for their Bills; It came into my Head, as young as I was, that it was a sad thing indeed to take a Man's Bills away for so much Money, and not have any Advantage by it neither; for I concluded that the Gentleman who own'd the Bills must loose all the Money, and it was strange he should keep the Bills, and make a Gentleman loose so much Money for nothing: I remember that I ruminated very much about it, and tho' I did not understand it very well, yet it lay upon my Mind, and I said every now and then to him, do, let the Gentleman have his Bills again, do, pray do, and so I Teiz'd him, with do, and pray do, till at last I cry'd about them; he said, what would you have me be found out and sent to *Bridewell,* and be Whip'd as your Brother Captain *Jack* was, I said no I wou'd not have you Whipt, but I would have the Man have his Bills, for they will do you no good, but the Gentleman will be undone it may be; *and then, I added again,* do, let him have them; he snapt me short, *Why,* says he, *how shall I get them to him? who dare carry them? I dare not to be sure, for they will stop me, and bring the* Goldsmith *to see if he does not know me, and that I received the Money, and so they will prove the Robbery, and I shall be hang'd, would you have me be hang'd* Jack?

I WAS silenc'd a good while with that, for when he said, would you have me be hang'd *Jack?* I had no more to say; but one Day after this, he call'd to me, Colonel *Jack,* said he, I have thought of a way how the Gentleman shall have his Bills again, and you and I shall get a good deal of Money by it, if you will be honest to me, as I was to you; indeed, *says I*, ROBIN,[91] that was his Name, I will be very honest, let me know how it is, for I would fain have him have his Bills.

WHY, *says he*, they told me that he had left word at the Clerk's Place in the Long Room, that he would give 30*l*. to any one that had the Bills, and would restore them, and would ask no Questions. Now if you will go, like a poor innocent Boy as you are, into the Long Room, and speak to the Clerk, it may do; tell him, if the Gentleman will do as he promis'd, you believe you can tell him who has it, and if they are civil to you, and willing to be as good as their Words, you shall have the Letter Case, and give it them.

I TOLD him aye, I would go with all my Heart; but Colonel *Jack, says he,* what if they should take hold of you, and threaten to have you whip'd, won't you discover me to them; no, *says I,* if they would whip me to Death I won't; well then, says he, *there's the Letter Case, do you go*; so he gave me Directions how to act, and what to say, but I would not take the Letter Case with me, least they should prove false, and take hold of me, thinking to find it upon me, and so Charge me with the Fact; so I left it with him; and the next Morning I went to the Custom-House, as was agreed; what my Directions were, will to avoid Repetition, appear in what happen'd; it was an Errand of too much Consequence indeed to be entrusted to a Boy, not only so young as I was, but so little of a Rogue as I was yet arriv'd to the Degree of.

Two things I was particularly arm'd with, which I resolv'd upon. (1.) That the Man should have his Bills again; for it seem'd a horrible thing to me that he should be made to lose his Money, which I suppos'd he must, purely because we would not carry the Letter Case home. (2.) That whatever happen'd to me, I was never to tell the Name of my Comrade *Robin*, who had been the Principal: With these two Peices of honesty, for such they were both in themselves, and with a manly Heart, tho' a Boy's Head, I went up into the Long Room in the Custom-House the next Day.

As soon as I came to the Place, where the thing was done, I saw the Man sit just where he had sat before, and it run in my Head, that he had sat there ever since; but I knew no better; so I went up and stood just at that Side of the writing Board, that goes up on that Side of the Room, and which I was but just Tall enough to lay my Arms upon.

WHILE I stood there, one thrust me this way, and another thrust me that way, and the Man that sat behind began to look at me; at last he call'd out to me; what does that Boy do there, get you gone Sirrah, are you one of the Rogues that stole the Gentleman's Letter Case a *Monday* last? Then he turns his Tale to a Gentleman that was doing Business with him, and goes on thus; here was Mr. — had a very unlucky Chance on *Monday* last, did not you hear of it; no, not I, *says the Gentleman*, Why? standing just there, where you do, *says he*, making his Entries, he pull'd out his Letter Case, and laid it down, as *he says*, but just at this Hand, while he reach'd over to the Standish[92] there for a Penful of Ink, and some Body stole away his Letter Case.

His Letter Case! *says t'other*, What? and was there any Bills in it?

AY, *says he*, there was Sir *Stephen Evans*'s Note in it for 300*l.* and another Goldsmith's Bill, for about 12*l.* and which is worse still for the Gentleman, he had two Foreign accepted Bills in it for a great Sum, I know not how much, I think one was a *French* Bill for 1200 Crowns.

AND who cou'd it be? *says the Gentleman.*

NO BODY knows, *says he*, but one of our Room-Keepers *says*, he saw a Couple of young Rogues like that, *pointing at me*, hanging about here, and that on a sudden they were both gone.

VILLIANS! *says he* again, Why? what can they do with them, they will be of no use to them; I suppose he went immediately, and gave notice to prevent the Payment.

YES, *says the Clerk*, he did; but the Rogues were too[a] nimble for him with the little Bill of 12*l.* odd Money, they went and got the Money for that, but all the rest are stopp'd, however, 'tis an unspeakable Damage to him for want of his Money.

WHY, he should publish a Reward for the Encouragement of those that have them to bring them again, they would be glad to bring them I warrant you.

HE has posted it up at the Door, that he will give 30*l.* for them.

AYE, but he should add, that he will promise, not to stop, or give any Trouble to the Person that brings them.

HE has done that too, *says he*, but I fear they won't trust themselves to be Honest, for fear he should break his Word.

Why, it is true he may break his Word in that Case, but no Man should do so; for then, no Rogue will venture to bring home any thing that is stolen, and so he would do an Injury to others after him.

I DURST pawn my Life for him, he would scorn it.

THUS far they Discours'd of it, and then went off to something else; I heard it all, but did not know what to do a great while; but at last, watching the Gentleman that went away, when he was gone, I run after him, to have spoken to him, intending to have broke it to him, but he went hastily into a Room or Two, full of People, at the hither End of the Long Room, and when I went to follow, the Door-keepers turn'd me Back, and told me

I must not go in there; so I went Back, and loyter'd about, near the Man that sat behind the Board, and hung about there, 'till I found the Clock struck Twelve, and the Room began to be thin of People; and at last he sat there Writing, but no Body stood at the Board before him, as there had all the rest of the Morning, then I came a little nearer, and stood close to the Board, as I did before, when looking up from his Paper, and seeing me, *says he to me*, you have been up and down there all this Morning, Sirrah, What do you want? You have some Business that is not very good, I doubt?

No, I han't, *said I.*

No, 'tis well if you han't, *says he*, Pray what Business can you have, in the Long Room, Sir, you are no Merchant?

I would speak with you, *said I.*

With me, *says*[a] *he*, What have you to say to me?

I have something to say, *said I*, if you will do me no Harm for it.

I do thee Harm Child, What Harm should I do thee? and spoke very kindly.

Won't you indeed Sir, *said I.*

No, not I Child! I'll do thee no Harm; what is it? do you know any Thing of the Gentleman's Letter Case.

I answer'd, but spoke softly, that he could not hear me, so he gets over presently, into the Seat next him, and opens a Place that was made to come out, and bad me come in to him; and I did.

Then he ask'd me again, if I knew any thing of the Letter-Case.

I spoke softly again, and said, Folks would hear him.

Then he whisper'd softly, and ask'd me again.

I told him, I believ'd I did; but that, indeed, I had it not, nor had no Hand in stealing it, but it was goten into the Hands of a Boy, that would have burnt it, if it had not been for me; and that I heard him say, that the Gentleman would be glad to have them again, and give a good deal of Money for them.

I did say so Child, *said he*, and if you can get them for him, he shall give you a good Reward, no less than 30*l.* as he has Promis'd.

But you said too Sir, to the Gentleman, just now, *said I*, that you was sure he would not bring them into any Harm that should bring them.

Gent. No, you shall come to no Harm; I will pass my Word for it.

Boy. Nor shan't they make me bring other People into trouble?

Gent. No, you shall not be ask'd the Name of any Body, nor to tell who they are.

Boy. I am but a poor Boy, and I would fain have the Gentleman have his Bills, and indeed, I did not take them away, nor I han't got them.

Gent. But can you tell how the Gentleman shall have them?

Boy. If I can get them, I will bring them to you, to Morrow Morning.

Gent. Can you not do it to Night?

Boy. I believe I may, If I knew where to come.

Gent. Come to my House Child.

Boy. I don't know where you Live.

Gent. Go along with me now, and you shall see.

So he carry'd me up into *Tower-street*,[93] and show'd me his House, and order'd me to come there at five a Clock at Night, which accordingly I did, and carry'd the Letter-Case with me.

When I came, the Gentleman ask'd me if I had brought the Book, *as he call'd it.*

It is not a Book, *said I.*

No, the Letter-Case, that's all one, *says he.*

You promis'd me, *said I,* you would not hurt me, *and cry'd.*

Don't be affraid Child, *says he,* I will not hurt thee, *poor Boy!* no Body shall hurt thee.

Here it is, *said I,* and pull'd it out.

He then brought in another Gentleman, who it seems own'd the Letter-Case, *and ask'd him,* If that was it? *and he said,* Yes.

Then, *ask'd me,* If all the Bills were in it.

I told him, I heard him say, there was one gone, but I believed there was all the rest.

Why do you believe so? *said he.*

Because, I heard the Boy, that I believe stole them, say, they were too big for him to meddle with.

The Gentleman then that own'd them, said, Where is the Boy?

Then the other Gentleman put in, *and said,* no, you must not ask him that, I pass'd my Word that you should not, and that he should not be oblig'd to tell it to any Body.

Well Child, *says he,* You will let us see the Letter-Case open'd, and whether the Bills are in it?

Yes, *says I.*

Then the first Gentleman said, how many Bills were there in it?

Only three, *says he,* besides the Bill of 12*l.* 10*s.* there was Sir *Stephen Evans*'s Note for 300*l.* and two Foreign Bills.

Well then, if they are in the Letter-Case, the Boy shall have 30*l.* shall he not? Yes, *says the Gentleman,* he shall have it very freely.

Come then, Child, *says he,* let me open it.

So I gave it him, and he open'd it, and there were all the three Bills, and several other Papers, fair and safe, nothing defac'd, or diminish'd, and the Gentleman said all was right.

Then said the first Man, then I am Security to the poor Boy for the Money; well, but, *says the Gentleman*, the Rogues have got the 12*l.* 10*s.* they ought to reckon that as Part of the 30*l.* had he ask'd me, I should have consented to it at first Word: But the first Man stood my Friend, Nay, *says he*, it was since you knew that the 12*l.* 10*s.* was receiv'd, that you offer'd 30*l.* for the other Bills, and publish'd it by the Cryer, and posted it up at the *Custom-House* Door, and I promis'd him the 30*l.* this Morning; they argu'd long, and I thought would have quarel'd about it.

However, at last they both yielded a little, and the Gentleman gave me 25*l.* in good Guineas; when he gave it me, he bad me hold out my Hand, and he told the Money into my Hand, and when he had done, he ask'd me if it was right, I said, I did not know, but I believ'd it was: Why, *says he*, can't you tell[94] it? I told him no, I never saw so much Money in my Life, nor I did not know how to tell Money: Why, *says he*, Don't you know that they are Guineas; no, *I told him*, I did not know how much a Guinea was.

Why, how then, *says he*, did you tell me you believ'd it was Right? *I told him*, because, I believ'd he would not give it me wrong.

Poor Child! *says he*, Thou knowest little of the World, indeed; what art thou?

I am a poor Boy, *says I*, and cry'd.

What is your Name, *says he*, but hold, I forgot, *said he*, I promised I would not ask your Name, so you need not tell me.

My Name is *Jack*, *said I*.

Why, have you no Sir-Name? *said he*.

What is that? *said I*.

You have some other Name, besides Jack, *says he*, han't you?

Yes, *says I*, They call me, *Col. Jack*.

But have you no other Name?

No, *said I.*

How come you to be call'd *Col. Jack*, pray.

They say, *said I*, my Father's Name was *Col.*

Is your Father or Mother alive? *said he.*

No, *said I*, my Father is dead.

Where is your Mother then, *said he.*

I never had e're a Mother, *said I.*

This made him laugh; what, *said he*, had you ne'er a Mother, what then?

I had a Nurse, *said I*, but she was not my Mother.

Well, *says he to the Gentleman*, I dare say, this Boy was not the Thief that stole your Bills.

Indeed, Sir, I did not steal them, *said I*, and Cry'd again.

No, no, Child, *said he*, we don't believe you did.

THIS is a cleaver Boy, *says he*, to the other Gentleman, and yet very Ignorant and Honest, 'tis pity some Care should not be taken of him, and something done for him; let us Talk a little more with him; so they sat down and drank Wine, and gave me some, and then the first Gentleman talk'd to me again.

WELL, *says he*, What wil't thou do with this Money now thou hast it?

I don't know, *said I*.

Where will you put it? *said he*.

In my Pocket, *said I*.

In your Pocket, *said he*, is your Pocket whole? shan't you lose it?

Yes, *said I*, my Pocket is whole.

And where will you put it, when you come Home?

I have no Home, *said I*, *and cry'd* again.

Poor Child! *said he then*, What doest thou do for thy Living?

I go of Errands, *said I*, for the Folks in *Rosemary-lane*.

And what dost thou do for a Lodging at Night?

I lye at the Glass-House, *said I*, at Night.

How lye at the Glass-House! have they any Beds there? *says he*.

I never lay in a Bed in my Life, *said I*, as I remember.

Why? *says he*, what do you lye on at the Glass-House?

The Ground, *says I*, and sometimes a little Straw, or upon the warm Ashes.

Here the Gentleman, that lost the Bills, *said*, this poor Child is enough to make a Man Weep for the Miseries of humane Nature, and be thankful for himself, he puts Tears into my Eyes; and into mine too, *says the other*.

Well, but *Hark ye* Jack? *says the first Gentleman*, do they give you no Money, when they send you of Errands?

They give me Victuals, *said I*, and that's better.

But what, *says he*, do you do for Cloths?

They give me sometimes old things, *said I*, such as they have to spare.

Why? you have ne're a Shirt on I believe, *said he*, have you?

No, I never had a Shirt, *said I*, since my Nurse dyed.

How long ago is that? *said he*.

Six Winters, when this is out, *said I*.

Why, how Old are you? *said he*.

I can't tell, *said I*.

Well, *says the Gentleman*, now you have this Money, won't you buy some Cloths, and a Shirt with some of it.

Yes, *said I*, I would buy some Cloths.

And, what will you do with the rest?

I can't tell, *said I*, and cry'd.

What doest cry for *Jack*, said he.

I am afraid, *said I*, and cryed still.

What art afraid of.

They will know I have Money.

Well, and what then.

Then I must sleep no more in the warm Glass-house, and I shall be starv'd[95] with cold.

But why must you sleep there no more?

They will take away my Money.[a]

Here the Gentlemen observ'd to one another, how naturally Anxiety and Perplexity attends those that have Money; I warrant you, *says the Clerk*, when this poor Boy had no Money, he slept all Night in the Straw or on the warm Ashes in the Glass-House, as soundly and as void of Care as it would be possible for any Creature to do; But now as soon as he has gotten Money, the Care of preserving it brings Tears into his Eyes, and Fear into his Heart.

THEY ask'd me a great many Questions more, to which I answer'd in my Childish way as well as I could, but so as pleas'd them well enough; at last I was going away with a heavy Pocket, and I assure you not a light Heart, for I was so frighted with having so much Money, that I knew[b] not what in the Earth to do with my self: I went away however, and walk'd a little way, but I could not tell what to do; so after rambling two Hours or thereabout, I went back again, and sat down at the Gentleman's Door, and there I cry'd as long as I had any Moisture in my Head to make Tears of, but never knock'd at the Door.

I had not sat long, I suppose, but some body belonging to the Family got knowledge of it, and a Maid came and talked to me, but I said little to her, only cry'd still; at length it came to the Gentleman's Ears; as for the Merchant he was gone; when the Gentleman heard of me, he call'd me in, and began to talk with me again, and ask'd me what I staid for.

I told him I had not staid there all that while, for I had been gone a great while, and was come again.

Well, *says he*, but what did you come again for?

I can't tell, *says I*.

And what do you cry so for, *said he*, I hope you have not lost your Money, have you?

No, I told him I had not lost it yet, but I was afraid I should.

And does that make you cry? *says he*.

I told him *yes*, for I knew I should not be able to keep it, but *they* would Cheat me of it, or *they* would Kill me, and take it away from me too.

They, says he, Who? what sort of Gangs of People art thou with?

I told him they were all Boys, but very wicked Boys, Thieves and Pick-Pockets, *said I*, such as stole this Letter Case, a sad Pack, I can't abide 'em.

Well, *Jack*, said he, what shall be done for thee? will you leave it with me, shall I keep it for you?

Yes, said I, with all my Heart, if you please.

Come then, *says he*, give it me, and that you may be sure I have it, and you shall have it honestly again, I'll give you a Bill for it, and for the Interest of it, and that you may keep safe enough; *nay*, added he, and if you lose it or any Body takes it from you, none shall receive the Money but your self, or any part of it.

I presently pull'd out all the Money, and gave it to him, only keeping about Fifteen Shillings for myself to buy me some Cloaths, and thus ended the Conference between us on the first occasion, at least for the first time: Having thus secured my Money to my full Satisfaction, I was then perfectly easie, and accordingly the sad Thoughts that afflicted my Mind before began to vanish away.

THIS was enough to let any one see how all the Sorrows and Anxieties of Men's Lives come about, how they rise from their Restless pushing at getting of Money, and the restless Cares of keeping it when they have got it. I that had nothing, and had not known what it was to have had any thing, knew nothing of the Care, either of getting, or of keeping; I wanted nothing, who wanted every thing;[96] I had no Care, no Concern about where I should get my Victuals, or how I should Lodge, I knew not what Money was, or what to do with it; and never knew what it was not to sleep, till I had Money to keep, and was afraid of losing it.

I HAD without doubt an opportunity at this time, if I had not been too foolish, and too much a Child to speak for myself; I had an opportunity, *I say*, to have got into the Service, or perhaps to be under some of the Care and Concern of these Gentlemen, for they seem'd to be very fond of doing something for me, and were surpriz'd at the Innocence of my Talk to them, as well as at the Misery (as they thought it) of my Condition.

BUT I acted indeed like a Child, and leaving my Money, *as I have said*, I never went near them for several Years after; what Course I took, and what befel me in that Interval, has so much Variety in it, and carries so much Instruction in it, that it requires[a] an Account of it by it self.

THE first happy Chance, that offer'd it self to me in the World, was now over; I had got Money, but I neither knew the Value of it, or the Use of it; the Way of Living I had begun, was so natural to me, I had no Notion of bettering it; I had not so much as any Desire of Buying me any Cloths, no not so much as a Shirt, and much less had I any Thought of getting any other Lodging, than that in the *Glass-House*, and loytering about the Street as I had done: For I knew no Good, and had tasted no Evil; *that is to say*, the Life I had led being not Evil in my Account.

IN this State of Ignorance, I return'd to my really miserable Life, so it was in it self, and was only not so to me, because I did not understand how to judge of it, and had known no better.

MY Comrade that gave me back the Bills, and who if I had not press'd him, design'd never to have restor'd them, never ask'd me what I had given me, but told me, if they gave me any thing it should be my own; for as *he said*, he would not run the venture of being seen in the restoring them, I deserv'd the Reward if there was any; neither did he trouble his Head with enquiring what I had, or whether I had any thing or no; so my Title to what I had got was clear.

I WENT now, up and down just as I did before; I had Money indeed in my Pocket, but I let no Body know it; I went of Errands chearfully, as before, and accepted of what any Body gave me with as much Thankfulness as ever; the only difference that I made with myself, was, that if I was a Hungry, and no Body employ'd me, or gave me any thing to Eat, I did not beg from Door to Door, as I did at first, but went to a boyling House, *as I said once before*, and got a Mess of Broth, and a piece of Bread, Price a Half-penny; very seldom any Meat; or if I treated myself, it was a Half-penny worth of Cheese; all which Expence did not Amount to above 2*d*. or 3*d*. a Week; for contrary to the usage of the rest of the Tribe, I was extremely Frugal, and I had not dispos'd of any of the Guineas, which I had at first; neither, *as I said* to the Custom-House Gentleman, could I tell what a Guinea was made of, or what it was worth.

AFTER I had been about a Month thus, and had done nothing, my Comrade, *as I call'd him*, came to me one Morning, Col. *Jack*, says he, When shall you and I take a walk again? when you will, *said I*: Have you got no Business yet? *says he*, no, *says I*, and so one thing bringing in another, he told me, I was a fortunate Wretch; and he believed I would be so again; but that he must make a new Bargain with me now, for *says he*, Col. the first time we always let a raw Brother come in for full share, to Encourage him, but afterward, except it be when he puts himself forward well, and runs equal Hazard, he stands to Courtisie;[97] but as we are Gentlemen, we always do very Honourably by one another; and if you are willing to trust it or leave it to me, I shall do handsomly by you, that you may depend upon. I told him, I was not able to do any thing, that was certain, for I did not understand it, and therefore I cou'd not expect to get any thing, but I would do as he bad me, so we walk'd Abroad together.

WE went no more to the *Custom house*, it was too bold a Venture; besides, I did not care to shew my self again, especially with him in Company; but we went directly to the *Exchange*, and we hanker'd about[98] in *Castle-Alley*, and in *Swithins-alley*, and at the Coffee-house-doors. 'Twas a very unlucky Day, for we got nothing all Day, but 2 or 3 Hankerchiefs, and came home to the old Lodging, at the *Glass-house*; nor had I had any thing to Eat or Drink all Day, but a piece of Bread, which he gave me, and some Water at the Conduit at the *Exchange gate*: So when he was gone from me, for he did not lye in the *Glass-house*, as I did, I went to my old Broth-house for my usual Bait;[99] and refresh'd my self, and the next Day early went to meet him again, as he appointed me.

BEING early in the Morning, he took his Walk to *Billingsgate*,[100] where it seems two Sorts of People make a great Crowd as soon as it is Light and at that time a Year, rather before Day light; *that is to say, Crimps*,[101] and the Masters of *Coal Ships*, who they call *Collyer Masters*; and Secondly, Fish-mongers, Fish-sellers and Buyers of Fish.

IT was the first of these People that he had his Eye upon: So he gives me my Orders, which was thus; go you, *says he*, into all the Ale-houses as we go along, and Observe, where any People are telling of Money, and when you find any, come and tell me; so he stood at the Door, and I went into the Houses: As the *Collyer Masters* generally Sell their Coals at the Gate, *as they call it*, So they generally receive their Money in those Ale-houses, and it was not long before I brought him Word of several; upon this he went in, and made his Observations, but found nothing to his purpose; at length I brought him Word, that there was a Man in such a House, who had received a great deal of Money of some body, I believ'd of several People, and that it lay all upon the Table in Heaps, and he was very busy Writing down the Sums, and putting it up in several Bags; is he? *says he*, I'll warrant him, I will have some of it, and in he goes, he Walks up and down the House, which had several open Tables and Boxes in it, and lissened to hear if he could what the Man's Name was, and he heard some body call him *Cullum*, or some such a Name; then he watches his Opportunity, and steps up to him, and tells him a long Story, that there was two Gentlemen at the *Gun-Tavern*[102] sent him to Enquire for him, and to tell him they desired to speak with him.

THE *Collier* Master had his Money lay before him, just as I had told him; and had two or three small Payments of Money, which he had put up in lit-tle Black Dirty Baggs, and lay by themselves; and as it was hardly broad Day, he found means in delivering his Message, to lay his Hand upon one of those Baggs, and carry it off perfectly undiscover'd.

WHEN he had got it, he came out to me, who stood but at the Door, and pulling me by the Sleeve, run *Jack*, says he, for our Lives, and away he Scours; and I after him, never resting or scarce looking about me, till we got quite up into *Fenchurch-street*, thro' *Lime-street*, into *Leaden-hall street*, down St. *Mary axe*,[103] to *London-Wall*, then[a] thro' *Bishop gate*, and down old *Bedlam*,[104] into *Moor-fields*. By this time we were neither of us able to run very fast, nor need we have gone so far, for I never found that any body Persued us: When we got into *Moorfields*, and began to take Breath, I ask'd him what it was frighted him so? *fright me*, you Fool, *says he, I have got a Devilish great Bag of Money*: A Bag! *said I*, ay, ay, said he, let us get out into the Fields, where no Body can see us, and I'll shew it you; so away he had me through *Long-alley*, and Cross *Hog-lane*, and *Holloway lane*, into the middle of the great Field, which since that, has been call'd the *Farthing-pye-house-field*: There we wou'd have sat down, but it was all full of Water; so we went on, cross'd the Road at *Anniseed-Cleer*, and went into the Field where now the Great Hospital stands:[105] And finding a by place, we sat down, and he Pulls out the Bag; thou art a lucky Boy, *Jack*, says he; thou deservest a good share of this Jobb[106] truly, for 'tis all long of thy lucky News, so he pours it all out into my Hat; for, as I told you, I now wore a Hat.

How he did to Whip away such a Bagg of Money from any Man that was Awake, and in his Senses, I cannot tell; But there was a great deal in it; and among it, a Paper full by it self: When the Paper dropt out of the Bag, hold, *says he*, that's Gold; and began to Crow and Hallow[107] like a mad Boy, but there he was Bauk'd; for it was a Paper of old Thirteen-pence-half-penny peices, half, and Quarter Peices, with Nine pences and Four-pence-half-penny's,[108] all old Crooked Money, *Scots* and *Irish* Coin, so he was disappointed in that; but as it was, there was about 17 or 18 Pound in the Bag as I understood by him, for I cou'd not tell Money, not I.

Well, he parted this Money into three, that is to say, into three Shares; two for himself, and one for me, and ask'd if I was Content, I told him yes, I had reason to be Contented; besides, it was so much Money added to that I had left of his former Adventure, that I knew not what to do with it, or with my self, while I had so much about me.

This was a most Exquisite Fellow for a Thief, for he had the greatest Dexterity at Conveying any thing away, that he scarse ever Pitch'd upon any thing in his Eye, but he carried it off with his Hands, and never that I know of, miss'd his Aim, or was catch'd in the Fact.

He was an Eminent Pick-pocket, and very Dextrous at the Ladies Gold Watches; but he generally push'd higher at such desperate Things as those, and he came off the cleanest, and with the greatest Success Imaginable; and it was in these Kinds of the wicked Art of Thieving, that I became his Scholar.

As we were now so Rich, he would not let me lye any longer in the *Glass-house*, or go Naked, and Ragged, as I had done; but oblig'd me to buy two Shirts, a Wastcoat, and a Great Coat, for a Great Coat was more for our purpose, in the Business we was upon than any other: So I Cloathed my self as he Directed, and he took me a Lodging in the same House with him, and we Lodg'd together in a little Garret fit for our Quality.

Soon after this, we Walk'd out again, and then we try'd our Fortune in the places by the *Exchange* a Second time. Here we began to act separately, and I undertook to Walk by my self, and the first thing I did accurately, was a trick I play'd, that argued some Skill, for a new Beginner, for I had never seen any Business of that Kind done before: I saw two Gentlemen mighty Eager in Talk, and one pull'd out a Pocket-book two or three times, and then slipt it into his Coat-pocket again, and then out it came again, and Papers were taken out, and others put in; and then in it went again, and so several times, the Man being still warmly Engag'd with another Man, and two or three others standing hard by them; the last time he put his Pocket-book into his Pocket, he might have been said to thro' it in, rather than put it in with his Hand, and the Book lay End way, resting upon some other Book, or something else in his Pocket; so that it did not go quite down, but one Corner of it was seen above his Pocket.

This Careless way of Men putting their Pocket-books into a Coat-pocket, which is so easily Div'd into, by the least Boy that has been us'd to the Trade, can never be too much blam'd; the Gentlemen are in great Hurries, their Heads and Thoughts entirely taken up, and it is impossible they should be Guarded enough against such little Hawks Eyed Creatures, as we were; and therefore, they ought either never to put their Pocket-books up at all, or to put them up more secure, or to put nothing of Value into them: I happen'd to be just opposite to this Gentleman in that they call *Swithins-alley*; or that Alley rather, which is between *Swithins-alley* and the *Exchange*; just by a Passage that goes out of the Alley into the *Exchange*: When seeing the Book pass, and repass, into the Pocket, and out of the Pocket, as above, it came immediately into my Head, certainly, I might get that Pocket-book out, if I were Nimble, and I warrant *Will* would have it, if he saw it go and come, to and again, as I did: But when I saw it Hang by the way, as I have said; Now, 'tis mine said I, to my self, and crossing the Alley, I brush'd smoothly but closely by the Man, with my Hand down flat to my own Side, and taking hold of it by the Corner that appear'd; the Book came so light into my Hand, it was impossible the Gentleman should feel the least motion, or any body else see me take it away. I went directly forward into the broad Place, on the North-side of the *Exchange*, then scour'd down *Bartholomew-lane*, so into *Token-house-yard*, into the Alleys, which pass thro' from thence to *London-wall*, so thro' *Moor-gate*, and sat down in the Grass, in the Second of the Quarters of *Moor-fields*; towards the middle Field; which was the Place that *Will* and I had appointed to meet at, if either of us got any Booty: When I came thither, *Will* was not come, but I saw him a coming in about half an Hour.

As soon as *Will* came to me, I ask'd him what Booty he had gotten; he look'd Pale, and as I thought frighted: But he return'd, I have got nothing, *not I*, but you lucky young Dog, *says he*, what have you got, have not you got the Gentleman's Pocket-book in *Swithins-Alley*: Yes, *says I*, and Laught at him; why, how did you know it: Know it! *says he*, why, the Gentleman is Raving and half Distracted: He Stamps and Crys, and Tears his very Cloths, *he says* he is utterly undone, and ruin'd, and the Folks in the Alley say, there is, I know not how many Thousand Pounds in it; what can be in it, *says* Will, *come let us see.*

WELL, we lay close in the Grass, in the Middle of the Quarter, so that no body minded us, and so we opened the Pocket-book, and there was a great many Bills and Notes under Men's Hands; some *Gold-smiths*, and some belonging to *Insurance Offices*, as they call them, and the like: But that which was, it seems, worth all the rest, was that in one of the Folds of the Cover of the Book, where there was a Case with several Partitions; there was a Paper full of loose Diamonds: The Man as we understood afterwards, was a *Jew*; who dealt in such Goods, and who indeed ought to have taken more Care of the keeping of them.

NOW was this Booty too great, even for *Will* himself to Manage; for tho' by this time, I was come to understand things better than I did formerly, when I knew not what belong'd to Money; yet, *Will* was better skill'd by far in those things than I. But this puzzl'd him too as well as me: Now were we something like the Cock in the Fable;[109] for all these Bills, and I think there was one Bill of Sir *Henry Furness's*[110] for 1200 Pounds, and all these *Diamonds*, which were worth above[a] 150*l. as they said*, I say, all these things were of no Value to us; one little Purse of Gold would have been better to us, than all of it: But, *come says Will*, let us look over the Bills for a little one.

WE look'd over all the Bills, and among them; we found a Bill under a Man's Hand for 32*l. come says Will*, let us go and Enquire where this Man Lives: So we went into the City again, and *Will* went to the *Post house*, and ask'd there, they told him he liv'd at *Temple-bar*;[111] Well, says *Will*, I will venture; I'll go and receive the Money, it may be he has not remembred to send to stop the Payment there.

BUT it came into his thoughts, to take another Course; *come says Will*, I'll go back to the Alley, and see if I can hear any thing of what has happen'd, for I believe the Hurry is not over yet; it seems the Man who lost the Book was carried into the *King's-Head-Tavern*,[112] at the End of that Alley, and a great Crowd was about the Door.

AWAY goes *Will*, and watches, and waits about the Place, and then seeing several People together, for they were not all dispers'd, he asks one or two what was the Matter; they tell him a long story of a Gentleman who had lost his Pocket-book, with a great Bag of *Diamonds* in it, and Bills for a great many Thousand Pounds, and I know not what; and that they had been just then Crying it,[113] and had offer'd a Hundred Pound Reward, to any one that would discover and restore it.

I WISH *said he*, to one of them, that Parled with him, I did but know who has it; I dont doubt but I would help him to it again; does he remember nothing of any body, Boy, or Fellow that was near him; if he cou'd but Describe him, it might do; some body that over heard him was so forward to assist the poor Gentleman, that they went up and let him know what a young Fellow, meaning *Will*, had been talking at the Door, and down comes another Gentleman from him, and taking *Will* aside, *ask'd him what he had said about it? Will* was a Grave sort of a young Man, that tho' he was an old Soldier at the Trade, had yet nothing of it in his Countenance, and he answer'd, that he was concerned in Business where a great many of the Gangs of little Pick-pockets haunted; and if he had but the least Discription of the Person that they Suspected, he durst say, he cou'd find him out, and might perhaps get the things again for him: Upon this, he desir'd him to go up with him to the Gentleman, which he did accordingly; and there he said he sat leaning his Head back in a Chair, Pale as a Cloth; disconsolate to a strange Degree, and as *Will* describ'd him, just like one under a Sentence.

WHEN they came to ask him whether he had seen no Boy, or shabby Fellow lurking near where he stood, or passing, and repassing? and the like, he answer'd, no, not any; neither could he remember that any Body had come near him; then said *Will*, it will be very hard, if not impossible, to find them out: However, said *Will*, if you think it worth while, I will put my self among those Rogues, tho' *says he*, I care not for being seen among them, but I will put in among them, and if it be in any of those Gangs, it is ten to one but I shall hear something of it.

THEY ask'd him then, if he had heard what Terms the Gentleman had offer'd to have it restor'd; he answer'd, no; (tho' he had been told at the Door,) they answer'd, he had offer'd a Hundred Pound; that is too much, *says Will*, but if you please to leave it to me; I shall either get it for you for less than that, or not be able to get it for you at all: Then the losing Gentleman said to one of the other, tell him, that if he can get it lower, the

Over-plus shall be to himself; *William* said, he would be very glad to do the Gentleman such a Service, and would leave the Reward to himself. Well, young Man, says one of the Gentlemen, what ever you appoint to the young Artist that has done this Roguery, for I warrant he is an Artist,[114] let it be who it will, he shall be paid, if it be within the Hundred Pound, and the Gentleman is willing to give you 50*l.* besides for your Pains.

TRULY, Sir, says *Will*, very Gravely, it was by meer Chance, that coming by the Door, and seeing the Crowd, I ask'd what the matter was; but if I should be Instrumental to get the unfortunate Gentleman his Pocket-book, and the things in it again, I shall be very glad; nor am I so Rich neither Sir, but 50*l.* is very well worth my while too: Then he took Directions who to come to, and where, and who to give his Account to, if he learnt any thing, *and the like.*

Will staid so long, that as he and I agreed, I went home, and he did not come to me till Night; for we had Consider'd before, that it would not be proper to come from them directly to me, least they should follow him, and apprehend me; if he had made no advances towards a Treaty, he would have come back in half an Hour, as we agreed; but staying late, we met at our Night-rendezvous, which was in *Rosemary-lane.*

WHEN he came, he gave me an Account of all the Discourse, and particularly what a Consternation the Gentleman was in, who had lost the Pocket-book, and that he did not doubt, but we should get a good round Sum for the Recovery of it:

WE Consulted all the Evening about it, and Concluded he should let them hear nothing of them the next Day at all; and that the third Day he should go, but should make no Discovery; only that he had got a Scent of it, and that he believ'd he should have it, and make it appear as Difficult as possible, and to start as many Objections as he could; accordingly, the third Day after, he met with the Gentleman, who he found had been uneasie at his long stay; and told him, they was afraid that he only Flatter'd them, to get from them; and that they had been too Easie in letting him go, without a farther Examination.

HE took upon him to be very Grave with them, and told them, that if that was what he was like to have for being so free, as to tell them he thought he might serve them, they might see that they had wrong'd him, and were mistaken by his coming again to them; that if they thought they cou'd do any thing by Examining him, they might go about it if they pleas'd now, that all he had to say to them, was, that he knew where some of the young Rogues Haunted, who were Famous for such things; and that by some Inquiries, offering them Money and the like, he believ'd they would be brought to betray one another, and that so he might pick it out for them, and this he would say before a Justice of Peace if they thought fit, and then all that he had to say farther to them, was to tell them, he had lost a Day or two in their Service; and had got nothing but to be suspected for his Pains; and that after that, he had done, and they might seek their Goods where they could find them.

THEY began to lissen[115] a little upon that, and ask'd him if he could give them any Hopes of recovering their Loss; he told them, that he was not afraid to tell them, that he believ'd he had heard some News of them, and that what he had done, had prevented all the Bills being Burnt Book and all; But that now he ought not to be ask'd any more Questions till they should be pleas'd to answer him a Question or two: They told him they would give him any Satisfaction they could, and bid him tell them what he desir'd.

WHY, Sir, *Says he*, how can you expect any Thief that had Robb'd you to such a Considerable Value as this, wou'd come and put himself into your Hands, confess he had your Goods, and restore them to you; if you do not give them Assurance, that you will not only give them the Reward you agree to, but also, give Assurance that they shall not be Stop'd, Question'd, or call'd to Account before a Magistrate.

THEY said they would give all possible Assurance of it; nay, *says he*, I do not know what Assurance you are able to give; for when a poor Fellow is in your Clutches, and has shown you your Goods, you may Seize upon him for a Thief, and it is plain he must be so; then you go take away your Goods, send him to Prison, and what amends can he have of you afterward?

THEY were entirely confounded with the difficulty, they ask'd him to try if he could get the Things into his Hands, and they would pay him the Money before he let them go out of his Hand, and he should go away Half an Hour before they went out of the Room.

NO Gentlemen, *says he*, that won't do now; if you had talk'd so before, you had talk'd of apprehending me for nothing, I should have taken your Words; but now it is plain you have had such a thought in your Heads, and how can I, or any one else be assur'd of Safety.

WELL, they thought of a great many particulars, but nothing would do; at length the other People who were present, put in, that they should give Security to him, by a Bond of 1000*l.* that they would not give the Person any Trouble whatsoever: He pretended they could not be Bound, nor could their Obligation be of any Value, and that their own Goods being once seen, they might Seize them; and what would it signify, *said he*, to put a poor Pick-pocket to Sue for his Reward: They could not tell what to say, but told him, that he should take the things off[a] the Boy, if it was a Boy; and they would be Bound to Pay him the Money promis'd. He Laught at them, and said, no Gentlemen, as I am not the Thief, so I shall be very loth to put my self in the Thiefs stead, and lye at your Mercy.

THEY told him they knew not what to do then; and that it would be very hard, he would not trust them at all; *he said*, he was very willing to trust them, and to serve them; but that it would be very hard to be ruin'd, and Charg'd with the Theft, for Endeavouring to serve them.

THEY then offer'd to give it him under their Hands, that they did not in the least Suspect him; that they would never Charge him with any thing about it; that they Acknowledg'd he went about to Enquire after the Goods at their Request; and that if he produced them, they would Pay him so much Money, at, and before the Delivery of them, without Obliging him to Name or produce that Person he had them from.

UPON this Writing Sign'd by three Gentlemen who were Present, and by the Person in particular who lost the things; the young Gentleman told them, he would go and do his utmost to get the Pocket-book, and all that was in it.

THEN he desir'd that they would in Writing before Hand, give him a particular of all the several things that were in the Book; that he might not have it said when he produc'd it, that there was not all; and he would have the said Writing Seal'd up, and he would make the Book be Seal'd up when it was given to him; This they agreed to, and the Gentleman accordingly drew up a particular of all the Bills that he remembred, *as he said*, was in the Book; and also of the *Diamonds*, as follows:

One Bill under Sir *Henry Furness*'s[116] Hand, for	1200*l.*
One Bill under Sir *Charles Duncomb*'s[117] Hand, for ⎫ 800*l.* 25*l.* Endorst off[118] ⎭	550
One Bill under the Hand of *J. Tassell*,[119] ⎫ Goldsmith ⎭	165
One Bill of Sir *Francis Child*,[120]	39
One Bill of one *Stewart*[121] that kept a *Wager Office*, ⎫ and *Insurance*. ⎭	350

A Paper containing 37 loose *Diamonds*, value about 250*l.*

A little Paper containing three large Rough *Diamonds*, and one large one, polish'd, and Cut, Value 185*l.*

FOR all these things, they promiss'd first to give him[a] what ever he agreed with the Thief to give him; not exceeding 50*l.* and to give him 50*l.* more for himself for procuring them.

NOW he had his Cue, and now he came to me, and told me honestly the whole Story, as above; so I deliver'd him the Book, and he told me that he thought it was reasonable we should not take the full Sum; because, he would seem to have done them some Service, and so make them the easier; all this I agreed to, so he went the next Day to the place, and the Gentlemen met him very punctually.

HE told them at first Word, he had done their Work, and as he hoped to their Mind; and told them, if it had not been for the *Diamonds*, he could have got it all for 10*l*; but that the *Diamonds* had shone so Bright in the Boy's Imagination, that he talk'd of running away to *France* or *Holland*, and living there all his Days like a Gentleman; at which they Laught: However, Gentlemen, *said he*, here is the Book, and so pull'd it out wrapt up in a Dirty peice of a Colour'd Handkerchief, as black as the Street could make it; and Seal'd with a peice of sorry Wax, and the Impression of a Farthing for a Seal.

UPON this, the Note being also unseal'd, at the same time he pull'd open the Dirty Rag, and shew'd the Gentleman his Pocket-Book; at which he was so over surpriz'd with Joy, notwithstanding all the preparatory Discourse, that he was fain to call for a Glass of Wine or Brandy, to Drink to keep him from Fainting.

THE Book being open'd, the Paper of *Diamonds* was first taken out; and there they were every one, only the little Paper was by itself, and the Rough *Diamonds* that were in it, were loose among the rest; but he own'd they were all there Safe.

THEN the Bills were call'd over, one by one, and they found one Bill for 80 Pound more than the Account mention'd; besides, several Papers which were not for Money, tho' of Consequence to the Gentleman; and he acknowledg'd that all was very honestly return'd, and now young Man, *said they*, you shall see we will deal as honestly by you; and so in the first place, they gave him 50*l*. for himself; and then they told out the 50*l*. for me.

HE took the 50*l*. for himself, and put it up in his Pocket, wrapping it in Paper, it being all in Gold: Then he began to tell over the other 50*l*. but when he had told out[122] 20*l*. Hold Gentlemen, *said he*, as I have acted fairly for you, so you shall have no reason to say, I do not do so to the End; I have taken 30*l*. and for so much I agreed with the Boy, and so there is 20*l*. of your Money again.

THEY stood looking one at another a good while, as surpriz'd at the honesty of it, for till that time they were not quite without a secret Suspicion that he was the Thief, but that peice of Policy cleared up his Reputation to them: The Gentleman that had got his Bills, said softly to one of them, give it him all, but the other said (softly too,) no, no, as long as he has got it abated, and is satisfied with the 50*l*. you have given him, 'tis very well, let it go as it is; this was not spoke so softly but he[a] heard it, and *he[b] said no* *too*, I am very well satisfied, I am glad I have got them for you, and so they began to part.

BUT just before they were going away, one of the Gentlemen said to him, young Man come, you see we are just to you, and have done fairly, as you have also, and we will not desire you to tell us who this cunning Fellow is that got such a Prize from this Gentleman; but as you have talk'd with him, prethee can you tell us nothing of how he did it, that we may beware of such Sparks again.

SIR, says *Will*, when I shall tell you what they say, and how the particular Case stood, the Gentleman would blame himself more than any Body else, or as much at least; The young Rogue that catch'd this Prize, was out it seems with a Comrade, who is a nimble experienced Pick-pocket as most in *London*, but at that time the Artist was some where at a distance, and this Boy never had pick'd a Pocket in his Life before; but *he says*, he stood over against the Passage into the *Exchange*, [123] on the East-Side, and the Gentleman stood just by the Passage; that he was very earnest in Talking with some other Gentleman, and often pull'd out this Book, and open'd it, and took Papers out, or put others in, and return'd it into his Coat-Pocket; that the last time it hitch'd at the Pocket-hole, or stop'd at something that was in the Pocket, and hung a little out, which the Boy, who had watch'd it a good while, perceiving, he passes by close to the Gentleman, and carry'd it smoothly off, without the Gentleman's perceiving it at all.

HE went on, *and said*, 'tis very strange Gentlemen should put Pocket-Books which have such things in them into those loose Pockets, and in so careless a manner; that's very true, *says the Gentleman*, and so with some other Discourse of no great signification he came away to me.

WE were now so rich that we scarce knew what to do with our Money, at least I did not, for I had no Relations, no Friend, no where to put any thing I had, but in my Pocket; as for *Will*, he had a poor Mother, but wicked as himself, and he made her Rich, and Glad with his good Success.

WE divided this Booty equally, for tho' the gaining it was Mine, yet the improving it was his, and his Management brought the Money; for neither he, or I could have made any thing proportionable of the thing, any other way; as for the Bills, there was no room to doubt, but unless they had been carried that Minute to the Goldsmiths for the Money, he would have come with Notice to stop the Payment, and perhaps have come while the Money was Receiving, and have taken hold of the Person; and then as to the Diamonds there had been no offering them to Sale, by us poor Boys to any Body, but those who were our known Receivers, and they would have given us nothing for them, compar'd to what they were worth; for as I understood afterwards, those who made a Trade thus of buying stolen Goods, took care to have false Weights and Cheat the poor Devil that stole them, at least an Ounce in Three.

UPON the whole, we made the best of it, many ways besides; I had a strange kind of uninstructed Conscience at that Time; for tho' I made no scruple of getting any thing in this manner from any Body, yet I could not bear destroying their Bills, and Papers, which were things that would do them a great deal of hurt, and do me no good; and I was so Tormented about it, that I could not rest Night or Day, while[124] I made the People easie, from whom the things were taken.

I WAS now rich, so rich that I knew not what to do with my Money, or with myself, I had liv'd so near and so close, that altho' as *I said*, I did now and then lay out Two-pence, or Three-pence for meer Hunger, yet I had so many People, who, *as I said*, employ'd me, and who gave me Victuals, and sometimes Clothes, that in a whole Year I had not quite Spent the 15 Shillings, which I had sav'd of the Custom House Gentleman's Money, and I had the 4 Guineas, which was of the first Booty before that, still in my Pocket, I mean the Money that I let fall into the Tree.

BUT now I began to look higher, and tho' *Will* and I went Abroad several times together, yet when small things offer'd, as Handkerchiefs, and such Trifles, we would not meddle with them, not caring to run the Risque for small Matters: It fell out one Day that as we were strouling about in *West-Smithfield*, on a *Friday*, there happen'd to be an antient Country Gentleman in the Market, selling some very large Bullocks; it seems they came out of *Sussex*, for we heard him say there were no such Bullocks in the whole County of *Sussex*; his Worship, *for so they call'd him*, had receiv'd the Money for these Bullocks at a Tavern, whose Sign I forget now, and having some of it in a Bag, and the Bag in his Hand, he was taken with a sudden fit of Coughing, and stands to Cough, resting his Hand with the Bag of Money in it, upon a Bulk-head of a Shop, just by the *Cloyster-Gate* in *Smithfield*,[125] *that is to say*, within three or four Doors of it; we were both just behind him, says *Will* to me, stand ready; upon this, he makes an artificial stumble, and falls with his Head just against the old Gentleman in the very Moment, when he was Coughing ready to be strangl'd, and quite Spent for want of Breath.

THE violence of the blow beat the old Gentleman quite down, the Bag of Money did not immediately fly out of his Hand, but I run to get hold of it, and gave it a quick snatch, pulled it clean away, and run like the Wind down the *Cloyster* with it, turn'd on the Left-Hand as soon as I was thro', and cut into *Little-Britain*, so into *Bartholomew-Close*, then cross *Aldersgate-street*, thro' *Paul's-Alley* into *Red-Cross-street*, and so cross all the Streets, thro' innumerable Alleys, and never stopp'd, till I got into the second Quarter of *Moor-fields*, our old agreed Rendezvous.

WILL, in the mean time fell down with the old Gentleman, but soon got up; the old Knight, *for such it seems he was*, was frighted with the fall, and his Breath so stopp'd with his Cough, that he could not recover himself to speak till some time, during which, nimble *Will* was got up again, and walk'd off; nor could he call out stop Thief, or tell any Body he had lost any thing for a good while; but Coughing vehemently, and looking red till he was almost black in the Face, he cry'd the Ro— *Hegh, Hegh, Hegh*, the Rogues *Hegh*, have got *Hegh, Hegh, Hegh, Hegh, Hegh, Hegh*, then he would get a little Breath, and at it again the Rogue – *Hegh, Hegh*, and after a great many *Heghs*, and *Rogues* he brought it out, have got away my Bag of Money.

ALL this while the People understood nothing of the matter, and as for the Rogues indeed, they had time enough to get clear away, and in about an Hour *Will* came to the Rendezvous; there we sat down in the Grass again, and turn'd out the Money, which prov'd to be 8 Guineas, and 5*l.* 8*s.* in Silver, so that it made just 14*l.* together; this we shar'd upon the Spot, and went to Work the same Day, for more; but whether it was that being flush'd with our Success, we were not so vigilant, or that no other opportunity offer'd, I know not, but we got nothing more that Night, nor so much as any thing offer'd it self for an attempt.

WE took many Walks of this kind, sometime together, at a little distance from one another, and several small Hits[126] we made, but we were so flush'd with our Success, that truly we were above meddling with Trifles, *as I said before*, no, not such things, that others would have been glad of; nothing but Pocket-Books, Letter-Cases, or Sums of Money would move us.

THE next Adventure was in the dusk of the Evening in a Court, which goes out of *Grace-Church-street* into *Lombard-street*, where the *Quaker's-Meeting House* is; there was a young Fellow, who as we learn'd afterward was a Wollen-Drapers Apprentice in *Grace-Church-street*; it seems he had been receiving a Sum of Money, which was very considerable, and he comes to a Goldsmith's-Shop in *Lombard Street* with it; paid in the most of it there, insomuch, that it grew Dark, and the Goldsmith began to be shutting in Shop, and Candles to be Lighted: We watch'd him in there, and stood on the other Side of the way to see what he did When he had paid in all the Money he intended; he stay'd still sometime longer to take Notes, as I suppos'd, for what he had paid, and by this time it was still darker than before; at last he comes out of the Shop, with still a pretty large Bag under his Arm, and walks over into the Court, which was then very Dark; in the middle of the Court is a boarded Entry, and farther, at the End of it a

Threshold, and as soon as he had set his Foot over the Threshold he was to turn on his Left Hand into *Grace-Church-street*.

KEEP up, says *Will* to me, be nimble, and as soon as he had said so, he flyes at the young Man, and Gives him such a violent Thrust, that push'd him forward with too great a force for him to stand, and as he strove to recover, the Threshold took his Feet, and he fell forward into the other part of the Court, as if he had flown in the Air, with his Head lying towards the *Quaker's-Meeting-House*; I stood ready, and presently felt out the Bag of Money, which I heard fall, for it flew out of his Hand, he having his Life to save, not his Money: I went forward with the Money, and *Will* that threw him down, finding I had it, run backward, and as I made along *Fen-Church-street, Will* overtook me, and we scour'd home together; the poor young Man was hurt a little with the fall, and reported to his Master, as we heard afterward that he was knock'd down, which was not true, for neither *Will*, or I had any Stick in our Hands; but the Master of the Youth was it seems so very thankful that his young Man was not knock'd down before he paid the rest of the Money, (which was above 100*l.* more) to the Goldsmith, who was Sir *John Sweetapple*,[127] that he made no great Noise at the Loss he had; and as we heard afterward, only warn'd his Prentice to be more careful, and come no more thro' such Places in the Dark; whereas the Man had really no such Deliverance as he imagined, for we saw him before, when he had all the Money about him, but it was no time of Day for such Work as we had to do, so that he was in no Danger before.

THIS Booty mounted to 29*l.* 16*s.* which was 14*l.* 18*s.* a peice, and added exceedingly to my Store, which began now to be very much too big for my Management; and indeed I began to be now full of Care for the preservation of what I had got: I wanted a trusty Friend to commit it to, but where was such a one to be found by a poor Boy, bred up among Thieves? if I should have let any honest Body know that I had so much Money, they would have ask'd me how I came by it, and would have been afraid to take it into their Hands, least I being some time or other catch'd in my Rogueries, they should be counted the Receivers of stolen Goods, and the encouragers of a Thief.

WE had however in the mean time a great many other successful Enterprizes, some of one kind, some of another, and were never so much as in danger of being apprehended; but my Companion *Will*, who was now grown a Man, and encourag'd by these Advantages fell into quite another Vein of Wickedness, getting acquainted with a wretched Gang of Fellows, that turn'd their Hands to every Thing that was vile.

Will was a lusty strong Fellow, and withal very bold and daring, would Fight any Body, and venture upon any thing, and I found he began to be above the mean Rank of a poor Pick-pocket, so I saw him but seldom; however, once coming to me in a very friendly familiar Manner, and asking me how I went on, I told him that I us'd the old Trade still, that I had had two or three good Jobbs, one with a young Woman, whose Pocket I had pick'd of eleven Guineas, and another a Country Woman just come out of a Stage-Coach, seeing her pull out her Bag to pay the Coachman, and that I follow'd her till I got an opportunity, and slipt it out so neatly, that tho' there was 8*l.* 17*s.* in it, yet she never felt it go; and several other Jobbs I told him off, by which I made pretty good Purchase: I always said you were a lucky Boy, Col. *Jack, says he,* but come you are grown almost a Man now, and you shall not be always at play at Push-pin,[128] I am got into better Business I assure you, and you shall come into it too, I'll bring you into a brave Gang *Jack, says he,* where you shall see we shall be all Gentlemen.

THEN he told me the Trade it self in short, which was with a Set of Fellows, that had two of the most desperate Works upon their Hands that belong'd to the whole Art of Thieving; *that is to say,* in the Evening they were Foot-pads, and in the Night they were House-breakers: *Will* told me so many plausible Stories, and talk'd of such great things, that in short, I who had been always us'd to do any thing he bid me do, went with him without any hesitation.

NOTHING is more certain, than that hitherto being partly from the gross Ignorance of my untaught Childhood, as I observ'd before, partly from the hardness, and wickedness of the Company I kept, and add to these, that it was the Business I might be said to be brought up to, I had, *I say,* all the way hitherto, no manner of thoughts about the Good or Evil of what I was embark'd in; consequently, I had no Sense of Conscience, no Reproaches upon my Mind for having done amiss.

YET I had something in me, by what secret Influence I knew not, kept me from the other degrees of Raking and Vice, and in short, from the general Wickedness of the rest of my Companions: For Example, I never us'd any ill Words, no Body ever heard me swear, nor was I given to drink, or to love strong drink; and I cannot omit a Circumstance that very much serv'd to prevent it; I had a strange original Notion, as I have mentioned in its Place, of my being a Gentleman; and several things had Casually happen'd in my way to encrease this Fancy of mine; it happen'd one Day, that being in the *Glass-house* Yard, between *Rosemary-lane* and *Ratcliff-high-way*, there came a Man dress'd very well, and with a Coach attending him, and he came, (as I suppose) to buy Glass-bottles, or some other Goods, as they sold; and in bargaining for his Goods, he swore most horrid Oaths at every two or three Words.

AT length the Master of the Glass, an antient grave Gentleman took the liberty to reprove him, which at first made him swear the worse; after a while the Gentleman was a little calmer, but still he swore very much, tho' not so bad as at first; after sometime, the Master of the *Glass-house* turn'd from him; really Sir, *says the good old Gentleman*, you swear so, and take God's Name in vain so, that I cannot bear to stay with you, I had rather you would let my Goods alone, and go some where else, I hope you won't take it Ill, but I don't desire to deal with any Body that does so, I am afraid my *Glass-House* should fall on your Head while you stay in it.

THE Gentleman grew good humour'd at the Reproof, and said, well come don't go away, I won't swear any more, *says he*, if I can help it, for I own, *say he*, I should not do it.

WITH that the old Gentleman look'd up at him, and returning, really Sir, *says he*, 'tis pity you that seem to be a fine Gentleman, well Bred and good Humour'd, should accustom your self to such an hateful Practice;[129] why it is not like a Gentleman to swear, 'tis enough for my black Wretches that Work there at the Furnace, or for these ragged nak'd black Guard Boys, pointing at me, and some others of the dirty Crew that lay in the Ashes; 'tis bad enough for them, *says he*, and they ought to be corrected for it too; but for a Man of Breeding, Sir, *says he*, a Gentleman! it ought to be look'd upon as below them; Gentlemen know better, and are taught better, and it is plain you know better; I beseech you Sir, when you are tempted to swear, always ask your self, is this like a Gentleman? does this become me as a Gentleman! do but ask your self that Question, and your Reason will prevail, you will soon leave it off.

I HEARD all this, and it made the Blood run Chill in my Veins, when he said Swearing was only fit for such as we were; in short, it made as great an Impression upon me, as it did upon the Gentleman; *and yet he took it very kindly too, and thank'd the old Gentleman for his Advice.* But from that time forward I never had the least Inclination to Swearing, or ill Words, and abhored it when I heard the other Boys do it; as to Drinking, I had no Opportunity, for I had nothing to Drink, but Water or small Beer,[130] that any body gave me in Charity, for they seldom gave away strong Beer; and after I had Money, I neither desir'd strong Beer, or car'd to part with my Money to Buy it.

THEN as to Principle, 'tis true I had no Foundation lay'd in me by Education; and being early led by my fate into Evil, I had the less Sense of its being Evil left upon my Mind: But when I began to grow to an Age of understanding, and to know that I was a Thief, growing up in all manner of Villany, and ripening a-pace for the Gallows, it came often into my thoughts that I was going wrong, that I was in the high Road to the Devil, and several times would stop short, and ask my self, if this was the Life of a Gentleman?

BUT these little things wore off again, as often as they came on, and I follow'd the old Trade again; especially when *Will* came to prompt me as I have observ'd, for he was a kind of a Guide to me in all these things, and I had by Custom and Application, together with seeing his way, learnt to be as acute a Workman as my Master.

BUT to go back where I left off, *Will* came to me as I have said, and telling me how much better Business he was fallen into, would have me go along with him, and I should be a Gentleman: *Will* it seems understood that Word in a quite differing manner from me; for his Gentleman was nothing more or less than a Gentleman Thief, a Villain of a higher Degree than a Pick-pocket; and one that might do something more Wicked, and better Entituling him to the Gallows, than could be done in our way: But my Gentleman that I had my Eye upon, was another thing quite, tho' I cou'd not really tell how to describe it neither.

HOWEVER the Word took with me,[131] and I went with him; we were neither of us Old, *Will* was about 24, and as for me I was now about 18, and pretty Tall of my Age.

THE first time I went with him, he brought me into the Company only of two more young Fellows; we met at the lower part of *Grays-Inn-Lane*, about an Hour before Sun-set, and went out into the Fields toward a place call'd *Pindar* of *Wakefield*,[132] where are abundance of Brick-Kilns: Here it was agreed to spread from the Field Path to the Road way, all the way towards *Pancrass Church*,[133] to observe any Chance Game, which as they call'd it, they might shoot Flying:[134] Upon the Path within the Bank, on the side of the Road going towards *Kentish Town*, two of our Gang, *Will*, and one of the other, met a single Gentleman walking a-pace towards the Town, being almost Dark: *Will* Cryed, *Mark ho*, which it seems was the Word, at which we were all to stand still at a distance, come in if he wanted help, and give a Signal if any thing appear'd that was Dangerous.

Will steps up to the Gentleman, stops him, and put the Question, that is, *Sir, your Money?* the Gentleman seeing he was alone, struck at him with his Cane, but *Will* a Nimble strong Fellow flew in upon him, and with Struggling, got him down, then he begg'd for his Life, *Will* having told him with an Oath, that he would Cut his Throat: In that Moment, while this was doing, comes a Hackney Coach along the Road; and the fourth Man who was that way, Crys, *Mark ho*, which was to intimate that it was a Prize, not a Surprize, and accordingly the next Man went up to assist him, where they stop'd the Coach, which had a Doctor of Physick[135] and a Surgeon in it, who had been to Visit some considerable Patient; and I suppose had had considerable Fees; for here they got two good Purses, one with 11 or 12 Guineas, the other Six, with some Pocket Money, two Watches, one Diamond Ring, and the Surgeons Plaister-box,[136] which was most of it full of Silver Instruments.

WHILE they were at this Work, *Will* kept the Man down, who was under him; and tho' he promis'd not to Kill him unless he offer'd to make a Noise, yet he would not let him stir till he heard the Noise of the Coach going on again, by which he knew the jobb was over on that Side: Then he Carried him a little out of the way, ty'd his Hands behind him, and bid him lye still and make no Noise, and he would come back in half an Hour and untie him upon his Word, but if he Cryed out he would come back and Kill him.

THE poor Man promis'd to lye still and make no Noise, and did so; and had not above 11*s.* 6*d.* in his Pocket, which *Will* took, and came back to the rest, but while they were together, I who was on the Side of the *Pindar* of *Wakefield*, cry'd *Mark ho*, too.

WHAT I saw, was a Couple of poor Women, one a kind of a Nurse, and the other a Maid-Servant going for *Kentish-Town*: As *Will* knew that I was but young at the work, he came flying to me, and seeing how easie a Bargain it was, *he said*, go *Col.* fall to Work; I went up to them, and speaking to the elderly Woman, Nurse, *said I*, don't be in such hast, I want to speak with you, at which they both stopp'd, and look'd a little frighted; don't be frighted Sweetheart, *said I*, to the Maid, a little of that Money in the bottom of your Pocket will make all easie, and I'll do you no harm; by this time *Will* came up to us, for they did not see him before; then they began to scream out; hold, *says I*, make no Noise, unless you have a mind to force us to murther you whether we will or no, give me your Money presently,[137] and make no Words, and we shan't hurt you; upon this, the poor Maid pull'd out 5*s.* 6*d.* and the old Woman a Guinea, and a Shilling, crying heartily for her Money, and said, it was all she had left in the World; well we took it for all that, tho' it made my very heart bleed to see what agony the poor Woman was in at parting with it, and I ask'd her where she liv'd, she said her Name was *Smith*, and she liv'd at *Kentish-Town*; I said nothing to her but bid them go on about their Business, and I gave *Will* the Money; so in a few Minutes we were all together again: Says one of the other Rogues, come, this is well enough, for one Road; its time to be gone; so we jog'd[138] away, crossing the Fields, out of the Path towards *Tottenham-Court*;[139] but hold, *says Will*, I must go and untye the Man, D—m him, *says one of them*, let him lye, no *says Will*, I won't be worse than my Word, I will untye him; so he went to the Place, but the Man was gone, either he had untyed himself, or some Body had pass'd by, and he had call'd for help, and so was unty'd, for he could not find him, nor make him hear, tho' he ventur'd to call twice for him aloud.

THIS made us hasten away the faster, and getting into *Tottenham Court* Road, they thought it was a little too near, so they made into the Town at St. *Giles*, and crossing to *Pickadilly*, went to *High-Park-Gate*;[140] here they ventured to rob another Coach; *that is to say*, one of the two other Rogues, and *Will* did it between the *Park Gate* and *Knight's-bridge*; there was in it, only a Gentleman and a Punk;[141] a Whore that he had pick'd up, it seems at the *Spring-Garden*[142] a little farther; they took the Gentleman's Money, and his Watch, and his Silver hilted Sword; but when they come to the Slut, she Damn'd them, and curs'd them for robbing the Gentleman of his Money, and leaving him none for her; as for her self, she had not one Sixpenny Peice about her, tho' she was indeed well enough dress'd too.

HAVING made this Adventure, we left that Road too, and went over the Fields to *Chelsea*; in the way from *Westminster* to *Chelsea*, we met three Gentlemen; but they were too strong for us to meddle with; they had been afraid to come over the Fields so late, (for by this time it was Eight a-Clock, and tho' the Moon gave some Light, yet it was too late, and too dark to be Safe,) so they hired three Men at *Chelsea*, two with Pitch-Forks, and the third, a Waterman, with a Boat-Hook-Staff to Guard them; we would have Steer'd clear of them, and car'd not to have them see us if we could help it, but they did see us, and cry'd, *Who comes there?* we answer'd Friends, and so they went on to our great Satisfaction.

WHEN we came to *Chelsea*, it seems we had other Work to do, which I had not been made privy to, and this was a House to be robb'd; they had some Intelligence it seems with a Servant in the House, who was of their Gang; this Rogue was a Waiting-man, or Foot-man, and he had a Watch word to let them in by; but this Fellow not for want of being a Villain, but by getting drunk, and not minding his part of the Work disappointed us, for he had Promis'd to rise at Two a-Clock in the Morning, and let us all in; but being very Drunk, and not come in at Eleven a-Clock his Master order'd him to be shut out, and the Doors lock'd up, and charg'd the other Servants not to let him in, upon any Terms whatsoever.

WE came about the House at One a-Clock to make our Observations, intending to go and lye under *Beaufort-House*[143] Wall till the Clock struck Two, and then to come again; but behold! when we came to the House, there lay the Fellow at the Door fast a-sleep, and very Drunk: *Will*, who I found was the Leader in all these things, wak'd the Fellow, who as he had had about two Hours Sleep was a little come to himself, and told them the Misfortune, as he call'd it, and that he could not get in; they had some Instruments about them, by which they could have broken in by Force, but

Will consider'd, that as it was but waiting till another time, and they should be let in quietly, they resolv'd to give it over for that time.

BUT this was a happy Drunken-bout for the Family, for the Fellow having let fall some Words in his Drink, for he was a Saucy one, as well as a Drunken one, and talk'd oddly, as that it had been better they had let him in, and he would make them pay dear for it, or some such thing; the Master hearing of it, turn'd him away in the Morning, and never let him come into his House again; *so I say,* it was a happy Drunkenness to the Family, for it sav'd them from being robb'd, and perhaps murther'd, for they were a cursed bloody Crew, and as I found were about Thirteen of them in all, whereof three of them made it their Business to get into Gentlemens Services, and so to open Doors in the Night, and let the other Rogues in upon them, to rob and destroy them.

I rambl'd this whole Night with them; they went from *Chelsea,* being disappointed there as above, to *Kensington;* there they broke into a Brew-house, and Wash-house, and by that means into an Out-Kitchen of a Gentleman's-House, where they unhang'd a small Copper,[144] and brought it off, and stole about a Hundred weight of Pewter, and went clear off with that too, and every one going their own by-ways, they found means to get safe to their several Receptacles where they used to dispose of such things.

WE lay still the next Day, and shar'd the Effects stolen that Night, of which my Share came to 8*l.* 19*s.* the Copper and Pewter being weigh'd, and cast up, a Person was at hand to take it as Money, at about half Value, and in the Afternoon, *Will* and I came away together: *Will* was mighty full of the Success we had had, and how we might be sure of the like this way every Day. But he observ'd that I did not seem so elevated at the Success of that Night's Ramble as I us'd to be, and also that I did not take any great Notice of the Expectations he was in, of what was to come, yet I had said little to him at that time.

BUT my Heart was full of the poor Woman's Case at *Kentish* Town, and I resolv'd, if possible to find her out, and give her her Money: With the abhorrence that fill'd my Mind at the Cruelty of that Act, there necessarily follow'd a little Distaste of the thing it self, and now it came into my Head with a double force, that this was the High Road to the Devil, and that certainly this was not the Life of a Gentleman!

Will and I parted for that time, but next Morning we met again, and *Will* was mighty Brisk and Merry; and now Col. *Jack, says he,* we shall be Rich very quickly; well, *says I,* and what shall we do, when we are Rich? do, *says he,* we will buy a Couple of good Horses, and go farther a Field; what do you mean by farther a Field, *said I?* why, *says he,* we will take the Highway like Gentlemen, and then we shall get a great deal of Money indeed; well, *says I*, what then? why then, *says he*, we shall live like Gentlemen.

BUT *Will*, *says I*, if we get a great deal of Money, shan't we leave this Trade off, and sit down, and be Safe and Quiet?

AY, says *Will*, when we have got a great Estate we shall be willing to lay it down; but where, *says I*, shall we be before that time comes, if we should drive on this cursed kind of Trade?

PRETHEE never think of that, *says Will*, if you think of those things, you will never be fit to be a Gentleman; he touch'd me there indeed, for it run much in my Mind still, that I was to be a Gentleman, and it made me Dumb for a while; but I came to my self after a little while, and I said to him, pretty Tartly, Why *Will*, do you call this way of Living the Life of a Gentleman?

WHY, *says Will*, why not?

WHY, *says I*, was it like a Gentleman for me to take that Two and Twenty Shillings from a poor antient Woman, when she beg'd of me upon her Knees not to take it, and told me it was all she had in the World to buy her Bread for her self and a sick Child which she had at home, do you think I could be so Cruel if you had not stood by, and made me do it? why, I cry'd at doing it, as much as the poor Woman did, tho' I did not let you see me.

YOU Fool you, *says Will*, you will never be fit for our Business indeed, if you mind such things as those, I shall bring you off of those things quickly; why, if you will be fit for Business, you must learn to fight when they resist, and cut their Throats when they submit; you must learn to stop their Breath, that they may beg and pray no more; what signifies pity? prethee, who will pity us when we come to the *Old Baily*? I warrant you that whining old Woman that beg'd so heartily for her Two and Twenty Shillings would let you or I beg upon our Knees, and would not save our Lives by not coming in for an Evidence against us; did you ever see any of them cry when they see Gentlemen go to the Gallows?

WELL, *Will*, *says I*, you had better let us keep to the Business we were in before; there was no such cruel doings in that, and yet we got more Money by it, then I believe we shall get at this.

NO, no, says *Will*, you are a Fool, you don't know what fine things we shall do in a little while.

UPON this Discourse we parted for that time, but I resolv'd with my self, that I would never be concern'd with him that Way any more; the Truth is, they were such a dreadful Gang, such horrid barbarous Villains, that even that little while that I was among them, my very blood run cold in my Veins at what I heard, particularly, the continu'd Raving and Damning one another, and themselves at every Word they spoke; and then the horrid

Resolutions of Murther, and cutting Throats, which I perceiv'd was in their Minds upon any Occasion that should present; this appear'd first in their Discourse upon the Disappointment they met with at *Chelsea*, where the two Rogues that were with us, ay, and *Will* too damn'd and rag'd, that they could not get into the House, and swore they would have cut the Gentleman's Throat, if they had got in, and shook Hands, damning and cursing themselves, if they did not murther the whole Family, as soon as *Tom* (that was the Man-Servant) could get an Opportunity to let them in.

TWO Days after this, Will came to my Lodging, for I had now got a Room by myself, had bought me tollerably good Cloaths, and some Shirts, and began to look like other Folks, but as it happen'd I was Abroad upon the Scout[145] another way; for tho' I was not harden'd enough for so black a Villain as *Will* would have had me be, yet I had not arriv'd to any Principle sufficient to keep me from a Life, in its degree wicked enough, which tended to the same Destruction, tho' not in so violent and precipitant Degrees: I had his Message deliver'd to me, which was to meet him the next Evening, at *such a Place*, and I came in time enough to meet, so I went to the Place, but resolv'd before hand, that I would not go any more with him among the Gang.

HOWEVER, to my great Satisfaction I miss'd him, for he did not come at all to the Place, but met with the Gang at another Place, they having sent for him in hast upon the Notice of some Booty, and so they went all away together; this was a Summons, it seems from one of the Creatures, which they had Abroad in a Family, where an Opportunity offer'd them to commit a notorious Robbery, down almost as far as *Hownslow*,[146] and where they wounded a Gentleman's Gardiner so, that I think he dyed, and robb'd the House of a very considerable Sum of Money and Plate.

THIS however was not so clean carried, nor did they get in so easie, but by the Resistance they met with, the Neighbours were all arm'd, and the Gentlemen Rogues were pursued, and being at *London* with the Booty, one of them was taken; *Will*, a dexterous Fellow, and Head of the Gang, made his Escape, and tho' in his Cloths with a great weight about him, of both Money and Plate, plung'd into the *Thames*, and swam over where there was no Path, or Road, leading to the River; so that no Body suspected any ones going that way; being got over, he made his way wet as he was into some Woods adjacent, and as he told me afterwards, not far from *Chertsy*, and stay'd lurking about in the Woods, or Fields there about, till his Cloaths were dry, then in the Night got down to *Kingstone*, and so to *Mortlack*, where he got a Boat to *London*.[147]

HE knew nothing that one of his Comerades[148] was taken; only he knew that they were all so closely pursued that they were oblig'd to disperse, and every one to shift for himself: He happened to come home in the Evening as good luck then directed him, just after search had been made for him by the Constables; his companion, who was taken, having upon promise of Favour, and of saving him from the Gallows, discover'd his Companions, and *Will* among the rest, as the principal Party in the whole Undertaking.

Will got notice of this just time enough to run for it, and not to be taken, and away he came to look for me; but as my good Fate still directed, I was not at home neither; however, he left all his Booty at my Lodging, and hid it in an old Coat, that lay under my Bedding, and left Word that my Brother *Will* had been there, and had left his Coat that he borrow'd of me, and that it was under my Bed.

I KNEW not what to make of it, but went up to go to Bed, and finding the Parcel, was perfectly frighted to see wrap'd up in it above a Hundred Pound in Plate, and Money, and yet knew nothing of Brother *Will, as he call'd himself,* nor did I hear of him in three or four Days.

AT the end of four Days, I heard by great Accident that *Will,* who us'd to be seen with me, and who call'd me Brother, was taken, and would be hang'd: Next Day a poor Man a Shoemaker, that us'd formerly to have a kindness for me, and to send me of Errands, and give me sometimes some Victuals, seeing me accidently in *Rosemary lane,* going by him, clap'd me fast hold by the Arm, hark ye young Man, *says he,* have I catch'd you, and hal'd[149] me a long as if I had been a Thief apprehended, and he the Constable; hark ye, *Col.* Jack, *says he again,* come a long with me, I must speak with you: What are you got into this Gang too? What are you turn'd House-breaker? come I'll have you hang'd to be sure.

THESE were dreadful Words to me, who tho' not guilty of the particular thing in Question, yet was frighted heartily before, and did not know what I might be charg'd with by *Will,* if he was taken, as I had heard that very Morning, he was; with these Words, the Shoemaker began to hale[150] and drag me a long as he us'd to do when I was a Boy.

HOWEVER recovering my Spirits, and provoked to the highest degree, I said to him again, what do you mean Mr. —? let me alone, or you will oblige me to make you do it, and with that, I stop'd short, and soon let him see I was grown a little too big to be hal'd about, as I us'd to be, when I run of his Errands, and made a Motion with my other Hand as if I would strike him in the Face.

HOW, *Jack! says he,* will you strike me? will you strike your old Friend? and then he let go my Arm, and Laugh'd; well, but hark ye *Col. says he,* I am in earnest, I hear bad News of you; they say you are gotten into bad Company, and that this *Will,* calls you Brother; he is a great Villain, and I hear he is Charg'd with a bloody Robbery, and will be hang'd, if he is taken; I hope you are not concern'd with him, if you are, I would advise you to shift for your self, for the Constable, and the Headborough[151] are after him to Day, and if he can lay any thing to you he will do it you may be sure; he will certainly hang you to save himself.

THIS was kind, and I thank'd him, but told him, this was a thing too Serious, and that had too much Weight in it to be jested with, as he had done before; and that some Ignorant Stranger might have seiz'd upon me, as a Person Guilty, who had no farther Concern in it, than just knowing the Man, and so I might have been brought into Trouble for nothing; at least People might have thought I was among them, whether I was or no, and it would have rendered me suspected, tho' I was Innocent.

HE acknowledg'd that, told me he was but in jest, and that he talk'd to me just as he us'd to do; However, Col. *says he*, I wont jest any more with you, in a thing of such a dangerous Consequence; I only advise you to keep the Fellow Company no more.

I THANK'D him, and went away, but in the greatest perplexity Imaginable; and now not knowing what to do with my self, or with the little ill-gotten Wealth which I had; I went musing, and alone into the Fields towards *Stepney*, my usual Walk; and there began to consider what to do, and as this Creature had left his Prize in my Garret, I began to think, that if he should be taken and should Confess, and send the Officers to Search there for the Goods, and they should find them, I should be undone, and should be taken up for a Confederate; whereas, I knew nothing of the matter, and had no Hand in it.

WHILE I was thus musing, and in great Perplexity, I heard some body Hallow to me; and looking about, I saw *Will* running after me: I knew not what to think at first; but seeing him alone was the more Encouraged, and I stood still for him; when he came up to me, I said to him, What's the matter *Will?* matter, *says Will*, matter enough, I am undone, when was you at Home?

I saw what you left there, *says I*, what is the meaning of it, and where got you all that? is that your being undone?

AY, *says Will*, I am undone for all that; for the Officers are after me, and I am a Dead Dog if I am taken, for *George* is in Custody, and he has Peach'd[152] me and all the others, to save his Life.

LIFE! *says I*, why should you loose your Life, if they should take you, pray what would they do to you?

DO to me, *says he*, they would Hang me, if the King had ne'er another Soldier in his Guards, I shall certainly be Hang'd, as I am now alive.

THIS frighted me terribly, and *I said*, and what will you do then? Nay, *says he*, I know not, I would get out of the Nation if I knew how; but I am a Stranger to all those things, and I know not what to do, not I; advise me, *Jack, says he,* prethee tell me whether[153] shall I go, I have a good mind to go to Sea.

YOU talk of going away, *says I,* what will you do with all that you have hid in my Garret, it must not lye there, *said I,* for if I should be taken up for it; and it be found to be the Money you Stole, I shall be ruin'd.

I CARE not what becomes of it, not I, *says Will;* I'll be gone, do you take it, if you will, and do what you will with it; I must Fly, and I cannot take it with me: I won't have it, not I, *says I,* to him, I'll go and fetch it to you if you will take it, *says I,* but I wont meddle with it; besides, there is Plate, what shall I do with Plate, *said I,* if I should offer to sell it any where, *said I,* they will stop me?

AS for that, *says Will,* I cou'd Sell it well enough, if I had it, but I must not be seen any where among my old Acquaintance; for I am blown,[154] and they will all betray me: But I will tell you where you shall go and Sell it if you will; and they will ask you no Questions, if you give them the Word that I will give you; so he gave me the Word, and Directions to a Pawn-broker, near *Cloth-fair;*[155] the Word was *GOOD TOWER STANDARD;*[156] having these Instructions, *he said,* to me, Col. *Jack,* I am sure you won't betray me; and I promise you if I am taken, and should be Hang'd, I won't name you, I will go to such a House, naming a House at *Bromley* by *Bow;* where he and I had often been, and there, *says he,* I'll stay till it is Dark; at Night I will come near the Streets, and I will lye under such a Hay-stack all Night, a place we both knew also very well; and if you cannot finish to come to me there, I will go back to *Bow.*

I WENT back and took the Cargo, went to the place by *Cloth fair,* and gave the Word, *GOOD TOWER STANDARD;* and without any words they took the Plate, weigh'd it, and paid me after the Rate of 2*s.* per Ounce for it; so I came away, and went to meet him; but it was too late to meet him at the first place; but I went to the Hay-stack, and there I found him fast a sleep.

I DELIVER'D him his Cargo, what it really amounted to, I knew not, for I never told it; but I went Home to my Quarters very late, and Tyr'd: I went to Sleep at first, but not withstanding, I was so weary I Slept little or none, for several Hours; at last being overcome with Sleep, I Dropt, but was immediately Rouz'd with Noise of People knocking at the Door, as if they would beat it down, and Crying and Calling out to the People of the House, Rise, and let in the Constable here, we come for your Lodger in the Garret.

I WAS frighted to the last degree, and started up in my Bed; but when I was awake, I heard no Noise at all, but of two *Watch-men* thumping at the

Doors with their Staves, and giving the Hour past Three a Clock, and a Rainy wet Morning *for such it was*: I was very glad when I found it was but a Dream, and went to Bed again, but was soon Rouz'd a Second time, with the same, very same Noise, and Words: Then being sooner awak'd than I was before, I Jump'd out of Bed and run to the Window, and found it was just an Hour more, and the *Watch-men* were come about past four a Clock, and they went way again very quietly; so I lay me down again, and slept the rest of the Night quietly enough.

I LAY'D no stress upon the thing call'd a Dream, neither till now did I understand that Dreams were of any Importance: But getting up the next Day, and going out with a Resolution to meet Brother *WILL*, who should I meet, but my former Brother, Capt. *Jack*? When he saw me, he came Close to me in his Blunt way; and says, do you hear the News? no, not I, *said I*, what News? your old Comrade and Teacher is taken this Morning and carried to *Newgate*; how! *says I*, this Morning! yes, *says he*, this Morning, at 4 a Clock, he is Charg'd with a Robbery and Murther some where beyond *Brentford*, and that which is worse, is, that he is Impeach'd by one of the Gang, who to save his own Life, has turn'd Evidence; and therefore you had best consider, *says the Capt.* what you have to do: What I have to do! *says I*, and what do you mean by that? Nay, Col. *says he*, don't be angry, you know best if you are not in Danger; I am glad of it, but I doubt not but you were with them: No, not I, *said I*, again, I assure you, I was not; well, *says he*, but if you were not with them this bout, you have been with them at other times; and 'twill be all one: Not I, *says I*, you are quite mistaken, I am none of their Gang; they are above my Quality; with such, and a little more talk of that kind we parted, and Capt. *Jack* went away; but as he went, I observ'd, he shook his Head, seem'd to have more Concern upon him, than I at first apprehended; and indeed, more than he cou'd be suppos'd to have, meerly on my Account, of which we shall hear more very quickly.

I WAS Extreamly allarm'd when I heard *Will* was in *Newgate*, and had I known where to have gone, would certainly have fled as far as Legs would have carry'd me; my very Joints trembl'd, and I was ready to sink into the Ground, and all that Evening, and that Night following, I was in the uttermost Consternation; my Head run upon nothing but *Newgate*, and the Gallows, and being Hang'd; which I said I deserv'd, if it were for nothing but taking that two and twenty Shillings from the poor old Nurse.

THE first thing my perplex'd Thoughts allow'd me to take care of, was my Money: This indeed lay in a little Compass, and I carried it generally all about me; I had got together as you will perceive by the past Account, above Sixty Pounds, for I spent nothing, and what to do with it I knew not;

at last it came into my Head, that I would go to my Benefactor, the Clerk, at the *Custom-house*, if he was to be found, and see if I could get him to take the rest of my Money; the only Business was to make a plausible Story to him, that he might not wonder how I came by so much Money.

BUT my Invention quickly supply'd that want; there was a Suit of Cloths at one of our Houses of Rendezvous, which was left there for any of the Gang to put on upon particular Occasions, as a Disguise: This was a Green Livery, Lac'd with Pink Colour'd Galloon,[157] and lin'd with the same; an Edg'd Hat,[158] a pair of Boots, and a Whip, I went and Dress'd my self up in this Livery, and went to my Gentleman, to his House in *Tower-street*; and there I found him in Health, and Well, just the same honest Gentleman, as ever.

HE star'd at me when first I came to him, for I meet him just at his Door; I say he star'd at me, and seeing me Bow, and Bow to him several times, with my Lac'd Hat under my Arm; at last not knowing me in the least, *says he*, to me, Dost thou want to speak with me, young Man? and I said, yes, Sir, I believe your Worship (I had learnt some Manners now) does not know me; I am poor Boy *Jack*; he look'd hard at me, and then Recollecting me presently, says he, *who* Col. *Jack! why where hast thou been all this while? why 'tis five or six Years since I saw you*: 'Tis above Six Years and please your Worship, *says I*.

Well, and where hast thou been all this while, *says he*?

I have been in the Country, Sir, *says I*, at Service?

WELL, Col. *Jack, says he*, you give long Credit, what's the Reason you han't fetch'd your Money all this while, nor the Interest? why, you will grow so rich in time by the Interest of your Money, you won't know what to do with it.

To that I said nothing, but Bow'd, and Scrap'd a great many times; well come, Col. *Jack, said he*, come in, and I will give you your Money, and the Interest of it too.

I Cring'd,[159] and Bow'd, and told him, I did not come to him for my Money; for I had had a good place or two, and I did not want my Money.

Well, Col. *Jack, said he*, and who do you Live with?

Sir *Jonathan Loxham*, said I, *Sir*, in *Somersetshire* and please your Worship: This was a name I had heard of, but knew nothing of any such Gentleman, or of the Country.[160]

Well, *says he*, but won't you have your Money *Jack*?

No, Sir, *said I*, if your Worship would please, for I have had a good place.

If I would please to do, what prethee? your Money is ready I tell thee.

No, Sir, *said I*, but I have had a good place.

Well, and what doest thou mean *Jack*? I do not understand thee.

Why, and please your Worship, my old Master, Sir *Jonathan*'s Father left me 30*l.* when he Died, and a Suit of Mourning,[161] and –

And what prethee *Jack*, what hast thou brought me more Money? for then he began to understand what I meant.

Yes, Sir, *said I*, and your Worship would be so good to take it, and put it all together, I have sav'd some too out of my Wages.

I TOLD you, *Jack, says he*, you would be rich, and how much hast thou sav'd, come let me see it.

To shorten the Story, I pull'd it out, and he was content to take it, giving me his Note, with Interest, for the whole Sum, which amounted to Ninety four Pounds, that is to say,

    25*l.*   The first Money.
     9   For Six Years Interest.
    60   Now paid him.
    ――――
    94 Pounds.

I CAME away exceeding Joyful, made him abundance of Bows, and Scrapes, and went immediately to shift[162] my Cloaths again, with a Resolution to run away from *London*, and see it no more for a great while; but I was surpris'd the very next Morning, when going cross *Rosemary-lane*, by the End of the Place, which is call'd *Rag-Fair*,[163] I heard one call *Jack*; he had said something before, which I did not hear, but upon hearing the Name *Jack*, I look'd about me, immediately saw three Men, and after them a Constable coming towards me with great Fury; I was in a great Surprize, and started to run, but one of them clap'd in upon me, and got hold of me, and in a Moment the rest surrounded me, and I was taken, I ask'd them what they wanted, and what I had done; they told me it was no Place to Talk of that there; but show'd me their Warrant, and bad me read it, and I should know the rest when I came before the Justice, so they hurried me away.

I took the Warrant, but to my great Affliction, I could know nothing by that, for I could not read, so I desir'd them to read it, and they read it that they were to Apprehend a known Thief, that went by the Name of one of the three *Jacks* of *Rag-Fair*, for that he was Charg'd upon Oath, with having been a Party in a notorious Robbery, Burglary, and Murther, committed so and so, in such a Place, and on such a Day.

IT was to no purpose for me to deny it, or to say I knew nothing of it, that was none of their Business they said; that must be disputed, they told me, before the Justice, where I would find that it was sworn positively against me, and then perhaps I might be better satisfied.

I HAD no remedy, but Patience, and as my Heart was full of Terror and Guilt, so I was ready to die with the weight of it; as they carried me a long, for as I very well knew that I was Guilty of the first Days work, tho' I was not of the last; so I did not doubt, but I should be sent to *Newgate*, and then I took it for granted I must be hang'd; for to go to *Newgate*, and to be hang'd were to me, as things which necessarily followed one another.

BUT I had a sharp Conflict to go thro' before it came to that Part, and that was before the Justice, where when I was come, and the Constable brought me in, the Justice ask'd me my Name; but, hold, *says he*, young Man, before I ask you your Name, let me do you Justice, you are not bound to answer till your Accusers come, so turning to the Constable, he ask'd for his Warrant.

WELL, *says the Justice*, you have brought this young Man here by Vertue of this Warrant; is this young Man the Person for whom this Warrant is granted?

Con. I believe so, and please your Worship.

Just. Believe so. Why are you not sure of it?

Con. An't please your Worship, the People said so, where I took him.

Just. It is a very particular kind of Warrant, it is to apprehend a young Man, who goes by the Name of *Jack*, but no Sir Name,[164] only that it is said, he is call'd Capt. *Jack*, or some other such Name. Now young Man, pray is your Name Capt. *Jack*? or are you usually call'd so?

I presently found, that the Men that took me knew nothing of me, and that the Constable had taken me up by Hear-say, so I took Heart and told the Justice, that I thought with submission, that it was not the present Question, what my Name was, but what these Men, or any one else had to lay to my Charge, whether I was the Person, who the Warrant empower'd to Apprehend or no.

HE smil'd, 'tis very true young Man, *says he*, it is very true, and on my Word, if they have taken you up, and do not know you, and there is no Body to Charge you, they will be mistaken to their own Damage.

THEN I told his Worship, I hop'd I should not be oblig'd to tell my Name till my Accuser was brought to Charge me, and then I should not conceal my Name.

IT is but Reason, said his good Worship, Mr. *Constable*, turning to the Officers; are you sure this is the Person that is intended in your Warrant? if you are not, you must fetch the Person that Accuses him, and on whose Oath the Warrant was granted: They us'd many Words to insinuate that I was the Person, and that I knew it well enough, and that I should be oblig'd to tell my Name.

I insisted on the unreasonableness of it, and that I should not be oblig'd to accuse myself, and the Justice told them in so many Words, that he could not force me to it, that I might do it if I would indeed; but you see, *says the Justice*, he understood too well, to be impos'd upon in that Case; so that in short, after an Hours Debating before his Worship, in which time I pleaded against four of them, the Justice told them they must produce the Accuser, or he must Discharge me.

I WAS greatly encouraged at this, and argued with the more Vigour for myself; at length the Accuser was brought Fettered as he was from the Goal, and glad I was when I saw him, and found that I knew him not, *that is to say*, that it was not one of the two Rogues that I went out with that Night, that we robb'd the poor old Woman.

WHEN the Prisoner was brought into the Room, he was set right against me.

DO you know this young Man? *says the Justice*.

NO, Sir, *says the Prisoner*, I never saw him in my Life.

HUM, *says the Justice*, Did not you Charge one that goes by the Name of *Jack*, or Capt. *Jack*, as concern'd in the Robbery and Murther, which you are in Custody for?

Pris. Yes, an't please your Worship, *says the Prisoner*.

Just. And is this the Man, or is he not?

Pris. This is not the Man, Sir, I never saw this Man before.

VERY good Mr. Constable, *says the Justice*, What must we do now?

I AM surpriz'd, *says the Constable*; I was at such a House, naming the House, and this young Man went by, the People cryed out there's *Jack*, that's your Man, and these People run after him, and apprehended him.

WELL, *says the Justice*, and have these People any thing to say to him? can they prove that he is the Person?

ONE said no, and the other said no; and in short, they all said no, Why then said the *Justice*, what can be done? the young Man must be Discharg'd; and I must tell you Mr. Constable, and you Gentlemen that have brought him hither, he may give you Trouble, if he thinks fit, for your being so rash; but look you young Man, *says the Justice*, you have no great Damage done you, and the Constable, tho' he has been Mistaken, had no ill-design, but to be Faithful to his Office; I think you may pass it by.

I TOLD his Worship, I would readily pass it by, at his Direction; but I thought the Constable, and the rest cou'd do no less than to go back to the Place where they had insulted me, and Declare publickly there that I was honourably acquitted, and that I was not the Man: This his Worship said was very Reasonable, and the Constable, and his Assistants promis'd to do it, and so we came all away good Friends, and I was clear'd with Triumph.

NOTE,

> 'THIS was the Time that as I mention'd above, the Justice talk'd to me, told me I was born to better Things, and that by my well managing of my own Defence, he did not question but I had been well Educated, and that he was sorry I should fall into such a Misfortune as this, which he hop'd however would be no Dishonour to me, since I was so handsomely acquitted.'

THO' his Worship was mistaken in the Matter of my Education, yet it had this good Effect upon me, that I resolv'd if it was possible I would learn to Read and Write, that I would not be such an uncapable Creature, that I should not be able to read a Warrant, and see whether I was the Person to be Apprehended or not.

BUT there was something more in all this, from what I have taken notice of; for in a Word, it appear'd plainly that my Brother Capt. *Jack*, who had the forwardness to put it to me, whether I was among them, or no, when in Truth he was there himself, had the only Reason to be afraid to flye, at the same time, that he advised me to shift for my self.

AS this presently occur'd to my Thoughts; so I made it my Business to enquire, and find him out, and to give him notice of it.

IN the mean time, being now Confident of my own Safety, I had no more Concern upon my Mind about myself; but now I began to be anxious for poor *Will*, my Master and Tutor in Wickedness, who was now fast by the Heels in *Newgate*, while I was happily at Liberty, and I wanted very much to go and see him, and accordingly did so.

I FOUND him in a sad Condition loaden with heavy Irons, and had himself no prospect or hope of Escaping; he told me he should die, but bid me be easie; for as it would do him no good to accuse me, who never was out with any of them, but that once; so I might depend upon it, he would not bring me into the Trouble; as for the Rogue, who had betray'd them all, he was not able to hurt me, for I might be satisfied he had never seen me in his Life; but Col. *Jack*, says he, I will tell you who was with us, and that is your Brother the Captain, and the Villain has certainly nam'd him, and therefore, *says he*, if you can give him timely Notice of it, do, that he may make his Escape.

HE said a great many things to warn me of following the steps he had led me; I was far out *Jack*, *said he*, when I told you to be a notorious Thief, was to live like a Gentleman; he chiefly discover'd[165] his concern that they had, as he fear'd killed the Gentleman's Gardiner, and that he in particular had given him a Wound in the Neck, of which he was afraid he would die.

HE had a great Sum of Money in Gold about him, being the same that I had carried back to him at the Hay-Stack; and he had concealed it so well, that those that took him had not found it, and he gave me the greatest Part of it, to carry to his Mother, which I very honestly delivered, and came away with a heavy Heart; nor did I ever see him since, for he was Executed in about three Weeks time after, being condemn'd that very next Sessions.

I HAD nothing to do now, but to find the Capt. who tho' not without some trouble, I at last got News of, and told him the whole Story, and how I had been taken up for him by mistake, and was come off, but that the Warrant was still out for him, and very strict search after him; *I say*, telling him all this, he presently discover'd by his surprize that he was Guilty, and after a few Words more, told me plainly it was all true; that he was in the Robbery, and that he had the greatest Part of the Booty in keeping, but what to do with it, or himself he did not know, and wanted me to tell him, which I was very unfit to do, for I knew nothing of the World; then he told me, he had a Mind to fly into *Scotland*, which was easie to be done, and ask'd me if I would go with him: I told him I would with all my Heart, if I had Money enough to bear the Charge; he had the Trade still in his Eyes by his answer, I warrant you, *says he*, we will make the Journey pay our Charge; I dare not think of going any more upon the Adventure, *says I*, besides, if we meet with any Misfortune out of our Knowledge, we shall never get out of it, we shall be undone; nay, *says he*, we shall find no Mercy here, if they can catch us, and they can do no worse Abroad, I am for venturing at all.

WELL, but Captain, *says I*, have you Husbanded your time so ill, that you have no Money to supply you in such a Time as this; I have very little indeed, *said he*, for I have had bad luck lately; but he lyed, for he had a great Share of the Booty they had got at their last Adventure, as above, and as the rest complain'd, he and *Will* had got almost all of it, and kept the rest out of their Shares, which made them the willinger to discover them.

HOWEVER it was, he own'd about 22*l.* he had in Money, and something that would yield Money, I suppose it was Plate; but he would not tell me what it was, or where it was, but he said, he durst not go to fetch it, for he should be betray'd and seiz'd, so he would venture without it; sure, *says he*, we shall come back again some time, or other.

I honestly produc'd all the Money I had, which was Sixteen Pound, and some odd Shillings: Now, *says I*, if we are good Husbands,[166] and Travel frugally, this will carry us quite out of Danger, for we had both been assur'd, that when we came out of *England*, we should be both Safe, and no

Body could Hurt us, tho' they had known us; but we neither of us thought it was so many weary steps to *Scotland*, as we found it.

I speak of myself, as in the same Circumstances of Danger, with Brother *Jack*, but it was only thus, I was in as much Fear as he, but not in quite as much Danger.

I cannot omit that in the Interval of these things, and a few Days before I carried my Money to the Gentleman in *Tower-street*, I took a Walk all alone into the Fields, in order to go to *Kentish-Town*, and do Justice to the poor old Nurse; it happen'd that before I was aware I cross'd a Field that came to the very Spot where I robb'd the poor old Woman, and that Maid, or where I should say *Will* made me rob them; my Heart had reproach'd me many a time with that cruel Action, and many a time I had promis'd to myself that I would find a way to make her Satisfaction, and restore her Money, and that Day I had Set a part for the Work; but was a little surpriz'd that I was so suddenly upon the unhappy Spot.

THE Place brought to my Mind the Villany I had committed there, and something struck me with a kind of Wish, I cannot say Prayer, for I know not what that meant, that I might leave off that curs'd Trade; and said to myself, O! that I had some Trade to live by, I would never rob no more, for sure 'tis a wicked abominable Thing.

HERE indeed I felt the loss of what just Parents do, and ought to do by all their Children; I mean being bred to some Trade, or Employment, and I wept many times, that I knew not what to do, or what to turn my Hand to, tho' I resolved to leave off the wicked Course I was in.

BUT to return to my Journey, I ask'd my way to *Kentish-Town*, and it happen'd to be of a poor Woman, that said she liv'd there, upon which Intelligence I ask'd, if she knew a Woman that lived there, whose Name was *Smith*? She answer'd, yes, very well, that she was not a settled Inhabitant, only a Lodger in the Town, but that she was an honest poor industrious Woman, and by her Labour and Pains, maintain'd a poor diseas'd Husband, that had been unable to help himself some Years.

WHAT a Villain have I been! *said I*, to myself, that I should rob such a poor Woman as this, and add Grief, and Tears to her Misery, and to the Sorrows of her House? This quicken'd my Resolution to restore her Money, and not only so, but I resolv'd I would give her something over and above her Loss; so I went forward, and by the Direction I had receiv'd, found her Lodging with very little Trouble; then asking for the Woman, she came to the Door immediately, for she heard me ask for her by her Name, of a little Girl that came first to the Door; I presently spoke to her, Dame, *said I*, was not you robb'd about a Year ago, as you was coming home from *London*, about *Pindar of Wakefields*? yes indeed I was, *says she*, and sadly frighted into the Bargain; and how much did you lose? *said I*, indeed, *says she*, I lost all the Money I had in the World; I am sure I work'd hard for it, it was Money for keeping a Nurse Child, that I had then, and I had been at *London* to receive it; but how much was it Dame? *said I*, why, *says she*, it was Two and Twenty Shillings and Six-Pence Half-penny; One and Twenty Shillings I had been to fetch, and the odd Money was my own before.

WELL, look you good Woman, what will you say if I should put you in a way to get your Money again; for I believe the Fellow that took it is fast enough[167] now, and perhaps I may do you a kindness in it, and for that I came to see you? O Dear, says the old Woman, I understand you, but indeed I cannot Swear to the Man's Face again; for it was Dark, and besides, I would not Hang the poor Wretch for my Money, let him live and Repent: That is very kind, *says I*, more than he deserves from you, but you need not be Concern'd about that, for he will be Hang'd, whether you appear against him or not: But are you willing to have your Money again that you lost? Yes, indeed, says the Woman, I should be glad of that, for I have not been so hard put to it for Money a great while, as I am now; I have much a do to find us Bread to Eat, though I work hard early and late, and with that she Cryed.

I THOUGHT it would have broke my very Heart, to think how this poor Creature work'd, and was a Slave at near Threescore, and that I a young Fellow of hardly Twenty, should Rob her of her Bread to Support my Idleness, and Wicked Life; and the Tears came from my Eyes, in spight of all my strugling to prevent it, and the Woman perceiv'd it too; poor Woman, *said I*, 'tis a sad thing such Creatures as these should plunder, and strip such a poor Object as thou art; well, he is at Leisure now to Repent it, I assure you; I perceive Sir, *says she*, you are very Compassionate, indeed, I wish he may Improve the time God has spar'd him, and that he may Repent, and I pray God give him Repentance, who ever he is, I forgive him, whether he can make me Recompence, or not, and I pray God forgive him, I won't do him any Prejudice, not I; and that she went on Praying for me.

WELL, Dame, come hither to me, *says I*, and with that I put my Hand in my Pocket, and she came to me: Hold up your Hand, *said I*, which she did, and I told[168] her Nine half Crowns into her Hand; there Dame, *said I*, is your 22s.ª 6d. you lost, I assure you, Dame, *said I*, I have been the chief Instrument to get it of him for you; for ever since he told me the Story of it among the rest of his wicked Exploits, I never gave him any rest till I made him promise me to make you Restitution: All the while I held her Hand, and put the Money into it, I look'd in her Face, and I perceiv'd her Colour come, and go, and that she was under the greatest Surprize of Joy Imaginable.

WELL, God bless him, *says she*, and spare him from the Disaster he is afraid of, if it be his will; for sure, this is an Act of so much Justice, and so Honest, that I never expected the like; she run on a great while so, and wept for him; when I told her, I doubted there was no room to expect his Life: Well, *says she*, then pray God give him Repentance, and bring him to Heaven, for sure he must have something that is Good at the Bottom; he has a Principle of Honesty at Bottom, to be sure; however, he may have been brought into bad Courses, by bad Company, and evil Example, or other Temptations: But I dare say he will be brought to Repentance, one time or other, before he Dies.

ALL this touch'd me nearer than she Imagin'd, for I was the Man that she pray'd for all this while; though she did not know it, and in my Heart I said *Amen* to it; for I was sensible that I had done one of the vilest Actions, in the World, in attacking a poor Creature in such a Condition, and not lissening[169] to her Entreaties, when she begg'd so heartily for that little Money we took from her.

IN a Word, the good Woman so mov'd me with her Charitable Prayers; that I put my Hand in my Pocket again for her, Dame, *said I*, you are so Charitable in your Petitions for this miserable Creature, that it puts me in Mind of one thing more, which I will do for him, whether he order'd me or not; and that is, to ask you Forgiveness for the Thief in robbing you, for it was an Offence, and a Trespass against you, as well as an Injury to you; and therefore I ask your Pardon for him, will you Sincerely and Heartily forgive him, Dame? I do desire it of you; and with that I stood up, and with my Hat off, ask'd her Pardon; O Sir, *says she*, do not stand up, and with your Hat off to me, I am a poor Woman, I forgive him, and all that were with him; for there was one or more with him, I forgive them with all my Heart; and I pray God to forgive them.

WELL, Dame, then, *said I*, to make you some Recompence for your Charity; there is something for you more than your Loss; and with that I gave her a Crown[170] more.

THEN I ask'd her, who that was, who was robb'd with her? She said, it was a Servant Maid that liv'd then in the Town, but she was gone from her place, and she did not know where she liv'd now: Well Dame, *says I*, if ever you do hear of her, let her leave Word where she may be found; and if I live to come and see you again, I will get the Money of him for her too; I think that was but little, was it not, no,[a] *says she*, it was but 5s. 6d. which I knew as well as she; well, *says I*, Dame, enquire her out if you have Opportunity; so she promis'd me she would, and away I came.

THE Satisfaction this gave me, was very much, but then a Natural Consequence attended it, which fill'd me with Reflection afterwards, and this was, that by the same Rule, I ought to make Restitution to all that I had wrong'd, in the like manner; and what cou'd I do, as to that? To this I knew not what to say; and so the Thought in time wore off, for in short it was impossible to be done: I had not Ability, neither did I know any of the People who I had so Injur'd, and that satisfying me for the present, I let it Drop.

I COME now to my Journey, with Capt. *Jack*, my suppos'd Brother: We set out from *London* on Foot, and Travel'd the first Day to *Ware*, for we had learnt so much of our Road, that the way lay thro' that Town; we were weary enough the first Day, having not been us'd at all to Travelling; but we made shift to walk once up and down the Town, after we came into it.

I SOON found, that his walking out to see the Town, was not to satisfie his Curiosity in viewing the Place; for he had no Notion of any thing of that Kind, but to see if he cou'd light of any Purchase, for he was so natural a Thief, that he cou'd see nothing on the Road, but it occur'd to him; how easily that might be taken, and how cleverly this might be carry'd off, *and the like.*

NOTHING offer'd in *Ware* to his Mind, it not being Market-Day, and as for me, tho' I made no great scruple of Eating and Drinking at the Cost of his Roguery, yet I resolv'd not to enter upon any thing, *as they call'd it*, nor to take the least thing from any Body.

WHEN the Captain found me resolv'd upon the Negative, he ask'd me, how I thought to Travel? I ask'd him what he thought of himself, that was sure to be hang'd, if he was taken, how small soever the Crime was, that he should be taken for? How can that be? *says he*, they don't know me in the Country; ay, *says I*, but do you think they do not send up Word to *Newgate* as soon as any Thief is taken in the Country, and so enquire who is escap'd from them, or who is fled, that they may be stopp'd? assure yourself, *says I*, the Jaylors Correspond with one another, with the greatest Exactness imaginable; and if you were taken here but for stealing a Basket of Eggs, you shall have your Accuser sent down to see if he knows you.

THIS terrify'd him a little for a while, and kept him honest, for three or four Days; but it was but for a few Days indeed; for he play'd a great many Rogues Tricks without me, till at last he came to his End without me too, tho' it was not till many Years after, as you shall hear in its Order;[171] but as these Exploits are no part of my Story, but of his, whose Life and Exploits are sufficient to make a Volume larger than this by itself; so I shall omit every thing, but what I was particularly concern'd in, during this tedious Journey.

FROM *Ware* we Travell'd to *Cambridge*, tho' that was not our direct Road, the occasion was this; in our way going thro' a Village, call'd *Puckeridge*, we baited at an *Inn*, at the Sign of the *Faulcon*, and while we were there, a Countryman comes to the *Inn*, and hangs[172] his Horse at the Door, while he goes in to Drink; we sat in the Gate-way, having called for a Mug of Beer, and drank it up: We had been talking with the Hostler about the way to *Scotland*, and he had bid us ask the Road to *Royston*; *but says he*, there is a Turning just here a little farther, you must not go that Way, for that goes to *Cambridge*.

WE had paid for our Beer, and sat at the Door, only to rest us, when on the sudden, comes a Gentleman's Coach to the Door, and three or four Horsemen; the Horsemen rod[173] into the Yard, and the Hostler was oblig'd to go in with them; *says he*, to the Captain, young Man pray take hold of the Horse, meaning the Countryman's Horse, I mention'd above, and take him out of the way, that the Coach may come up; he did so, and beckon'd to me to follow him; we walked together to the Turning; *says he*, to me, do you step afore, and turn up the *Lane*, I'll overtake you; so I went on up the *Lane*, and in a few Minutes he was got up upon the Horse, and at my Heels, come get up, *says he*, we will have a lift, if we don't get the Horse by the Bargain.

I MADE no difficulty to get up behind him, and away we went at a good round Rate, it being a good strong Horse: We lost no time for an Hours riding, and more, by which time we thought we were out of the reach of being pursued, and as the Countryman, when he should miss his Horse, would hear that we enquir'd the way to *Royston*, he would certainly pursue us that way, and not towards *Cambridge*, we went easier after the first Hours riding, and coming thro' a Town or two we alighted by Turns, and did not ride Double thro' the Villages.

NOW as it was impossible for the Captain to pass by any thing that he could lay his Hand on, and not take it, so now having a Horse to carry it off too, the Temptation was the stronger; going thro' a Village, where a good Housewife of the House had been Washing, and hung her Cloths out upon a Hedge, near the Road, he could not help it, but got hold of a Couple of good Shirts, that were but about half dry, and over-took me upon the Spur;[174] for I walk'd on Foot before; I immediately got up behind, and away we Gallop'd together as fast as the Horse would well go; in this Part of our Expedition his good luck or Mine, carried us quite out of the Road, and having seen no Body to ask the way of, we lost ourselves, and wandered I know not how many Miles to the Right Hand, till Partly by that means, and Partly by the Occasion following, we came quite into the Coach Road to *Cambridge*, from *London*, by *Bishop-Stortford*; the particular

Occasion that made me wander on was thus; the Country was all open Cornfields, no Enclosures; when being upon a little rising Ground, I Bad him stop the Horse, for I would get down, and walk a little to ease my Legs, being tyr'd with riding so long behind without Stirrups; when I was down, and look'd a little about me; I saw plainly the Great white Road, which we should have gone at near two Miles from us.

ON a sudden, looking a little back to my Left, upon that Road, I saw four or five Horsemen, riding full Speed, some a good way before the other, and hurrying on as People in a full pursuit.

IT immediately struck me; Ha, Brother *Jack, says I,* get off of the Horse this Moment, and ask why afterwards; so he jumps off, What's the matter? *says he,* the matter, *says I,* look yonder, 'tis well we have lost our Way; do you see how they ride, they are pursuing us you may depend upon it, either, *says I,* you are pursued from the last Village for the two Shirts, or from *Puckeridge,* for the Horse. He had so much Presence of Mind, that without my mentioning it to him, he puts back the Horse behind a great white-Thorn Bush, which grew just by him; so that they could by no means see the Horse, which we being just at the Top of the Hill they might otherwise have done, and so have pursued that way at a venture.

BUT as it was impossible for them to see the Horse, so was it as impossible for them to see us at that distance, who sat down on the Ground to look at them the more securely.

THE Road winding about, we saw them a great way, and they rod as fast as they could make their Horses go; when we found they were gone quite out of Sight, we mounted, and made the best of our way also; and indeed, tho' we were two upon one Horse, yet we abated no speed where the way would admit of it, not enquiring of any Body the way to any where, till after about two Hours riding, we came to a Town, which upon Enquiry, they call'd *Chesterford,* and here we stopp'd, and ask'd not our way to any Place, but whether that Road went, and were told it was the Coach Road to *Cambridge;* also that it was the Way to *New-Market,* to St. *Edmunds-Bury,*[175] to *Norwich* and *Yarmouth,* to *Lyn,* and to *Ely,* and the like.

WE staid here a good while believing ourselves secure, and afterwards towards Evening went forward to a Place, call'd *Bourn-Bridge,* where the Road to *Cambridge* turns away out of the Road to *New-Market,* and where there are but two Houses only, both of them being *Inns.* Here the Captain *says to me,* Hark ye, you see we are pursued towards *Cambridge,* and shall be stop'd if we go thither; now *New-Market* is but ten Miles off, and there we may be safe, and perhaps get an opportunity to do some Business.

LOOK ye, *Jack, said I,* talk no more of doing Business, for I will not joyn with you in any thing of that Kind; I would fain get you to *Scotland,* before you get a Halter about your Neck, I will not have you hang'd in *England*, if I can help it, and therefore I won't go to *New-Market*, unless you will promise me to make no false steps there: Well, *says he*, if I must not, then I won't; but I hope you will let us get another Horse, won't you? that we may Travel faster; no, *says I*, I won't agree to that, but if you will let me send this Horse back fairly, I will tell you how we shall hire Horses after-wards, for one Stage, or two, and then take them as far as we please; 'tis only sending a Letter to the Owner to send for him, and then, if we are stopp'd, it can do us but little Hurt.

YOU are a wary Politick[176] Gentleman, *says the Captain*, but, *I say*, we are better as we are; for we are out of all Danger of being stopp'd on the Way after we are gone from this Place.

WE had not Parl'd[177] thus long; but tho' in the Dead of the Night, came a Man to the other *Inn* Door, for as above, there are two *Inns* at that Place, and call'd for a Pot of Beer, but the People were all in Bed, and would not Rise; he ask'd them if they had seen two Fellows come that way upon one Horse: The Man[178] *said he had*, that they went by in the Afternoon, and ask'd the Way to *Cambridge*, but did not stop only to drink one Mug: O! *says he*, are they gone to *Cambridge*? then I'll be with them quickly: I was awake in a little Garret of the next Inn, where we Lodg'd; and hearing the Fellow call at the Door, got up, and went to the Window, having some uneasiness at every Noise I heard; and by that means heard the whole Story: Now, the case is plain, our Hour was not come, our Fate had Deter-min'd other things for us, and we were to be reserv'd for it; the matter was thus; when we first came to *Bourn-Bridge*, we call'd at the first House, and ask'd the Way to *Cambridge*, Drank a Mug of Beer, and went on, and they might see us turn off to go the way they Directed; but Night coming on, and we being very Weary, we thought we should not find the way; and we came back in the Dusk of the Evening, and went into the other House, being the first as we came back, as that where we call'd before, was the first, as we went forward.

YOU may be sure I was allarm'd now, as indeed I had Reason to be; the Captain was in Bed, and fast a Sleep, but I Wak'd him, and Rouz'd him with a Noise that frighted him enough; Rise, *Jack, said I*, we are both Ruin'd, they are come after us hither; indeed, I was wrong to terrify him at that Rate; for he started, and jumpt out of Bed, and run directly to the Window, not knowing where he was; and not quite awake, was just going to Jump out of the Window, but I laid hold of him; what are you going to do? *Says I*, I won't be taken, *says he*, let me alone, *where are they?*

THIS was all Confusion, and he was so out of himself with the Fright; and being overcome with Sleep, that I had much to do to prevent his jumping out of the Window: However, I held him fast, and thoroughly waken'd him, and then all was well again, and he was presently compos'd.

THEN I told him the Story, and we sat together upon the Bed-side; considering, what we should do: Upon the whole, as the Fellow that call'd, was apparently gone on to *Cambridge*; we had nothing to fear, but to be quiet till Day break, and then to Mount and be gone.

ACCORDINGLY, as soon as Day peep'd, we were up, and having happily inform'd ourselves of the Road at the other House; and being told that the Road to *Cambridge* turn'd off on the left Hand, and that the Road to *New-Market* lay strait forward; I say, having learn't this, the Captain told me he would walk away on Foot towards *New-Market*; and so when I came to go out, I should appear as a single Traveller; accordingly he went out immediately, and away he walk'd, and he Travell'd so hard, that when I came to follow, I thought once that he had Dropp'd me, for tho' I Rid hard, I got no sight of him for an Hour; at length having pass'd the great Bank call'd the *Divel's-Ditch*,[179] I found him, and took him up behind me, and we Rode Double till we came almost to the end of *New-Market* Town; just at the hither House in the Town, stood a Horse at a Door, just as it was at *Puckeridge*: Now, *says Jack*, if the Horse was at the other end of the Town, I would have him, as sure as we had the t'other at *Puckeridge*; but it would not do, so he got down, and Walk'd thro' the Town on the right Hand side of the Way.

HE had not got half thro' the Town, but the Horse having some how or other got loose, came Trotting gently on by himself, and no body following him; the Captain, an old Soldier at such Work, as soon as the Horse was got a pretty way before him, and that he saw no Body follow'd, sets up a run after the Horse; and the Horse hearing him follow, run the faster; then the Captain calls out, stop the Horse, and by this time the Horse was got almost to the farther end of the Town, the People of the House where he stood not missing him all the while.

UPON his calling out stop the Horse, the Poor People of the Town, such as were next Hand, run from both sides the Way and stopp'd the Horse for him, as readily as cou'd be; and held him for him, till he came up; he very Gravely comes up to the Horse, hits him a Blow or two, and calls him Dog for running away; gives the Man 2*d.* that catch'd him for him, Mounts, and away he comes after me.

THIS was the oddest Adventure that cou'd have happen'd, for the Horse stole the Capt. the Capt. did not steal the Horse; when he came up to me, now Col. *Jack, says he,* what say you to good luck, would you have had me refus'd the Horse, when he came so Civily to ask me to Ride? No, no, *said*

I, you have got this Horse by your Wit, not by Design, and you may go on now I think, you are in a safer Condition than I am, if we are taken.

THE next Question was, what Road we should take; here were four ways before us, and we were alike Strangers to them all; first on the right Hand, and at about a little Mile from the Town, a great Road went off to St. *Edmund's-Bury*; strait on, but enclining afterwards to the right, lay the Great Road to *Barton Mills*, and *Thetford*, and so to *Norwich*; and full before us lay a great Road also to *Brandon* and *Lynn*, and on the left, lay a less Road to the City of *Ely*, and into the Fens.

IN short, as we knew not which Road to take, nor which way to get into the great North Road which we had left, so we by meer unguided Chance took the way to *Brandon*, and so to *Lynn*: At *Brand*, or *Brandon* we were told that passing over at a place call'd *Downham Bridge*, we might cross the Fenn Country to *Wisbich*; and from thence go along that Bank of the River *Nyne* to *Peterborough*, and from thence to *Stamford*, where we were in the Northen Road again; and likewise, that at *Lynn*, we might go by the Washes into *Lincolnshire*, and so might Travel North. But upon the whole, this was my Rule, that when we enquir'd the way to any particular Place, to be sure we never took that Road, but some other; which the accidental Discourse we might have should bring in, and thus we did here, for having chiefly ask'd our way into the Northern Road, we resolv'd to go directly for *Lynn*.

WE arriv'd here very easy and safe, and while we was considering of what way we should Travel next; we found we were got to a Point, and that there was no way now left, but that by the Washes into *Lincolnshire*, and that was represented as very Dangerous; so an Opportunity offering of a Man that was Travelling over the Fenns; we took him for our Guide, and went with him to *Spalding*, and from thence to a Town call'd *Deeping*, and so to *Stamford* in *Lincolnshire*.

THIS is a large populous Town, and it was Market Day when we came to it; so we put in at a little House, at the hither end of the Town, and Walk'd into the Town.

HERE it was not possible to restrain my Captain from playing his Feats of Art, and my Heart ak'd for him; I told him I would not go with him, for he would not promise, and I was so terribly concern'd at the Apprehensions of his ventrous[180] Humour, that I would not so much as stir out of my Lodging; but it was in vain to perswade him; he went into the Market, and found a *Mountebank*[181] there, which was what he wanted; how he pick'd two Pockets there in one Quarter of an Hour and brought to our Quarters a Peice of new *Holland*, of eight or nine Ells;[182] a Peice of Stuff,[183] and played three or four Pranks[184] more, in less than two Hours; and how afterward he robb'd a Doctor of Physick,[185] and yet came off clear in them all; this I say, *as above*, belongs to his Story, not to Mine.

I scolded heartily at him, when he came back, and told him he would certainly ruin himself, and me too before he left off, and threaten'd in so many Words, that I would leave him, and go back, and carry the Horse to *Puckeridge*, where we borrow'd it, and so go to *London* by myself.

HE promis'd amendment, but as we resolv'd now we were in the Great Road to Travel by Night, so it being not yet Night, he gives me the slip again, and was not gone half an Hour, but he comes back with a Gold Watch in his Hand; come, *says he*, Why an't you ready? I am ready to go as soon as you will; and with that he pulls out the Gold Watch: I was amaz'd at such a Thing, as that in a Country Town, but it seems there was Prayers at one of the Churches in the Evening, and he placing himself, as the Occasion directed, found the way to be so near the Lady, as to get it from her Side, and walk'd off with it unperceived.

THE same Night we went away, by Moon-light, after having the Satisfaction to hear the Watch cry'd, and ten Guineas offer'd for it again, he would have been glad of the ten Guineas, instead of the Watch; but durst not venture to carry it home. Well, *says I*, you are afraid, and but you have Reason,[186] give it me, I will venture to carry it again; but he would not let me; but told me, that when he came into *Scotland* we might sell any thing there without Danger, which was true indeed, for there they ask'd us no Questions.

WE set out, *as I said*, in the Evening by Moon-light, and Travell'd hard, the Road being very plain and large, till we came to *Grantham*, by which time it was about two in the Morning, and all the Town, as it were dead a sleep, so we went on for *Newark*, where we reach'd about 8 in the Morning, and there we lay down and slept most of the Day, and by this sleeping so continually, in the Day time, I kept him from doing a great deal of Mischief, which he would otherwise have done.

FROM *Newark*, we took Advice of one that was accidently comparing the Roads,[187] and we concluded that the Road by *Nottingham*, would be the best for us; so we turn'd out of the Great Road, and went up the Side of the *Trent* to *Nottingham*: Here he play'd his Pranks again in a manner, that it was the greatest wonder imaginable to me, that he was not surpriz'd, and yet he came off clear; and now he had got so many bulky Goods that he bought him a Portmanteau to carry them in: It was in vain for me to offer to restrain him any more; so after this he went on his own way.

AT *Nottingham*, I say, he had such Success, that made us the hastier to be going, than otherwise we would have been, least we should have been baulk'd, and should be laid hold of; from Thence we left the Road, which leads to the North again, and went away by *Mansfield* into *Scarsdale*, and *Yorkshire*.

I SHALL take up no more of my own Story, with his Pranks, they very well merit to be told by themselves; but I shall observe only what relates to our Journey. In a Word, I drag'd him along as fast as I could, till I came to *Leeds* in *Yorkshire*, here tho' it be a large, and populous Town, yet he could make nothing of it, neither had he any Success at *Wakefield*; and he told me, in short, that the North Country People were certainly all Thieves: Why so? *said I*, The People seem to be just as other People are; *No, no, says he*, they have their Eyes so about them, and are all so sharp, they look upon every Body that comes near them to be a Pick-Pocket, or else they would never stand so upon their Guard; and then again, *says he*, they are so poor, there is but little to be got, and I am afraid, *says he*, the farther we go North, we shall find it worse. Well, *said I*, What do you infer from thence? I argue from thence? *says he*, that we shall do nothing there, and I had as good go back into the South, and be hang'd, as into the North to be starv'd.

WELL, we came at length to *New-Castle* upon *Tyne*. Here on a Market-day was a great Throng of People, and several of the Towns-People going to Market to buy Provisions, and here he play'd his Pranks, cheated a Shop-keeper of 15 or 16*l.* in Goods, and got clear away with them; stole a Horse, and sold that he came upon, and play'd so many Pranks, that I was quite frighted for him; I say for him, for I was not concern'd for myself, having never stirr'd out of the House where I Lodg'd, at least not with him, nor without some or other with me, belonging to the *Inn*, that might give an Account of me.

NOR did I use this Caution in vain, for he had made himself so publick by his Rogueries, that he was way-laid every where to be taken, and had he not artfully at first given out, that he was come from *Scotland*, and was going toward *London*, enquiring that Road, and the like, which amus'd[188] his Pursuers for the first Day, he had been taken, and in all probability had been hang'd there; but by that Artifice he got half a Days time of them; and yet as it was, he was put so to it, that he was fain to plunge Horse and all into the River *Tweed*, and swim over, and thereby made his Escape: It was true, that he was before upon *Scots* Ground, *as they call'd it*, and consequently they had no power to have carried him off, if any Body had oppos'd them; yet as they were in a full Chase after him, could they have come up with him, they would have run the Risque of the rest, and they cou'd but have deliver'd him up, if they had been Questioned about it; however, as he got over the *Tweed*, and was landed safe, they could neither follow him, the Water being too High at the usual Place of going over, nor could they have attempted to have brought him away, if they had taken him: The place where he took the River, was where there is a *Ford* a little below *Kelso*, but the Water being up, the *Ford* was not passable, and he had no time to go to the *Ferry-Boat*, which is about a Furlong off, opposite to the Town.[189]

HAVING thus made his Escape, he went to *Kelso*, where he had appointed me to come after him.

I followed with a heavy Heart, expecting every Hour to meet him upon the Road, in the Custody of the Constables, and such People, or to hear of him in the Goal; but when I came to a Place on the Border, call'd *Woller-haugh-head*,[190] there I understood how he had been Chas'd, and how he had made his Escape.

WHEN I came to *Kelso*, he was easie enough to be found, for his having desperately swam the *Tweed*, a rapid and large River, made him much talk'd of, tho' it seems they had not heard of the occasion of it, nor any thing of his Character; for he had wit enough to conceal all that, and live as retir'd as he could till I came to him.

I WAS not so much rejoyc'd at his Safety, as I was provok'd at his Conduct; and the more, for that I could not find he had yet the least Notion of its having been void of common Sense with respect to his Circumstances, as well as contrary to what he promis'd me; however, as there was no beating any thing into his Head by Words, I only told him, that I was glad he was at last gotten into a Place of Safety, and I ask'd him then how he intended to manage himself in that Country? He said in few Words, he did not know yet, he doubted[191] the People were very poor; but if they had any Money, he was resolv'd to have some of it.

BUT do you know too, *says I*, that they are the severest People upon Criminals of your kind in the World? he did not value that, *he said*, in his blunt short way, he would venture it; upon this, *I told him*, that seeing it was so, and he would run such ventures, I would take my leave of him, and be gone back to *England*: He seem'd Sullen, or rather it was the roughness of his untractable Disposition; he said I might do what I would, he would do, as he found opportunity; however, we did not Part immediately, but went on towards the Capital City;[192] on the Road we found too much Poverty, and too few People to give him room to expect any Advantage in his way, and tho' he had his Eyes about him, as sharp as a Hawk, yet he saw plainly there was nothing to be done; for as to the Men, they did not seem to have much Money about them; and for the Women, their Dress was such, that had they any[a] Money, or indeed any Pockets, it was impossible to come at them; for wearing large Plads[193] about them, and down to their Knees, they were wrap'd up so close, that there was no coming to make the least attempt of that kind.

Kelso was indeed a good Town, and had abundance of People in it, and yet tho' he staid one *Sunday* there, and saw the Church, which is very large and throng'd with People; yet as he told me, there was not one Woman to be seen in all the Church with any other Dress than a Plaid, except in two Pews, which belong'd to some Noblemen, and who when they came out, were so surrounded with Footmen and Servants, that there was no coming near them, any more than there was any coming near the King surrounded by his Guards.

WE set out therefore with this Discouragement, which I was secretly glad of, and went forward for *Edinborough*; all the way thither we went thro' no considerable Town, and it was but very course[194] Travelling for us, who were Strangers, for we met with Waters, which were very Dangerous to pass, by Reason of hasty Rains, at a Place, call'd *Lauderdale*,[195] and where my Captain was really in danger of drowning, his Horse being driven down by the Stream, and fell under him, by which he wetted and spoil'd his stolen Goods, that he brought from *New-Castle*, and which he had kept dry, strangely by holding them up in his Arms, when he swam the *Tweed*; but here it wanted but little, that he and his Horse had been lost, not so much by the depth of the Water, as the fury of the Current; but he had a Proverb in his Favour,[196] and he got out of the Water, tho' with difficulty enough, not being born to be drown'd, as I shall observe afterwards in its Place.

WE came to *Edinborough*, the third Day from *Kelso*, having stopp'd at an *Inn* one whole Day, at a Place, call'd, *Soutra-Hill*, to dry our Goods, and refresh our selves: We were oddly Saluted at *Edinborough*, the next Day after we came thither; My Captain having a desire to walk, and look about him, ask'd me if I would go, and see the Town? I told him yes; so we went out, and coming thro' a Gate, that they call the *Nether-Bow* into the Great High-street, which went up to the *Cross*; we were surpriz'd to see it throng'd with an infinite Number of People: Ay, *says my Captain*, this will do; however, as I had made him promise to make no Adventures that Day, otherwise, I told him I would not go out with him; so I held him by the sleeve, and would not let him stir from me.

THEN we came up to the *Mercart-Cross*,[197] and there besides the great Number of People who pass'd, and repass'd, we saw a great Parade or kind of Meeting, like an *Exchange*, of Gentlemen, of all Ranks, and Qualities, and this Encourag'd my Captain again, and he pleas'd himself with that Sight.

IT was while we were looking, and wondering at what we saw here, that we were surpriz'd with a Sight; which we little expected; we observ'd the People running on a sudden, as to see some strange Thing just coming along, and strange it was indeed; for we see two Men naked from the Wast upwards, run by us as swift as the Wind, and we imagin'd nothing, but that it was two Men running a Race for some mighty Wager; on a sudden, we found two long small Ropes or Lines, which hung down at first pull'd strait, and the two Racers stopp'd, and stood still, one close by the other; we could not imagine what this meant, but the Reader may judge at our surprize when we found a Man follow after, who had the ends of both those Lines in his Hands, and who, when he came up to them, gave each of them two frightful Lashes with a Wire-whip, or Lash, which he held in the other Hand; and then the two poor naked Wretches run on again to the length of their Line or Tether, where they waited for the like Salutation; and in this manner they Danc'd the length of the whole Street, which is about half a Mile.

THIS was a dark Prospect to my Captain, and put him in Mind, not only of what he was to expect, if he made a slip in the way of his Profession, in this Place; but also of what he had suffer'd, when he was but a Boy; at the famous place, call'd *Bridewell*.[198]

BUT this was not all, for as we saw the Execution, so we were curious to Examine into the Crime too; and we ask'd a young Fellow who stood near us, what the two Men had done, for which they suffer'd that Punishment. The Fellow, an unhappy ill natur'd *Scotch-man*; perceiv'd by our Speech, that we were *English-men*; and by our Question, that we were Strangers, told us with a malicious Wit, that they were two *English-men*; and that they were Whip'd so for Picking-pockets; and other petty Thieveries, and that they were afterwards to be sent away, over the Border into *England*.

NOW this was every Word of it False, and was only form'd by his nimble Invention, to insult us as *English-men*; for when we enquir'd farther, they were both *Scotch-men*, and were thus Scourg'd for the usual Offences, for which we give the like Punishment in *England*; and the Man who held the Line, and Scourg'd them, was the City Hangman;[199] who (by the Way) is there an Officer of Note, has a constant Sallary, and is a Man of Substance, and not only so, but a most Dextrous Fellow in his Office; and makes a great deal of Money of his Employment.

THIS sight however, was very shocking to us; and my Captain turn'd to me, come, *says he*, let us go away? I won't stay here any longer; I was glad to hear him say so, but did not think he had meant or intended what he said: However, we went back to our Quarters, and kept pretty much within, only that in the Evenings we Walk'd about: But even then my Captain found no Employment, no Encouragement; two or three times indeed, he made a Prize of some Mercery and Millenary Goods:[200] But when he had them, he knew not what to do with them; so that in short, he was forc'd to be honest, in spight[201] of his good will, to be otherwise.

WE remain'd here about a Month; when on a sudden my Captain was gone, Horse and all, and I knew nothing what was become of him; nor did I ever see or hear of him for eighteen Months after, nor did he so much as leave the least notice for me; either, whether[202] he was gone, or whether he would return to *Edinborough* again, or no.

I TOOK his leaving me very heiniously, not knowing what to do with my self, being a Stranger in the Place, and on the other Hand, my Money abated a-pace too: I had for the most part of this time, my Horse upon my Hands to keep; and as Horses yield but a sorry Price in *Scotland*, I found no Opportunity to make much of him; and on the other Hand, I had a secret Resolution, if I had gone back to *England*, to have restor'd him to the Owner, at *Puckeridge*, by *Ware*; and so I should have wrong'd him of nothing, but of the use of him for so long time: But I found an Occasion to answer all my Designs, about the Horse to Advantage.

THERE came a Man to the *Stabler* (so they call the People at *Edinborough*, that take in Horses to keep) and wanted to know if he could hear of any return'd Horses for *England*; my Landlord (so we call'd him) came bluntly to me one Day, and ask'd me *if my Horse was my own?* it was an odd Question as my Circumstances stood, and puzzl'd me at first; and I ask'd him why, and what was the matter? Because, *says he*, if it be a hir'd Horse in *England*, as is often the Case with *English* Men, who come to *Scotland*, I could help you to send it back, and get you something for riding it, so he express'd himself.

I WAS very glad of the Occasion; and in short, took Security there of the Person, for delivering the Horse safe and sound, and had 15*s. Sterling* for the riding him: Upon this Agreement I gave order to leave the Horse at the *Falcon* at *Puckeridge*, and where I heard many Year after, that he was honestly left, and that the Owner had him again, but had nothing for the Loan of him.

BEING thus eas'd of the Expence of my Horse, and having nothing at all to do; I began to consider with myself, what would become of me, and what I could turn my Hand to: I had not much diminish'd my Stock of Money for tho' I was all the way so wary, that I would not Joyn with my Captain in his desperate Attempts, yet I made no scruple to live at his Expence, which as I came out of *England*, only to keep him Company had been but just, had I not known that all he had to spend upon me, was what he robb'd honest People off, and that I was all that while a Receiver of stolen Goods; but I was not come off so far then[a] as to scruple that Part at all.

IN the the next Place, I was not so anxious about my Money running low, because, I knew what a Reserve I had made at *London*; but still I was very willing to have engag'd in any honest Employment for a Livelihood; for I was Sick indeed of the wandering Life which I had led, and was resolv'd to Thieve no more; but then two or three things, which I had offer'd me, I lost, because I could not Write or Read.[203]

THIS afflicted me a great while very much, but the *Stabler*, as I have call'd him deliver'd me from my Anxiety that way, by bringing me to an honest, but a poor young Man, who undertook to teach me, both to Write and Read, and in a little time too, and for a small Expence, if I would take pains at it; I promised all possible Diligence and to Work, I went with it; but found the Writing much more difficult to me than the Reading.

HOWEVER, in Half a Years time, or thereabouts; I could Read and Write too tollerably well, insomuch, that I began to think I was now fit for Business, and I got by it into the Service of a certain Officer of the Customs, who employed me for a time, but as he set me to do little, but pass and repass between *Leith* and *Edinborough*, with the Accounts which he kept for the Farmers of the Customs[204] there, leaving me to live at my own Expence, till my Wages should be due, I run out the little Money I had left, in Cloths and Subsistance, and a little before the Years End, when I was to have 12*l*. *English* Money, truly my Master was turn'd out of his Place, and which was worse, having been Charged with some Mis-applications,[205] was oblig'd to take Shelter in *England*, and so we that were Servants, for there were three of us, were left to shift for ourselves.

THIS was a hard Case for me, in a strange Place, and I was reduc'd by it, to the last Extremity: I might have gone for *England*, an *English* Ship being there; the Master profer'd me to give me my passage (upon telling him my distress) and to take my Word for the Payment of 10*s*. when I came there; but my Captain appear'd just then under new Circumstances which oblig'd him not to go away, and I was loth to leave him; it seems we were yet farther to take our Fate together.

I HAVE mention'd, that he left me, and that I saw him, no more for Eighteen Months: His Ramble, and Adventures were many in that time; he went to *Glasgow*, play'd some remarkable Pranks there, escap'd almost Miraculously from the Gallows, got over to *Ireland*, wander'd about there, turn'd Raparee,[206] and did some villanious Things there, and escap'd from *London-Derry*, over to the *Highlands*, in the North of *Scotland*, and about a Month before I was left destitute at *Leith*, by my Master; behold! my Noble Capt. *Jack* came in there, on Board the Ferry-Boat, from *Fife*, being after all his Adventures, and Successes advanc'd to the Dignity of a Foot-Soldier, in a Body of Recruits rais'd in the North, for the Regiment of *Douglas*.[207]

AFTER my Disaster, being reduc'd almost as low as my Captain, I found no better Shift before me, at least for the present, than to enter myself a Soldier too, and thus we were Rank'd together, with each of us a Musquet upon our Shoulders, and I confess that thing did not fit so ill upon me, as I thought at first it would have done; for tho' I far'd Hard, and lodg'd Ill, for the last especially is the Fate of poor Soldiers in that Part of the World; yet to me, that had been us'd to Lodge on the Ashes in the Glass-House, this was no great matter; I had a secret Satisfaction at being now under no Necessity of stealing, and living in fear of a Prison, and of the lash of the Hangman; a thing which from the time I saw it in *Edinborough*, was so terrible to me, that I could not think of it without horror, and it was an inexpressible ease to my Mind, that I was now in a certain way of Living, which was honest, and which I could say, was not unbecoming a Gentleman.

WHATEVER was my Satisfaction in that Part, yet other Circumstances did not equally concur to make this Life suit me; for after we had been about Six Months in this Figure, we were inform'd that the Recruits were all to march for *England*, and to be shipp'd off at *New-Castle*, or at *Hull*, to join the Regiment which was then in *Flanders*.

I should tell you that before this, I was extreamly delighted with the Life of a Soldier; and I took the Exercise so naturally, that the Serjeant that taught us to handle our Arms, seeing me so ready at it, ask'd me if I had never carryed Arms before; I told him no, at which he swore, tho' Jesting, they call you Col. *says he*, and I believe you will be a Col. or you must be some Colonel's Bastard, or you would never handle your Arms as you do, at once or twice showing.

THIS pleas'd me extreamly, and encourag'd me, and I was mightily taken with the Life of a Soldier; but when my Captain came, and told me the News, that we were to march for *England*, and to be shipp'd off for *Flanders* at *New-Castle* upon *Tyne*, I was surpriz'd very much, and new Thoughts began to come in my Mind; as first, my Captain's Condition was particular, for he durst not appear publickly at *New-Castle*, as he must have done if he had march'd with the Battalion (for they were a Body of above 400, and therefore, call'd themselves a Battalion, tho' they were but Recruits, and belonged to the several Companies abroad) *I say*, he must have march'd with them, and been publickly seen, in which Case he would have been apprehended, and delivered up: In the next Place, I remember'd that I had almost a Hundred Pound in Money in *London*, and if it should have been ask'd all the Soldiers in the Regiment which of them would go to *Flanders*, a private Centinel[208] if they had a 100*l*. in their Pockets, I believ'd none of them would answer in the Affirmative; a Hundred Pound being at that time sufficient to buy a Colours[209] in any New Regiment, tho' not in that Regiment which was on an old Establishment: This whetted my Ambition, and I Dream't of nothing but being a Gentleman Officer, as well as a Gentleman Soldier.

THESE two Circumstances concurring, I began to be very uneasy, and very unwilling in my Thoughts to go over a poor Musquetier into *Flanders,* to be knock'd on the Head at the Tune of Three and Six-pence a Week: While I was dayly musing on the Circumstances of being sent away, as above, and considering what to do, my Captain comes to me one Evening; Hark ye, *Jack, says he,* I must speak with you, let us take a walk in the Fields a little out from the Houses; we were Quarter'd at a Place, call'd *Park-End,* near the Town of *Dunbar,* about 20 Miles from *Berwick* upon *Tweed,* and about Sixteen Miles from the River *Tweed,* the nearest way.

WE walk'd together here, and talk'd seriously upon the matter; the Captain told me how his Case stood, and that he durst not march with the Battalion into *New-Castle;* that if he did, he should be taken out of the Ranks, and tryed for his Life, and that I knew as well as he; I could go privately to *New-Castle, says he,* and go thro' the Town well enough, but to go publickly, is to run into the Jaws of Destruction: *Well, says I, that is very true, but what will you do?* Do! *says he, do you think I am so bound by honour, as a Gentleman Soldier, that I will be hang'd for them,* no, no, *says he,* I am resolv'd to be gone; and I would have you go with us: *said I,* What do you mean by us? why, here is another honest Fellow, an *English* Man also, *says he,* that is resolv'd to Desert too, and he has been a long while in their Service, and says, he knows how we shall be us'd Abroad, and he will not go to *Flanders, says he,* not he.

WHY, *says I,* you will be shot to Death for Deserters if you are taken; and they will send out Scouts for you in the Morning all over the Country, so that you will certainly fall into their Hands; as for that, *says he,* my Comrade is thoroughly acquainted with the Way; and has undertaken to bring us to the Bank of *Tweed,* before they can come up with us, and when we are on the other side of the *Tweed,* they can't take us up.

AND when would you go away, *says I?*

THIS Minute, *says he,* no time to be lost; 'tis a fine Moon-shining Night.

I have none of my Baggage, *says I,* let me go back and fetch my Linnen, and other things.

YOUR Linnen is not much, I suppose, *says he,* and we shall easily get more in *England* the old Way.

NO, *says I,* no more of your old Ways; it has been owing to those old Ways, that we are now in such a strait.

WELL, well, *says he*, the old Ways are better than this starving Life of a Gentleman, as we call it.

BUT, *says I*, we have no Money in our Pockets; how shall we Travel?

I have a little, *says the Captain*, enough to help us on to *New-Castle*; and if we can get none by the Way, we will get some Collier Ship to take us in, and carry us to *London* by Sea.

I like that the best of all the Measures you have laid yet, *said I*, and so I consented to go, and went off with him immediately: The cunning Rogue having lodg'd his Comrade a Mile off under the Hills, had drag'd me, talking with him by little and little that way; till just when I consented, he was in sight, and he said, look there's my Comrade; who I knew presently, having seen him among the Men.

BEING thus gotten under the Hills, and a Mile of the way, and the Day just shot in,[210] we kept on a pace; resolving if possible to get out of the reach of our Pursuers, before they should miss us, or know any thing of our being gone.

WE ply'd our time so well, and travell'd so hard; that by five a Clock in the Morning we were at a little Village, whose Name I forget; But they told us, that we were within eight Miles of the *Tweed*; and that as soon as we should be over the River, we were on *English* Ground.

WE refresh'd a little here, but march'd on with but little stay; however, it was half an Hour past eight in the Morning before we reach'd the *Tweed*; so it was at least twelve Miles, when they told us it was but Eight: Here we overtook two more of the same Regiment who had Deserted from *Haddingtown*;[211] where another part of the Recruits were quarter'd.

THOSE were *Scots-men*, and very Poor, having not one Penny in their Pockets; and had no more when they made their Escape, but 8*s.* between them; and when they see us, who they knew to be of the same Regiment, they took us to be Pursuers, and that we came to lay hold of them; upon which they stood upon their Defence, having the Regiment Swords on, as we had also, but none of the Mounting[212] or Cloathing; for we were not to receive the Cloathing, till we came to the Regiment in *Flanders*.

IT was not long before we made them understand, that we were in the same Circumstances with themselves, and so we soon became one Company; and after resting some time on the *English* side of the River, (for we were heartily tyr'd, and the other were as much Fateagu'd as we were;) I say, after resting a while, we set forward towards *New Castle*, whether we resolv'd to go to get our Passage by Sea to *London*; for we had not Money to hold us out any farther.

OUR Money was Ebb'd very Low, for tho' I had one piece of Gold in my Pocket, which I kept reserv'd for the last Extremity; yet it was but half a

Guinea, and my Captain had born all our Charges as far as his Money would go; so that when we came to *New Castle*, we had but Six-pence left in all to help ourselves; and the two *Scots* had begg'd their way, all along the Road.

WE contriv'd to come into *New-Castle* in the Dusk of the Evening; and even then we durst not venture into the publick Part of the Town, but made down towards the River, something below the Town where some *Glass-houses*[213] stand: Here we knew not what to do with ourselves; but Guided by our Fate, we put a good Face upon the Matter, and went into an *Ale-house*, sat down and call'd for a Pint of Beer.

THE House was kept by a Woman only, *that is to say*, we saw no other, and as she appear'd very Frank, and Entertain'd us Cheerfully, we at last told her our Condition; and ask'd her, if she cou'd not help us to some kind Master of a Collier, that would give us a Passage to *London* by Sea; the Subtil Devil, who immediately found us proper Fish for her Hook, gave us the kindest Words in the World; and told us, she was heartily sorry she had not seen us one Day sooner; that there was a Collier Master of her particular Acquaintance that went away, but with the Morning-Tide; that the Ship was fallen down to *Shields*,[214] but she believ'd was hardly over the Bar yet, and she would send to his House, and see if he was gone on Board, for sometimes the Masters do not go away till a Tide after the Ship, and she was sure if he was not gone, she cou'd prevail with him to take us all in; but then she was afraid we must go on Board immediately, the same Night.

WE begg'd of her to send to his House, for we knew not what to do, and if she cou'd oblige him to take us on Board, we did not care what time of Night it was: for as we had no Money, we had no Lodging, and we wanted nothing, but to be on Board.

WE look'd upon this as a mighty Favour, that she sent to the Master's House; and to our greater Joy, she brought us Word about an Hour after, that he was not gone, and was at a Tavern in the Town, whether[215] his Boy had been to fetch him; and that he had sent Word he would call there in the way Home.

THIS was all in our Favour, and we were extreamly pleas'd with it; about an Hour after the Landlady being in the Room with us, her Maid brings us Word the Master was below, so down she goes to him, telling us she would go and tell him our Case, and see to perswade him to take us all on Board; after some time, she comes up with him, and brings him into the Room to us; where are these honest Gentlemen Soldiers, *says he*, that are in such Distress? We stood all up and paid our Respects to him; Well, Gentlemen, and is all your Money spent?

INDEED it is, *said one of our Company*; and we shall be infinitely obliged to you, Sir, if you will give us a Passage, we will be very willing to do any thing we can in the Ship, though we are not Seamen.

WHY, *says he*, were none of you ever at Sea in your Lives?

NO, *says we*, not one of us.

YOU will be able to do me no Service then, *says he*, for you will be all Sick: Well, however, *says he*, for my good Landlady's sake, *here I'll do it*: But are you all ready to go on Board, for I go on Board this very Night?

YES, Sir, *says we* again, we are ready to go this Minute.

NO, no, *says he*, very kindly, we'll Drink together; come Landlady, *says he*, make these honest Gentlemen a Sneaker[216] of Punch.

WE look'd at one another, for we knew we had no Money, and he perceiv'd it; come, come, *says he*, don't be concern'd at your having no Money, my Landlady here, and I, never part with dry Lips: Come good Wife, *says he*, make the Punch as I bid you.

WE thank'd him, and said, God Bless you Noble Captain, a hundred times over; being overjoy'd with such good Luck: While we were Drinking the Punch, he calls the Landlady, come, *says he*, I'll step Home, and take my things, and bid them Good-bye, and order the Boat to come at high Water and take me up here; and pray good Wife, *says he*, get me something for Supper, sure if I can give these honest Men their Passage, I may give them a Bit of Victuals too, it may be they han't had much for Dinner.

WITH this away he went, and in a little while we heard the Jack[217] a going; and one of us going down Stairs for a Spye, brought us Word there was a good Leg of Mutton at the Fire: In less than an Hour our Captain came again, and came up to us, and blam'd us that we had not drank all the Punch out; come, *says he*, don't be bashful, when that's out we can have another, when I am obliging poor Men, I love to do it handsomely.

WE drank on, and drank the Punch out, and more was brought up, and he push'd it about a pace; then came up a Leg of Mutton, and I need not say that we eat heartily, being told several times, that we should pay nothing; after Supper was done, he bids my Landlady ask if the Boat was come? and she brought word no, it was not High Water by a good deal; no, *says he*, well then give us some more Punch, so more Punch was brought in, and, as was afterwards confess'd something was put into it, or more Brandy than ordinary, that by that time the Punch was drunk out, we were all very Drunk, and as for me I was asleep.

ABOUT the time that was out, we were told the Boat was come, so we tumbl'd out, almost over one another into the Boat, and away we went, and our Captain with us in the Boat; most of us, if not all, fell asleep; till after sometime, tho' how much or how far going we knew not, the Boat stopp'd, and we were wak'd, and told we were at the Ship side; which was true, and with much help and holding us, for fear we should fall over Board, we were all gotten into the Ship; all I remember of it was this, that as soon as we were on Board, our Captain, as we call'd him, call'd out thus, here Boatson[218] take care of these Gentlemen, and give them good Cabbins, and let them turn in and go to sleep, for they are very weary; and so indeed we were, and very Drunk too, being the first time I had ever drank any Punch in my Life.

WELL, care was taken of us, according to order, and we were put into very good Cabbins, where we were sure to go immediately to sleep; in the mean time the Ship, which was indeed just ready to go, and only on notice given, had come to an Anchor for us at *Shields*, weigh'd, stood over the Bar, and went off to Sea, and when we wak'd, and began to peep abroad, which was not till near Noon the next Day we found ourselves a great way at Sea, the Land in sight indeed, but at a great distance, and all going merrily on for *London*, as we understood it; we were very well us'd, and well satisfy'd with our Condition for about three Days, when we began to enquire whether we were not almost come, and how much longer it would be, before we should come into the River? What River? *says one of the Men*, why, the *Thames*, says my Captain *Jack*; the *Thames*, says the Seamen, What do ye mean by that? What han't you had time enough to be sober yet? so Captain *Jack* said no more, but look'd about him like a Fool, when a while after, some other of us ask'd the like Question, and the Seamen, who knew nothing of the Cheat, began to smell a Trick, and turning to the other *Englishman* that came with us, pray, *says he*, Where do you fancy you are going, that you ask so often about it? why to *London*, says he, where should we be going? we agreed with the Captain to carry us to *London*.

NOT with the Captain, *says he*, I dare say; poor Men, you are all cheated; and I thought so when I saw you come Aboard with that Kidnapping Rogue *Gilliman*; poor Men! *adds he*, you are all Betray'd, Why, you are going to *Virginia*, and the Ship is bound to *Virginia*.

THE *Englishman* falls a storming, and raving like a mad Man, and we gathering round him, let any Men guess if they can, what was our surprise, and how we were confounded when we were told how it was; in short, we drew our Swords, and began to lay about us, and made such a Noise, and Hurry[219] in the Ship, that at last the Seamen were obliged to call out for help; the Captain commanded us to be disarmed in the first Place, which was not however done without giving, and receiving some Wounds, and afterwards he caus'd us to be brought to him into the great Cabbin.

HERE he talk'd calmly to us, that he was really very sorry, for what had befallen us, that he perceiv'd we had been Trappan'd,[220] and that the Fellow, who had brought us on Board was a Rogue that was employ'd by a sort of wicked Merchants, not unlike himself; that he suppos'd he had been represented to us, as Captain of the Ship, and ask'd us if it was not so? we told him yes, and gave him a large Account of ourselves, and how we came to the Woman's House to enquire for some Master of a *Collier* to get a Passage to *London*, and that this Man engag'd to carry us to *London* in his own Ship, and the like, as is related above.

HE told us he was very sorry for it, and he had no hand in it;[a] but it was out of his Power to help us, and let us know very plainly what our Condition was; namely, that we were put on Board his Ship as Servants to be deliver'd at *Maryland*, to such a Man, who he named to us; but that however if we would be quiet, and orderly in the Ship, he would use us well in the Passage, and take care we should be us'd well when we came there, and that he would do any thing for us that lay in his Power; but if we were unruly and refractory we could not expect but he must take such Measures as to oblige us to be satisfied; and that in short, we must be Hand-cuffed, carried down between the Decks, and kept as Prisoners, for it was his Business to take care that no Disturbance must be in the Ship.

MY Captain rav'd like a mad Man; swore at the Captain, told him he would not fail to cut his Throat either on Board, or a Shore, whenever he came within his reach, and that if he could not do it now, he would do it after he came to *England* again, if ever he durst show his Face here again, for he might depend upon it, if he was carryed away to *Virginia*, he should find his way to *England* again; that if it was 20 Year after, he would have Satisfaction of him: Well, young Man, *says the Captain smiling*, 'tis very honestly said, and then[b] I must take care of you while I have you here; and afterwards, I must take care of my self; do your worst, *says Jack boldly*, I'll pay you home for it one time or other; I must venture that young Man, says he still, calmly, but for the present you and I must talk a little; so he bids the Boatswain, who stood near him, secure him, which he did; I spoke to him to be easie and patient, and that the Captain had no Hand in our Misfortune.

NO Hand in it! D—m him, *said he*, aloud, do you think he is not Confederate in this Villainy? Would any honest Man receive Innocent People on Board his Ship, and not enquire of their Circumstances, but carry them away, and not speak to them? and now he knows how Barbarously we are treated; Why does he not set us on Shore again? I tell you he is the Villain, and none but him; Why does he not compleat his Villainy, and Murther us, and then he will be free from our Revenge? But nothing else shall ever deliver him from my Hands; but sending us to the D—l, or going thither himself; and I am honester in telling him so fairly, than he has been to me, and am in no Passion any more than he is.

THE Captain was a little shock'd at his boldness, for he talk'd a great deal more of the same Kind; with a great deal of Spirit, and Fire, and yet, without any Disorder in his Temper; indeed I was surpriz'd at it, for I never had heard him talk so well, and so much to the Purpose in my Life: The Captain was, *I say*, a little shock'd at it; however, he talk'd very handsomely to him, and told him, look ye, young Man, I bear with you the more, because I am sensible your Case is very hard, and yet, I cannot allow your Threatning me neither; and you oblige me by that, to be severer with you than I intended; however, I will do nothing to you, but what your Threatning my Life makes necessary: The Boatswain call'd out to have him to the Geers,[221] as they call'd it, and to have him Tast the *Cat-a-nine-tales*;[222] all which were Terms we did not understand till afterwards, we were told he should have been Whipp'd and Pickl'd,[223] for they said it was not to be suffer'd; but the Captain said, no, no, the young Man has been really Injur'd, and has Reason to be very much provok'd: But I have not Injur'd him, *says he*, and then he protested he had no Hand in it; that he was put on Board, and we also by the Owner's Agent, and for their Account; That it was true, that they did always deal in Servants, and carryed a great many every Voyage; but that it was no profit to him as Commander, but they were always put on Board by the Owners, and that it was none of his Business to enquire about them, and to prove that he was not concern'd in it, but was very much troubled at so base a thing, and that he would not be Instrumental to carry us away against our Wills, if the Wind and the Weather would permit he would set us on shore again, tho' as it blow'd then, the Wind being at South-West, and a hard Gale, and that they were already as far as the *Orkneys*, it was impossible.

BUT the Captain was the same Man; he told him, that let the Wind blow how it would, he ought not to carry us away against our consents, and that as to his Pretences of his Owners, and the like, it was saying of nothing to him; for it was he the Captain that carryed us away, and that whatever Rogue Trappan'd us on Board, now he knew it, he ought no more to carry us away, than Murther us, and that he demanded to be set on Shore, or else he the Captain was a Thief, and a Murtherer.

THE Captain continu'd mild still, and then I put in with an Argument, that had like to have brought us all back, if the Weather had not really hindered it; which when I came to understand Sea Affairs better, I found was indeed so, and that had been impossible. I told the Captain that I was sorry that my Brother was so warm, but that our usuage was Villainous, which he could not deny; then I took up the air of what my Habit did not agree with,[224] I told him, that we were[a] not People to be sold for Slaves, that tho' we had the Misfortune to be in a Circumstance that oblig'd us to conceal ourselves, having disguised ourselves to get out of the Army, as being not willing to go into *Flanders*; yet, that we were Men of Substance, and able to Discharge ourselves from the Service, when it came to that, and to convince him of it, I told him I would give him sufficient Security, to pay 20*l.* a piece, for my Brother and my self; and in as short time as we could, send from the Place he should put in at *London*, and receive a Return; and to show that I was able to do it, I pull'd out my Bill for 94*l.* from the Gentleman of the Custom-House, and who to my infinite Satisfaction, he knew as soon as he saw the Bill; he was astonish'd at this, and lifting up his Hands, by what Witchcraft, *says he*, were you brought hither!

As to that, *says I*, we have told you the Story, and we add nothing to it, but we insist upon it, that you will do this Justice to us now: Well, *says he*, I am very sorry for it, but I cannot answer putting back the Ship; neither if I could, *says he*, is it Practicable to be done.

While this Discourse lasted, the two *Scotsmen*, and the other *Englishman* were silent, but as I seem'd to Acquiesce, the *Scotchsmen* began to talk to the same purpose, which I need not repeat, and had not mention'd, but for a merry Passage that followed; after the *Scotchsmen* had said all they could, and the Captain still told them they must submit; And will you then carry us to *Virginia*? *Yes*, says the Captain, and will we be sold says the *Scotsman*, when we come there? Yes, *says the Captain*; Why, then, Sir, says the *Scotsman* the Devil will have you at the hinder End of the Bargain; *say you so*, says the Captain smiling, well, well, *let the Devil and I alone to agree about that*, do you be quiet, and behave Civilly as you should do, and you shall be us'd as kindly both here, and there too as I can: The poor *Scotchsmen* could say little to it, nor I, nor any of us; for we saw there was no Remedy, but to leave the Devil and the Captain to agree among themselves, as the Captain had said, as to the honesty of it.

Thus, in short, we were all, *I say*, oblig'd to Acquiesce; but my Captain, who was so much the more obstinate when he found that I had a Fund to make such an offer upon, nor could all my perswasions prevail with him: The Captain of the Ship and he had many pleasant Dialogues about this in the rest of the Voyage, in which *Jack* never treated him with any Language, but that of Kidnapper, and Villain, nor talk'd of any thing, but of taking his Revenge of him; but I omit that Part tho' very Diverting as being no part of my own Story.

In short, the Wind continu'd to blow hard, tho' very fair, till, as the Seamen said, we were pass'd the Islands, on the North of *Scotland*, and that we began to Steer away Westerly, and then in a few Days, (which I came to understand since) as there was no Land any way, for many Hundred Leagues, so we had no Remedy but Patience, and to be as easy as we could; only my surly Captain *Jack* continued the same Man all the way.

WE had a very good Voyage, no Storms all the way, and a Northerly Wind almost 20 Days together; so that in a Word, we made the Capes of *Virginia* in two and Thirty Days, from the Day we steer'd West, as I have said, which was in the Latitude of 60 Degrees, 30 Minutes; being to the North of the Isle of *Great Britain*, and this they said was a very quick Passage.

NOTHING material happen'd to me, during the Voyage, and indeed when I came there I was oblig'd to act in so narrow a Compass, that nothing very material could Present it self.

WHEN we came a shore, which was in a great River, which they call *Potomack*,[225] the Captain ask'd us, but me more particularly, whether I had any thing to propose to him now? *Jack* answer'd *yes, I have something to propose to you* Captain; that is, that I have promis'd you to cut your Throat, and depend upon it I will be as good as my Word: Well, well, *says the Captain*, If I can't help it you shall; so he turn'd away to me, I understood him very well what he meant; but I was now out of the reach of any Relief, and as for my Note it was now but a bit of Paper of no value, for no Body could receive it but myself: I saw no Remedy, and so talk'd coldly to him of it, as of a thing I was indifferent about; and indeed I was grown indifferent, for I considered all the way on the Voyage, that as I was bred a Vagabond, had been a Pickpocket, and a Soldier, and was run from my Colours, and that I had no settled Abode in the World, nor any Employ to get any thing by, except that wicked one I was bred to, which had the Gallows at the Heels of it; I did not see, but that this Service might be as well to me as other Business; and this I was particularly satisfied with when they told me, that after I had Served out the five Years Servitude,[226] I should have the Courtisie of the Country, *as they call'd it*; that is a certain Quantity of Land to Cultivate and Plant for myself;[227] so that now I was like to be brought up to something, by which I might live without that wretched thing, call'd stealing; which my very Soul abhorr'd, and which I had given over, as I have said ever since that wicked time, that I robb'd the poor Widow of *Kentish* Town.

IN this Mind I was, when I arriv'd at *Virginia*, and so when the Captain enquired of me what I intended to do, and whether I had any thing to propose, *that is to say*, he meant whether I would give him my Bill, which he wanted to be Fingering very much; I answer'd coldly, my Bill would be of no use to me now, for no Body would advance any thing upon it, only this I would say to him, that if he would carry me and Captain *Jack* back to *England*, and to *London* again, I would pay him the 20*l.* off of my Bill for each of us: This he had no mind to; *For as to your Brother*, says he, *I would not take him into my Ship for twice* 20l. *he is such a hardened desperate Villain*, says he, *I should be oblig'd to carry him in Irons as I brought him hither.*

THUS we parted with our Captain, *or Kidnapper, call him as you will*: We were then deliver'd to the Merchants, to whom we were Consign'd, who again dispos'd of us as they thought fit, and in a few Days we were separated.

AS for my Captain *Jack*, to make short of the Story, that desperate Rogue had the Luck to have a very easie good Master; whose Easiness, and good Humour he abus'd very much, and in particular, took an Opportunity to run away with a Boat, which his Master entrusted him and another with, to carry some Provisions down the River to another Plantation, which he had there: This Boat, and Provisions they ran away with, and sail'd North to the bottom of the Bay, *as they call it*, and into a River, call'd *Sasquehanuagh*,[228] and there quitting the Boat, they wandered thro' the Woods, till they came into *Pensilvania*, from whence they made shift to get Passage to *New-England*, and from thence Home; where falling in among his old Companions, and to the old Trade; he was at length taken and hang'd, about a Month before I came to *London*, which was near 20 Years afterward.

MY Part was harder at the Beginning, tho' better at the latter End; I was dispos'd of, *that is to say* sold, to a rich Planter, whose Name was *Smith*, and with me, the other *Englishman*, who was my Fellow Deserter, that *Jack* brought me to when we went off from *Dunbar*.

WE were now Fellow Servants, and it was our Lot to be carryed up a small River or Creek, which falls into *Potowmack* River, about eight Miles from the great River: Here we were brought to the Plantation, and put in among about 50 Servants, as well *Negroes*, as others, and being delivered to the Head-man, or Director, or Manager of the Plantation, he took care to let us know that we must expect to Work, and very hard too; for it was for that Purpose his Master bought Servants, and for no other: I told him very submissively, that since it was our Misfortune to come into such a miserable Condition as we were in, we expected no other; only we desir'd, we might be show'd our Business, and be allowed to learn it gradually, since he might be sure we had not been us'd to Labour; and I added that when he knew particularly by what Methods we were brought, and betrayed into such a Condition, he would perhaps see Cause, at least to shew us that Favour, if not more: This I spoke with such a moving Tone, as gave him a Curiosity to enquire into the particulars of our Story, which I gave him at large, a little more to our Advantage too, than ordinary.

THIS Story as I hop'd it would, did move him to a sort of Tenderness, but yet he told us that his Master's Business must be done, and that he expected we must Work, as above; that he could not dispense with that, upon any account whatever; accordingly to Work we went, and indeed we had three hard Things attending us; namely, we work'd Hard, lodg'd Hard, and far'd Hard; the first I had been an utter Stranger to, the last I could shift well enough with.

DURING this Scene of Life, I had time to reflect on my past Hours, and upon what I had done in the World, and tho' I had no great Capacity of making a clear Judgment, and very little reflections from Conscience, yet it made some impressions upon me; and particularly that I was brought into this miserable Condition of a Slave; by some strange directing Power, as a Punishment for the Wickedness of my younger Years, and this thought was increas'd upon the following occasion: The Master whose Service I was now gaged[229] in, was a Man of Substance and Figure in the Country, and had abundance of Servants, as well as *Negroes*, as *English*; in all I think he had near 200, and among so many, as some grew every Year infirm and unable to Work, others went off upon their time being expir'd, and others died; and by these and other Accidents the Number would diminish, if they were not often Recruited and fill'd, and this obliged him to buy more every Year.

IT happen'd while I was here, that a Ship arrived from *London*, with several Servants, and among the rest was seventeen Transported Fellons,[230] some burnt in the Hand,[231] others not; eight of whom my Master bought for the time specified in the Warrant for their Transportation, respectively, some for a longer, some a shorter term of Years.

OUR Master was a great Man in the Country, and a Justice of Peace; tho' he seldom came down to the Plantation where I was, yet as the new Servants were brought on Shore, and delivered at our Plantation, his Worship came thither, in a kind of State[232] to see and Receive them: When they were brought before him, I was call'd among other Servants, as a kind of a Guard to take them into Custody, after he had seen them, and to carry them to the Work; they were brought by a Guard of Seamen from the Ship, and the second Mate of the Ship came with them, and deliver'd them to our Master, with the Warrant for their Transportation, as above.

WHEN his Worship had read over the Warrants, he call'd them over by their Names, One by One, and having let them know by his reading the Warrants over again to each Man respectively, that he knew for what Offences they were Transported; he talk'd to every one separately very gravely, let them know how much Favour they had receiv'd in being sav'd from the Gallows, which the Law had appointed for their Crimes, that they were not Sentenced to be Transported, but to be hang'd, and that Transportation was granted them upon their own Request and humble Petition.

THEN he laid before them, that they ought to look upon the Life they were just a going to enter upon, as just beginning the World again; that if they thought fit to be diligent, and sober, they would after the time they were order'd to Serve was expir'd, be encourag'd by the Constitution of the Country, to Settle and Plant for themselves, and that even he himself would be so kind to them, that if he liv'd to see any of them serve their Time faithfully out, it was his custom to assist his Servants, in order to their Settling in that Country, according as their Behaviour might Merit from him, and they would see and know several Planters round about them, who now were in very good Circumstances, and who formerly were only his Servants, in the same Condition with them, and came from the same Place; that is to say, *Newgate*, and some of them had the Mark of it in their Hands, but were now very honest Men, and liv'd in very good Repute.

AMONG the rest of his new Servants, he came to a young Fellow not above 17 or 18 Years of Age, and his Warrant mention'd that he was, tho' a young Man, yet an old Offender; that he had been several times Condemn'd, but had been Respited or Pardon'd, but still he continued an incorrigible Pick-pocket; that the Crime for which he was now Transported was for Picking a Merchant's Pocket-Book, or Letter Case out of his Pocket, in which was Bills of *Exchange*, for a very great Sum of Money; that he had afterward receiv'd the Money upon some of the Bills; but that going to a Goldsmith in *Lombard street* with another Bill, and having demanded the Money, he was stopp'd, Notice having been given of the Loss of them; that he was condemn'd to Die for the Felony, and being so well known for an old Offender, had certainly died, but the Merchant upon his earnest Application, had obtain'd that he should be Transported, on Condition that he restor'd all the rest of the Bills, which he had done accordingly.

OUR Master talk'd a long time to this young Fellow; mention'd with some surprize, that he so young should have follow'd such a wicked Trade so long, as to obtain the Name of an old Offender, at so young an Age, and that he should be stil'd incorrigible, which is to signify, that notwithstanding his being Whipt two or three times, and several times punish'd by Imprisonment, and once burnt in the Hand, yet nothing would do him any good; but that he was still the same. He talk'd mighty Religiously to this Boy, and told him, God had not only spar'd him from the Gallows, but had now mercifully deliver'd him from the Opportunity of committing the same Sin again, and put it into his Power to live an honest Life, which perhaps he knew not how to do before; and tho' some part of this Life now might be laborious, yet he ought to look on it to be no more, then being put out Apprentice to an honest Trade, in which, when he came out of his Time he might be able to Set up for himself, and live honestly.

THEN he told him, that while he was a Servant, he would have no Opportunity to be dishonest, so when he came to be for himself, he would have no Temptation to it, and so after a great many other kind things said to him and the rest they were dismist.

I WAS exceedingly mov'd at this Discourse of our Masters, as any Body would judge I must be, when it was directed to such a young Rogue, born a Thief, and bred up a Pick pocket like my self, for I thought all my Master said was spoken to me, and sometimes it came into my Head, that sure my Master was some extraordinary Man, and that he knew all things that ever I had done in my Life.

BUT I was surpriz'd to the last degree, when my Master dismissing all the rest of us Servants, Pointed at me, and speaking to his head Clerk, *here says he*, bring that young Fellow hither to me.

I HAD been near a Year in the Work, and I had ply'd it so well, that the Clerk, or head Man, either flatter'd me, or did really believe that I behav'd very well; but I was terribly frighted to hear myself call'd out, aloud, just as they us'd to call for such as had done some Misdemeanour, and were to be Lash'd, or otherwise Corrected.

I CAME in like a Malefactor indeed, and thought I look'd like one just taken in the Fact, and carry'd before the Justice; and indeed when I came in, for I was carry'd into an Inner-Room, or Parlour in the House to him; his Discourse to the rest was in a large Hall, where he sat in a Seat like a Lord Judge upon the Bench, or a Petty King upon his Throne.

WHEN I came in, *I say*, he ordered his Man to withdraw, and I standing half naked, and bare-headed with my Haugh or Hoe in my Hand, (the Posture and Figure I was in at my Work,) near the Door, he bad me lay down my Hoe, and come nearer; then he began to look a little less Stern and Terrible, than I fancy'd him to look before; or perhaps both his Countenance then, and before might be to my Imagination, differing from what they really were; for we do not always Judge those things by the real Temper of the Person, but by the Measure of our Apprehensions.

Hark ye young Man, How old are you? *says my Master*, and so our Dialogue began.

Jack. Indeed Sir, I do not know.

Mast. What is your Name?

Jack. They call me COLONEL* here, but my Name is JACK, an't please your Worship.

Mast. But prethee, what is thy Name?

* I was not call'd Col. *Jack as at London*, but *Colonel*, and they did not know me by any other Name.

Jack. Jack.

Mast. What is thy Christian Name then *Colonel*, and thy Sir Name *Jack?*

Jack. Truly Sir, to tell *your Honour* the Truth, I know little, or nothing of myself,* nor what my true Name is; but thus I have been call'd ever since I remember; which is my Christian-Name, or which my Sir-Name, or whether I was ever Christen'd, or not, I cannot tell.

Mast. Well, however, that's honestly answer'd. Pray how came you hither, and on what Account are you made a Servant here?

Jack. I wish your Honour could have Patience with me, to hear the whole Story; it is the hardest, and most unjust thing that ever came before you.

Mast. Say you so, tell it me at large then, I'll hear it, I Promise that, if it be an Hour long.

    THIS encourag'd me, and I began at my being a Soldier, and being per-sawded to Desert at *Dunbar*, and gave him all the Particulars, as they are related above, to the time of my coming on Shore, and the Captain talking to me about my Bill after I arriv'd here: He held up his Hands several times as I went on, expressing his abhorrence of the Usage I had met with at *New-Castle*, and enquir'd the Name of the Master of the Ship, for *said he*, that Captain for all his smooth Words must be a Rogue; so I told him his Name, and the Name of the Ship, and he took it down in his Book, and then we went on.

Mast. But pray answer me honestly too, to another Question, What was it made you so much concern'd at my talking to the Boy there, the Pick-pocket?

Jack. An't please your Honour, it mov'd me, to hear you talk so kindly to a poor Slave.

Mast. And was that all, speak truly now?

Jack. No, indeed, but a secret Wish came into my Thoughts, that you that were so good to such a Creature as that, could but one way or other know my Case, and that if you did, you would certainly pity me, and do something for me.

Mast. Well, but was there nothing in his Case that hit with your own, that made you so affected with it, for I saw Tears come from your Eyes, and it was that made me call, to speak to you.

Jack. Indeed Sir, I have been a wicked idle Boy, and was left Desolate in the World; but that Boy is a Thief, and condemn'd to be hang'd, I never was before a Court of Justice in my Life.

---

  * *NOTE*, He did not now talk quite so blindly, and Childishly, as when he was a Boy, and when the Custom-House Gentleman talked to him about his Names.

Mast. Well, I won't Examine you too far, if you were never before a Court of Justice, and are not a Criminal Transported, I have nothing farther to enquire of you: You, have been ill used, that's certain and was it that, that affected you?

Jack. Yes indeed, please your *Honour [*we all call'd him his Honour, or his Worship.]

Mast. Well, now I do know your Case, What can I do for you?

Mast. You speak of a Bill of 94*l.* of which you would have given the Captain, 40*l.* for your Liberty, Have you that Bill in your keeping still?

Jack. Yes Sir, *here it is, [I pull'd it out of the Wastband of my Drawers, where I always found means to preserve it, wrap'd up in a piece of Paper, and pin'd to the Wastband, and yet almost worn out too, with often pining, and removing,] so^a I gave it to him to read, and he read it.

Mast. And is this Gentleman in being that gave you the Bill?

Jack. Yes Sir, he was alive, and in good Health, when I came from *London*, which you may see by the Date of the Bill, for I came away the next Day.

Mast. I do not wonder that the Captain of the Ship, was willing to get this Bill of you when you came on Shore here.

Jack. I would have given it into his possession, if he would have carryed me, and my Brother back again to *England*, and have taken what he ask'd for us out of it.

Mast. Ay, but he knew better than that too, he knew if you had any Friends there, they would call him to an Account for what he had done; but I wonder he did not take it from you while you were at Sea, either by Fraud or by Force.

Jack. He did not attempt that indeed.

Mast. Well, young Man, I have a mind to try if I can do you any Service in this Case; on my Word, if the Money can be paid, and you can get it safe over, I might put you in a way how to be a better Man than your Master, if you will be honest and diligent.

Jack. As I behave myself in your Service Sir, you will I hope judge of the rest.

Mast. But perhaps you Hanker after returning to *England*.

Jack. No indeed Sir, if I can but get my Bread honestly here, I have no mind to go to *England*, for I know not how to get my Bread there, if I had I had not Listed^233 for a Soldier.

Mast. Well, but I must ask you some Questions about that Part hereafter, for 'tis indeed something strange, that you should List for a Soldier, when you had 94*l.* in your Pocket.

Jack. I shall give your Worship as particular Account of that, as I have of the other Part of my Life, if you please, but 'tis very long.

Mast. Well, we will have that another time; but to the Case in Hand, Are you willing I should send to any Body at *London*, to talk with that Gentleman that gave you the Bill; not to take the Money of him, but to ask him only whether he has so much Money of yours in his Hands? and whether he will Part with it, when you shall give Order, and send the Bill, or a *Duplicate of it* (*that is, says he,* the Copy) and it was well he did say so, *for I did not understand the Word* [Duplicate] at all.[a]

Jack. Yes Sir, I will give you the Bill it self if you please, I can trust it with you, tho' I cou'd not with him.

Mast. No, no, young Man, I won't take it from you.

Jack. I wish your Worship would please to keep it for me, for if I should lose it, then I am quite undone.

Mast. I will keep it for you *Jack* if you will, but then you shall have a Note under my Hand, signifying that I have it, and will return it you upon Demand, which will be safe to you as the Bill, I won't take it else.

SO I gave my Master the Bill, and he gave me his Note for it, and he was a faithful Steward for me, as you will hear in its Place: After this Conference, I was dismissed, and went to my Work, but about two Hours after, the Steward or the Overseer of the Plantation came riding by, and coming up to me as I was at Work, pull'd a Bottle out of his Pocket, and calling me to him, gave me a Dram of Rum; when in good Manners, I had taken but a little Sup, he held it out to me again, and bad me take another, and spoke wonderous civilly to me, quite otherwise than he us'd to do.

THIS encouraged me, and hearten'd me very much, but yet I had no particular View of any thing, or which way I should have any Relief.

A DAY or two after, when we were all going out to our Work in the Morning, the Overseer call'd me to him again, and gave me a Dram, and a good peice of Bread, and bad me come off from my Work about One a-Clock, and come to him to the House, for he must speak with me.

WHEN I came to him, I came to be sure in the ordinary Habit of a poor half naked Slave; Come hither young Man, *says he,* and give me your Hoe, when I gave it him; well, *says he,* you are to Work no more, in this Plantation.

I look'd surpriz'd, and as if I was Frighted, What have I done, Sir? *said I,* and whether[234] am I to be sent away.

NAY, nay, *says he,* and look'd very pleasantly, do not be frighted, 'tis for your good, 'tis not to hurt you, I am order'd to make an Overseer of you, and you shall be a Slave no longer.

ALAS! *says I,* to him, I, an Overseer! I am in no Condition for it, I have no Cloaths to put on, no Linnen, nothing to help myself.

WELL, well, *says he,* you may be better us'd than you are aware of, come hither with me; so he led me into a vast great Ware-house, or rather Set of Ware-houses, one within another, and calling the Ware-house-keeper, *here says he,* you must Cloth this Man, and give him every thing necessary, upon the Foot[235] of Number Five, and give the Bill to me, our Master has order'd me to allow it, in the Account of the West Plantation: That was it seems the Plantation where I was to go.

ACCORDINGLY, the Ware-house Keeper carryed me into an Inner Ware-house, where were several Suites of Cloths of the Sort his Orders mention'd; which were plain but good sorts of Cloths ready made, being of a good Broad Cloth, about 11*s.* a Yard in *England*, and with this he gave me three good Shirts, two Pair of Shoes, Stockings and Gloves, a Hat, six Neckcloths, and in short, every thing I could want; and when he had look'd every thing out, and fitted them, he lets me into a little Room by it self; here *says he,* go in there a Slave, and come out a Gentleman; and with that carryed every thing into the Room, and shutting the Door, bid me put them on, which I did most willingly; and now you may believe, that I began to hope for something better than ordinary.

IN a little while after this, came the Overseer, and gave me Joy of my new Cloths, and told me I must go with him; so I was carried to another Plantation larger than that where I work'd before, and where there were two Overseers, or Clerks, One within Doors, and Two without: This last was remov'd to another Plantation, and I was plac'd there in his room, *that is to say,* as the Clerk without Doors, and my Business was to look after the Servants and *Negroes*,[a] and take Care that they did their Business, provide their Food, and in short, both Govern and Direct them.

I WAS elevated to the highest degree in my Thoughts at this Advancement, and it is impossible for me to express the Joy of my Mind upon this Occasion; but there came a difficulty upon me, that shock'd me so violently, and went so against my very Nature, that I really had almost forfeited my Place about it, and in all Appearance the Favour of our Master, who had been so generous to me; and this was, that when I entered upon my Office, I had a Horse given me, and a long Horse-whip, like what we call in *England* a Hunting-whip; the Horse was to ride up and down all over the Plantation to see the Servants and *Negroes* did their Work, and the Plantation being so large, it could not be done on Foot, at least so often, and so effectually as was requir'd; and the Horse-whip was given me to correct and lash the Slaves and Servants, when they proved Negligent, or Quarrelsome, or in short were guilty of any Offence: This part turn'd the very blood within my Veins, and I could not think of it with any temper; that I, who was but Yesterday a Servant or Slave like them, and under the Authority of the same Lash, should lift up my Hand to the Cruel Work, which was my Terror but the Day before: This I say, I cou'd not do; insomuch, that the *Negroes* perceiv'd it, and I had soon so much Contempt upon my Authority, that we were all in Disorder.

THE Ingratitude of their Return, for the Compassion I shew'd them, provok'd me, I Confess, and a little harden'd my Heart, and I began with the *Negroes*, two of whom I was oblig'd to Correct; and I thought I did it most Cruelly; but after I had Lash'd them till every Blow I struck them, hurt my self, and I was ready to Faint at the Work, the Rogues Laught at me, and one of them had the Impudence to say behind my Back, that if he had the Whipping of me, he would show me better how to Whip a *Negro*.

WELL, however, I had no Power to do it in such a Barbarous manner, as I found it was necessary to have it done; and the Defect began to be a Detriment to our Masters Business, and now I began indeed to see, that the Cruelty, so much talk'd of, used in *Virginia* and *Barbadoes*, and other Colonies, in Whipping the *Negro* Slaves,[236] was not so much owing to the Tyranny, and Passion, and Cruelty of the *English*, as had been reported; the *English* not being accounted to be of a Cruel Disposition, and really are not so: But that it is owing to the Brutallity, and obstinate Temper of the *Negroes*, who cannot be mannag'd by Kindness, and Courtisy; but must be rul'd with a Rod of Iron, beaten with *Scorpions*, as the Scripture calls it;[237] and must be used as they do use them, or they would Rise and Murther all their Masters, which, their Numbers consider'd, would not be hard for them to do, if they had Arms and Ammunition suitable to the Rage and Cruelty of their Nature.

BUT I began to see at the same time, that this Brutal temper of the *Negroes* was not rightly manag'd; that they did not take the best Course with them, to make them sensible, either of Mercy, or Punishment; and it was Evident to me, that even the worst of those tempers might be brought to a Compliance, without the Lash, or at least without so much of it, as they generally Inflicted.

OUR Master was really a Man of Humanity himself, and was sometimes so full of Tenderness, that he would forbid the Severities of his Overseers and Stewards; but he saw the Necessity of it, and was oblig'd at last to leave it to the Discretion of his upper Servants: yet he would often bid them be Merciful, and bid them consider the Difference of the Constitution of the Bodies of the *Negro*'s; some being less able to bear the Tortures of their Punishment than others, and some of them less Obstinate too, than others.

HOWEVER, some body was so officious as to inform him against me upon this Occasion, and let him know, that I Neglected his Affairs, and that the Servants were under no Government; by which means his Plantation was not duly manag'd, and that all things were in Disorder.

THIS was a heavy Charge for a young Overseer, and his Honour came like a Judge, with all his Attendants, to look into things, and hear the Cause: However, he was so just to me, as that before he Censur'd me, he resolv'd to hear me fully; and that not only Publickly, but in Private too; and the last part of this was my particular good Fortune, for as he had formerly allow'd me to speak to him with Freedom; so I had the like Freedom now, and had full Liberty to Explain, and Defend my self.

I knew nothing of the Complaint against me, till I had it from his own Mouth; nor any thing of his coming, till I saw him in the very Plantation, viewing his Work, and viewing the several Peices of Ground that were order'd to be New Planted; and after he had Rod[238] all round, and seen things in the Condition, which they were to be seen in; how every thing was in its due Order, and the Servants and *Negroes* were all at Work, and every thing appearing to his Mind, he went into the House.

AS I saw him come up the Walks, I ran towards him, made my Homage, and gave him my humble Thanks for the Goodness he had shew'd me, in taking me from the Miserable Condition I was in before, and Employing and Entrusting me in his Business; and he look'd pleasant enough, tho' he did not say much at first, and I attended him thro' the whole Plantation, gave him an Account of every thing as he went along, answer'd all his Objections, and Enquiries, every where in such a manner, as it seems, he did not expect: And, as he acknowledg'd afterward, every thing was very much to his Satisfaction.

THERE was an Overseer, as I observ'd, belonging to the same Plantation, who was, tho' not over me, yet in a Work Superior to mine; for his Business was to see the *Tobacco* pack'd up, and deliver it either on Board the Sloops, or otherwise, as our Master order'd, and to receive *English* Goods from the Grand Ware-house, which was at the other Plantation, because, that was nearest the Water-side; and in short, to keep the Accounts: This Overseer, an Honest and upright Man, made no Complaint to him of his Business being Neglected, as above, or of any thing like it, tho' he Enquir'd of him about it, and that very strictly too.

I should have said, that as he Rid over the Plantation; he came in his round to the Place where the Servants were usually Corrected, when they had done any Fault; and there stood two *Negroes* with their Hands ty'd behind them, as it were under Sentence; and when he came near them, they fell on their Knees, and made pitiful Signs to him for Mercy: Alas!

Alas! *says he*, turning to me, why did you bring me this way? I do not love such Sights, what must I do now? I must Pardon them; prethee, what have they done? I told him the particular Offences, which they were brought to the Place for; one had Stole a Bottle of Rum, and had made himself Drunk with it, and when he was Drunk, had done a great many Mad things, and had attempted to knock one of the white Servants Brains out with a Hand-spike;[239] but that the white Man had avoided the Blow, and striking up the *Negroes* Heels,[240] had seiz'd him, and brought him Prisoner thither, where he had lain all Night; and that I had told him he was to be Whipp'd that Day, and the next three Days, twice every Day.

AND could you be so Cruel, *says his Honour*, why, you would Kill the poor Wretch! and so beside the Blood which you would have to answer for, you would lose me a lusty Man *Negro*, which Cost me at least 30 or 40*l.* and bring a Reproach upon my whole Plantation; nay, and more than that, some of them in Revenge would Murther me, if ever it was in their Power.

SIR, *says I*, if those Fellows are not kept under by Violence, I believe you are Satisfied, nothing is to be done with them; and it is reported in your Works, that I have been rather their Jest, than their Terror, for want of using them as they deserve; and I was resolv'd how muchsoever it is against my own Disposition, that your Service should not suffer for my unseasonable Forbearance; and therefore, if I had Scourg'd him to Death:— Hold, *says he*, no, no, by no means, any such Severity in my Bounds; remember young Man, you were once a Servant, deal as you would acknowledg'd it would be just to deal with you in his Case, and mingle always some Mercy; I desire it, and let the Consequence of being too gentle, be plac'd to my Account.

THIS was as much as I cou'd desire, and the more, because what pass'd, was in Publick, and several, both *Negroes* and white Servants, as well as the particular Persons, who had accused me, heard it all, tho' I did not know it: A Cruel Dog of an Overseer, *says one of the white Servants behind*, he would have Whipp'd poor *Bullet-head*, (*so they call'd the* Negro, that was to be Punish'd) to Death, if *his Honour* had not happen'd to come to Day.

HOWEVER, I urg'd the Notorious Crime this Fellow was Guilty of,[a] and the Danger there was in such Forbearance, from the Refactory and incorrigible Temper of the *Negroes*, and press'd a little the Necessity of making Examples; but *he said*, well, well, do it the next time, but not so, I said no more.

THE other Fellows Crime was trifling, compar'd with this; and the Master went forward, talking of it to me, and I following him, till we came to the House; when after he had been sat down a while, he call'd me to him: And not suffering my Accusers to come near, till he had heard my Defence, he began with me thus.

Mast. Hark ye, young Man, I must have some Discourse with you: Your Conduct is Complain'd of, since I set you over this Plantation; I thought your Sence of the Obligation I had laid on you, would have secur'd your Diligence, and Faithfulness to me.

Jack. I am very sorry any Complaint should be made of me, because the Obligation I am under to *your Honour*, (and which I freely Confess) does bind me to your Interest in the strongest manner Imaginable; and however I may have mistaken my Business, I am sure I have not willingly Neglected it.

Mast. Well, I shall not Condemn you, without hearing you, and therefore I call'd you in now, to tell you of it.

Jack. I humbly Thank *your Honour*, I have but one Petition more, *and that is*, that I may know my Accusation, and if you please, my Accusers.

Mast. The first, you shall, *and that is*, the Reason of my talking to you in Private; and if there is any need of a farther Hearing, you shall know your Accusers too: What you are charg'd with, is just contrary to what appear'd to me just now, and therefore you and I must come to a new understanding about it; for I thought I was too cunning for you, and now I think you have been too Cunning for me.

Jack. I hope *your Honour* will not be offended, that I do not fully understand you.

Mast. I believe you do not; come tell me Honestly, did you really intend to Whip the poor *Negro* twice a Day, for four Days together; *that is to say*, to Whip him to Death, for that would have been the *English* of it, and the End of it.

Jack. If I may be permitted to Guess, Sir, I believe I know the Charge that is brought against me; and that *your Honour* has been told, that I have been too gentle with the *Negroes*, as well as with other Servants; and that when they have deserv'd to be us'd with the accustom'd Severity of the Country, I have not given them half enough; and that by this Means they are careless of your Business, and that your Plantation is not well look'd after, *and the like.*

Mast. Well, you Guess right, go on.

Jack. The first Part of the Charge I Confess, but the last I Deny; and appeal to *your Honour's* strictest Examination, into every part of it.

Mast. If the last Part could be true, I would be glad the first were; for it would be an infinite Satisfaction to me, that my Business not being Neglected, nor our safety Endanger'd, those poor Wretches cou'd be us'd with more Humanity, for Cruelty is the Aversion of my Nature; and it is the only uncomfortable thing that attends me, in all my Prosperity.

Jack. I freely acknowledge, Sir, that at first, it was impossible for me to bring my self to that Terrible Work: How could I, that was but just come out of the Terror of it my self, and had but the Day before been a poor Naked miserable Servant my self, and might be to Morrow reduc'd to the same Condition again; How cou'd I use *this Terrible Weapon on the naked Flesh of my Fellow Servants, as well as Fellow Creatures? As least, Sir, when my Duty made it absolutely Necessary, I cou'd not do it without the utmost Horror: I beseech you Pardon me, if I have such a Tenderness in my Nature, that tho' I might be fit to be your Servant; I am incapable of being an Executioner, having been an Offender myself.

Mast. Well, but how then can my Business be done? And how will this terrible Obstinacy of the *Negroes*, who they tell me, can be no otherwise governed, be kept from Neglect of their Work, or even Insolence and Rebellion?

Jack. This brings me, Sir, to the latter part of my Defence; and here, I hope *your Honour* will be pleased to call my Accusers, or that you will give your self the Trouble of taking the exactest View of your Plantation, and see, or let them shew you, if any thing is Neglected, if your Business has suffer'd in any thing, or if your *Negroes* or other Servants are under less Government than they were before; and if on the contrary, I have found out that happy Secret, to have good Order kept, the Business of the Plantation done, and that with Diligence, and Dispatch, and that the *Negroes* are kept in Awe, the natural Temper of them Subjected, and the Safety and Peace of your Family secur'd; as well by gentle Means, as by Rough, by moderate Correction, as by Torture, and Barbarity; by a due Awe of just Discipline, as by the Horror of unsufferable Torments, I hope *your Honour* will not lay that Sin to my Charge.[241]

Mast. No indeed, you would be the most acceptable Mannager that ever I employed; But how then does this consist with the cruel Sentence you had pass'd on the poor Fellow, that is in your Condemn'd Hole yonder, who was to be Whipp'd eight times in four Days?

Jack. Very well, Sir; first Sir, he remains under the terrible Apprehensions of a Punishment, so Severe, as no *Negro* ever had before; this Fellow, with your leave, I intended to Release to Morrow, without any Whipping at all, after Talking to him in my way about his Offence, and raising in his Mind a Sense of the value of Pardon; and if this makes him a better Servant than the severest Whipping will do, then[a] I presume you would allow I have gain'd a Point.

---

* Here he shew'd him the Horse-whip that was given him, with his New Office.

Mast. AY, but what if it should not be so, for these Fellows have no Sense of Gratitude?

Jack. That is, Sir, because they are never Pardon'd, if they Offend; they never know what Mercy is, And what then have they to be Grateful for?

Mast. Thou art in the right indeed, where there is no Mercy shew'd, there is no Obligation laid upon them.

Jack. Besides, Sir, if they have at any time been let go, which is very seldom, they are not told what the Case is; they take no pains with them to imprint Principles of Gratitude on their Minds, to tell them what Kindness is shewn them, and what they are Indebted for it, and what they might Gain in the End by it.

Mast. But do you think such usage would do? would it make any impression? you perswade your self it would; but you see 'tis against the receiv'd Notion of the whole Country.

Jack. There are it may be Publick and National Mistakes and Errors in Conduct, and this is One.

Mast. Have you try'd it? you cannot say it is a Mistake, till you have try'd and prov'd it to be so.

Jack. Your whole Plantation is a Proof of it. This very Fellow had never acted as he did, if he had not gotten Rum in his Head, and been out of the Government of himself; so that indeed all the Offence I ought to have punish'd him for, had been that of stealing a Bottle of Rum, and drinking it all up; in which Case, like *Noah*,[242] he did not know the strength of it, and when he had it in his Head he was a mad Man, he was as one Raging and Distracted; so that for all the rest he deserv'd Pity, rather than Punishment.

Mast. Thou art right, certainly right, and thou will be a rare Fellow if thou canst bring these Notions into Practise; I wish you had try'd it upon any one particular *Negroe*, that I might see an Example, I would give 500*l*. it could be brought to bear.

Jack. I desire nothing, Sir, but your Favour, and the Advantage of obliging you, I will show you an Example of it, among your own *Negro's*, and all the Plantation will acknowledge it.

Mast. You make my very Heart glad within me, *Jack*; if you can bring this to pass, I here give you my Word, I'll not only give you your own Freedom, but make a Man of you for this World, as long as you live.

UPON this, I Bow'd to him very respectfully, and told him the following Story. There is a *Negroe*, Sir, in your Plantation, who has been your Servant several Years before I came; he did a Fault that was of no great Consequence in itself, but perhaps would have been worse, if they had indeed gone farther, and I had him brought into the usual Place, and ty'd him by the Thumbs for Correction, and he was told that he should be Whipp'd and Pickl'd[243] in a dreadful manner.

AFTER I had made proper Impressions on his Mind, of the Terror of his Punishment, and found that he was sufficiently humbled by it, I went into the House, and caus'd him to be brought out, just as they do when they go to Correct the Negroes on such Occasions; when he was strip'd and ty'd up, he had two Lashes given him, that were indeed very cruel Ones, and I call'd to them to hold; hold said I, to the two Men that had just began to lay on upon the poor Fellow, hold said I, let me talk with him.

So he was taken down, then I began, and represented to him how kind you, that were his *Great Master had been to him; that you had never done him any Harm, that you had us'd him gently, and he had never been brought to this Punishment in so many Year, tho' he had done some Faults before; that this was a notorious Offence, for he had stolen some Rum, and made himself, and two other Negroes Drunk† mad, and had abus'd two Women Negroes, who had Husbands in our Master's Service, but in another Plantation; and play'd several other Pranks,[244] and for this I had appointed him this Punishment.

HE shook his Head, and made Signs, that he was muchee sorree,[245] as he call'd it, And what will you say, or do, said I, if I should prevail with the Great Master to Pardon you? I have a mind to go and see if I can beg for you: He told me he would lye down, let me kill him, me will, says he, run go, fetch, bring for you as long as me live: This was the opportunity I had a mind to have, to trye whether as Negroes have all the other Faculties of reasonable Creatures, they had not also some Sense of Kindness, some Principles of natural Generosity, which in short, is the Foundation of Gratitude; for Gratitude is the Product of generous Principles.[246]

YOU please me with the beginning of this Story, says he, I hope you have carryed it on.

YES, Sir, says I, it has been carryed on farther perhaps, than you may imagine, or will think has been possible in such a Case.

BUT I was not so Arrogant, as to assume the Merit to myself; no, no, said I, I do not ask you to go, or run for me, you must do all that for our Great Master, for it will be from him entirely that you will be Pardon'd, if you are Pardon'd at all; for your Offence is against him, and what will you

---

* So the Negroes call the Owner of the Plantation, or at least so they call'd him, because he was a great Man in the Country, having three or four large Plantations.

† To be Drunk in a Negroe, is to be Mad, for when they get Rum they are worse than Raving, and fit to do any manner of Mischief.

say, will you be Grateful to him, and run, go, fetch, bring, for him as long as you live, as you have said you would for me.

YES indeed, says he, *and muchee do, muchee do, for you too* (he would not leave me out) *you ask him for me.*

WELL, I put off all his promis'd Gratitude to me, from myself, as was my Duty, and plac'd it to your Account, told him I knew you was *muchee Good, muchee Pitiful*, and I would perswade you if I could; and so told him I would go to you, and he should be Whipp'd no more till I came again; but hark ye, *Mouchat*, says I, that was the Negro's *Name*, they tell me when I came hither, that there is no showing kindness to any of you *Negro*'s, that when we spare you from Whipping you Laugh at us, and are the worse.

HE look'd very serious at me, and said, *O, that no so*, the Masters say so, *but no be so; no be so*, indeedè, indeedè, *and so we Parlee'd.*

Jack. Why do they say so then? to be sure they have try'd you all.

Negro. No, no, they no try, they say so, but no trye.

Jack. I hear them all say so.

Negro. Me tell you the True, they have no Merciéè, they Beat us Cruel, all Cruel, they never have show Mercèè. How can they tell we be no better?

Jack. What do they never spare?

Negro. Master, me speakee de true, they never give Merciéè, they always Whippee, Lashee, Knockee down, all Cruel: *Negroe* be muchee better Man do muchee better Work, but they tell us no Mercee.

Jack. But what do they never show any Mercy?

Negro. No, never, no never, all whipee, all whipee, Cruel, worse than they whippee de Horse, whipee de Dog.

Jack. But would they be better if they did?

Negro. Yes yes, *Negroe* be muchee better if they be Merciéè; when they whippee, whippee, *Negroe* muchee cry, muchee hate, would kill if they had de Gun; but when they makee de Mercy, then *Negroe* tell de great Tankee, and love to Worke, and do muchee Work; and because be good Master to them.

Jack. They say no; you would Laugh at them, and Mock when they shew Mercy.

Negro. How! they say when they shew Merciéè; they never shew Merciéé, me never see them shew one Merciéè, since me live.

Now, Sir, *said I*, if this be so, really they go I dare say, contrary to your Inclination; for I see you are but too full of Pity for the Miserable; I saw it in my own Case, and upon a Presumption, that you had rather have your Work done from a Principle of Love, than Fear, without making your Servants Bleed for every Triffle, if it were possible; I say, upon this Presumption, I dealt with this *Mouchat*, as you shall hear.

Mast. I have never met with any thing of this Kind, since I have been a Planter; which is now above 40 Year, I am delighted with the Story, go on, I expect a pleasant Conclusion.

Jack. The Conclusion, Sir, will be, I believe as much to your Satisfaction, as the beginning; for it every way answer'd my Expectation, and will yours also; and shew you how you might be faithfully serv'd if you pleas'd, for 'tis certain you are not so serv'd now.

Mast. No, indeed, they serve me but just as they do the Devil, for fear I should hurt them; but 'tis contrary to an ingenious Spirit,[247] to delight in such Service; I abhor it, if I could but know how to get any other.

Jack. It is easy, Sir, to shew you, that you may be serv'd upon better Principles; and Consequently be better serv'd, and more to your Satisfaction; and I dare undertake to convince you of it.

Mast. Well, go on with the Story.

Jack. After I had talk'd thus to him, I said, well *Mouchat,* I shall see how you will be afterward; if I can get our Great Master to be Merciful to you at this time.

Negro. Yes, you shall see, you *mucheé* see, *mucheé* see.

UPON this, I call'd for my Horse, and went from him, and made as if I Rode away to you, who they told me was in the next Plantation; and having staid four or five Hours, I came back and talk'd to him again; told him that I had waited on you, and that you had heard of his Offence, was highly Provok'd, and had resolv'd to Cause him to be severely Punish'd for an Example to all the *Negroes* in the Plantation: But that I had told you how Penitent he was, and how good he would be if you would Pardon him; and had at last had prevail'd on you: That you had told me what all People said of the *Negroes*; how, that to shew them Mercy, was to make them think you were never in Earnest with them, and that you did but Triffle and Play with them; However, that I had told you what he had said of himself; and that it was not true of the *Negroes,* and that the white Men said it, but that they could not know, because they did never shew any Mercy, and therefore had never try'd: That I had perswaded you to shew Mercy, to try whether kindness would prevail as much as Cruelty; and now, Mouchat, *said I,* you will be let go, pray let our Great Master see that I have said true; so I order'd him to be unty'd, gave him a Dram of Rum out of my Pocket-bottle, and order'd them to give him some Victuals.

WHEN the Fellow was let loose, he came to me, and kneel'd down to me, and took hold of my Legs and of my Feet, and laid his Head upon the Ground; and Sob'd, and Cry'd, like a Child that had been Corrected, but could not speak for his Life; and thus he continu'd a long time: I would have taken him up, but he would not Rise, but I Cry'd as fast as he, for I could not bear to see a poor Wretch lye on the Ground to me, that was but a Servant the other Day like himself; at last, but not till a quarter of an Hour, I made him get up, and then he spoke. *Me muchee know good Great Master,* muchee good *you Master: No* Negro *unthankful,* me Dye *for them, do me so muchee kind.*

I dismiss'd him then, and bad him go to his Wife, for he was Marry'd, and not Work that Afternoon; but as he was going away, I call'd him again, and talk'd thus to him.

NOW, *Mouchat, says I,* you see the white Men can shew Mercy: Now you must tell all the *Negroes,* what has been reported of them; that they Regard nothing but the Whip; that if they are us'd gently, they are the Worse, not the Better; and that this is the Reason, why the white Man shew them no Mercy; and convince them, that they would be much better treated, and us'd kindlier if they would shew themselves as grateful, for kind usage, as humble after Torment, and see if you can Work on them.

ME go, me go, *says he,* me muchèè talk to them, they be muchèè glad as me be, and do great Work, to be us'd kind by de Great Master.

Mast. Well, but now what Testimony have you of this Gratitude you speak of? have you seen any alteration among them.

Jack. I come next to that Part Sir, about a Month after this, I caus'd a Report to be spread abroad in the Plantation, that I had offended you the Great Master, and that I was turn'd out of the Plantation, and was to be hang'd; your Honour knows that sometime ago, you sent me upon your particular Business into *Potuxent* River,[248] where I was absent 12 Days, then I took the opportunity to have this Report spread about among the *Negroes* to see how it would work.

Mast. What? to see how *Mouchat* would take it.

Jack. Yes, Sir, and it made a Discovery indeed; the poor Fellow did not believe it presently, but finding I was still Absent, he went to the Head Clerk, and standing at his Door, said nothing, but look'd like a Fool of 10 Year old; after some time, the upper Overseer came out, and seeing him stand there, at first said nothing, supposing he had been sent of some Errand; but observing him to stand stock still, and that he was in the same Posture and Place, during the time that he had pass'd and repass'd two or three times, he stops short the last time of his coming by, What do you want, *says he* to him, that you stand idle here so long?

ME speakèè, me tell something, *says he.*

THEN the Overseer thought some Discovery was at Hand, and began to listen to him, What would you tell me, *says he?*

ME tell Pray, *says he,* Where be de other Master?

HE meant, he would ask where he was; What other Master do you mean, *says the Clerk*? what do you want to speak with the Great Master? he can't be spoke with by you; Pray what is your Business, cannot you tell it to me?

NO, no; me no speakèè the Great Master, the other Master, *says Mouchat*.

WHAT, the *Colonel? says the Clerk*.

Yes, yes, the *Colonel, says he*.

WHY don't you know that he is to be hang'd to Morrow, *says the Clerk*, for making the great Master angry*.

YES, yes, *says Mouchat*, me know, me know, but me won't speak, me tell something.

WELL. What would you say, *says the Clerk*.

O! me no, let him makèè de Great Master angry, with that he kneel'd down to the Clerk.

WHAT ails you? *says the Clerk*, I tell you he must be hang'd.

NO, no, *says he*, no hang de Master, me kneel for him to Great Master

YOU† Kneel for him! *says the Clerk*, What do you think the great Master will mind you? he has made the great Master angry, and must be hang'd, I tell you, what signifies your begging.

Negroe. O! me pray, me pray the great Master for him.

Clerk. Why, what ails you, that you would pray for him?

Neg. O! he beggèè the great Master for me, now me beggèè for him; the great Master muchee good, muchee good; he pardon me when the other Master beggee me; now he pardon him, when me beggee for him again.

Clerk. No, no, your begging won't do; will you be hang'd for him? if you will do that, something may be.

Negr. YES, yes, me be hang, for de poor Master that beggeé for me, *Mouchat* shall hang, the great Master shall hangee mee, whippee mee, any thing to save the poor Master that beggee me, yes, yes, indeed.

Clerk. Are you in earnest *Mouchat*?

Negr. Yes indeed, me Telleé de true, the great Master shall know me tellee de true, for he shall see the *White-Man* hanggee me *Mouchat*, poor *Negroe Mouchat* will be hangee, be whippee, any thing for the poor Master that beggee for me.

WITH this the poor Fellow cry'd most pitifully, and there was no room to Question his being in earnest; when on a sudden, I appear'd, for I was

---

* Note, he understood the Plot, and took the opportunity to tell him that, to see what he would say.

† He understood him, he meant he would beg your Honour for me, that I might not be hang'd for Offending you.

fetch'd to see all this Transaction: I was not in the House at first, but was just come home from the Business you sent me of, and heard it all, and indeed neither the Clerk, nor I could bear it any longer; so he came out to me, go to him, *says he*, you have made an Example that will never be forgot, that a *Negroe* can be Grateful; go to him, *adds he*, for I can talk to him no longer; so I appear'd, and spoke to him presently, and let him see that I was at Liberty; but to hear how the poor Fellow behav'd, your Honour cannot but he pleas'd.

Mast. Prethee go on I am pleas'd with it all, 'tis all a new Scene of *Negroe* Life to me, and very moving.

Jack. For a good while he stood as if he had been Thunder-struck, and stupid;[249] but looking steadily at me, tho' not speaking a Word, at last he Mutters to himself with a kind of a Laugh, Ay, ay, *says he, Mouchat* see, *Mouchat* no see; me wakee, me no wakee; no hangee, no hangee, he live truly, very live; and then on a sudden he runs to me, snatches me away as if I had been a Boy of ten Years old, and takes me up upon his back, and run away with me, till I was fain to cry out to him to stop; then he sets me down, and looks at me again, then falls a Dancing about me, as if he had been bewitch'd, just as you have seen them do about their Wives and Children when they are Merry.

WELL, then he began to talk with me, and told me what they had said to him, how I was to be hang'd; well, says I, *Mouchat*, and would you have been satisfied to be hang'd to save me, yes, yes, *says he*, be truly hangee, to beggee you.

BUT why do you love me so well *Mouchat? said I.*

DID you no beggee me, *he says*, at the great Master? you savee me, make great Master muchee good, muchee kind, no whippee me, me no forget, me be whip'd, be hang'd, that you no be hang'd, me dye, that you no dye, me no let any bad be with you, all while that me live.

NOW, Sir, your Honour may judge, whether kindness well manag'd would not oblige these People as well as Cruelty; and whether there are Principles of Gratitude in them, or no.

Mast. But what then can be the Reason, that we never believed it to be so before?

Jack. Truly, Sir, I fear that *Mouchat* gave the true Reason.

Mast. What was that Pray? that we were too Cruel.

Jack. That they never had any Mercy shew'd them; that we never try'd them, whether they would be grateful or no; that if they did a Fault, they were never spar'd, but punish'd with the utmost Cruelty; so that they had no Passion, no Affection to Act upon, but that of Fear, which necessarily brought Hatred with it; but that if they were used with Compassion, they would Serve with Affection, as well as other Servants: Nature is the same, and Reason Governs in just Proportions in all Creatures; But having never been let Taste what Mercy is, they know not how to act from a Principle of Love.

Master. I am convinc'd, it is so; But now, pray tell me, how did you put this in Practice with the poor *Negro's* now in Bonds yonder, when you pass'd such a cruel Sentence upon them, that they should be whipp'd twice a Day, for four Days together, was that shewing Mercy?

Jack. My Method was just the same, and if you please to inquire of Mr. —, your other Servant, you will be satisfy'd that it was so; for we agreed upon the same Measures as I took with *Mouchat*; Namely, first to put them into the utmost Horror and Apprehensions of the Cruelest Punishment that they had ever heard of, and thereby enhaunce the Value of their Pardon, which was to come as from your self, but not without our great Intercession: Then I was to argue with them, and Work upon their Reason, to make the Mercy that was shew'd them sink deep into their Minds, and give lasting Impressions; explain the Meaning of Gratitude to them, and the Nature of an Obligation, and the like, as I had done with *Mouchat*.

Master. I am answer'd, your Method is certainly Right, and I desire you may go on with it for I desire nothing (on this side Heaven) more than to have all my *Negroes* serve me from Principles of Gratitude, for my Kindness to them: I abhor to be fear'd like a Lion, like a Tyrant, it is a Violence upon Nature every way, and is the most disagreable Thing in the World to a generous Mind.

Jack. But, Sir, I am doubtful that you may not believe that I intended to act thus with those poor Fellows; I beseech you to send for Mr. —, that he may tell you, what we had agreed on before I speak with him.

Master. What Reason have I to doubt that?

Jack. I hope you have not, but I should be very Sorry you should think me capable of Executing such a Sentence as you have heard me own, I had pass'd on them; and there can be no way effectually to clear it up, but this.

Master. Well, seeing you put so much Weight upon it, he shall be *call'd for.

Jack. I hope, Sir, you are now, not only satisfy'd of the Truth of the Account I gave, relating to the Method we had agreed on; but of its being so proper, and so likely to answer your End.

---

* He was called, and being order'd by the Master, to tell the Measures that were concerted between them, for the Punishment, or Management of those *Negroes*; he gave it just as *Jack* had done before.

Master. I am fully satisfy'd, and shall be glad to see that it answers the End; for, as I have said, nothing can be more agreeable to me, nothing has so much robb'd me of the Comfort of all my Fortunes, as the Cruelty used in my Name, on the Bodies of those poor Slaves.

Jack. It is certainly wrong, Sir; it is not only wrong, as it is barbarous and cruel; but it is wrong too, as it is the worst way of Managing, and of having your Business done.

Master. It is my Aversion, it fills my very Soul, with Horror; I believe, if I should come by, while they were using those Cruelties on the poor Creatures, I should either sink down at the Sight of it, or fly into a Rage, and kill the Fellow that did it; tho' it is done too, by my own Authority.

Jack. But, Sir, I dare say, I shall convince you also that it is wrong, in Respect of Interest; and that your Business shall be better discharg'd, and your Plantations better order'd, and more Work done by the *Negroes*, who shall be engaged by Mercy and Lenity, than by those, who are driven, and dragg'd by the Whips, and the Chains of a merciless Tormentor.

Master. I think the Nature of the Thing speaks it self, doubtless it should be so, and I have often thought it would be so, and a thousand Times wish'd it might be so; but all my *English* People pretend otherwise, and that it is impossible to bring the *Negroes* to any Sence of Kindness, and Consequently not to any Obedience of Love.

Jack. It may be true, Sir, that there may be found here and there a *Negro* of a senceless, stupid, sordid Disposition; perfectly Untractable, undocible,[250] and incapable of due Impressions; especially incapable of the Generosity of Principle which I am speaking of; you know very well, Sir, there are such among Christians, as well as among *Negroes*, whence else came the *English* Proverb; *that if you save a Thief from the Gallows, he shall be the first to Cut your Throat.*[251] But, Sir, if such a Refractory, undocible Fellow comes in our way, he must be dealt with, first, by the smooth ways, to Try him; then by the Violent way to Break his Temper, as they Break a Horse; and if nothing will do, such a Wretch should be Sold off, and others Bought in his Room; for the Peace of the Plantation should not be broken for one Devilish temper'd Fellow; and if this was done, I doubt not, you should have all your Plantation carried on, and your Work done, and not a *Negro* or a Servant upon it, but what would not only Work for you, but even Die for you, if there was an Occasion for it, as you see this poor *Mouchat* would have done for me.

Mast. Well, go on with your Measures, and may you succeed, I'll promise you I will fully make you amends for it; I long to have these Cruelties out of use, in my Plantation especially, as for others, let them do as they will.

OUR Master being gone, I went to the Prisoners, and first, I suffer'd them to be told that the Great Master had been there, and that he had been enclin'd to Pardon them, till he knew what their Crime was; but then he said it was so great a Fault that it must be Punish'd: Besides, the Man that talk'd to them, told them, that the Great Master said, that he knew if he had Pardon'd them, they would but be the Worse, for that the *Negroes* were never thankful for being spar'd, and that there were no other ways to make them Obedient, but Severity.

ONE of the poor Fellows, more sensible than the other; answer'd, if any *Negroe* be Bader for kindly us'd, they should be Whipped till they were muchèè better, but that he never knew that, for he never knew the *Negroe* be kindly use.

THIS was the same thing as the other had said, and indeed, was but too true, for the Overseers really knew no such thing as Mercy; and that Notion of the *Negroes* being no other way to be govern'd but by Cruelty, had been the Occasion, that no other Method was ever try'd among them.

AGAIN, if a slack Hand has been at any time been held upon them; it had not been done with Discretion, or as a point of Mercy; and manag'd with the Assistance of Argument to convince the *Negroes* of the Nature and Reason of it, and to shew them what they ought to do in Return for it: But it was perhaps the effect of Negligence, ill Conduct, and want of Application to the Business of the Plantation; and then 'twas no wonder that the *Negroes* took the Advantage of it.

WELL, I carried on the Affair with these two *Negroes*, just as I did with *Mouchat*, so I need not repeat the particulars, and they were deliver'd with infinite Acknowledgments and Thanks, even to all the Extravagancies of Joy usual in those People on such Occasion; and such was the Gratitude of those two pardon'd Fellows, that they were the most Faithful, and most Diligent Servants ever after, that belong'd to the whole Plantation, *Mouchat* excepted.

IN this manner I carried on the Plantation fully to his Satisfaction; and before a Year more was expir'd, there was scarse any such thing as Correction known in the Plantation; except upon a few Boys who were incapable of the Impressions, that good Usuage would have made, even upon them too, till they had liv'd to know the Difference.

IT was some time after this Conference, that our Great Master, *as we call'd him*, sent for me again to his Dwelling-house, and told me he had had an Answer from *England* from his Friend, to whom he had written about my Bill: I was a little afraid that he was going to ask me leave to send it to *London*: But he did not say any thing like that: But told me that his Friend had been with the Gentleman, and that he own'd the Bill, and that he had all the Money in his Hand, that the Bill had mention'd; but that he had promis'd the young Man, that had given him the Money, (meaning me,) not to pay the Money to any Body but himself, tho' they should bring the Bill; the Reason of which was, that I did not know who might get the Bill away from me.

BUT now, Col. *Jack, says he*, as you Wrote him an Account where you was, and by what wicked Arts you were Trapann'd;²⁵² and that it was impossible for you to have your Liberty till you cou'd get the Money: My Friend at *London* has written to me, that upon making out a due Copy of the Bill here, attested by a notary, and sent to him, and your Obligation likewise attested; whereby you oblige your self to Deliver the Original to his Order, after the Money is paid, he will pay the Money.

I told him I was willing to do whatever his Honour directed; and so the proper Copies were drawn, as I had been told were requir'd.

BUT now, what will you do with this Money, *Jack? says he* smiling, will you Buy your Liberty of me,²⁵³ and go to Planting?

I was too cunning for him, now indeed, for I remember'd what he had promis'd me; and I had too much Knowledge of the Honesty of his Principles, as well as of the Kindness he had for me; to doubt his being **as** good as his Word; so I turn'd all this Talk of his upon him another way; I knew that when he ask'd me if I would Buy my Liberty and go to Planting, it was to try if I would leave him; so, I said, as to buying my Liberty, Sir, *that is to say,* going out of your Service, I had much rather Buy more time in your Service, and I am only unhappy that I have but two Year to serve.

COME, come, Col. *says he*, don't flatter me, I love plain Dealing, Liberty is precious to every Body; if you have a Mind to have your Money brought over, you shall have your Liberty to begin for your self, and I will take care you shall be well us'd by the Country, and get you a good Plantation.

I still insisted, that I would not quit his Service for the best Plantation in *Maryland*; that he had been so good to me, and I believ'd I was so useful to him, that I cou'd not think of it; and at last, I added, I hop'd he cou'd not believe but I had as much Gratitude as a *Negro*.

HE smil'd, and said, he would not be serv'd upon those Terms; that he did not forget what he had promis'd, nor what I had done in his Plantation; and that he was resolv'd in the first place to give me my Liberty, so he Pulls out a peice of Paper, and throws it to me, there, *says he*, there's a Certificate of your coming on Shore, and being Sold to me for five Years,²⁵⁴ of which you have liv'd three with me, and now you are your own Master.

I Bow'd, and told him, that I was sure if I was my own Master, I would be his Servant as long as he would accept of my Service; and now we strain'd Courtisies;²⁵⁵ and he told me I should be his Servant still: But it should be on two Conditions. (1.) That he would give me 30*l.* a Year, and my Board, for my managing the Plantation I was then employ'd in; and (2.) That at the same time he would procure me a new Plantation to begin upon for my own Account; for Col. *Jack, says he,* smiling, tho' you are but a young Man, yet 'tis time you were doing something for your self.

I answer'd, that I cou'd do little at a Plantation for my self, unless I Neglected his Business, which I was resolv'd not to do on any Terms whatever: But that I would serve him Faithfully if he would accept of me as long as he liv'd: So you shall, *says he,* again, and serve your self too; and thus we parted for that time.

HERE I am to observe in the general, to avoid dwelling too long upon a Story; that as the two *Negroes* who I deliver'd from Punishment, were ever after the most Diligent, and Laborious poor Fellows in the whole Plantation, as above; except *Mouchat,* of whom I shall speak more by and by, so they not only were Grateful themselves for their good usuage, but they Influenc'd the whole Plantation: So that the Gentle usuage and Lenity, with which they had been treated, had a Thousand times more Influence upon them, to make them Diligent, than all the Blows and Kicks, Whippings, and other Tortures could have, which they had been us'd to, and now the Plantation was famous for it; so that several other Planters began to do the same, tho' I cannot say it was with the same Success; which might be for want of taking Pains with them, and working upon their Passions in a right manner; it appeared that *Negroes* were to be reason'd into things as well as other People, and it was by thus managing their Reason, that most of the Work was done.

HOWEVER, (as it was) the Plantations in *Maryland,* were the better for this Undertaking, and they are to this Day less Cruel and Barbarous to their *Negroes,* than they are in *Barbados,* and *Jamaica*; and 'tis observ'd the *Negroes* are not in these Colonies so desperate, neither do they so often run away, or so often Plot mischief against their Master, as they do in those.[256]

I HAVE dwelt the longer upon it, that if possible Posterity might be perswaded to try gentler Methods with those miserable Creatures, and to use them with Humanity; assuring them, that if they did so, adding the common Prudence that every particular Case would direct them to for itself, the *Negroes* would do their Work faithfully, and chearfully; they would not find any of that refractoriness, and sullenness in their Temper, that they pretend now to complain of; but they would be the same as their Christian Servants, except that they would be the more Thankful and Humble, and Laborious of the Two.

I Continue'd in this Station between five and six Year after this,[257] and in all that time we had not one *Negroe* whipp'd, except as I observ'd before, now and then an unluckly[258] Boy, and that only for Triffles; I cannot say, but we had some ill-natured ungovernable *Negroes*; but if at any time such Offended, they were Pardon'd the first Time, in the manner as above; and the second Time were ordered to be turn'd out of the Plantation; and this was remarkable that they would Torment themselves at the Apprehensions of being turn'd away, more by a great deal, than if they had been to be whipp'd, for then they were only Sullen and Heavy; nay, at length we found the fear of being turn'd out of the Plantation, had as much Effect to Reform them, *that is to say*, make them more diligent, than any Torture would have done; and the Reason was Evident, namely, because in our Plantation, they were us'd like Men, in the other like Dogs.

MY Master own'd the Satisfaction he took in this blessed Change, as he call'd it, as long as he lived, and as he was so engag'd, by seeing the *Negroes* Grateful, he shew'd the same Principle of Gratitude to those that serv'd him, as he look'd for in those that he serv'd; and particularly to me, and so I come briefly to that Part: The first thing he did after giving me my Liberty, *as above*, and making me an allowance, was to get the Country Bounty to me, that is to say, of a Quantity of Land to begin, and Plant for myself.[259]

BUT this he manag'd Away by himself, and as I found afterwards took up, *that is*, purchased in my Name, about 300 Acres of Land in a more convenient Place, than it would have otherwise been Allotted me; and this he did by his Interest with the Lord Proprietor;[260] so that I had an extent of Ground mark'd out to me, not next, but very near one of his own Plantations: When I made my acknowledgement for this to him, he told me plainly, that I was not beholding to him for it at all; for he did it, that I might not be oblig'd to neglect his Business for the carrying on my own, and on that Account he would not reckon to me what Money he paid, which however, according to the Custom of the Country was not a very great Sum, I think about 40 or 50*l*.

THUS he very generously gave me my Liberty, advanc'd this Money for me, put me into a Plantation for myself, and gave me 30*l*. a Year Wages for looking after one of his own Plantations.

BUT Colonel, *says he*, to me, giving you this Plantation is nothing at all to you, if I do not assist you to support it, and to carry it on, and therefore I will give you Credit for what ever is needful to you for the carrying it on; such as Tools, Provisions for Servants, and some Servants to begin; Materials to build Out-Houses, and Conveniences of all Sorts for the Plantation, and to buy Hogs, Cows, Horses for Stock, and the like, and I'll take it out of your Cargo, which will come from *London*, for the Money of your Bill.

THIS was highly obliging and very kind, and the more so, as it afterwards appear'd; in order to this, he sent two Servants of his own, who were Carpenters, as for Timber, Boards, Planks, and all Sorts of such Things in a Country almost all made of Wood, they could not be wanting: These run me up a little wooden House in less than three Weeks time, where I had three Rooms, a Kitchin, an Out-House, and two large Sheds at a distance from the House, for Store-houses, almost like Barns, with Stables at the End of them; and thus I was Set up in the World, and in Short, removed by the degrees that you have heard from a Pick-pocket, to a Kidnapp'd miserable Slave in *Virginia*; (for *Maryland*, is *Virginia*, speaking of them at a distance,) then[a] from a Slave to a Head Officer, and Overseer of Slaves, and from thence to a Master Planter.

I HAD now as above, a House, a Stable, two Ware-houses, and 300 Acres of Land; but *as we say*, bare Walls make giddy Hussy's,[261] so I had neither Axe or Hatchet, to cut down *the Trees; Horse, or Hog, or Cow to put upon the Land; not a Hoe, or a Spade to break Ground, nor a Pair of Hands, but my own to go to Work upon it.

BUT Heaven and kind Masters, make up all those things to a diligent Servant; and I mention it, because People, who are either Transported, or otherwise Trappan'd[262] into those Places, are generally thought to be rendered miserable, and undone; whereas, on the contrary, I would encourage them upon my own Experience to depend upon it, that if their own Diligence in the time of Service, gains them but a good Character, which it will certainly do, if they can deserve it, there is not the poorest, and most despicable Felon that ever went over, but may after his time is serv'd, begin for himself, and may in time be sure of raising a good Plantation.

FOR Example, I will now take a Man in the meanest Circumstances of a Servant, who has serv'd out his 5 or 7 Years, (suppose a Transported Wretch for 7 Years.) The custom of the Place was then (what it is since I know not) that on his Master's certifying that he had serv'd his time out faithfully he had 50 Acres of Land allotted him, for Planting, and on this Plan he begins.

SOME had a Horse, a Cow, and three Hogs given, or rather lent them as a Stock for the Land, which they made an allowance for, at a certain Time and Rate.

CUSTOM has made it a Trade, to give Credit to such Beginners as these, for Tools, Cloths, Nails, Iron-work, and other things necessary for

* *Note* all the Land before it is planted is over grown with high Trees, which must be cut down, and grubb'd up, before any thing call'd Planting can be begun.

their Planting; and which the Persons so giving Credit to them, are to be paid for out of the Crop of *Tobacco* which they shall Plant; nor is it in the Debtors power to Defraud the Creditor of Payment in that manner; and as *Tobacco* is their Coin, as well as their Product; so all things are to be Purchas'd at a certain quantity of *Tobacco*, the Price being so Rated.[263]

THUS the naked[264] Planter has Credit at his Beginning, and immediately goes to Work, to cure[265] the Land, and Plant *Tobacco*; and from this little Beginning, have some of the most considerable Planters in *Virginia* and in *Maryland* also, rais'd themselves, namely, from being without a Hat, or a Shoe, to Estates of 40 or 50000 Pound; and in this Method, I may add, no Diligent Man ever Miscarried, if he had Health to Work, and was a good Husband;[266] for he every Year encreases a little, and every Year adding more Land, and Planting more *Tobacco*, which is real Money, he must Gradually encrease in Substance, till at length he gets enough to Buy *Negroes*, and other Servants, and then never Works himself any more.

IN a Word, every *Newgate* Wretch, every Desperate forlorn Creature; the most Despicable ruin'd Man in the World, has here a fair Opportunity put into his Hands to begin the World again, and that upon a Foot of certain Gain, and in a Method exactly Honest; with a Reputation, that nothing past will have any Effect upon; and innumerable People have thus rais'd themselves from the worst Circumstance in the World; Namely, from the *Condemn'd Hole* in *Newgate*.[267]

BUT I Return to my own Story, I was now a Planter, and encourag'd by a kind Benefactor, for, that I might not be wholly taken up with my new Plantation, he gave me freely, and without any Consideration my grateful Negro *Mouchat*: He told me it was a Debt due to the Affection that poor Creature had always had for me; and so indeed, it was, for as the Fellow would once have been Hang'd for me, so now, and to his last he lov'd me so much, that it was apparent he did every thing with Pleasure that he did for me; and he was so overcome of Joy when he heard he was to be my *Negro*, that the People in the Plantation really thought it would turn his Head, and that the Fellow would go Distracted.

BESIDES this, he sent me two Servants more, a Man and a Woman, but these he put to my Account, as above: *Mouchat*, and these two fell immediately to Work for me; and they began with about 2 Acres of Land, which had but little Timber on it at first, and most of that was Cut down by the two *Carpenters* who built my House, (or shed, rather, for so it should be call'd.)

THESE two Acres I got in good Forwardness,[268] and most of it well Planted with *Tobacco*; tho' some of it we were oblig'd to plant with Garden Stuff for Food; such as Potatoes, Carrots, Cabbages, Peas, Beans, &c.

IT was a great Advantage to me, that I had so Bountiful a Master, who help'd me out in every Case; for in this very first Year I receiv'd a Terrible Blow, for my Bill as I have observ'd, having been Coppy'd, and Attested in Form, and sent to *London*: My kind Friend and *Custom house* Gentleman paid me the Money; and the Merchant at *London*, by my Good Masters Direction, had laid it all out in a sorted Cargo of Goods for me, such as would have made a Man of me all at once; but to my Inexpressible Terror and Surprize, the Ship was Lost, and that just at the Entrance into the Capes, *that is to say*, the Mouth of the Bay; some of the Goods were recover'd, but spoil'd, and in short, nothing but the Nails, Tools, and Iron-work were good for any thing, and tho' the Value of them was pretty Con-siderable in Proportion to the rest, yet, my loss was irreparably Great, and indeed, the Greatness of the loss to me consisted in its being Irreparable.

I was perfectly Astonish'd at the first News of the loss, knowing that I was in Debt to my Patron, or Master, so much, that it must be several Years before I should recover it; and as he brought me the bad News him-self, he perceiv'd my Disorder, *that is to say*, he saw I was in the utmost Confusion, and a kind of Amazement, and so indeed I was, because I was so much in Debt; But he spoke Chearfully to me; come, *says he*, do not be so Discourag'd, you may make up this Loss: No, Sir, *says I*, that never can be, for 'tis my all, and I shall never be out of Debt; well, *says he*, you have no Creditor, however, but me, and now remember, I once told you, I would make a Man of you, and I will not Disappoint you for this Dissaster.

I thank'd him, and did it with more Ceremony and Respect than ever; because I thought my self more under the Hatches[269] than I was before. But he was as good as his Word, for he did not Baulk me in the least of any thing I wanted, and as I had more Iron-work sav'd out of the Ship, in pro-portion, than I wanted, I supplied him with some part of it, and took up some Linnen, and Cloaths, and other Necessaries from him in Exchange.

AND now I began to encrease Visibly; I had a large Quantity of Land Cur'd, *that is*, Freed from Timber; and a very good Crop of *Tobacco* in view, and I got three Servants more, and one *Negroe*; so that I had five white Servants, and two *Negroes*, and with this my Affairs went very well on.

THE first Year, indeed, I took my Wages, or Sallary, *that is to say*, of 30*l.* a Year, because I wanted it very much; but the second and third Year I resolv'd not to take it, on any Account whatsoever, but to leave it in my Benefactors Hands, to clear off the Debt I had Contracted.

AND now I must Impose a short Digression on the Reader, to Note, That notwithstanding all the Disadvantages of a most wretched Education, yet Now when I began to feel my self, as I may say, in the World; and to be arriv'd to an Independant State, and to foresee, that I might be something Considerable in time; I say, Now I found differing Sentiments of things taking Place in my Mind; and first, I had a solid Principle of Justice and Honesty, and a secret Horror at things pass'd, when I look'd back upon my former Life: That Original something, I knew not what, that used formerly to Check me in the first meannesses of my Youth, and us'd to Dictate to me when I was but a Child, that I was to be a Gentleman, continued to Operate upon me Now, in a manner I cannot Describe; and I continually remember'd the Words of the ancient *Glass-maker*, to the Gentleman, that he reprov'd for Swearing, that to be a Gentleman, was to be an *Honest Man*,[270] that without Honesty, Human Nature was Sunk and Degenerated; the Gentleman lost all the Dignity of his Birth, and plac'd himself, even below an Honest Beggar: These Principles growing upon my Mind in the present Circumstances I was in, gave me a secret Satisfaction, that I can give no Description of; it was an inexpressible Joy to me, that I was now like to be, not only a Man, but an Honest Man; and it yielded me a greater Pleasure, that I was Ransom'd from being a Vagabond, a Thief, and a Criminal, as I had been from a Child, than that I was deliver'd from Slavery, and the wretched State of a *Virginia* Sold Servant: I had Notion enough in my Mind, of the Hardships of the Servant, or Slave, because I had felt it, and Work'd thro' it; I remember'd it as a State of Labour and Servitude, Hardship and Suffering. But the other shock'd my very Nature, chil'd my Blood, and turn'd the very Soul within me: The thought of it was like Reflections upon Hell, and the Damn'd Spirits; it struck me with Horror, it was Odious and Frightful to look back on, and it gave me a kind of a Fit, a Convulsion or nervous Disorder, that was very uneasy to me.

BUT to look forward, to Reflect, how things were Chang'd; how Happy I was, that I cou'd live by my own Endeavours, and was no more under the Necessity of being a Villain, and of getting my Bread at my own Hazard, and the Ruin of Honest Families; this had in it something more than commonly pleasing and agreeable, and in particular, it had a Pleasure, that till then I had known nothing of: It was a sad thing to be under a Necessity of doing Evil, to procure that subsistance, which I could not Support the want of, to be oblig'd to run the venture of the Gallows, rather than the venture of Starving, and to be always wick'd, for fear of want.

I cannot say that I had any serious Religious reflections, or that these things proceeded yet from the uneasiness of Conscience, but from meer Reasonings with myself, and from being arriv'd to a Capacity of making a right Judgement of things more than before; yet I own I had such an abhorrence of the wicked Life I had led, that I was secretly easie, and had a kind of Pleasure in the Dissaster that was upon me about the Ship, and that tho' it was a loss I could not but be glad, that those ill gotten Goods were gone, and that I had lost what I had stolen; for I look'd on it as none of mine, and that it would be fire in my Flax[271] if I should mingle it with what I had now, which was come honestly by, and was as it were sent from Heaven, to lay the Foundation of my prosperity, which the other would be only as a Moth to consume.[272]

AT the same time my Thoughts dictated to me, that tho' this was the Foundation of my new Life, yet that this was not the Superstructure, and that I might still be born for greater things than these; that it was Honesty, and Virtue alone that made Men Rich and Great, and gave them a Fame, as well as a Figure in the World, and that therefore I was to lay my Foundation in these, and expect[273] what might follow in time.

To help these Thoughts, as I had learn'd to Read, and Write when I was in *Scotland*; so I began now to love Books, and particularly I had an Opportunity of Reading some very considerable Ones; such as *Livy's* Roman History, the History of the *Turks*, the *English* History of *Speed*, and others; the History of the *Low Country* Wars, the History of *Gustavus Adolphus*, King of *Sweden*, and the History of the *Spaniard's* Conquest of *Mexico*,[274] with several others, some of which I bought at a Planter's House, who was lately dead, and his Goods sold, and others I borrowed.

I consider'd my present State of Life to be my meer[275] Youth, tho' I was now above 30 Year old, because in my Youth, I had learn'd nothing; and if my daily Business which was now great, would have permitted, I would have been content to have gone to School; however, Fate that had yet something else in Store for me, threw an Opportunity into my Hand; namely, a clever Fellow, that came over a transported Felon, from *Bristol*, and fell into my Hands for a Servant: He had led a loose Life, that he acknowledged, and being driven to Extremities took to the Highway, for which, had he been taken, he would have been Hang'd, but falling into some low priz'd Rogueries afterwards for want of Opportunity for worse, was catch'd, Condemn'd, and Transported, and as, *he said*, was glad he came off so.

HE was an excellent Schollar, and I perceiving it, ask'd him one time, if he could give a Method how I might learn the Latin Tongue? *He said*, smiling, yes, he could Teach it me in three Months, if I would let him have

Books, or even without Books, if he had time; I told him, a Book would become his Hands better than a Hoe, and if he could promise to make me but understand Latin enough to read it, and understand other Languages by it, I would ease him of the Labour, which I was now oblig'd to put him to, especially if I was assur'd that he was fit to receive that Favour of a kind Master: In short, I made him to me, what my Benefactor made me to him, and from him I gain'd a Fund of Knowledge, infinitely more valuable than the Rate of a Slave, which was what I paid for it, but of this hereafter.

WITH these Thoughts I went chearfully about my Work: As I had now five Servants, my Plantation went on, tho' gently, yet safely, and encreas'd gradually; tho' slowly; but the third Year with the Assistance of my old Benefactor, I purchas'd two *Negroes* more, so that now I had seven Servants, and having cur'd Land sufficient for supply of their Food, I was at no difficulty to maintain them, so that my Plantation began now to enlarge itself, and as I liv'd without any Personal Expense, but was maintain'd at my old Great Master's, *as we call'd him*, and at his Charge, with 30*l*. a Year besides, so all my Gain was laid up for Encrease.

IN this Posture I went on for 12 Year,[276] and was very successful in my Plantation, and had gotten by means of my Master's favour, who now I call'd my Friend, a Correspondent in *London*, with whom I Traded, Shipp'd over my Tobacco, to him, and receiv'd *European* Goods in returns such as I wanted, to carry on my Plantation, and sufficient to sell to others also.

IN this interval, my good Friend and Benefactor died, and I was left very disconsolate, on account of my Loss, for it was indeed a great Loss to me; he had been a Father to me, and I was like a forsaken Stranger without him, tho' I knew the Country, and the Trade too well enough, and had for sometime chiefly carried on his whole Business for him, yet I seem'd now at a loss; my Councellor, and my chief Supporter was gone, and I had no Confident to communicate myself to, on all Occasions, as formerly; but there was no Remedy. I[a] was however in a better Condition to stand alone than ever; I had a very large Plantation, and had near 70 *Negroes*, and other Servants: In a Word, I was grown really Rich, considering my first Circumstances that began, *as I may say*, with nothing: *That is to say*, I had nothing of Stock, but I had a great Beginning, for I had such a Man's Friendship, and Support in my Beginning, that indeed, I needed no other Stock, and if I had had 500*l*. to have begun with, and not the Assistance, Advice, and Countenance of such a Man, I had not been in a better Condition; but he promis'd to make a Man of me, and so he did, and in one Respect, *I may say*, I merited it of him, for I brought his Plantation into such order, and the Government of his *Negroes*, into such a Regulation, that if he had given 500*l*. to have had it done, he would have thought his Money well bestow'd;

his Work was always in order going forward to his Mind; every thing was in a thriving Posture; his Servants all lov'd him, even *Negroes* and all, and yet there was no such thing, as a cruel Punishment, or Severities known among them.

IN my own Plantation it was the same thing, I wrought so upon the Reason, and the Affections of my *Negroes*, that they serv'd me chearfully, and by Consequence, Faithfully, and Diligently; when in my Neighbour's Plantation, there was not a Week hardly pass'd without such horrible Outcryes, Roarings and Yellings of the Servants, either under Torture, or in Fear of it, that their *Negroes* would in Discourse with ours, wish themselves dead, and gone, (as it seems they believ'd they should after Death) into their own Country.[277]

IF I met with a sullen stupid Fellow, as sometimes it was unavoidable, I always parted with him, and sold him off; for I would not keep any, that Sense of kind Usage would not oblige; but I seldom met with such bad ones, for by talking to them in a plain Reasoning way, I found the Temper of the Roughest of them would break and soften; the Sense of their own Interest would prevail with them first, or last; and if it had not, the contrary Temper was so general among my People, that their own Fellows and Countrymen would be against them, and that serv'd to bring them to Reason, as soon as any other thing; and this, those who think it worth their while, will easily find, (*viz.*) that having prevail'd Effectually over one leading Man among them to be tractable, and pleas'd, and grateful, he shall make them all like him, and that in a little while, with more ease than can be imagin'd.

I WAS now a Planter, and also a Student; my Pedagogue I mention'd above, was very diligent, and prov'd an extraordinary Man indeed, he Taught me not only with Application, but with admirable Judgement in the Teaching part, for I have seen it in many Instances since that time, that every good Schollar is not fitted for a School-master, and that the Art of Teaching is quite different from that of Knowing the Language Taught.

BUT this Man had both, and prov'd of great Use to me, and I found Reason in the worth of the Person to be very kind to him, his Circumstances consider'd: I once took the liberty to ask him how it came to pass, that he who must have had a liberal Education, and great Advantages to have advanc'd himself in the World, should be capable of falling into such miserable Circumstances as he was in, when he came over? I us'd some Caution in entring upon an enquiry, which, *as I said*, might not be pleasant to him to relate, but that I would make him amends, by telling him, that if he desir'd not to enter into it with me, I would readily excuse him, and would not take it ill at all; this I did, because to a Man under such Afflictions, one should always be Tender, and not put them upon relating any thing of themselves, which was grievous to them, or which they had rather was conceal'd.

BUT he told me, that it was true, that to look back upon his past Life, was indeed *renovare dolorem*;[278] but that such Mortifications were now useful to him, to help forward that Repentance which he hop'd he was sincerely entered upon; and that tho' it was with horror he look'd back upon mispent Time, and ill applied Gifts, which a bountiful Creator had bless'd him with, and spar'd to him for a better Improvement, yet he thought he ought to load himself with as much of the shame, as it pleas'd God to make his Lot, since he had already loaded himself with the Guilt in a shameless manner; till God (he still hop'd in Mercy to him) had cut him short, and brought him to publick Disgrace, tho' he could not say he had been brought to Justice, for then he had been sent into Eternity in despair, and not been sent to *Virginia*, to repent of the wickedest Life that ever Man liv'd:– He would have gone on, but, I found his Speech interrupted by a passionate struggle within, between his Grief and his Tears.

I took no more Notice of it, than to tell him, that I was sorry I had ask'd him about it, but that it was my Curiosity; when I saw that ignorant, untaught, untractable Creatures come into Misery and Shame, I made no enquiry after their Affairs, but when I saw Men of Parts and Learning take such Steps, I concluded it must be occasion'd by something exceeding wicked; so indeed, *said he*, the Judge said to me when I beg'd Mercy of him in Latin, he told me that when a Man furnish'd with such Learning falls into such Crimes, he is more inexcusable than other Men; because his Learning recommending him, he could not want Advantages, and had the less temptation to Crime.

BUT, Sir, *said he*, I believe my Case was what I find is the Case of most of the wicked Part of the World (*viz.*) that to be reduc'd to Necessity is to be wicked[279] for Necessity is not only the Temptation, but is such a Temptation as human Nature is not empower'd to resist: How good then, *says he*, is that God, which takes from you Sir, the Temptation, by taking away the Necessity?

I was so sensible of the Truth of what he said, *knowing it by my own Case*, that I could not enter any farther upon the Discourse; but he went on voluntarily: *This Sir*, says he, I am so sensible of, that I think the Case I am now reduc'd to, much less miserable than the Life which I liv'd before, because I am deliver'd from the horrid Necessity of doing such ill things, which was my Ruin, and Dissaster then, even for my Bread, and am not now oblig'd to ravish my Bread out of the Mouths of others by Violence and Disorder; but am fed tho' I am made to Earn it by the hard Labour of my Hands, and I thank God for the Difference. He paws'd here but went on thus,

How much is the Life of a Slave in *Virginia*, to be preferr'd to that of the most prosperous Thief in the World! here I live miserable, but honest; suffer wrong, but do no wrong; my Body is punish'd, but my Conscience is not loaded; and as I us'd to say, that I had no Leisure to look in, but I would begin when I had some Recess, sometime to spare; now God has found me leisure to Repent; he run on in this manner a great while, giving Thanks, I believe most heartily, for his being deliver'd from the wretch'd Life he had liv'd, tho' his Misery were to be ten Fold, as much as it was.

I Was sincerely Touch'd with his Discourse on this Subject, I had known so much of the real difference of the Case, that I could not but be affected with it, tho' till now I confess I knew little of the religious Part: I had been an Offender as well as he, tho' not altogether in the same Degree, but I knew nothing of the Penitence; neither had I look'd back upon any thing, as a Crime; but as a Life dishonourable, and not like a Gentleman, which run much in my Thoughts, as I have several times mention'd.

Well, but now, *says I*, you talk Penitently, and I hope you are sincere, but what would be your Case, if you were deliver'd from the miserable Condition of a Slave sold for Money, which you are now in? should you not, think you, be the same Man?

Blessed be God, *says he*, that if I thought I should, I would sincerely pray that I might not be Deliver'd, and that I might for ever be a Slave rather than a Sinner.

Well, but *says I*, suppose you to be under the same necessity, in the same starving Condition, Should you not take the same Course?

He replied very sharply, that shows us the need we have of the Petition in the Lord's Prayer: *Lead us not into Temptation;*[280] and of *Solomon's* or *Agar's* Prayer: *Give me not Poverty, least I Steal.*[281] I should ever beg of God not to be left to such Snares as Human Nature cannot resist. But I have some hope that I should venture to Starve, rather than to Steal; but I also beg to be deliver'd from the Danger, because I know not my own Strength.

This was honestly spoken, indeed; and there really were such visible Tokens of Sincerity in all his Discourse, that I could not suspect him: On some of our Discourses on this Subject, he pull'd out a little Dirty Paper Book, in which he had wrote down such a Prayer in Verse, as I doubt few Christians in the World could Subscribe to; and I cannot but Record it, because I never saw any thing like it in my Life, the Lines are as follows:

> Lord! whatsoever Sorrows Rack my Breast,
> Till Crime removes too, let me find no Rest;

How Dark so e'er, my State, or sharp my Pain,
O! let not Troubles Cease, and Sin Remain.
  For Jesus sake, remove not my Distress,
Till free Triumphant Grace shall Reposess
The Vacant Throne, from whence my Sins Depart,
And make a willing Captive of my Heart;
Till Grace Compleatly shall my Soul Subdue,
Thy Conquest full, and my Subjection True.[282]

THERE were more Lines on the same Subject, but these were the beginning; and these touching me so sensibly, I have remember'd them distinctly ever since, and have I believe repeated them to my self a Thousand times.

I press'd him no more you may be sure, after an answer so very particular, and affecting as this was; it was easy to see the Man was a sincere Penitent, not sorrowing for the Punishment he was suffering under; for his Condition was no part of his Affection, he was rather thankful for it, as above; but his Concern was a feeling and affecting Sence of the Wicked and Abominable Life he had led, the abhorr'd Crimes he had Committed, both against God and Man, and the little Sence he had had of the Condition he was in, that even till he came to the Place where he now was.

I ask'd him if he had no Reflections of this kind, after, or before his Sentence, he told me, *Newgate, for the Prison at* Bristol *is call'd, so it seems, as well as that at* London, was a place that seldom made Penitents, but often made Villains worse, till they learn'd to defie God and Devil. But, that however, he cou'd look back with this Satisfaction; that he could say, he was not altogether insensible of it, even then; but nothing that amounted to a thorough Serious looking up to Heaven: That he often indeed look'd in, and reflected upon his past mispent Life, even before he was in Prison, when the Intervals of his wicked Practises gave some time for Reflection, and he would sometimes say to himself, Whether am I going? To what, will all these things bring me at last? And where will they End? Sin and Shame follow one another, and I shall certainly come to the Gallows; *then said he*, I wou'd strike upon my Breast, and say: O wicked Wretch, when wilt thou Repent! And would answer my self as often; Never! Never! Never! Except it be in a Goal, or at a Gibbet.

THEN *said he*, I would Weep, and Sigh, and look back a little upon my wretched Life, the History of which would make the World amaz'd; but Alas! the prospect was so Dark, and it fill'd me with so much Terror, that I cou'd not bear it; then, I would fly to Wine and Company for relief, that Wine brought on Excess, and that Company being always wicked Company like my self, brought on Temptation; and then all Reflection Vanish'd, and I was the same Devil as before.

HE spoke this with so much Affection, that his Face was ever smiling, when he talk'd of it, and yet his Eyes had Tears standing in them, at the same time, and all the time; for he had a delightful Sorrow, if that be a proper Expression, in speaking of it.

THIS was a strange Relation to me, and began to affect me after a manner that I did not understand; I lov'd to hear him talk of it, and yet it always left a kind of a Dead Lump behind it upon my Heart, which I cou'd give no Reason for, nor imagine to what it should tend; I had a heaviness on my Soul without being able to describe it, or to say, what ailed me.

WELL, he went on with his Relation, after this, *says he*, I fell into the Hands of Justice for a Triffle, a peice of Sport in our Crime; and I, that for a hundred Robberies, as well on the Highway, as otherwise, the particulars of which would fill a Book to give an Account of, ought, whenever I was taken to be Hang'd in Chains, and who, if it had been Publick, could not have fail'd of having Twenty People come in against me, was privately Hurried into a Country Goal, under a wrong Name; try'd for a small Fact[283] within Benefit of Clergy,[284] and in which I was not principally Guilty, and by this means obtained the favour of being Transported.

AND what think you, *said he*, has most sensibly affected me, and brought on the blessed Change that I hope I may say, God has wrought in my Soul: Not the Greatness of my Crimes, but the Wonders of that merciful Providence, which when it has Mercy in store for a Man, often brings him into the Briars, into Sorrow and Misery for lesser Sins; that Men may be led to see how they are spar'd from the Punishment due to them, for the greater Guilt which they know lies upon them; do you think that when I receiv'd the Grant of Transportation, I cou'd be insensible what a Miracle of Divine Goodness such a thing must be, to one who had so many ways deserv'd to be Hang'd, and must infallibly have Died, if my true Name had been known, or if the least Notice had been given, that it was such a Notorious Wretch as I, that was in Custody? There began the first Motive of Repentance, for certainly the Goodness of our Great Creator in sparing us, when we forfeit our Lives to his Justice, and his Merciful bringing us out of the Miseries which we Plunge ourselves into, when we have no way to Extricate ourselves, his bringing those very Miseries to be the means of our Deliverance, and working Good to us out of Evil, when we are working the very Evil out of his Good: I say, these things are certainly the strongest Motives to Repentance that are in the World; and the sparing Theives from the Gallows, certainly makes more Penitents than the Gallows it self.

IT is true, *continu'd he*, that the Terror of Punishment works strongly upon the Mind: In view of Death, Men are fill'd with Horror of Soul, and immediately they call that Repentance which I doubt is too often mistaken; being only a kind of Anguish in the Soul, which breeds a Grief for the Punishment that is to be suffer'd; an Amazement founded upon the dreadful View of what is to follow: But the Sense of Mercy is quite another thing, this Seizes all the Passions, and all the Affections, and Works a sincere Unfeigned Abhorrence of the Crime, as a Crime; as an Offence against our Benefactor, as an Act of Baseness and Ingratitude to him, who has given us Life, and all the Blessings and Comforts of Life; and who has Conquer'd us by continuing to do us good, when he has been Provok'd to destroy us.

THIS, Sir, *says he*, has been the Fountain of that Repentance, which I so much Rejoyce in: This is the delightful Sorrow, *says he*, that I spoke of just now; and this makes Smiles sit on my Face, while Tears run from my Eyes; a Joy that I can no otherwise Express, than by telling you, Sir, that I never liv'd a happy Day since I came to an Age of acting in the World, till I Landed in this Country, and work'd in your Plantation: Naked and Hungry, Weary and Faint, oppress'd with Cold in one Season, and Heat in the other; then I began to see into my own ways, and see the Difference between the Hardships of the Body, and the Torment of the Mind: Before I Revell'd in fulness, and here, I struggl'd with hard fare; then I wallow'd in Sloth and Voluptuous Ease; here, I labour'd till Nature sometimes was just sinking under the Load; but with this Difference in the Felicity of either Case; Namely, that there I had a Hell in my Soul, was fill'd with Horror and Confusion, was a daily Terror to my self, and always expected a miserable End; Whereas here, I had a bless'd Calm of Soul, an Emblem, and forerunner of Heaven: Thankful and Humble, adoring that Mercy that had snatch'd me out of the Jaws of the Devil; these took up my Thoughts, and made my most weary Hours Pleasant to me, my Labour light, and my Heart Chearful; I never lay down on my hard Lodging, but I prais'd God with the greatest Excess of Affection, not only, that it was not the *Condemn'd-Hole*; and that I was delivered from the Death I had deserv'd; But that it was not *Shooters hill*,[285] that I was not still a Robber, a Terror to Just and honest Men; a Plunderer of the Innocent, and the Poor; a Thief, and a Villain, that ought to be Rooted out from the Earth, for the Safety of others; But that I was deliver'd from the horrid Temptation of Sinning, to Support my Luxury, and making one Vice Necessary to another; and this I bear Witness, is sufficient to Sweeten the bitterest Sorrow, and make any Man be thankful for *Virginia*, or a worse Place, if that can be.

HE then entertain'd me with an Opinion of his, that if it were possible for the Face of Heaven and Hell to be Disclos'd and laid open, and that Men could be made capable of seeing distinctly, and separately, the Joys and Glory, and utmost Felicity of One, and the Horrors of the Other; and to make a Judgment of both, according to the Power of human Reasoning, the first would have a stronger and more powerful Effect to Reform the World, than the latter: But this we had farther Discourses about on[a] many Occasions.

IF it should be enquir'd, how I was capable of hearing all this, and having no Impressions made upon my Mind by it, especially, when it so many ways suited my own Case, and the Condition of the former part of my Life; I shall answer that presently by it self: However, I took no notice of it to him, for he had quite other Notions of me, than I had of my self; nor did I, as is usual in such Cases, enter into any Confidence with him on my *own* Story, only that I took sometimes the Occasion to let him know, that I did not come over to *Virginia* in the Capacity of a Criminal, or that I was not Transported; which considering how many of the Inhabitants there were so, who then liv'd in good Circumstances, was needful enough to be done.

BUT as to myself it was enough, that I was in Condition now, 'twas no matter to any Body, what I had been; and as it was grown pretty much out of Memory, from what original dissaster, I came into the Country, or that I was ever a Servant, otherwise than Voluntary, and that it was no Business of mine to expose myself; so I kept that Part close; but for all that, it was impossible for me to conceal the Disorder I was in, as often as he talk'd of these things; I had hitherto gone on upon a Notion of things founded only in their appearance, as they affected me with Good, or Evil; esteeming, the happy and unhappy Part of Life to be those that gave me Ease, or Sorrow, without regarding, or indeed much understanding how far those Turns of Life were influenced by the giver of Life; or how far they were all directed by a Sovereign God, that Governs the World, and all the Creatures it had made.

AS I had no Education but as you have heard, so I had had no Instruction, no Knowledge of Religion, or indeed of the meaning of it; and tho' I was now in a kind of search after Religion, it was a meer looking, *as it were*, into the World to see what kind of a thing, or Place it was, and what had been done in it; but as to him that made it, there had truly been scarce a Creature among all he had made, with Souls in them, that were so intirely without the knowledge of God as I was, and made so little enquiry about it.

BUT the serious affectionate Discourse of this young Man, began to have different Effects upon me; and I began to say to myself, this Man's reflections are certainly very just, but what a Creature am I, and what have I been doing? I that never once did this in all my Life! that never said so much, *God, I thank thee* for all that I have been sav'd from, or all that I have been brought to in this World; and yet my Life has been as full of Variety, and I have been as miraculously deliver'd from Dangers and Mischiefs, and as many of them, as ever he has; and if it has all been brought to pass by an invisible Hand in Mercy to me, what have I been doing, and where have I liv'd? that I only should be the most Thoughtless, and Unthankful of all God's Creatures!

THIS indeed began to grow upon me, and made me very melancholy; but as to Religion, I understood so little about it, that if I had resolv'd upon any such thing, as a new Course of Life, or to set about a religious Change, I knew not at which End to begin, or what to do about it.

ONE Day it happen'd, that my Tutor, for so I always call'd him, had the Bible in his Hand, and was looking in it, as he generally did many times every Day, tho' I knew not for what, seeing the Bible, I took it out of his Hands, and went to look in it; which I had done so little before, that I think I might safely say, I had never read a Chapter in it, in all my Life; he was talking of the Bible then, as a Book only; as where he had it, and how he brought it to *Virginia*, and in some extasie, he took it, and kiss'd: This blessed Book! *says he*, this was all the Treasure I brought out of *England* with me, and a comfortable Treasure, it has been to me, *added he*, I would not have been without it in my Sorrows, for any other Treasure in the World, and so he went on at Large.

I THAT had no Notion of what he meant, only, *as I have said above*, some Young Infant Thoughts, about the Works of Providence in the World, and its merciful Dealings with me, took the Book out of his Hand, and went to look into it, and the Book open'd at the *Acts* 26. v. 28. where *Fælix* says to *St.* Paul, *almost thou perswadest me to be a Christian.* I think, *says I*, here's a Line hits me to a Tittle, upon the long Account, you have given of yourself, and I must say them to you, as the Governor here said; and so I read the Words to him. He blush'd at the Text, and returns, I wish I could answer you in the very Words the Apostle return'd to him in the next Ver. *I would thou wert both almost, and altogether such as I am, except these Bonds.*

I WAS now more than Thirty Year old,[286] by my own Account, and as well as it was possible for me to keep a reckoning of my Age, who had no Body left, that ever knew my beginning, I was, *I say*, above 30 Year old, and had gone thro some Variety in the World; but as I was perfectly abandoned in my Infancy, and utterly without Instruction in my Youth; so I was intirely ignorant of every thing that was worthy the name of Religion in the World; and this was the first time that ever any Notion of Religious

Things entered into my Heart; but I was surpriz'd at this Man's talk, and that several ways; particularly, he talk'd so feelingly of his pass'd Circumstances, and they were so like my own, that every time he made a religious Inference from his own Condition, and argued from one Condition of his to another, it struck into my Thoughts like a Bullet from a Gun, that I had certainly as much to be thankful for, and to repent of, as he had, except only that I had no knowledge of better things to be thankful for, which he had; but in return for that, I was deliver'd, and set up in the World, made a Master, and easy, and was in good Circumstances, being rais'd from the very same low distress'd Condition as he was in, I mean a sold Servant; but that he remain'd so still, so that if his Sin had been greater than mine, so his Distress was still greater.

THIS Article of Gratitude struck deep, and lay heavy upon my Mind; I remembered that I was Grateful to the last degree to my old Master, who had rais'd me from my low Condition, and that I lov'd the very name of him, or as might be said, the very Ground he trod on; but I had not so much as once thought of any higher obligation; no, nor, so much as like the Pharisee had said, one *God I thank thee*,[287] to him, for all the Influence which his Providence must have had in my whole Affair.

IT occurr'd to me presently, that if none of all these things befall us without the direction of a divine Power, as my new Instructor had told me at large; and that God had order'd every thing, the most Minute, and least Transaction of Life, insomuch, *That not a Hair of our Heads shall fall to the Ground without his Permission*;[288] I say, it occurr'd to me, that I had been a most unthankful Dog to that Providence, that had done so much for me; and the Consequence of the Reflection was immediately this; how justly may that Power, so disoblig'd, take away again his Wooll, and his Flax, with which I am now clothed, and reduce me to the misery of my first Circumstances.

THIS perplex'd me much, and I was very pensive, and sad, in which however, my new Instructor was a constant Comforter to me, and I learn'd every day something or other from him, upon which I told him one Morning, that I thought he must leave off teaching me Latin, and Teach me Religion.

HE spoke with a great deal of Modesty of his being uncapable of Informing me of any thing that I did not know, and propos'd to me to read the Scriptures every Day, as the sure and only Fund of Instruction: I answer'd; that in the Words of the *Eunuch* to St. *Philip*, when the Apostle ask'd him, if he understood what he read? *How can I, unless some one Guide me?*[289]

WE talk'd frequently upon this Subject, and I found so much Reason to believe he was a Sincere Convert, that I can speak of him as no other, in all

I have to say of him; However, I cannot say my Thoughts were yet Ripen'd, for an Opperation of that kind; I had some uneasiness about my past Life, and I liv'd now, and had done so before I knew him, a very regular Sober Life, always taken up in my Business, and running into no Excesses; but as to commencing Penitent, as this Man had done, I cannot say, I had any Convictions upon me, sufficient to bring it on, nor had I a Fund of religious Knowledge to support me in it; so it wore off again Gradually, as such things generally do, where the first Impressions are not deep enough.

IN the mean time as he Read over long Lectures of his own Disasters to me, and applied them all seriously to me, so our Discourse was always very Solid and Weighty, and we had nothing of Levity between us, even when we were not concern'd in religious Discourses: He read History to me, and where Books were wanting, he gave me Ideas of those things which had not been Recorded by our modern Histories, or at least, that our Number of Books would not reach; by these things he rais'd an unquenchable Thirst in me, after seeing something that was doing in the World, and the more because all the World was at that time engag'd more or less, in the great War wherein the *French* King might be said to be engag'd with, and against all the Powers of *Europe*.[290]

NOW, I look'd upon my self as one Buried alive, in a remote Part of the World, where I could see nothing at all, and hear but a little of what was seen, and that little, not till at least half a Year after it was done, and sometimes a Year or more; and in a Word, the old Reproach often came in my way; Namely, that even this was not yet, the Life of a Gentleman.

IT was true, that this was much nearer to it, than that of a Pick-pocket, and still nearer than that of a sold Slave: But in short, this would not do, and I cou'd receive no Satisfaction in it; I had now a second Plantation, a very considerable one, and it went forward very well; I had on it almost 100 Servants already, of sundry Sorts, and an Overseer, that I had a great deal of Reason to say, I might depend upon, and but that, I had a third in Embrio, and newly begun, I had nothing to hinder me from going where I pleas'd.

HOWEVER, I now began to Frame my Thoughts for a Voyage to *England*; resolving then to Act as I should see Cause, but with a secret Resolution, to see more of the World, if possible, and reallize those things to my Mind, which I had hitherto only entertain'd remote Ideas of, by the helps of Books.

ACCORDINGLY, I push'd forward the Settlement of my third Plantation, in order to bring it to be in a Posture, to be either let to a Tennant, or left in Trust with an Overseer, as I should find occasion.

HAD I resolved to leave it to an Overseer, or Steward, no Man in the World could have been fit for it, like my Tutor; but I could not think of parting with him, who was the Cause of my desire of Travelling, and who I concluded to make my Partner in my Travels.

IT was three Year after this, before I could get things in order, fit for my leaving the Country; in this time I deliver'd my Tutor from his Bondage, and would have given him his Liberty, but to my great disappointment I found that I could not empower him to go for *England*, till his time was expir'd, according to the Certificate of his Transportation,[291] which was Register'd, so I made him one of my Overseers, and thereby rais'd him gradually to a Prospect of living in the same manner, and by the like steps that my good Benefactor rais'd me; only, that I did not assist him to enter upon Planting for himself as I was assisted, neither was I upon the Spot to do it; but his Man's Diligence and honest Application, even unassisted deliver'd himself, any farther than, as *I say*, by making him an Overseer, which was only a present Ease and Deliverance to him from the hard Labour, and Fare, which he endured as a Servant.[292]

HOWEVER, in this Trust he behav'd so faithfully, and so diligently, that it recommended him in the Country; and when I came back, I found him in Circumstances very differing from what I left him in, besides his being my principal Mannager for near twenty Years, as you shall hear in its Place.

I mention these things the more at large, that if any unhappy Wretch, who may have the Disaster to fall into such Circumstances as these, may come to see this Account, they may learn the following short Lessons from these Examples.

1. THAT *Virginia*, and a State of Transportation, may be the happiest Place and Condition they were ever in, for this Life, as by a sincere Repentance, and a diligent Application to the Business they are put to; they are effectually deliver'd from a Life of a flagrant Wickedness, and put in a perfectly new Condition, in which they have no Temptation to the Crimes they formerly committed, and have a prospect of Advantage for the future.

2. THAT in *Virginia*, the meanest, and most despicable Creature after his time of Servitude is expir'd, if he will but apply himself with Diligence and Industry to the Business of the Country, is sure (Life and Health suppos'd) both of living Well and growing Rich.

AS this is a foundation, which the most unfortunate Wretch alive is entitul'd to, a Transported Felon, is in my Opinion a much happier Man, than the most prosperous untaken Thief in the Nation; nor are those poor young People so much in the wrong, as some imagine them to be, that go voluntarily over to those Countries,[293] and in order to get themselves carried over, and plac'd there, freely bind themselves there; especially if the Persons into whose Hands they fall, do any thing honestly by them; for as it is to be suppos'd that those poor People knew not what Course to take before, or had miscarried in their Conduct before; here they are sure to be immediately provided for, and after the expiration of their time, to be put into a Condition to provide for themselves; but I return to my own Story, which now begins a new Scene.

I WAS now making Provision for my going to *England*, after having settled my Plantation in such Hands, as was fully to my satisfaction; my first Work was to furnish myself with such a Stock of Goods, and Money, as might be sufficient for my occasions Abroad, and particularly might allow to make large Returns to *Maryland*, for the Use and Supply of all my Plantations; but when I came to look nearer into the Voyage, it occurr'd to me, that it would not be prudent to put my Cargo all on Aboard the same Ship that I went in; so I Shipp'd at several times five Hundred Hogsheads[294] of Tobbacco in several Ships for *England*, giving Notice to my Correspondent[295] in *London*, that I would Embark about such a time to come over myself, and ordering him to Ensure for a considerable Sum, proportion'd to the value of my Cargo.

ABOUT two Months after this I left the Place, and Embark'd for *England*, in a stout Ship, carrying 24 Guns, and about six Hundred Hogsheds of Tobacco, and we left the Capes of *Virginia*, on the first of *August* —: We had a very sour[296] and rough Voyage for the first Fortnight, tho' it was in a Season so generally noted for good Weather.

AFTER we had been about eleven Days at Sea, having the wind most part of the Time blowing very hard at West or between the West and N.W. by which we were carried a great way farther to the Eastward, than they usually go in their Course for *England*, we met with a furious Tempest, which held us five Days, blowing most of the time excessive hard, and by which, we were oblig'd to run away afore the Wind, *as the Seamen call it*, wheresoever it was, our Lot to go; by this Storm, our Ship was greatly damag'd, and some Leaks we had, but not so bad, but that by the diligence of the Seamen they were stopp'd: However, the Captain after having beaten up[297] again, as well as he could against the Weather and the Sea going very high, at length he resolved to go away for the *Bermudas*.

I WAS not Seaman enough to understand what the Reason of their Disputes was, but in their running for the Islands, it seems they over-shot the Latitude, and could never reach the Island of *Bermudas* again; the Master and the Mate differed to an extremity about this; their reckonings, being more than usually wide of one another, the Storm having driven them a little out of their Knowledge; the Master being a positive Man, insulted the Mate about it, and threatn'd to expose him for it, when he came to *England*: The Mate was an excellent Sea Artist,[298] and an experienc'd Sailor, but withal a modest Man; and tho' he insisted upon his being right, did it in respectful Terms, and as it became him; but after several days Dispute, when the Weather came to abate, and the Heavens to clear up that they could take their Observations, and know where they were, it appear'd that the Mates account was right, and the Captain was mistaken, for they were then in the Latitude of 29 Degrees, and quite out of the Wake[299] of the *Bermudas*.

THE Mate made no Indecent use of the Discovery at all, and the Captain being convinc'd, carry'd it civilly to him, and so the Heats were over among them; but the next Question was, What they should do next? some were for going one Way, some another, but all agreed they were not in Condition to go on the direct Course for *England*, unless they could have a Southerly, or South-west Wind, which had not been our Fate since we came to Sea.

UPON the whole, they resolv'd by consent to stand away for the *Canaries*, which was the nearest Land they could make, except the *Cape de Verd* Islands,[300] which were too much to the Southward for us, if it could be avoided.

UPON this, they stood away N. E. and the Wind hanging still Westerly, or to the Northward of the West, we made good Way, and in about 15 Days sail we made the *Pico Teneriffe* being a monstrous Hill in one of the *Canary* Islands:[301] Here we refresh'd our selves, got fresh Water, and some fresh Provisions, and plenty of excellent Wine, but no Harbour to run into, to take care of the Ship, which was Leaky, and tender, having had so much very bad Weather; so we were oblig'd to do as well as we could, and put to Sea again, after Riding at the *Canaries* four Days only.

FROM the *Canaries*, we had tollerable Weather, and a smooth Sea, till we came into the Soundings,[302] so they call the Mouth of the *British* Channel, and the Wind blowing hard at the N. and N. W. oblig'd us to keep a larger Offing,[303] as the Seamen call it, at our Enterance into the Channel, when behold! in the gray of the Morning, a *French* Cruiser, or Privateer of 26 Guns appear'd, and crowded after us with all the Sail they could make: In short, our Captain exchang'd a Broadside or two with them, which was terrible Work to me; for I had never seen such before, the *Frenchman's* Guns having Raked us, and kill'd and wounded six of our best Men.

IN short, after a Fight long enough to show us, that if we would not be taken, we must resolve to sink by her Side, for there was no room to expect

Deliverance; and a Fight long enough to save the Master's Credit, we were taken, and the Ship carried away for St. *Malo's*.[304]

I WAS not much concern'd for the loss I had in the Ship, because I knew I had sufficient in the World somewhere or other; but as I was effectually strip'd of every thing I had about me, and even almost my Cloaths from my back, I was in but a very indifferent Condition; but some Body informing the Captain of the Privateer, that I was a Passenger, and a Merchant, he call'd for me, and inquir'd into my Circumstances, and coming to hear from myself, how I had been us'd, oblig'd the Seamen to give me a Coat and Hat, and a pair of Shoes, which they had taken off me, and himself gave me a Morning Gown of his own, to wear while I was in his Ship, and to give him his due treated me very well.

I HAD however, besides my being taken, the Mortification to be detain'd on Board the Cruiser, and seeing the Ship I was in[305] Mann'd with *Frenchmen*, and sent away, as above, for St. *Malo*, and this was a greater Mortification to me afterwards, when being brought into St. *Malo's*, I heard that our own Ship was Retaken in her Passage to St *Malo's* by an *Englishman* of War, and carryed to *Portsmouth*.

WHEN our Ship was sent away, the *Rover*[306] Cruis'd abroad again in the Mouth of the Channel for some time, but met with no Purchase; at last they made a Sail,[307] which prov'd to be one of their Nation, and one of their own Trade, from whom they learn'd (the News having been carried to *England*, that some *French* Privateers lay off and on, in the Soundings,) that three *Englishmen* of War were come out from *Plymouth*, on purpose to Cruise in the Channel, and that they would certainly meet with us. Upon this Intelligence, the *Frenchman*, a bold brave Fellow, far from shrinking from his Work, stands away North East for St. *Georges* Channel[308] and in the Latitude of 48 and a half, unhappily enough, meets with a large and rich *English* Ship, bound home from *Jamaica*; it was in the gray of the Morning, and very clear when a Man on the Round-Top,[309] cry'd out *au voile*, a Sail; I was in hopes indeed it had been the *Englishmen* of War, and by the Hurry and Clutter[310] they were in, to get all ready for a Fight, I concluded it was so, and got out of my Hammock, for I had no Cabbin to lye in, that I might see what it was, but I soon found that my hopes were vain, and it was on the wrong Side; for that being on our Larboard Bow, the Ship lying then Northward, to make the Coast of *Ireland*; by the time I was turn'd out I could perceive they had all their Sails bent, and full, having begun to Chace, and making great way; on the other Hand, it was Evident the Ship saw them too, and knew what they were, and to avoid them, stretch'd away with all the Canvas they could lay on, for the Coast of *Ireland*, to run in there for Harbour.

OUR Privateer, it was plain, infinitely out sail'd her, running two Foot for her one, and towards Evening came up with them; had they been able to have held it but six Hours longer, they would have got into *Limerick* River, or somewhere under Shore; so that we should not have ventured upon them, but we came up with them, and the Captain when he see there was no Remedy, bravely brought to,[a] and prepar'd to Fight;[311] she was a Ship of 30 Guns, but deep in the Sea, cumber'd between Deck with Goods, and could not run out her lower Deck Guns, the Sea also going pretty high, tho' at last she ventur'd to open her Gun-room Ports, and Fire with three Guns on a Side; but her worst fate was, she sail'd heavy, being deep Loaden, and the *Frenchman* had run up by her Side, and pour'd in his Broad-side, and was soon ready again; However, as she was well Mann'd too, and that the *English* Sailors bestirr'd themselves, they gave us their Broad-sides too very nimbly and heartily, and I found the *Frenchman* had a great many Men kill'd at the first Brush, but the next was worse, for the *English* Ship, tho' she did not sail so well as the *Frenchman*, was a bigger Ship, and strong built, and as we (the *French*) bore down upon them again, the *English* run boldly on Board us, and lay'd Thwart our Hause,[312] lashing themselves fast to us; then it was that the *English* Captain run out his lower Tire[313] of Guns, and indeed tore the *Frenchman* so, that had he held it, the Privateer would have had the worst of it; but the *Frenchman* with admirable readiness indeed, and Courage, the Captain appearing every where, with his Sword in his Hand, bestirr'd themselves, and loosing themselves from the *English* Ship, thrusting her off with Brooms, and pouring their small Shot so thick, that the other could not appear upon Deck; *I say*, clearing themselves thus, they came to lye a Broadside of each other, when by long firing the *English* Ship was at length disabled, her Missen-Mast and Bole-sprit[314] shot away, and which was worst of all, her Captain kill'd, so that after a Fight which held all Night, for they fought in the Dark, and part of the next Day, they were oblig'd to Strike.[315]

I was civily desir'd by the *French* Captain to go down into the Hold, while the Fight held, and besides the Civility of it, I found he was not willing I should be upon Deck; perhaps he thought I might have some Opportunity to do hurt, tho' I know not how it could be: However, I was very ready to go down, for I had no Mind to be Kill'd; especially by my own Friends, so I went down and sat by the Surgeon, and had the Opportunity to find, that the first Broad-side the *English* Fir'd, seven wounded Men were brought down to the Surgeon, and three and Thirty more afterward; *that is to say*, when the *English* lay Thwart their Bow, and after they Cleared themselves, there was about Eleven more; so that they had one and fifty Men Wounded, and about two and Twenty Kill'd, the *Englishman* had eighteen Men Kill'd and Wounded, among whom, was the Captain.

THE *French* Captain however, triumph'd in this Prize, for it was an exceeding Rich Ship, having Abundance of Silver on Board; and after the Ship was taken, and they had Plundered all the great Cabbin afforded, which was very Considerable, the Mate promis'd the Captain, that if he would give him his Liberty, he would discover Six Thousand peices of Eight[316] to him Privately, which none of the Men should know of; the Captain engag'd, and gave it under his Hand to set him at Liberty, as soon as he came on Shore; accordingly in the Night after all was either turn'd in, *as they call it*, or Employ'd on the Duty of the Watch, the Captain, and the Mate of the Prize went on Board, and having faithfully Discover'd the Money which lay in a Place made on purpose to Conceal it; the Captain resolv'd to let it lye till they arriv'd, and then he Convey'd it on Shore for his own use; so that the Owners nor the Seamen ever came to any Share of it, which by the way was a Fraud in the Captain; but the Mate paid his Ransom by the Discovery, and the Captain gave him his Liberty very Punctually as he promis'd, and two Hundred peices of Eight to carry him into *England*, and to make good his Losses.

WHEN he had made this Prize, the Captain thought of nothing more, than how to get safe to *France* with her; for she was a Ship sufficient to Enrich all his Men, and his Owners also. The Account of her Cargo by the Captains Books, of which I took a Copy, was in general:

> 260 Hhds[317] Sugar.
> 187 Smaller Cask of Sugar.
> 176 Barrels of *Indico*.[318]
>   28 Cask of *Piemento*.[319]
>   42 Baggs of Cotton-Wooll.
>   80 C. Weight of *Elephants* Teeth.
>   60 Small Cask of Rum.
> 18000 Peices of Eight, besides the 6000 Conceal'd.
> Several parcels of Drugs, Tortoise-shell, Sweet-meats call'd Succads,[320] Chocolate, Lime-juice, and other things of considerable Value.

THIS was a Terrible loss among the *English* Merchants, and a noble Booty for the Rogues that took it; but as it was in open War, and by fair Fighting as they call it, there was no Objection to be made against them, and to give them their Due, they Fought bravely for it.

THE Captain was not so bold as to meeting the *English*-Men of War before, but he was as wary now; for having a Prize of such Value in his

Hands, he was resolv'd not to lose her again, if he could help it; so he stood away to the Southward, and that so far, that I once thought he was resolv'd to go into the Streights,[321] and Home by *Marseilles*. But having sail'd to the Latitude of 45. 3qrs. or thereabouts, he stood away East, into the Bottom of the Bay of *Biscay*, and carried us all into the River of *Bourdeaux*, where on Notice of his Arrival with such a Prize, his Owners or Principals came Overland to see him, and where they consulted what to do with her; the Money they secur'd to be sure, and some of the Cargo; but the Ships sail'd afterwards along the Coast to St. *Malo*, taking the Opportunity of some *French* Men of War which were Cruising on the Coast, to be their Convoy as far as *Ushant*.[322]

HERE the Captain rewarded and dismiss'd the *English* Mate, *as I have said*, who got a Passage from thence to *Diep*[323] by Sea, and after that into *England*, by the help of a Passport, thro' *Flanders*, to *Ostend*; the Captain it seems, the more willingly Ship'd him off, that he might not Discover to others, what he had Discover'd to him.

I was now at *Bourdeaux* in *France*, and the Captain ask'd me one Morning, what I intended to do. I^a did not understand him at first, but he soon gave me to understand, that I was now either to be deliver'd up to the State as an *English* Prisoner, and so be carried to *Dinant*[324] in *Britanny*, or to find means to have my self Exchang'd, or to pay my Ransom; and this Ransom he told me at first, was 300 Crowns.

I knew not what to do, but desir'd he would give me time to Write to *England*, to my Friends; for that I had a Cargo of Goods sent to them, by me, from *Virginia*, but I did not know but it might have fallen into such Hands as his were, and if it was, I knew not what would be my Fate; he readily granted that, so I Wrote by the Post, and had the Satisfaction in Answer to it, to hear that the Ship I was taken in, had been retaken, and carried into *Portsmouth*; which I doubted would have made my new Master more strict, and perhaps insolent, but he said nothing of it to me, nor I to him, tho' as I afterwards understand, he had Advice of it before.

HOWEVER, this was a help to me, and serv'd to more than Pay my Ransom to the Captain; and my Correspondent in *London* hearing of my being alive, and at *Bourdeaux*, immediately sent me a Letter of Credit upon an *English* Merchant at *Bourdeaux*, for what ever I might have Occasion for: As soon as I received this, I went to the Merchant, who Honour'd the Letter of Credit, and told me, I should have what Money I pleas'd. But as I, who was before a meer Stranger in the Place, and knew not what Course to take, had now as it were a Friend to Communicate my Affairs to, and Consult with; as soon as I told him my Case, Hold, *says he*, if that be your Case, I may perhaps find a way to get you off without a Ransom.

THERE was it seems, a Ship Bound Home to *France* from *Martinico*, taken off of Cape *Finisterre* by an *Englishman* of War, and a Merchant of *Rochelle* being a Passenger, was taken on Board, and brought into *Plymouth*: This Man had made great Sollicitation by his Friends to be Exchang'd, pleading Poverty, and that he was unable to Pay any Ransom; my Friend told me something of it, but not much, only bad me not be too forward to Pay any Money to the Captain, but pretend I cou'd not hear from *England*: This I did, till the Captain appear'd Impatient.

AFTER some time, the Captain told me I had us'd him ill; that I had made him expect a Ransom, and he had treated me Courteously, and been at Expence to Subsist me, and that I held him in Suspence, but that in short, if I did not procure the Money, he would send me to *Dinant*, in Ten Days, to lye there as the King's Prisoner, till I should be Exchang'd: My Merchant gave me my Cue, and by his Direction I answer'd, I was very sensible of his Civility, and sorry he should lose what Expences he had been at; but that I found my Friends forgot me, and what to do I did not know, and that rather than Impose upon him, I must Submit to go to *Dinant*, or where he thought fit to send me; but that if ever I obtain'd my Liberty, and came into *England*, I would not fail to Reimburse him what Expence he had been at for my Subsistance; and so in short, made my Case very bad in all my Discourse: He shook his Head, and said little, but the next Day Enter'd me in the List of *English* Prisoners, to be at the King's Charge, as appointed by the Intendant of the Place, and to be sent away into *Britainny*.

I was then out of the Captains Power, and immediately the Merchant with two others, who were Friends to the Merchant Prisoner, at *Plymouth*, went to the Intendant, and Gain'd an Order for the Exchange, and my Friend giving Security for my being Forth-coming, in Case the other was not Deliver'd; I had my Liberty immediately, and went Home with him to his House.

THUS we Bilk'd[325] the Captain of his Ransom Money: But however, my Friend went to him, and letting him know that I was Exchang'd by the Governors Order, paid him whatever he cou'd say he was in Disburse on my Account; and it was not then in the Captains Power to Object, or to claim any thing for a Ransom.

I got Passage from hence to *Dunkirk*, on Board a *French* Vessel, and having a Certificate of an Exchang'd Prisoner from the Intendant[326] of *Bourdeaux*: I had a Passport given me, to go into the *Spanish* Netherlands, and so whether I pleas'd.

ACCORDINGLY I came to *Ghent*, in *April* —, just as the Armies were going to take the Field; I had no dislike to the Business of the Army, but I thought I was a little above it now; and had other things to look to, for that in my Opinion, no Body went into the Field but those that cou'd not live at Home; and yet I resolv'd to see the manner of it a little too, so having made an Acquaintance with an *English* Officer, Quarter'd at *Ghent*, I told him my Intention, and he Invited me to go with him, and offer'd me his Protection as a Voluntier, that I should Quarter with him in his Tent, and live as I would, and either carry Arms, or not, as I saw Occasion.

THE Campaign was none of the hardest that had been, or were like to be; so that I had the Diversion of seeing the Service, as it was proper to call it, without much Hazard, indeed, I did not see any considerable Action, for there was not much Fighting that Campaign; as to the Merit of the Cause on either side, I knew nothing of it, nor had I suffer'd any of the Disputes about it, to enter into my Thoughts: The Prince of *Orange* had been made King of *England*,[327] and the *English* Troops were all on his Side; and I heard a great deal of Swearing and Damming for King *William* among the Soldiers, but as for Fighting, I observ'd the *French* Beat them several times, and particular the Regiment my Friend belong'd to was surrounded in a Village where they were Posted I know not upon what Occasion, and all taken Prisoners: But by great good hap, I being not in Service, and so not in Command, was stroll'd away that Day to see the Country about, for it was my Delight, to see the strong Towns, and observe the Beauty of their Fortifications; and while I Diverted my self thus, I had the happy Deliverance of not being taken by the *French* for that time.

WHEN I came back, I found the Enemy possess'd of the Town, but as I was no Soldier, they did me no harm, and having my *French* Passport in my Pocket, they gave me leave to go to *Newport*, where I took the Packet-Boat, and came over to *England*, Landing at *Deal* instead of *Dover*, the Weather forcing us into the *Downs*, and thus my short Campaign ended, and this was my second Essay at the Trade of Soldiering.

WHEN I came to *London*, I was very well receiv'd by my Friend, to whom I had consign'd my Effects, and I found my self in very good Circumstances; for all my Goods, which as above, by several Ships I had Consign'd to him, came safe to Hand; and my Overseers that I had left behind, had Ship'd at several times 400 Hhds[328] of *Tobacco* to my Correspondent in my Absence, being the Product of my Plantations, or Part of it, for the time of my being Abroad; so that I had above a Thousand Pounds in my Factors Hands, 200 Hhds of *Tobacco* besides left in Hand, not Sold.

I HAD nothing to do now, but entirely to conceal myself, from all that had any knowledge of me before, and this was the easiest thing in the World to do; for I was grown out of every Body's knowledge, and most of those I had known were grown out of mine: My Captain, who went with me, or rather, who carryed me away, I found by enquiring at the proper

Place, had been rambling about the World, came to *London*, fell into his old Trade, which he could not forbear, and growing an eminent Highway-man, had made his Exit at the Gallows, after a Life of 14 Years most exquisite and successful Rogueries; the particulars of which would make as I observ'd an admirable History; my other Brother *Jack*, who I called Major follow'd the like wicked Trade, but was a Man of more Gallantry, and Generosity, and having committed innumerable Depredations upon Mankind, yet had always so much Dexterity, as to bring himself off, till at length he was laid fast in *Newgate*, and loaded with Irons, and would certainly have gone the same way as the Captain; but he was so dexterous a Rogue, that no Goal, no Fetters would hold him; and he with two more, found means to knock off their Irons, work'd their way thro' the Wall of the Prison, and let themselves down on the Out-side in the Night; so escaping, they found means to get into *France*, where he followed the same Trade, and that with so much Success, that he grew famous by the Name of *Anthony*, and had the Honour with three of his Comrades, who he had Taught the *English* way of Robbing generously, *as they called it*, without Murthering or Wounding, or Ill using those they robb'd, *I say*, he had the Honour to be broke upon the Wheel at the *Greve*[329] in *Paris*.

ALL these things I found Means to be fully inform'd of, and to have a long Account of the particulars of their Conduct, from some of their Comrades, who had the good Fortune to Escape, and who I got the Knowledge of, without letting them so much as guess at who I was, or upon what Account I enquir'd.

I WAS now at the height of my good Fortune; indeed I was in very good Circumstances, and being of a frugal Temper from the beginning, I Sav'd things together, as they came, and yet liv'd very well too; particularly I had the Reputation of a very considerable Merchant, and one that came over vastly Rich from *Virginia*, and as I frequently brought Supplies for my several Families and Plantations there, as they wrote to me for them, so I pass'd, I say, for a great Merchant.

I liv'd single indeed, and in Lodgings, but I began to be very well known, and tho' I had subscrib'd my Name only *Jack* to my particular Correspondent, yet the *French*, among whom I liv'd near a Year, *as I have said* not understanding what *Jack* meant, call'd me Monsieur *Jacque*, and Colonel *Jacques*, and so gradually Colonel *Jacque*; so I was call'd in the Certificate of Exchanging me with the other Prisoner, so that I went so also in Flanders; upon which, and seeing my Certificate of Exchange, as above, I was call'd Colonel *Jacques* in *England*, by my Friend, who I call'd Correspondent; and thus I pass'd for a Foreigner, and a Frenchman, and I was infinitely fond of having every Body take me for a *Frenchman*; and as I spoke French very well, having learn'd it by continuing so long among them; so I went constantly to the *French-Church*[330] in London, and spoke French upon all occasions, as much as I could, and to compleat the appearance of it, I got me a French Servant to do my Business, I mean as to my Merchandise, which only consisted in receiving and disposing of Tobacco, of which I had about 500 to 600 Hogsheads a Year from my own Plantations, and in supplying my People with Necessaries, as they wanted them.

IN this private Condition I continued about two Year more, when the Devil owing me a Spleen,[331] ever since I refus'd being a Thief, paid me home, with my Interest, by laying a Snare in my way, which had almost ruined me.

THERE dwelt a Lady, in a House opposite to the House I lodg'd in, who made an extraordinary Figure, indeed she went very well Dress'd, and was a most beautiful Person; she was well Bred, Sung admirably fine, and sometimes I could hear her very distinctly, the Houses being over against one another, in a narrow Court not much unlike *Three King Court* in *Lombard Street*.

THIS Lady put herself so often in my way, that I could not in good Manners forbear taking Notice of her, and giving her the Ceremony of my Hat, when I saw her at her Window, or at the Door, or when I pass'd her in the Court, so that we became almost acquainted at a distance; sometimes she also visited at the House I lodg'd at, and it was generally contriv'd, that I should be introduced when she came; and thus by degrees we became more intimately acquainted, and often convers'd together in the Family, but always in Publick, at least for a great while.

I WAS a meer Boy in the Affair of Love, and knew the least of what belong'd to a Woman, of any Man in *Europe* of my Age; the thoughts of a Wife, much less of a Mistress, had never so much as taken the least hold of my Head, and I had been till now as perfectly unacquainted with the Sex, and as unconcern'd about them, as I was when I was ten Year old, and lay in a Heap of Ashes at the Glass-House.

BUT I know not by what Witch-Craft in the Conversation of this Woman, and her singling me out upon several Occasions, I began to be ensnared, I knew not how, or to what End;[a] and was on a sudden so embarrass'd in my Thoughts about her, that like a Charm she had me always in her Circle;[332] if she had not been one of the subtilest Women on Earth, she could never have brought me to have given myself the least Trouble about her, but I was drawn[b] in by the Magick of a Genius capable to Deceive a more wary Capacity than mine, and it was impossible to resist her.

SHE attack'd me without ceasing, with the fineness of her Conduct, and with Arts which were impossible to be ineffectual; she was ever, as it were, in my View; often in my Company, and yet kept herself so on the Reserve, so surrounded continually with Obstructions, that for several Months after she could perceive I sought an Opportunity to speak to her, she rendered it impossible, nor could I ever break in upon her, she kept her Guard so well.

THIS rigid Behaviour was the greatest Mystery that could be, considering at the same time, that she never Declined my seeing her, or Conversing with me in Publick; but she held it on, she took care never to sit next me, that I might slip no Paper into her Hand, or speak softly to her; she kept some body or other always between, that I could never come up to her; and thus as if she was resolv'd really to have nothing to do with me, she held me at the Bay several Months.

ALL this while nothing was more certain then that she intended to have me, if she could catch, and it was indeed a kind of a Catch, for she manag'd all by Art, and drew me in with the most resolute backwardness, that it was almost impossible not to be deceiv'd by it; on the other Hand, she did not appear to be a Woman despicable, neither was she poor, or in a Condition that should require so much Art to draw any Man in, but the Cheat was really on my Side; for she was unhappily told, that I was vastly Rich, a great Merchant, and that she would live like a Queen, which I was not at all Instrumental in putting upon her, neither did I know that she went upon that Motive.

SHE was too cunning to let me perceive how easie she was to be had; on the contrary she run all the hazards of bringing me to neglect her entirely, that one would think any Woman in the World could do; and I have wondered often since that, how it was possible it should fail of making me perfectly Averse to her; for as I had a perfect indifferency for the whole Sex, and never till then entertain'd any Notion of them, they were no more to me than a Picture hanging up against a Wall.

As we Convers'd freely together in Publick, so she took a great many Occasions to rally[333] the Men, and the weakness they were guilty of, in leting the Woman insult them as they did; she thought if the Men had been Fools, Marriage had been only Treaties of Peace between two Neighbours, or Alliances Offensive or Defensive, which must necessarily have been carried on sometimes by Interviews, and personal Treaties; but oftner by Ambassadors, Agents, and Emissaries on both Sides; but that the Women had out-witted us, and brought us upon our knees, and made us whine after them, and lower our selves, so as we could never pretend to gain our equallity again.

I TOLD her I thought it was a Decency to the Ladies to give them the Advantage of denying a little, that they might be Courted, and that I should not like a Woman the worse for denying me. I expect it Madam, *says I*, when I wait on you to Morrow, intimating, that I intended it; you shan't be deceiv'd Sir, *says she*, for I'll deny now, before you ask me the Question.

I WAS dash'd so effectually, with so malicious, so devilish an Answer, that I return'd with a little sullenness, I shan't Trespass upon you yet Madam, and I shall be very careful not to offend you when I do.

IT is the greatest Token of your Respect Sir, *says she*, that you are able to bestow upon me, and the most agreeable too, except one, which I will not be out of hopes of obtaining of you in a little time.

WHAT is in my Power to oblige you in Madam, *said I*, you may command me at any time, especially, the way we are Talking of; this I spoke still with a Resentment very Sincere.

'TIS only, Sir, that you would promise to Hate me, with as much Sincerity, as I will endeavour to make you a suitable Return.

I granted that Request, Madam, seven Year before you ask'd it, *said I*, for I heartily Hated the whole Sex, and scarce know how I came to abate that good Disposition in Compliment to your Conversation; but I assure you that abatement is so little, that it does no Injury to your Proposal.

THERE'S some Mystery in that indeed, Sir, *said she*, for I desir'd to assist your Aversion to Women in a more particular manner, and hop'd it should never abate under my Management. We said a Thousand ill-natured things after this, but she out-did me, for she had such a Stock of bitterness upon her Tongue, as no Woman ever went beyond her, and yet all this while she was the pleasantest, and most obliging Creature in every Part of our Conversation that could possibly be, and meant not one Word of what she said, no, not a Word: But I must confess, it no way answer'd her End, for it really cooled all my Thoughts of her, and I that had liv'd in so perfect an indifferency to the Sex all my Days, was easily return'd to that Condition again, and began to grow very cold and negligent in my usual Respects to her upon all Occasions.

SHE soon found she had gone too far with me; and in short, that she was extreamly out in her Politicks,[334] that she had to do with one that was not listed yet among the whining Sort of Lovers, and knew not what it was to Adore a Mistress, in order to abuse her; and that it was not with me, as it was with the usual Sort of Men in Love, that are warm'd by the cold, and rise in their Passions, as the Ladies fall in their Returns; on the contrary, she found that it was quite alter'd; I was Civil to her, as before, but not so forward, when I saw her at her Chamber Window, I did not throw mine open, as I usually had done to Talk with her; when she Sung in the Parlour, where I could easily hear it, I did not Listen; when she Visited at the House where I lodg'd, I did not always come down, or if I did, I had business which oblig'd me to go Abroad, and yet all this while, when I did come into her Company, I was as intimate as ever.

I could easily see that this madded her to the Heart, and that she was perplex'd to the last degree, for she found that she had all her Game to play over again; that so absolute a Reservedness, even to Rudeness and Ill-manners, was a little too much; but she was a meer Posture Mistress[335] in Love, and could put herself into what Shapes she pleas'd.

SHE was too[a] wise to show a fondness or forwardness, that look'd like kindness, she knew that was the meanest, and the last Step a Woman can take, and lays her under the Foot of the Man she pretends to; Fondness is not the last Favour indeed, but it is the last Favour but one, that a Woman can grant, and lays her almost as low, I mean it lays her at the Mercy of the Man, she shows it to, but she was not come to that neither: This Camelion put on another Colour, turn'd on a sudden the gravest, soberest, majestick Madam, so that any one would have thought she was advanced in Age in one Week, from Two and Twenty, to Fifty, and this she carried on with so much Government of her self, that it did not in the least look like Art, but if it was a Representation of Nature only, it was so like Nature itself, that no body living can be able to distinguish; she Sung very often in her Parlour, as well by her self as with two young Ladies, who came often to see her; I could see by their Books, and her Guitar in her Hand, that she was Singing, but she never open'd the Window as she was wont to do; upon my coming to my Window, she kept her own always shut, or if it was open, she would be sitting at Work[336] and not look up, it may be once in Half an Hour.

IF she saw me by Accident all this while, she would smile and speak as chearfully as ever, but it was but a Word or two, and so make her Honours and be gone; so that in a Word, we Convers'd just as we did after I had been there a Week.

SHE tired me quite out at this Work, for tho' I began the strangness indeed, yet I did not design the carrying it on so far, but she held it to the last, just in the same manner as she began it: She came to the House where I Lodg'd, as usual, and we were often together, Supp'd together, Play'd at Cards together, Danc'd together; for in *France* I accomplish'd myself with every thing that was needful, to make me what I believ'd myself to be even from a Boy, I mean a Gentleman; *I say*, we Convers'd together, *as above*, but she was so perfectly another thing than what she us'd to be in every Part of her Conversation, that it presently occurr'd to me, that her former Behaviour was a kind of a Rant, or Fit; that either it was the Effect of some extraordinary Levity that had come upon her, or that it was done to Mimick the Coquets of the Town, believing it might take with me, who she

thought was a *Frenchman*, and that it was what I lov'd; but her new Gravity
was her real natural Temper, and indeed became it her so much better, or as
I should say, she acted it so well, that it really brought me back, to have,
not as much only, but more mind to her, than ever I had before.

HOWEVER, it was a great while before I discover'd myself,[337] and I stay'd
indeed to find out, if possible, whether this Change was Real or Counterfeit? for I could not easily believe it was possible the Gay Humour she us'd
to appear in could be a Counterfeit; it was not therefore till a Year and
almost a Quarter, that I came to any Resolution in my Thoughts about her,
when on a meer Accident we came to a little Conversation together.

SHE came to Visit at our House as usual, and it happen'd all the Ladies
were gone abroad;[338] but as it fell out, I was in the Passage, or Entry of the
House, going towards the Stairs, when she knock'd at the Door; so step-
ping back, I open'd the Door, and she without any Ceremony came in and
run forward into the Parlour, supposing the Women had been there; I went
in after her, as I could do no less, because she did know that the Family was
Abroad.

UPON my coming in, she ask'd for the Ladies, I told her, I hop'd she
came to Visit me now, for that the Ladies were all gone abroad; are they,
said she, as if surpris'd (tho' as I understood afterwards she knew it before,
as also that I was at home) and then rises up to be gone; no Madam, *said I*,
Pray do not go; when Ladies come to Visit me, I do not use to tyre them of
my Company so soon; that's as Ill-natured, *says she*, as you could possibly
talk, pray don't Pretend I came to Visit you, I am satisfy'd who I came to
Visit, and satisfy'd that you know it; yes Madam, *said I*, but if I happen to
be all of the Family that's left at home, then you came to Visit me.

I never receive Visits from those that I hate, *says she*.

YOU have me there indeed, *said I*, but you never gave me leave to tell
you why I hated you: I hated you because you would never give me an
Opportunity to tell you I lov'd you; sure you took me for some frightful
Creature that you would never come near enough, so much as to Whisper
to you that I love you.

I never care to hear any thing so disagreeable, *says she*, tho' it be spoken
ever so softly.

WE rallyed[339] thus for an Hour; in short, she showed the abundance of
her Wit, and I an abundant defficiency of mine; for tho' three or four times
she provok'd me to the last degree, so that once I was going to tell her I
had enough of her Company, and if she pleas'd I would wait upon her to
the Door; yet she had always so much Witchcraft on her Tongue, that she
brought herself off again; till to make the Story short, we came at last to
talk seriously on both Sides about Matrimony, and she heard me freely pro-

pose it, and answered me directly upon many occasions: For Example, she told me, I would carry her away to *France*, or to *Virginia*, and that she could not think of leaving *England*, her native Country; I told her I hop'd she did not take me for a Kidnapper: By the way, I did not tell her how I had been Kidnapp'd myself: She said no, but the Consequence of my Affairs, which were it seems mostly Abroad, might oblige me to go, and she could never think of Marrying any Man, that she could not be content to go all over the World with, if he had occasion to go himself: This was handsomely expressed indeed; I made her easie in that Point, and thus we began the grand Parlee,[340] which indeed she drew me into with the utmost Art and Subtilty, such as was peculiar to herself, but was infinitely her Advantage in our Treating of[341] Marriage; for she made me effectually Court her, tho' at the same time in her Design she Courted me with the utmost skill, and such Skill it was that her Design was perfectly impenetrable to the last Moment.

In short, we came nearer and nearer every time we met, and after one casual Visit more, in which I had the mighty Favour of talking with her alone, I then waited on her every Day at her own House or Lodgings rather; and so we set about the Work to a purpose, and in about a Month we gave the World the slip, and were privately Marry'd to avoid Ceremony, and the publick Inconveniency of a Wedding.

We soon found a House proper for our dwelling, and so went to House-keeping; we had not been long together, but I found that gay Temper of my Wife return'd, and she threw off the Mask of her Gravity, and good Conduct, that I had so long Fancy'd was her meer natural Disposition, and now having no more occasion for Disguises, she resolv'd to seem nothing but what really she was, a wild untam'd Colt, perfectly loose, and careless to conceal any part, no, not the worst of her Conduct.

She carry'd on this Air of Levity to such an Excess, that I could not but be dissatisfy'd at the Expence of it, for she kept Company that I did not like, liv'd beyond what I could support, and sometimes lost at Play[342] more than I car'd to pay: Upon which, one Day, I took Occasion to mention it, but lightly; and said to her, by way of Rallery,[343] that we liv'd merrily, for as long as it would last; she turn'd short upon me, what do ye mean, *says she*, Why, you don't pretend to be uneasy do ye? No, no, Madam, not I, by no means, 'tis no business of mine you know, *said I*, to enquire what my Wife spends, or whether she spends more than I can afford, or less, I only desire the Favour to know as near as you can guess, how long you will please to take to dispatch me, for I would not be too long a dying.

I don't know what you talk of, *says she*, you may die as leisurely, or as hastily as you please when your time comes, I an't a going to kill you, as I know of.

BUT you are a going to starve me Madam, *said I*,[a] and Hunger is as leisurely a Death, as breaking upon the Wheel.[344]

I starve you, Why are not you a great *Virginia* Merchant, and did not I bring you 1500*l*. What would you have? sure, you can maintain a Wife out of that can't you?

YES, Madam, *says I*, I could maintain a Wife, but not a Gamster, tho' you had brought me 1500*l*. a Year, no Estate is big enough for a Box and Dice.[345]

SHE took Fire at that, and flew out in a Passion, and after a great many bitter Words, told me in short, that she saw no occasion to alter her Conduct, and as for my not maintaining her, when I could not maintain her longer, she would find some way or other to maintain herself.

SOMETIME after the first Rattle[346] of this kind, she vouchsafed to let me know that she was pleas'd to be with Child; I was at first glad of it, in hopes it would help to abate her Madness; but it was all one, and her being with Child only added to the rest, for she made such Preparations for her lying in, and the other Appendixes of a Childs being born, that in short, I found she would be down right Distracted, and I took the Liberty to tell her one Day, that she would soon bring herself and me to Destruction, and entreated her to consider that such Figures [347] as those were quite above us, and out of our Circle; and in short, that I neither could, nor would allow such Expences; that at this Rate, two or three Children would effectually ruin me, and that I desir'd her to consider what she was doing.

SHE told me with an Air of disdain, that it was none of her Business to consider any thing of that matter, that if I could not allow it, she would allow it her self, and I might do my worst.

I begg'd her to consider things for all that, and not drive me to Extremities, that I married her to love and cherish her, and use her as a good Wife ought to be us'd, but not to be ruin'd, and undone by her. In a Word, nothing could molifie her, nor any Argument perswade her to Moderation, but withal took it so heiniously that I should pretend to restrain her, that she told me in so many Words, she would drop her Burthen with me,[348] and then if I did not like it, she would take care of herself, she would not live with me an Hour, for she would not be restrain'd not she, and talk'd a long while at that Rate.

I told her, as to her Child, which she call'd her Burthen, it should be no Burthen to me, as to the rest, she might do as she pleas'd; it might however do me this Favour, that I should have no more Lyings-Inn at the rate of 136*l.* at a time, as I found she intended it should be now; she told me she cou'd not tell that, if she had no more by me, she hop'd she should by some Body else; say you so Madam, *said I*, then they that get them, shall keep them? She did not know that neither, *she said*, and so turn'd it off Jearing, and as it were Laughing at me.

THIS last Discourse Nettl'd me, I must Confess, and the more, because I had a great deal of it, and very often, till in short, we began at length to enter into a Friendly Treaty about Parting.

NOTHING cou'd be more Criminal than the several Discourses we had upon this Subject; she demanding a separate Maintenance, and in particular at the Rate of 300*l.* a Year, and I demanded Security of her, that she should not run me in Debt; she Demanded the keeping of the Child, with an Allowance of 100*l.* a Year for that, and I Demanding that I should be secur'd from being Charg'd for keeping any she might have by some Body else, as she had threaten'd me.

IN the Interval, and during these Contests, she Drop'd her Burthen, *as she call'd it*, and brought me a Son, a very fine Child.

SHE was Content during her lying in, to abate a little, tho' it was but a very little indeed, of the great Expence she had intended; and with some Difficulty and Perswasion was content with a Suit of Child-bed-linnen of 15*l.* instead of one she had intended of Threescore; and this she magnified as a particular Testimony of her Condescension, and a yielding to my Avaricious Temper, *as she call'd it*.

BUT after she was up again, it was the same thing, and she went on with her Humour to that Degree, that in a little time she began to carry it on to other Excesses, and to have a sort of Fellows come to Visit her, which I did not like, and once in particular, stay'd Abroad all Night: The next Day when she came Home, she began to Cry out first; told me where (as she said) she lay, and that the Occasion was a Christening, where the Company had a Feast, and stay'd too late; that if I was dissatisfied, I might inform my self there of all the particulars, where she lay, *and the like*; I told her coldly, Madam, you do well to Suggest my being dissatisfied, for you may be sure I am, and you cou'd expect no other; that as to going to your Haunts to inform my self, that's not my Business; 'tis your Business to bring Testimonies of your Behaviour, and to prove where you lay, and in what Company, 'tis enough to me that you lay out of your own House, without your Husbands Knowledge or Consent, and before you and I Converse again, I must have some Satisfaction of the particulars.

SHE answer'd, with all her Heart, she was as Indifferent as I, and since I took so ill her lying at a Friend's House, on an extraordinary Occasion, she gave me to understand that it was what she would have me expect, and what she would have the Liberty to do, when she thought fit.

WELL, Madam, *said I*, if I must expect what I cannot allow, you must expect I shall shut my Doors by Day, against those that keep out of them at Night.

SHE would try me, *she said*, very speedily, and if I shut the Doors against her, she would find a way to make me open them.

WELL, Madam, *says I*, you threaten me hard, but I would advise you to consider before you take such Measures, for I shall be as good as my Word: However, it was not long that we cou'd live together upon these Terms; for I found very quickly what Company she kept, and that she took a Course which I ought not to bear; so I began the Separation first, and refus'd her my Bed: We had indeed refrain'd all Converse as Husband and Wife for about two Months before; for I told her very plainly, I would Father no Brats that were not of my own getting; and Matters coming thus Gradually to an Extremity, too great to continue as it was she went off one Afternoon, and left me a Line in Writing, signifying that Affairs were come to such a pass between us, that she did not think fit to give me the Opportunity of shutting her out of Doors, and that therefore, she had retir'd her self to such a Place; naming, a Relation of her own, as scandalous as her self; and that she hop'd I would not give her the trouble to Sue for her Support, in the ordinary Course of Law; but that as her Occasions requir'd, she should draw Bills upon me, which she expected I would not refuse.

I was extremely satisfied with this proceeding, and took care to let her hear of it, tho' I gave no answer at all to her Letter, and as I had taken care before, that whenever she play'd such a Prank as this, she should not be able to carry much with her; so after she was gone, I immediately broke up House-keeping, sold my Furniture by Publick out-cry,[349] and in it every thing in particular that was her own, and set a Bill upon my Door, giving her to understand by it, that she had pass'd *the Rubicon*,[350] that as she had taken such a step of her own Accord, so there was no room left her, ever to think of coming back again,

THIS was what any one may believe I should not have done, if I had seen any Room for a Reformation, but she had given me such Testimonies of a Mind alienated from her Husband in particular, Espousing her own unsufferable Levity, that there was indeed no possibility of our coming afterwards to any Terms again.

HOWEVER, I kept a Couple of trusty Agents so near her, that I fail'd not to have a full Account of her Conduct, tho' I never let her know any thing of me, but that I was gone over to *France*; as to her Bills which she said she would draw upon me, she was as good as her Word in drawing one of 30*l.*

which I refus'd to accept,[351] and never gave her leave to trouble me with another.

IT is true, and I must acknowledge it, that all this was a very Melancholy Scene of Life to me, and but that she took Care by carrying her self to the last Degree Provoking, and continually to Insult me, I cou'd never have gone on to the parting, with so much Resolution, for I really lov'd her very sincerely, and could have been any thing but a Beggar, and a Cuckold with her, but those were intollerable to me, especially, as they were put upon me with so much Insult, and Rudeness.

BUT my Wife carried it at last to a Point that made all things light and easy to me, for after above a Years Separation, and keeping such Company as she thought fit, she was pleas'd to be with Child again, in which she had, however, so much Honesty, as not to pretend that she had had any thing to do with me; what Wretched Life she led after this, and how she brought her self to the utmost Extremity of Misery and Distress, I may speak of hereafter.

I had found soon after our Parting, that I had a great deal of Reason to put my self into a Posture at first, not to be impos'd upon by her; for I found very quickly that she had run her self into Debt in several Places very Considerably; and that it was upon a Supposition, that I was liable to those Debts: But I was gone, and it was Absolutely necessary I should do so; upon which, she found her self oblig'd out of her wicked Gains, however, whatever she made of them, to Discharge most those Debts her self.

AS soon as she was deliver'd of her Child, in which my Intelligence was so good, that I had gotten sufficient Proof of it; I Sued her in the Ecclesiastick Court, in order to obtain a Divorce,[352] and as she found it impossible to avoid it, so she declin'd the Defence, and I gain'd a legal Decree, *or what they call it*, of Divorce, in the usual time of such Process, and now I thought my self a Freeman once again, and began to be Sick of Wedlock, with all my Heart.

I liv'd retir'd, because I knew she had Contracted Debts, which I should be oblig'd to Pay,[353] and I was resolv'd to be gone out of her reach, with what Speed I cou'd, but it was necessary that I should stay till the *Virginia* Fleet came in; because I look'd for at least 300 Hhds of *Tobacco* from thence, which I knew would heal all my Breaches; for indeed, the Extravagance of three Years with this Lady, had sunk me most effectually; even far beyond her own Fortune, which was Considerable, tho' not quite 1500*l. as she had call'd it*.

BUT all the Mischiefs I met with on Account of this Match, were not over yet, for when I had been parted with her about three Months, and had refus'd to accept her Bill of 30*l.* which I mention'd above, tho' I was remov'd from my first Lodgings too, and thought I had effectually secur'd myself from being found out, yet there came a Gentleman well Dress'd to my Lodgings one Day, and was let in before I knew of it, or else I should scarce have admitted him.

HE was led into a Parlour, and I came down to him in my Gown and Slippers; when I came into the Room, he call'd me as familiarly by my Name, as if he had known me twenty Year, and pulling out a Pocket-Book, he shows me a Bill upon me, drawn by my Wife, which was the same Bill for thirty Pound that I had refus'd before.

SIR, *says I*, this Bill has been presented before, and I gave my answer to it then.

ANSWER! Sir, *says he, with a kind of jeering taunting Air*, I don't understand what you mean by an answer, it is not a Question Sir, it is a Bill to be paid.

WELL, Sir, *says I*, it is a Bill, I know that, and I gave my answer to it before.

SIR, Sir, says he, *very saucily*, your Answer, there's no Answer to a Bill, it must be paid, Bills are to be paid, not to be answered, they say you are a Merchant, Sir, Merchants always pay their Bills.

I begun to be angry too a little, but I did not like my Man, for I found he began to be Quarrelsome; however *I said*, Sir, I perceive you are not much us'd to presenting Bills; Sir, a Bill is always first presented, and presenting, is a Question, 'tis asking if I will accept, or pay the Bill, and then whether I say yes, or no, 'tis an answer one way, or other; after 'tis accepted, it indeed requires no more answer but Payment when 'tis due; if you please to inform yourself, this is the usage which all Merchants or Tradesmen of any kind who have Bills drawn upon them, Act by.

WELL Sir, *says he*, and what then? what is this to the paying me the thirty Pounds?

WHY, Sir, *says I*, it is this to it, that I told the Person that brought it, I should not pay it.

NOT pay it, *says he*, but you shall pay it; ay, ay, you will pay it.

SHE that draws it, has no Reason to draw any Bills upon me, I am sure, *said I*, and I shall pay no Bills she draws, I assure you.

UPON this he turns short upon me, Sir, she that draws this Bill is a Person of too much Honour to draw any Bill without Reason, and 'tis an Affront to say so of her, and I shall expect satisfaction of you for that by itself, but first the Bill Sir, the Bill, you must pay, the Bill, Sir.

I return'd as short, Sir, I Affront no Body, I know the Person as well as you, I hope, and what I have said of her, is no Affront, she can have no Reason to draw Bills upon me, for I owe her nothing.

I omit intermingling the Oaths he lac'd his Speech with, as too foul for my Paper, but he told me he would make me know, she had Friends to stand by her, that I had abus'd her, and he would let me know it, and do her Justice; but first, I must pay his Bill.

I answer'd in short, I would not pay the Bill, nor any Bills he should draw.

With that he steps to the Door, and shuts it, and swore by G—d he would make me pay the Bill before we parted, and laid his Hand upon his Sword, but did not draw it out.

I confess I was frighted to the last degree, for I had no Sword, and if I had, I must own that tho' I had learn'd a great many good things in *France* to make me look like a Gentleman, I had forgot the main Article, of learning, how to use a Sword, a thing so universally practis'd there; and to say more, I had been perfectly unacquainted with Quarrels of this Nature; so that I was perfectly surpris'd when he shut the Door, and knew not what to say or do.

However as it happen'd, the People of the House hearing us pretty loud, came near the Door, and made a Noise in the Entry, to let me know they were at Hand, and one of the Servants going to open the Door, and finding it lock'd, call'd out to me, *Sir, for Godsake open the Door*, What is the matter? *Shall we fetch a Constable?* I made no Answer, but it gave me Courage, so I sat down compos'd, in one of the Chairs, and said to him, Sir, this is not the way to make me pay the Bill, you had much better be easy, and take your satisfaction another way.

He understood me of Fighting, which upon my Word, was not in my Thoughts, but I meant that he had better take his Course at Law.

With all my heart, *says he*, they say, you are a Gentleman, and they call you Colonel; now if you are a Gentleman, I accept your Challenge, Sir, and if you will walk out with me I'll take it for full payment of the Bill, and will decide it as Gentlemen ought to do.

I Challenge you, Sir, *said I*, not I, I made no Challenge, I said, this is not the way to make me pay a Bill, that I have not accepted, *that is*, that you had better seek your satisfaction at Law.

Law! *says he*, Law! Gentleman's Law is my Law; in short, Sir, you shall pay me, or Fight me; and then, as if he had mistaken, he turns short upon me; nay, *says he*, you shall both Fight me and pay me, for I will maintain her Honour; and in saying this, he bestow'd about six or seven Damme's and Oaths, by way of Parenthesis.

This interval deliver'd me effectually, for just at^a the Word *fight me*, for I will maintain her Honour, the Maid had brought in a Constable with three or four Neighbours to assist him.

HE heard them come in, and began to be a little in a Rage, and ask'd if I intended to Mob him, instead of paying, and laying his Hand on his Sword told me, if any Man offered to break in upon him, he would run me thro' the first Moment, that he might have the fewer to deal with afterwards.

I told him he knew I had call'd for no help, believing he could not be in earnest in what he had said, and that if any Body attempted to come in upon us, it was to prevent the Mischief he Threaten'd, and which he might see I had no Weapons to resist.

UPON this the Constable call'd, and charg'd us both in the King's Name to open the Door, I was sitting in a Chair, and offer'd to rise, he made a Motion, as if he would draw, upon which I sat down again, and the Door not being open'd, the Constable set his Foot against it and came in.

WELL, Sir, *says my Gentleman*, And what now? What's your Business here? Nay, Sir, *says the Constable*, you see my Business, I am a Peace-Officer, all I have to do is to keep the Peace, and I find the People of the House, frighted for fear of Mischief should be between you, have fetch'd me to prevent it; what Mischief have they suppos'd you should find, *says he*; I suppose, *says the Constable*, they were afraid you should Fight; that's because they did not know this Fellow here, he never fights, they call him Colonel, *says he*, I suppose he might be born a Colonel, for I dare say, he was born a Coward; he never Fights, he dares not see a Man, if he would have fought he would have walk'd out with me; but he scorns to be Brave, they would never have talk'd to you of Fighting, if they had known him; I tell you Mr. Constable he is a Coward, and a Coward is a Rascal; and with that he came to me, and strok'd his Finger down my Nose pretty hard, and laugh'd and mock'd most horridly, as if I was a Coward; now for ought I knew it might be true, but I was now what they call a Coward made desperate, which is one of the worst of Men in the World to Encounter with, for being in a Fury I threw my Head in his Face, and Closing with him, threw him fairly on his Back, by main Strength, and had not the Constable step'd in, and taken me off, I had certainly stamp'd him to Death, with my Feet, for my Blood was now all in a Flame, and the People of the House were frighted now as much the other way, least I should kill him, tho' I had no Weapon at all in my Hand.

THE Constable too reprov'd me in his turn, but I said to him, Mr. *Constable*, don't you think I am sufficiently Provok'd? Can any Man bear such things as these? I desire to know who this Man is, and who sent him hither.

I am, *says he*, a Gentleman, and come with a Bill to him for Money, and he refuses to Pay it; well, says the *Constable*, very Prudently, that's none of my Business, I am no Justice of Peace to hear the Cause, be that among your selves; but keep your Hands off of one another, and that's as much as

I desire; and therefore, Sir, says the *Constable* to him, if I may advise you, seeing he will not Pay the Bill, and that must be Decided between you as the Law directs, I would have you leave it for the present, and go quietly away.

HE made many Impertinent Harangues about the Bill, and insisted, that it was drawn by my own Wife; I said angrily, then it was drawn by a Whore, he Bullied me upon that, told me I durst not tell him so any where else; and I answer'd, I would very soon Publish her for a Whore to all the World, and Cry her down,[354] and thus we scolded for near half an Hour, for I took Courage when the *Constable* was there, for I knew that he would keep us from Fighting, which indeed I had no Mind to, and so at length I got Rid of him.

I was heartily vext at this Rencounter, and the more, because I had been found out in my Lodging, which I thought I had effectually Conceal'd: However, I resolv'd to remove the next Day, and in the mean time I kept within Doors all that Day till the Evening, and then I went out in order not to return thither any more.

BEING come out into *Grace-church-street*, I observ'd a Man follow'd me, with one of his Legs tied up in a String, and Hopping along with the other, and two Crutches; he begg'd for a Farthing, but I inclining not to give him any thing, the Fellow follow'd me still, till I came to a Court, when I answer'd hastily to him, I have not for you, pray don't be so troublesome; with which Words he knock'd me down with one of his Crutches.

BEING stunn'd with the blow I knew nothing what was done to me afterwards; but coming to myself again, I found I was wounded very frightfully in several Places, and that among the rest my Nose was slit upwards, one of my Ears cut almost off, and a great cut with a Sword on the Side of my Forehead, also a stab into the Body, tho' not Dangerous.

WHO had been near me, or struck me, besides the Cripple that struck me with his Crutch I knew not, nor do I know to this Hour, but I was terribly wounded, and lay bleeding on the Ground, sometime, till coming to my self I got strength to cry out for help, and People coming about me, I got some Hands to carry me to my Lodging, where I lay by it more than two Months, before I was well enough to go out of Doors, and when I did go out, I had Reason to believe that I was waited for by some Rogues, who watch'd an opportunity to repeat the injury I had met with before.

THIS made me very uneasie, and I resolv'd to get myself out of Danger, if possible, and to go over to *France*, or home, *as I call'd it*, to *Virginia*; so to be out of the way of Villains, and Assassinations; for every time I stirr'd out here, I thought I went in danger of my Life, and therefore, as before I went out at Night, thinking to be conceal'd, so now I never went out, but in open Day that I might be safe, and never without one or two Servants to be my Life Guard.

BUT I must do my Wife a peice of Justice here too, and that was that hearing of what had befallen me she wrote me a Letter, in which she treated me more Decently than she had been wont to do, said she was very sorry to hear how I had been used, and the rather because she understood it was on presenting her Bill to me; she said she hop'd I could not in my worst Dispositions think so hardly of her, as to believe it was done by her Knowledge, or Consent, much less by her Order, or Direction; that she abhorr'd such things, and Protested if she had the least Knowledge, or so much as a guess at the Villains concern'd she would Discover them to me; she let me know the Persons Name to whom she gave the Bill, and where he liv'd, and left it to me to oblige him to discover the Person who had brought it and us'd me so ill, and wish'd I might find him, and bring him to Justice, and have him punish'd with the utmost severity of the Law.

I TOOK this so kindly of my Wife, that I think in my Conscience, had she come after it herself, to see how I did, I had certainly taken her again; but she satisfy'd herself with the Civility of another Letter, and desiring me to let her know as often as I could how I was, adding, that it would be infinitely to her satisfaction to hear I was recover'd of the hurt I had receiv'd, and that he was hang'd at *Tyburn*, who had done it.

SHE us'd some Expressions, signifying as I understood them, her Affliction at our parting, and her continu'd Respect for me, but did not make any Motion towards returning; then she us'd some Arguments, to move me to pay her Bills, intimating that she had brought me a large Fortune, and now had nothing to subsist, which was very severe.

I Wrote her an Answer to this Letter, tho' I had not to the other, letting her know how I had been us'd, that I was satisfied upon her Letter, that she had no hand in it; that it was not in her Nature to treat me so, who had never injur'd her, us'd any Violence with her, or been the Cause, or desire of our parting; that as to her Bill, she could not but know how much her Expensive way of living had straitn'd, and reduc'd me, and would if continu'd have ruin'd me, that she had in less than three Years spent more than as much as she brought to me and would not abate her Expensive way tho' calmly intreated by me, with Protestations, that I could not Support so great an Expence, but Chose rather to break up her Family, and go from me, than to restrain herself to reasonable Limits, tho' I used no Violence with her, but Entreaties, and earnest Perswasions, back'd with good Reasons; letting her know how my Estate was, and convincing her that it must reduce us to Poverty at least; that however, if she would recall her Bill, I would send her 30*l*. which was the Sum mention'd in her Bill, and according to my Ability would not let her want, if she pleas'd to live within due Bounds; but then I let her know also, that I had a very bad Account of her Conduct, and that she kept Company with a scandalous Fellow, who I nam'd to her; that I was loth to believe such things of her, but that to put an entire End to the Report, and Restore her Reputation, I let her know that still after all I had heard, if she would resolve to live without Restraints within the reasonable Bounds of my Capacity, and Treat me with the same Kindness and Affection, and Tenderness, as I always had Treated her, and ever would; I was willing to receive her again, and would forget all that was past, but that if she declin'd me now, it would be for ever, for if she did not accept my offer, I was resolv'd to stay here no longer, where I had been so ill Treated on many Occasions; but was preparing to go into my own Country, where I would spend my Days in Quiet, and in a Retreat from the World.

SHE did not give such an Answer to this, as I expected; for tho' she thank'd me for the 30*l.* yet she insisted upon her Justification in all other Points, and tho' she did not refuse to return to me, yet she did not say she Accepted it, and in short, said little or nothing to it, only a kind of Claim to a Reparation of her Injur'd Reputation, *and the like.*

THIS gave me some Surprize at first, for I thought indeed, any Woman in her Circumstances would have been very willing to have put an End to all her Miseries, and to the Reproach that was upon her, by a Reconciliation; especially, considering she subsisted at that time but very meanly: But there was a particular Reason, which prevented her return, and which she cou'd not Plead to me in her Letter, yet was a good Reason against accepting an offer, which she would otherwise have been glad of, and this was that, as I have mention'd above, she had fallen into bad Company, and had prostituted her Vertue to some of her Flatterers, and in short, was with Child; so that she durst not venture to accept my offer.

HOWEVER, as I observe above, she did not absolutely refuse it, intending (as I understood afterward,) to keep the Treaty of it on Foot, till she could Drop her Burthen, as she had call'd it before; and having been deliver'd privately, have accepted my Proposal afterward: And indeed, this was the most Prudent step she cou'd take, or, as we may say, the only step she had left to take: But I was too many for her here too, my Intelligence about her was too good, for her to Conceal such an Affair from me, unless she had gone away before she was visibly Big, and unless she had gone farther off too than she did, for I had an Account to a Tittle, of the time when and Place where, and the Creature of which she was deliver'd, and then my Offers of taking her again were at an End, tho' she Wrote me several very Penitent Letters, acknowledging her Crime, and begging me to forgive her;

but my Spirit was above all that now, nor cou'd I ever bear the Thoughts of her after that: But persued a Divorce, and accordingly obtain'd it, as I have mention'd already.

THINGS being at this pass, I resolv'd, as I have observ'd above, to go over to *France*, after I had receiv'd my Effects from *Virginia*, and accordingly I came to *Dunkirk* in the Year — and here I fell into Company with some *Irish* Officers of the Regiment of *Dillon*,[355] who by little and little Enter'd me into the Army, and by the help of Lieutenant General — an *Irishman*, and some Money, I obtain'd a Company in his Regiment, and so went into the Army directly.

I was exceedingly pleas'd with my new Circumstances, and now I us'd to say to my self, I was come to what I was Born to, and that I had never till now liv'd the Life of a Gentleman.

OUR Regiment, after I had been some time in it, was Commanded into *Italy*,[356] and one of the most considerable Actions that I was in, was the Famous Attack upon *Cremona*,[357] in the *Millanese*,[358] where the *Germans*[359] being Privately, and by Treachery let into the Town in the Night, thro' a kind of Common-Shoar,[360] surpriz'd the Town, and got possession of the greatest Part of it, surprizing the Mareschal Duke *de Villeroy*,[361] and taking him Prisoner as he came out of his Quarters, and beating the few *French* Troops, which were left, into the Citadel: But were in the middle of their Victory so boldly, and resolutely attack'd by two *Irish* Regiments, who were Quarter'd in the *Street* leading to the River *Po* and who kept Possession of the Water-Gate, or *Po* Gate of the Town, by which the *German* Reinforcements should have come in, that after a most desperate Fight, the *Germans* had their Victory wrung out of their Hands, and not being able to break thro' us to let in their Friends, were oblig'd at length to quit the Town again, to the eternal Honour of those *Irish* Regiments, and indeed of their whole Nation, and for which we had a very handsome Compliment from the King of *France*.

I now had the satisfaction of knowing, and that for the first time too, that I was not that cowardly low spirited Wretch, that I was, when the Fellow Bullied me in my Lodgings, about the Bill of 30*l.* had he attack'd me now, tho' in the very same Condition, I should naked and unarm'd as I was have flown in the Face of him, and trampl'd him under my Feet; but Men never know themselves till they are tried, and Courage is acquir'd by time, and Experience of things.

Philip de Comines[362] tells us, that after the Battle of *Monteleri*, the Count de *Charolois*,[363] who till then had an utter Aversion to the War, and abhorr'd it, and every thing that belong'd to it, was so chang'd by the Glory he obtain'd in that Action, and by the Flattery of those about him, that afterwards, the Army was his Mistress, and the Fateigues of the War his chief Delight; 'tis too great an Example for me to bring in my own Case, but so it was, that they Flattered me so with my bravery as they call'd it on the Occasion of this Action, that I fancy'd myself Brave, whether I was so or not, and the Pride of it made me Bold, and Daring to the last Degree on all Occasions; but what added to it, was, that some Body gave a particular Account to the Court of my being Instrumental to the saving the City and the whole *Cremonese*, by my extraordinary Defence of the *Po* Gate, and by my Managing that Defence after the Lieutenant Colonel, who Commanded the Party where I was Posted was kill'd; upon which, the King sent me a publick Testimony of his accepting my Service, and sent me a Breviat[364] to be a Lieutenant Colonel, and the next Courier brought me actually a Commission for Lieutenant Colonel in the Regiment of —.

I WAS in several Skirmishes and petty Encounters before this, by which I gain'd the Reputation of a good Officer, but I happen'd to be in some particular Posts too, by which I got somewhat that I lik'd much better, and that was a good deal of Money.

OUR Regiment was sent from *France* to *Italy* by Sea, we embark'd at *Thoulon*, and Landed at *Savona* in the Territory of *Genoa*, and march'd from thence to the Dutchy of *Millan*: At the first Town we were sent to take Possession of, which was *Alexandria*,[365] the Citizens rose upon our Men in a most furious manner, and drove the whole Garrison, which consisted of 800 Men, that is *French*, and Soldiers in the *French* Service quite out of the Town.

I was Quarter'd in a Burghers House, just by one of the Ports[366] with Eight of my Men, and a Servant; where calling a short Council with my Men, we resolv'd to maintain the House we was in, whatever it Cost, till we receiv'd Order to quit it from the Commanding Officer; and upon this, when I saw our Men cou'd not stand their Ground in the Street, being press'd hard by the Citizens, I turn'd out of Doors all the Family, and kept the House, as a Castle which I was Governor in; and as the House join'd to the City Gate, I resolv'd to maintain it, so as to be the last that should quit the Place, my own Retreat being secur'd by being so near the Port.

HAVING thus emptyed the House of the Inhabitants, we made no Scruple of filling our Pockets with whatever we could find there, in a Word, we left nothing we could carry away; among which, it came to my Lot to Dip into the Burghers Cabinet, whose House it was where we were; and there I took about the Quantity of 200 Pistols[367] in Money and Plate, and other things of Value. There was great Complaint made to Prince *Vaudemont*,[368] who was then Governor of the *Millanese* of this Violence; but as the Repulse the Citizens gave us, was contrary to his Order, and to the general Design of the Prince, who was then wholy in the Interest of King *Philip*,[369] the Citizens cou'd obtain nothing, and I found, that if we had Plunder'd the whole City, it would have been the same thing; for the Governor had Order to take our Regiment in, and it was an Act of open Rebellion to resist us as they did; however, we had orders not to Fire upon the Burghers, unless constrain'd to it by evident Necessity, and we rather chose to quit the Place, as we did, then Dispute it with a Desperate Body of Fellows, who wanted no Advantage of us, except only that, of having Possession of two Bastions, and one Port for our Retreat; first they were Treble our Number, for the Burghers being join'd by seven Companies of the regular Troops, made up above 1600 Men, besides Rabble which was many more; whereas, we were about 800 in all; they also had the Cittadel and several Peices of Cannon, so that we cou'd have made nothing of it, if we had attack'd them; but they submitted three or four Days after to other Forces, the Soldiers within turning upon them, and taking the Cittadel from them.

AFTER this, we lay still in Quarters 8 Months, for the Prince having secur'd the whole *Millanese* for King *Philip*, and no Enemy appearing for some time, had nothing to do, but to receive the Auxiliar Troops of *France*; and as they came, extend himself every way as he cou'd, in order to keep the Imperialists (who were preparing to fall into *Italy* with a great Army) as much at a Distance as possible, which he did, by taking Possession of the City of *Mantua*, and of most of the Towns on that Side, as far as the Lake *dela Guarda*, and the River *Addige*.

WE lay in *Mantua* some time, but were afterwards drawn out by Order of the Count *de Tesse*,[370] (afterwards Marshal of *France*) to Form the *French* Army, till the Arrival of the Duke *de Vandosme*,[371] who was to Command in Chief. Here we had a Severe Campaign, *Anno* 1701. having Prince *Eugene* of *Savoy*,[372] and an Army of 40000 *Germans*, all old Soldiers to deal with, and tho' the *French* Army was more Numerous than the Enemy, by 25000 Men, yet being on the Defensive, and having so many Posts to Cover, not knowing exactly where the Prince of *Savoy*, who commanded the Imperial Army would attack us; it oblig'd the *French* to keep their Troops so divided, and so remote from one another, that the *Germans* push'd on their Design with great Success as the Histories of those Times more fully relate.

I WAS at the Action at *Carpi, July* 1701,[373] where we were worsted by the *Germans*; indeed, were forc'd to quit our Encampment, and give up to the Prince the whole River of *Addige*, and where our Regiment sustain'd some Loss, but the Enemies got little by us, and Monsieur *Catinate*,[374] who Commanded at that time drew up in order of Battle the next Day in sight of the *German* Army, and gave them a defiance, but they would not stir, tho' we offer'd them Battle two Days together, for having gain'd the Passage over the *Addige*, by our quitting *Rivoli*, which was then useless to us, their Business was done.

FINDING they declin'd a decisive Action, our Generals press'd them in their Quarters, and made them fight for every Inch of Ground they gain'd, and at length in the *September* following, we attack'd them in their entrench'd Posts of *Chiar*,[375] here we broke into the very heart of their Camp, where we made a very terrible Slaughter, but I know not by what Mistake among our Generals, or Defect in the Execution of their Orders, the Brigade of *Normandy*, and our *Irish* Brigade, who had so Bravely enter'd the *German* Intrenchments were not supported as we should have been, so that we were oblig'd to sustain the shock of the whole *German* Army, and at last to quit the Advantage we had gain'd, and that not without Loss, but being timely reinforc'd by a great Body of Horse, the Enemy were in their Turn beaten off too, and driven back into their very Camp: The *Germans* boasted of having a great Victory here, and indeed in repulsing us after we had gain'd their Camp they had the advantage, but had Monsieur *de Tesse* succoured us in time, as old *Catinat* said he ought to have done, with 12000 Foot which he had with him, that Days Action had put an End to the War, and Prince *Eugene* must have been glad to have gone back to *Germany* in more hast than he came, if perhaps we had not cut him short by the way.

BUT the Fate of things went another way, and the *Germans* continu'd all that Campaign to push forward, and advance one Post after another, till they beat us quite out of the *Millanese*.

THE latter part of this Campaign we made only a party War,[376] the *French* according to their volatile Temper, being every Day abroad, either Forraging or surprizing the Enemies foragers, plundering, or circumventing the Plunders of the other Side, and that tho' they very often come short home; for the *Germans* had the better of them on several Occasions, and indeed so many lost their lives upon those petty Encounters, that I think including those who dyed of Distempers gotten by hard Service, and bad Quarters, lying in the Field, even till the middle of *December*, among Rivers, and Bogs in a Country so full of Canals and Rivers, as that Part of *Italy* is known to be, *I say*, we lost more Men, and so did the Enemy also, than would have been lost in a general decisive Battle.

THE Duke of *Savoy*,[377] to give him his due, press'd earnestly to put it to a Day, and come to a Battle with Prince *Eugene*, but the Duke *de Villeroy*, Monsieur *Catinate*, and the Count *de Tesse*, were all against it, and the principal Reason was, that they knew the weakness of the Troops, who had suffer'd so much on so many Occasions, that they were in no Condition to give Battle to the *Germans*; so after, as *I say*, about three Months Harrassing one another with Parties we went into Winter Quarters.

BEFORE we march'd out of the Field, our Regiment with a Detachment of Dragoons of 600, and about 250 Horse went without a Design to intercept Prince *Commercy*,[378] a General of Note under Prince *Eugene* of *Savoy*; the Detachment was intended to be only Horse and Dragoons, but because it was the Imperialists good luck to beat many of our Parties, and as was given out, many more than we beat of theirs; and because it was believed that the Prince, who was an Officer of good Note among them would not go abroad, but in very Company, the *Irish* Regiment of Foot was order'd to be added, that if possible they might meet with their Match.

I WAS commanded about two Hours before, to pass about 200 Foot, and 50 Dragoons, at a small Wood, where our General had intelligence that the Prince[a] would Post some Men, to secure his Passage, which accordingly I did; but Count *Tesse* not thinking our Party strong enough, had march'd himself with a Thousand Horse, and 300 Grenadiers to Support us, and it was very well he did so; for Prince *Commercy* having Intelligence of the first Party, came forward sooner than they expected, and fell upon them, and had entirely Routed them, had not the Count hearing the firing, advanc'd with the Thousand Horse he had with such Expedition, as to support his Men in the very heat of the Action, by which means the *Germans* were defeated, and forc'd to retire; but the Prince made a pretty good Retreat, and after the Action came on to the Wood, where I was posted, but the surprise of his Defeat had prevented his sending a Detachment to secure the Pass at the Wood, as he intended.

THE Count *de Tesse*, understanding that we were sent, *as above*, to the Wood, follow'd them close at the Heels to prevent our being cut off, and if it were possible that we should give them any Check at the Wood, to fall in, and have another Brush with them; it was near Night before they came to the Wood, by which means they could not discern our Number, but when they came up to the Wood, 50 Dragoons advanc'd to discover the Pass, and see if all was clear: These we suffer'd to pass a great way into the Defile, or Lane, that went thro' the Wood, and then clapping in between them, and the Enterance, cut off their Retreat so effectually, that when they discover'd us, and fir'd, they were instantly surrounded and cut in peices; the Officer who commanded them, and eight Dragoons only being made Prisoners.

THIS made the Prince halt, not knowing what the Case was, or how strong we were, and to get better Intelligence, sent 200 Horse to surround or Skirt the Wood, and beat up our Quarter, and in the intrim, the Count *de Tesse* appear'd, in his Rear: We found the strait he was in, by the Noise of our own Troops at a Distance, so we resolv'd to Engage the 200 Horse immediately; accordingly our little Troop of Horse drew up in the Entrance of the Lane, and offer'd to Skirmish, and our Foot lying behind the Hedge, which went round the Wood, stood ready to act as occasion should offer; the Horse being attack'd gave way, and retir'd into the Lane, but the *Germans* were too old for us there, they contented themselves to push us to the Enterance, but would not be drawn into a narrow Pass without knowing whether the Hedges were Lin'd or no.

BUT the Prince finding the *French* in his Rear, and not being strong enough to Engage again, resolv'd to force his way thro', and commanded his Dragoons to alight, and enter the Wood to clear the Hedges on either Side the Lane, that he might pass with his Cavalry; this they did so vigorously, and were so much too strong for us, that tho' we made good our Ground a long time, yet our Men were almost half of them cut in pieces. However, we gave time to the *French* Cavalry to come up, and to fall on the Prince's Troops, and cut them off, and take a great many Prisoners, and then retreated in our Turn, opening a Gap for our own Horse to break in; 300 of the Dragoons were kill'd, and 200 of them taken Prisoners.

IN the first heat of this Action, a *German* Officer of Dragoons well follow'd, had knock'd down three of my Men that stood next me, and offering me Quarter, I was oblig'd to accept it, and gave him my Sword, for our Men were upon the Point of quitting their Post, and shifting every one[379] as they could; but the Scale was turn'd, for our Cavalry breaking in, *as above*, the Dragoons went to wreck, and the Officer who had me Prisoner, turning to me said, *we are all Lost*; I asked him if I could serve him, stand still a little, *says he*, for his Men fought most desperately indeed, but about 200 *French* Horse appearing in his Rear too, *he said*, to me in *French*, I will be your Prisoner, and returning me my Sword, gave me also his own; a Dragoon that stood near him was just going to do the like when he was shot dead, and the Horse coming up, the Field was cleared in an Instant, but Prince *Commercy* went off with the rest of his Party, and was pursued no farther.

THERE were sixteen or seventeen of our Men releas'd, as I was, from being taken; but they had not the luck I had, to take the Officer that had them in keeping; he had been so generous to me, as not to ask what Money I had about me, tho' I had not much, if he had; but I lost by his Civility, for then I could not have the Assurance to ask him for his Money tho' I understood he had near a 100 Pistols about him; but he very handsomely at Night, when we came to our Tents made me a Present of 20 Pistols, and in return I obtain'd leave for him to go to Prince *Eugen*'s Camp upon his Parole, which he did, and so got himself exchang'd.

IT was after this Campaign that I was Quartered at *Cremona*, when the Action happen'd there, of which I have spoken already, and where our *Irish* Regiment did such Service, that they sav'd the Town from being really sur-priz'd, and indeed beat the *Germans* out again after they had been Masters of three Quarters of the Town six Hours, and by which they gain'd a very great Reputation.

BUT I hasten on to my own History, for I am not writing a Journal of the Wars, in which I had no long Share.

THE Summer after this, our two *Irish* Regiments were drawn out into the Field, and had many a sore Brush with the *Germans*, for Prince *Eugene*, a vigilant General, gave us little Rest, and gain'd many Advantages by his continual moving up and down, Harrassing his own Men, and ours too; and whoever will do the *French* Justice, and knew how they had behaved, must ackowledge, they never declin'd the *Germans*, but fought them upon all Occasions, with the utmost Resolution and Courage, and tho' it cost the Blood of an infinite Number of fine Gentlemen, as well as private Soldiers, yet the Duke *de Vendome*, who now Commanded, tho' King *Philip* was him-self in the Army this Campaign, made the Prince of *Savoy* a full return in his own kind, and drove him from Post to Post, till he was just at the Point of quitting the whole Country of *Italy*; all that gallant Army Prince *Eugene* brought with him into *Italy*, which was the best without doubt, for the goodness of the Troops that ever were there, laid their Bones in that Coun-try, and many Thousands more after them; till the Affairs of *France* declining in other Places, they were forc'd in their Turn to give way to their Fate, as may be seen in the Histories of those Times, *as above*, but 'tis none of my Business.

THE part that I bore in these Affairs was but short and sharp, we took the Field about the beginning of *July* 1702, and the Duke *de Vendome* order'd the whole Army to draw the sooner together, in order to relieve the City of *Mantua*, which was block'd up by the Imperialists.

PRINCE *Eugene* was a Politick, and indeed a fortunate Prince, and had the Year before pushed our Army upon many Occasions; but his good Fortune began to fail him a little this Year, for our Army was not only more Numer-ous than his, but the Duke was in the Field before him, and as the Prince had held *Mantua* closely block'd up all the Winter, the Duke resolv'd to relieve the Town, cost what it would: As *I said*, the Duke was first in the Field, the Prince was in no Condition to prevent his raising the Blockade by force; so he drew off his Troops, and leaving several strong Bodies of Troops to protect *Bersello*, which the Duke *de Vendomse* threaten'd, and *Borgofort*, where his Magazine lay, he drew all the rest of his Forces together, to make Head against us; by this time the King of *Spain*, was come into the Army, and the Duke *de Vendomse* lay, with about 35000 Men, near *Luzara*, which he had resolv'd to attack, to bring Prince *Eugene* to a Battle: The Prince of *Vaudemont* lay Entrench'd with 20000 more at *Rivalto*, behind *Mantua*, to cover the Frontiers of *Millan*, and there was near 12000 in *Mantua* itself; and Monsieur *Pracontal*[380] lay with 10000 Men, just under the Cannon of one of the Forts, which Guard the Causeway, which leads into the City of *Mantua*: So that had all these joyn'd, as they would have done in a few Days more, the Prince must have been put to his shifts, and would have had enough to do, to have maintain'd himself in *Italy*; for he was Master of no one Place in the Country, that could have held out a formal Seige of fifteen Days open Trenches, and he knew all this very well, and therefore it seems, while the Duke of *Vendosme*, resolv'd if possible to bring him to a Battle, and to that End, made Dispositions to attack *Luzara*; we were surpriz'd to find the 15th of *June*, 1702, the whole Imperial Army appear'd in Batalia,[381] and in full March to attack us.

As it happen'd, our Army was all marching in Columns towards them, as we had done for two Days before, and I should have told you, that three Days before, the Duke having Notice that General *Visconti*,[382] with three Imperial Regiments of Horse, and one of Dragoons, was posted at *San-Victoria*, on the *Tessona*, he resolv'd to attack them, and this Design was carried so secretly that while Monsieur *Visconti*, tho' our Army was three Leagues another way, was passing[a] towards the *Modenese*, he found himself unexpectedly attack'd by 6000 Horse, and Dragoons of the *French* Army: He defended himself very Bravely, for near an Hour; when being over powr'd,[b] and finding he should be forc'd into Disorder, he sounded a Retreat, but the Squadrons had not fac'd about to make their Retreat scarce a Quarter of an Hour, when they found themselves surrounded with a great Body of Infantry, who had entirely cut off their Retreat, except over the Bridge of *Tassona*, which being throng'd with their Baggage, they could neither get backward or forward; so they Thrust and tumbl'd over one another, in such a manner, that they could preserve no kind of Order; but abundance fell into the River, and were drowned, many were kill'd, and more taken Prisoners, so that in a Word the whole three Regiments of Horse, and one of Dragoons, were entirely Defeated.

THIS was a great Blow to the Prince, because they were some of the choicest Troops of his whole Army: We took about 400 Prisoners, and all their Baggage, which was a very considerable Booty, and about 800 Horses; and no doubt these Troops were very much wanted in the Battle that insued on the 15th; as I have said: Our Army being in full March, as *above*, to attack *Luzara*, a Party of the *Germans* appear'd, being about 600 Horse, and in less than an Hour more, their whole Army in order of Battle.

OUR Army form'd immediately, and the Duke posted the Regiments as they came up, so much to their Advantage, that Prince *Eugene* was oblig'd to alter his Dispositions, and had this particular Inconvenience upon his Hands, (*viz.*) to attack an Army superior to his own, in all their most advantagious Posts; whereas had he thought fit to have waited but one Day, we should have met him half way; but this was owing to the Pride of the *German* Generals, and their being so Opiniated of the goodness of their Troops: The Royal Army was Posted with the Left to the great River *Po*, on the other Side of which the Prince of *Vaudemont*'s Army lay, Canonading of the intrenchments which the Imperialists had made at *Borgo-Fort*, and hearing that there was like to be a general Battle, he detach'd 12 Battalions, and about 1000 Horse to Reinforce the Royal Army; all which to our great Encouragement had time to joyn the Army, while Prince *Eugene* was making his new Dispositions for the attack; and yet it was the coming of these Troops which caus'd Prince *Eugene* to resolve to begin the Fight, expecting to have come to an Action before they cou'd come up, but he was disappointed in the Reason of Fighting, and yet was oblig'd to Fight too, which was an Error in the Prince, that it was too late to retrieve.

IT was five a-Clock in the Evening before he could bring up his whole Line to Engage, and then after having Canonaded us to no great purpose half an Hour, his Right commanded by the Prince *de Comercy* attack'd our Left Wing with great Fury: Our Men receiv'd them so well, and seconded one another so punctually, that they were Repulsed with a very great Slaughter, and the Prince *Comercy*, being (unhappily for them) kill'd in the first Onset, the Regiments for want of Orders, and surpris'd with the fall of so great a Man, were push'd into disorder, and one whole Brigade was entirely broke.

BUT their second Line advancing under General *Herbeville*,[383] restor'd things, in the first; the Battalions rallyed, and they came boldly on to Charge a second time, and being Seconded, with new Reinforcements from their main Body, our Men had their Turn, and were push'd to a Canal, which lay on their left Flank, between them and the *Po*, behind which they rally'd, and being supported by new Troops, as well Horse as Foot; they fought on both Sides, with the utmost obstinacy, and with such Courage and Skill, that it was not possible to judge who should have had the better, could they have been able to have fought it out.

ON the Right of the Royal Army was Posted, the Flower of the *French* Cavalry; Namely, the *Gens de Arms*, the Royal Carabineers, and the Queen's Horse-Guards, with 400 Horse more, and next them the Infantry, among which were our Brigade; the Horse advanc'd first to Charge and they carried all before them Sword in Hand, receiving the Fire of two Imperial

Regiments of Curiassers, without firing a Shot, and falling in among them, bore them down by the strength of their Horses, putting them into Confusion, and left so clear a Field for us to follow, that the first Line of our Infantry stood drawn up upon the Ground, which the Enemy at first possest.

IN this first attack the Marquiss *de Crequi*,[384] who Commanded the whole Right Wing, was killed; a Loss, which fully ballanc'd the Death of the Prince *de Commercy*, on the Side of the *Germans*; after we had thus pushed the Enemies Cavalry, *as above*, their Troops, being rally'd by the Dexterity of their Generals, and supported by three Imperial Regiments of Foot, they came on again to the Charge with such Fury, that nothing could withstand them; and here two Battalions of our *Irish* Regiments were put into Disorder, and abundance of our Men kill'd, and here also I had the Misfortune to receive a Musquet shot, which broke my left Arm, and, that was not all, for I was knock'd down by a Gyant like a *German* Soldier, who when he thought he had kill'd me, set his Foot upon me, but was immediately shot dead by one of my Men, and fell just upon me, which, my Arm being broken, was a very great mischief to me, for the very weight of the Fellow, who was almost as big as a Horse, was such, that I was not able to stir.

OUR Men were beaten back after this, from the Place where they stood, and so I was left in Possession of the Enemy, but was not their Prisoner, (*that is to say*, was not found) till next Morning, when a Party being sent, as usual with Surgeons to look after the wounded Men, among the Dead, found me almost smothered with the dead *Germans*, and others that lay near me; however, to do them justice, they us'd me with humanity, and the Surgeons set my Arm very Skilfully, and well; and after four or five Days I had liberty to go to *Parma* upon my Parole.

BOTH the Armies continued fighting, especially on our Left, till it was so dark, that it was impossible to know, who they fir'd at, or for the Generals to see what they did; so they abated firing Gradually, and as it may be truly said, the Night parted them.

BOTH Sides claim'd the Victory, and both conceal'd their Losses, as much as was possible, but 'tis certain that never Battle was fought with greater Bravery, and Obstinacy than this was, and had there been Day light to have fought it out, doubtless there would have been many Thousand Men more kill'd on both Sides.

ALL the *Germans* had to entitle them to the Victory was, that they made our Left retire, as I have said to the Canal, and to the high Banks, or Mounds on the edge of the *Po*; but they had so much Advantage in the

Retreat, that they fir'd from thence among the thickest of the Enemy, and cou'd never be forc'd from their Posts.

THE best Testimony the Royal Army had of the Victory, and which was certainly the better of the two, was, that two Days after the Fight, they attack'd *Guastalla*, as it were in View of the *German* Army, and forc'd the Garrison to surrender, and to swear not to Serve again for six Months, which they being 1500 Men, was a great Loss to the *Germans*, and yet Prince *Eugene* did not offer to Relieve it; and after that we took several other Posts, which the Imperialists had Possession of, but were oblig'd to Quit them upon the approach of the *French* Army, not being in Condition to Fight another Battle that Year.

MY Campaign was now at an End, and tho' I came Lame off, I came off much better than abundance of Gentlemen, for in that bloody Battle we had above 400 Officers kill'd or wounded, whereof three were General Officers.

THE Campaign held on till *December*, and the Duke *de Vendomse* took *Borgo Fort*, and several other Places from the *Germans*, who in short, lost Ground every Day in *Italy*; I was a Prisoner a great while, and there being no Cartel[385] settled, Prince *Eugene* order'd the *French* Prisoners to be sent into *Hungary*, which was a Cruelty that could not be reasonably exercised on them; however, a great many by that Banishment, found means to make their Escape to the *Turks*, by whom they were kindly receiv'd, and the *French* Ambassador at *Constantinople* took care of them, and Shipp'd them back again into *Italy* at the King's Charge.

BUT the Duke *de Vendomse* now took so many *Germans* Prisoners, that Prince *Eugene* was tyr'd[a] of sending his Prisoners to *Hungary*, and was oblig'd to be at the Charge of bringing some of them back again, who he had sent thither, and come to agree to a general Exchange of Prisoners.

I was, as I have said, allow'd for a time to go to *Parma*, upon my Parole, where I continu'd for the recovery of my Wound, and broken Arm, forty Days, and was then oblig'd to render my self to the Commanding Officer at *Ferrara*, where Prince *Eugene* coming soon after, I was with several other Prisoners of War, sent away into the *Milanese* to be kept for an Exchange of Prisoners.

IT was in the City of *Trent*, that I continu'd about eight Months, the Man in whose House I Quartered, was exceeding Civil to me, and took a great deal of care of me, and I liv'd very easie; here I contracted a kind of Familiarity, perfectly undesign'd by me, with the Daughter of the Burgher at whose House I had Lodg'd, and I know not, by what fatallity that was upon me, I was prevail'd with afterward to Marry her: This was a peice of Honesty on my Side, which I must acknowledge, I never intended to be guilty of; but the Girl was too cunning for me; for she found means to get some Wine into my Head more than I us'd to drink, and tho' I was not so disorder'd with it, but that I knew very well what I did, yet in an unusual height of good Humour, I consented to be Married. This impolitick piece of Honesty put me to many Inconveniences, for I knew not what to do with this new Clog, which I had loaded myself with, I could neither stay with her, or take her with me, so that I was exceedingly perplex'd.

THE time came soon after that I was releas'd by the *Chartel*,[386] and so was oblig'd to go to the Regiment, which then was in Quarters in the *Milanese*, and from thence, I got leave to go to *Paris* upon my Promise to raise some Recruits in *England* for the *Irish* Regiments, by the help of my Correspondence there; having thus leave to go to *Paris*, I took a Passport from the Enemy's Army, to go to *Trent*, and making a long Circuit, I went back thither, and very honestly pack'd up my Baggage, Wife, and all, and brought her away thro' *Tyrol*, into *Bavaria*, and so thro' *Suabia*, and the black Forest into *Alsatia* from thence, I came into *Louvain*, and so to *Paris*.

I HAD now a secret Design to quit the War, for I really had enough of fighting; but it was counted so Dishonorable a Thing to quit, while the Army was in the Field, that I could not Dispense with it, but an intervening Accident made that Part easie to me: The War was now renewed between *France*, and *England* and *Holland*, just as it was before; and the *French* King meditating nothing more than how to give the *English* a Diversion, fitted out a strong Squadron of Men of War, and Frigates at *Dunkirk*, on Board of which he embark'd a Body of Troops, of about 6500 Men, besides Voluntiers, and the new King, as we call'd him, tho' more generally he was called the Chevalier *de* St. *George*[387] was Shipp'd along with them, and all for *Scotland*.

I pretended a great deal of Zeal for this Service, and that if I might be permitted to sell my Company in the *Irish* Regiment I was in, and have the *Chevalier's* Brevet for a Colonel, in Case of raising Troops for him in *Great Britain*, after his arrival, I would embark Voluntier, and Serve at my own Expence; the latter gave me a great advantage with the *Chevalier*; for now I was esteem'd as a Man of Consideration, and one that must have a considerable Interest in my own Country; so I obtain'd leave to sell my Company, and having had a good round Sum of Money remitted me from *London*, by the way of *Holland*, I prepar'd a very handsome Equipage, and away I went to *Dunkirk* to embark.

I WAS very well receiv'd by the *Chevalier*, and as he had an Account that I was an Officer in the *Irish* Brigade, and had serv'd in *Italy*, and consequently was an old Soldier, all this added to the Character which I had before, and made me have a great deal of Honour paid me, tho' at the same time I had no particular attachment to his Person, or to his Cause, nor indeed did I much consider the Cause, of one Side or other, if I had, I should hardly have risqu'd not my Life only, but Effects too, which were all as I might say, from that Moment forfeited to the *English* Government and was too evidently in their Power to confiscate at their Pleasure.

HOWEVER having just receiv'd a Remittance from *London*, of 300*l*. Sterling, and sold my Company in the *Irish* Regiment for very near as much, I was not only insensibly drawn in, but was perfectly Voluntier in that dull Cause, and away I went with them at all hazards; it belongs very little to my History to give an Account of that fruitless Expedition, only to tell you that being so closely, and effectually Chas'd by the *English* Fleet, which was Superior in force to the *French*, I may say, that in escaping them, I escaped being hang'd.

IT was the good Fortune of the *French*, that they over-shot the Port they aim'd at, and intending for the *Frith* or *Forth*, or as it is call'd the *Firth* of *Edinburg*, the first Land they made was as far North as a Place call'd *Montrose*, where it was not their Business to Land, and so they were oblig'd to come back to the *Frith*, and were gotten to the Entrance of it, and came to an Anchor for the Tide; but this Delay or Hindrance gave time to the *English* Fleet, under Sir *George Bing*[388] to come up to the *Frith*, and they came to an Anchor, just as we did, only waiting to go up the *Firth* with the Flood.

HAD we not over-shot the Port, as above, all our Squadron had been destroy'd in two Days, and all we could have done, had been to have gotten into the *Peer* or *Haven* at *Leith*, with the smaller Fregates, and have Landed the Troops and Ammunition, but we must have set fire to the Men of War, for the *English* Squadron was not above 24 Hours behind us, or thereabout.

UPON this surprize the *French* Admiral set Sail from the North Point of the *Firth*, where we lay, and crowding away to the North, got the Start of the *English* Fleet, and made their escape, with the Loss of one Ship only, which being behind the rest, could not get away; when we were satisfy'd the *English* left Chasing us, which was not till the third Night, when we alter'd our Course, and lost Sight of them, we stood over to the Coast of *Norway*, and keeping that Shore on Board[389] all the way to the Mouth of the *Baltick*, we came to an Anchor again, and sent two Scouts Abroad to learn News, to see if the Sea was clear, and being satisfy'd that the Enemy did not Chase us, we kept on with an easier Sail, and came all back again to *Dunkirk*, and glad I was to set my Foot on Shore again, for all the while we were thus flying for our Lives, I was under the greatest Terror immaginable, and nothing but Halters and Gibbets run in my Head, concluding, that if I had been taken, I should certainly have been hang'd.

BUT the care was now over, I took my leave of the *Chevalier*, and of the Army, and made hast to *Paris*; I came so unexpectedly to *Paris*, and to my own Lodgings that it was my Misfortune to make a Discovery, relating to my Wife, which was not at all to my satisfaction, for I found her Ladyship had kept some Company, that I had Reason to believe were not such as an honest Woman ought to have Convers'd with, and as I knew her Temper, by what I had found of her myself, I grew very Jealous and Uneasie about her; I must own it touch'd me very nearly, for I began to have an extraordinary value for her, and her Behaviour was very taking, especially after I had brought her into *France*; but having a Vein of Levity, it was impossible to prevent her running into such things, in a Town, so full of what they call Gallantry as *Paris*.

IT vext me also to think that it should be my Fate to be a Cuckold, both Abroad and at Home, and sometimes I would be in such a Rage about it, that I had no Government of myself, when I thought of it; whole Days, and I may say sometimes whole Nights I spent musing and considering what I should do to her, and especially what I should do to the Villain, wherever he was that had thus abus'd and suplanted me: Here indeed I committed Murther more than once, or indeed than a hundred times, in my imagination, and as the Devil is certainly an apparent Prompter to wickedness, if he is not the first Mover of it in our Minds; he teiz'd me Night and Day with Proposals to kill my Wife.

THIS horrid Project he carried up so high, by raising fierce Thoughts, and fomenting the Blood upon my Contemplation of the word Cuckold, that in short, I left debating whether I should Murther her or no, as a thing out of the Question, and Determined; and my Thoughts were then taken up only with the Management how I should kill her, and how to make my escape after I had done it.

ALL this while I had no sufficient Evidence of her Guilt, neither had I so much as charg'd her with it, or let her know I suspected her, otherwise, than as she might perceive it in my Conduct, and in the Change of my Behaviour to her, which was such, that she could not but perceive that something troubled me, yet she took no notice of it to me, but receiv'd me very well, and shew'd herself to be very glad of my return; nor did I find she had been Extravagant in her Expences while I was Abroad; but Jealousie, as the wise Man says, *is the wrath of a Man*;[390] her being so good a Hussy[391] of what Money I had left her, gave my distemper'd Fancy an Opinion that she had been maintain'd by other People, and so had had no Occasion to spend.

I must confess she had a difficult Point here upon her, tho' she had been[392] really honest; for as my Head was prepossess'd of her dishonesty, if she had been Lavish, I should have said, she had spent it upon her Gentlemen; and as she had been Frugal, I said, she had been Maintain'd by them: Thus, *I say*, my Head was Distemper'd, I believ'd myself Abus'd, and nothing could put it out of my Thoughts Night or Day.

ALL this while, it was not visibly broken out between us, but I was so fully possess'd with the belief of it, that I seem'd to want no Evidence, and I look'd with an evil Eye upon every Body that came near her, or that she convers'd with: There was an Officer of the *Guards du Corps* that lodg'd in the same House with us, a very honest Gentleman, and a Man of Quality; I happen'd to be in a little Drawing-Room, adjoyning to a Parlour where my Wife sat at that time, and this Gentleman came into the Parlour, which as he was one of the Family, he might have done without Offence, but he not knowing that I was in the drawing-Room, sat down and talk'd with my Wife; I heard every word they said, for the Door between us was open, nor could I say that there pass'd any thing between them, but cursory Discourse; they talk'd of casual things, of a young Lady a Burgher's Daughter of 19, that had been Married the Week before to an Advocate in the Parliament of *Paris*, vastly Rich, and about 63, and of another, a Widow Lady of Fortune in *Paris*, that had married her deceas'd Husbands Valet de Chamber, and of such casual Matters, that I could find no Fault with now at all.

BUT it fill'd my Head with jealous Thoughts, and fir'd my Temper: Now I fancy'd he us'd too much freedom with her, then that she us'd too much freedom to him, and once or twice I was upon the Point of breaking in upon them, and Affronting[393] them both, but I restrain'd myself; at length he talk'd something merrily of the Lady throwing away her Maidenhead, as I understood it, upon an old Man; but still it was nothing indecent, but I, who was all on fire already could bear it no longer, but started up, and came into the Room, and catching at my Wive's words, *say you so*, Madam, said I, *was he too old for her!* and giving the Officer a look, that I Fancy was something a Kin to the Face on the Sign, call'd the *Bull and Mouth* within *Aldersgate*, I went out into the Street.

THE Marquiss, so he was stil'd, a Man of Honour, and of Spirit too, took it, *as I meant it*, and follow'd me in a Moment, and Hem'd[394] after me in the Street; upon which I stopp'd, and he came up to me, Sir, *said he*, our Circumstances are very unhappy in *France*, that we cannot do ourselves Justice here, without the most severe Treatment in the World; but come on it what will, you must explain yourself to me on the Subject of your Behaviour just now.

I WAS a little cool'd, as to the Point of my Conduct to him in the very few Moments that had pass'd, and was very sensible, that I was wrong to him, and, *I said*, therefore to him very frankly, Sir, you are a Gentleman, who I know very well, and I have a very great respect for you; but I had been disturb'd a little about the Conduct of my Wife, and were it your own Case, What would you have done less?

I AM sorry for any dislike between you, and your Wife, *says he*, But what is that to me? Can you Charge me with any Indecency to her, except my talking so, and so, at which he repeated the Words, and as I knew you were in next Room, and heard every Word, and that all the Doors were open, I thought no Man could have taken amiss so Innocent an Expression.

I could no otherwise take it amiss, *said I*, than as I thought it imply'd a farther Familiarity, and that you cannot expect should be born by any Man of Honour; however, Sir, *said I*, I spoke only to my Wife, I said nothing to you, but gave you my Hat as I pass'd you.

YES, *said he*, and a look as full of Rage as the Devil, Are there no Words in such looks?

I CAN say nothing to that, *said I*, for I cannot see my own Countenance; but my Rage as you call it was at my Wife, not at you.

BUT hark you, Sir, *said he, growing warm as I grow Calm*, your anger at your Wife, was for her Discourse with me, and I think that concerns me too, and I ought to Resent it.

I think not, Sir, *said I*, nor had I found you in Bed with my Wife, would I have Quarreled with you; for if my Wife will let you lye with her, 'tis she is the Offender, what have I do with you; you could not lye with her if she was not willing, and if she is willing to be a Whore I ought to punish her, but I should have no Quarrel with you, I'll lye with your Wife if I can; and then I am even with you.

I spoke this all in good Humour, and in order to pacify him, but it would not do; but he would have me have give him satisfaction, *as he call'd it*, I told him I was a Stranger in the Country, and perhaps, should find little Mercy in their Course of Justice; that it was not my Business to fight any Man in his Vindicating his keeping Company with my Wife, for that the Injury was mine, in having a bad Woman to deal with; that there was no Reason in the thing; that after any Man should have found the way into my Bed, I, who am injur'd should go, and Stake my Life upon an equal Hazard against the Men who have abus'd me.

NOTHING would prevail with this Person to be quiet, for all this; but I had affronted him, and no satisfaction could be made him, but that at the Point of the Sword, so we agreed to go away together to *Lisle* in *Flanders*: I was now Soldier enough, not to be afraid to look a Man in the Face, and as the Rage at my Wife inspir'd me with Courage, so he let fall a Word that fir'd, and provok'd me beyond all Patience; for speaking of the distrust I had of my Wife, he said unless I had good Information, I ought not to suspect my Wife; I told him, if I had good Information, I should be past Suspicion; he replyed, if he was the happy Man that had so much of her Favour, he would take care then to put me past the Suspicion. I[a] gave him as rough an Answer, as he could desire, and he return'd in *French, nous Verrons aux Lisle*, that is to say, we will talk further of it at *Lisle*.

I told him, I did not see the benefit, either to him, or me, of going so far as *Lisle* to decide this Quarrel, since now I perceiv'd he was the Man I wanted, that we might decide this Quarrel *aux Champ*, upon the Spot, and whoever had the Fortune to fell the other, might make his escape to *Lisle*, as well afterwards, as before.

THUS we walk'd on, talking very ill naturedly on both Sides, and yet very mannerly, till we came clear of the *Suburbs* of *Paris*, on the way to *Charenton*; when seeing the way clear, I told him under those Trees was a very fit Place for us, pointing to a row of Trees adjoyning to Monsieur —*s* Garden-wall; so we went thither, and fell to Work immediately; after some Fencing he made a home Thrust at me, and run me into my Arm, a long slanting Wound, but at the same time receiv'd my Point into his Body, and soon after fell; he spoke some Words before he drop'd; first he told me I had kill'd him, then he said, he had indeed wrong'd me, and as he knew it, he ought not to have fought me; he desir'd I would make my Escape immediately, which I did into the City, but no farther, no body as I thought having seen us together: In the Afternoon, about six Hours after the Action, Messengers brought News one on the Heels of another, that the Marquiss was mortally wounded, and carried into a House at *Charenton*; that account, saying he was not dead, surpris'd me a little, not doubting but that concluding I had made my Escape he would own who it was; however, I discover'd nothing of my Concern, but going up into my Chamber, I took out of a Cabinet there what Money I had, which indeed was so much as I thought would be sufficient for my Expences; but having an accepted Bill for 2000 Livres, I walk'd sedately to a Merchant who knew me, and got 50 Pistols of him upon my Bill, letting him know my Business call'd me to *England*, and I would take the rest of him when he had receiv'd it.

HAVING furnish'd myself thus, I provided me a Horse for my Servant, for I had one very good one of my own, and once more ventured Home to my Lodging, where I heard again that the Marquiss was not dead: My Wife all this while cover'd her Concern for the Marquiss so well, that she gave me no room to make any remark upon her; but she saw evidently the Marks of Rage, and deep Resentment in my Behaviour after some little stay, and perceiving me making Preparations for a Journey; she said to me, Are you going out of Town? yes Madam, *says I*, that you may have room to Mourn for your Friend, the Marquiss; at which she started, and shew'd she was indeed in a most terrible Fright: And making a thousand Crosses about herself, and with a great many callings upon the *Blessed Virgin*, and her Country *Saints*, she burst out at last, is it *possible!* Are you the Man that has kill'd the Marquiss? then you are undone, and I too.

YOU may, Madam, be a loser by the Marquiss being kill'd, but I'll take care to be as little a looser by you as I can; 'tis enough, the Marquiss has honestly confest your Guilt, and I have done with you; she would have thrown herself into my Arms, protesting her Innocence, and told me she would flye with me, and would Convince me of her Fidelity, by such Testimonies as I cou'd not but be satisfy'd with, but I thrust her violently from me, *alle*[395] *Infame!* said I, go infamous Creature, and take from me the Necessity I should be under, if I stay'd of sending you to keep Company with your dear Friend the Marquiss. I thrust her away with such Force that she fell backward upon the Floor, and cry'd out most terribly, and indeed she had Reason, for she was very much hurt.

IT griev'd me indeed to have thrust her away with such Force, but you must consider me now in the Circumstances of a Man enrag'd, and as it were out of himself Furious and Mad: However, I took her up from the Floor, and laid her on the Bed, and calling up her Maid, bad her go and take care of her Mistress; and going soon after out of Doors, I took Horse, and made the best of my way, not towards *Calais* or *Dunkirk*, or towards *Flanders*, whether it might be suggested I was fled, and whether they did pursue me, the same Evening; but I took the direct Road for *Lorrain*, and riding all Night and very hard, I pass'd the *Main* the next Day at Night at *Chalons*, and came safe into the Duke of *Lorrain's* Dominions the third Day; where I rested one Day, only to consider what Course to take, for it was still a most difficult thing to pass any way, but that I should either be in the King of *France's* Dominions, or be taken by the *French* Allies as a Subject of *France*; but getting good Advice from a Priest at *Bar le Duc,* who tho' I did not tell him the particulars of my Case, yet guess'd how it was, it being as he said very usual for Gentlemen in my Circumstances to fly that way, upon this Supposition, this kind *Padre* got me a Church Pass, *that is to say,* he made me a Purveyor for the Abbey of – and as such got me a Passport to go to *Deux Ponts,*[396] which belong'd to the King of *Sweden*: Having such Authority there, and the Priest's recommendation to an Ecclesiastick in the Place, I got Passports from thence in the King of *Sweden's* Name to *Cologne*, and then I was thoroughly safe, so making my way to the *Netherlands*, without any difficulty, I came to the *Hague*, and from thence, tho' very privately, and by several Names, I came to *England*: And thus I got clear of my *Italian* Wife, Whore I should have call'd her, for after I had made her so my self, how should I expect any other of her.

BEING arriv'd at *London*, I wrote to my Friend at *Paris*, but dated my Letter from the *Hague*, where I order'd him to Direct his Answers: The chief Business of my writing was to know if my Bill was paid him, to enquire if any pursuit was made after me, and what other News he had about me, or my Wife, and particularly how it had far'd with the Marquiss.

I receiv'd an Answer in a few Days, importing that he had receiv'd the Money on my Bill, which he was ready to pay as I should direct, that the Marquiss was not dead, but said he, you have kill'd him another way, for he has lost his Commission in the Guards, which was worth to him 20000 Livres, and he is yet a close Prisoner in the *Bastile*; that pursuit was order'd after me upon suspicion, that they had follow'd me to *Amiens*, on the Road to *Dunkirk*, and to *Chateau de Cambresis*, on the way to *Flanders*; but missing me that way, had given it over; that the Marquiss had been too well instructed to own that he had fought with me, but said, that he was assaulted on the Road, and unless I could be taken, he would take his Trial, and come off, for want of Proof, that my flying was Circumstance indeed, that mov'd strongly against him, because it was known that we had had some Words that Day, and were seen to walk together; but that nothing being prov'd on either Side, he would come off with the Loss of his Commission; which, however, being very Rich, he could bear well enough.

As to my Wife, he wrote me Word, she was inconsolable, and had cry'd her self to Death almost; but *he added* (very ill natur'd indeed) and whether it was for me, or for the Marquiss, that he could not determine: *He likewise told me*, She was in very bad Circumstances, and very low, So that if I did not take some Care of her, she would come to be in very great Distress.

THE latter Part of this Story mov'd me indeed, for, I thought however it was, I ought not to let her Starve; and besides, Poverty was a Temptation which a Woman could not easily withstand, and I ought not to be the Instrument to drive her to a horrid Necessity of Crime, if I could prevent it.

UPON this, I wrote to him again, to go to her, and talk with her, and learn as much as he could of her particular Circumstances; and that if he found she was really in Want, and particularly, that she did not live a scandalous Life, he should give her twenty Pistoles, and tell her, if she would engage to live retir'd and honestly, she should have so much annually, which was enough to subsist her.

SHE took the first twenty Pistoles, but bad him tell me, that I had wrong'd her, and unjustly charg'd her; and I ought to do her Justice; and I had ruin'd her, by exposing her in such a Manner as I had, having no Proof of my Charge, or Ground for any Suspicion; that as to twenty Pistoles a Year, it was a mean Allowance, to a Wife that had travelled over the World, as she had done with me, and the like; and so expostulated with him, to obtain forty Pistoles a Year of me, which I consented to; but she never gave me the Trouble of paying above one Year; for after that, the Marquiss was so fond of her again, that he took her away to himself; and as my Friend wrote me Word, had settled 400 Crowns a Year on her, and I never heard any more of her.

I was now in *London*, but was oblig'd to be very retir'd, and change my Name, letting no Body in the Nation know who I was, except my Merchant, by whom I corresponded with my People in *Virginia*, and particularly that my Tutor, who was now become the head Mannager of my Affairs, and was in very good Circumstances himself also by my Means; but he deserved all I did, or could do for him; for he was a most faithful Friend, as well as Servant, as ever Man had, in that Country at least.

I was not the easiest[397] Man alive, in the retir'd sollitary manner I now liv'd in; and I experienced the Truth of the Text, *That it is not good for Man to be alone*;[398] for I was extreamly Melancholly and Heavy, and indeed, knew not what to do with my self; particularly, because I was under some Restraint; that I was to afraid to go Abroad; at last I resolv'd to go quite away, and go to *Virginia* again, and there live retired as I could.

BUT when I came to consider that Part, more narrowly, I could not prevail with my self to live a private Life: I had got a wandring kind of Taste, and Knowledge of Things begat a Desire of encreasing it, and an exceeding Delight I had in it; tho' I had nothing to do in the Armies or in the War, and did not design ever to meddle with it again; yet I could not live in the World, and not enquire what was doing in it; nor could I think of living in *Virginia*, where I was to hear my News twice a Year, and read the publick Accounts, of what was just then upon the Stocks, as the History of things past.

THIS, was my Notion, I was now in my native Country, where my Circumstances were easy; and tho' I had had ill Luck Abroad, for I brought little Home with me; yet by little good Mannagement, I might soon have Money by me. I had no Body to keep but my self, and my Plantations in *Virginia*, generally return'd me from 400 to 600*l*. a Year, one Year above 700*l*. and to go thither, I concluded, was to be bury'd a-live; so I put off all Thoughts of it, and resolv'd to settle somewhere in *England*, where I might know every Body, and no Body know me. I was not long in concluding where to pitch, for as I spoke the *French* Tongue perfectly well, having been so many Years among them, it was easy for me to pass for a *French* Man. So I went to *Canterbury*,[399] call'd my self an *English* Man, among the *French*;

and a *French* Man among the *English*; and on that Score, was the more perfectly concealed, going by the Name of Monsieur *Charnot*, with the *French*,
was call'd Mr. *Charnock* among the *English*.

HERE, indeed, I liv'd perfectly *Incog*.[400] I made no particular Acquaintance, so as to be intimate, and yet I knew every Body, and every Body
knew me; I discours'd in Common, talk'd *French* with the *Walloons*;[401] and
English, with the *English*; and living retir'd and sober, was well enough
receiv'd by all Sorts; but as I medled with no Bodies business, so no Body
meddl'd with mine; I thought I liv'd pretty well.

BUT I was not fully satisfy'd, a settled family Life was the thing I Lov'd,
had made two pushes at it, as you have heard, but with ill Success; yet the
Miscarriage of what was pass'd did not discourage me at all but I resolv'd
to marry. I look'd out for a Woman as suitable as I could, but always found
something or other to shock my Fancy, except once a Gentleman's Daughter of good Fashion, but I met with so many repulses of one kind or
another, that I was forc'd to give it over, and indeed tho' I might be said to
be a Lover in this Suit, and had mannag'd myself so well with the young
Lady, that I had no difficulty left, but what would soon have been adjusted,
yet her Father was so difficult, made so many Objections, was to Day not
pleas'd one way, to Morrow another, that he would stand by nothing that
he himself had propos'd, nor could he ever[a] be brought to be of the same
Mind two Days together; so that we at last put an End to the Pretentions,
for she would not Marry without her Father's consent, and I would not
steal her, and so that Affair ended.

I cannot say, but I was a little vex'd at the Disappointment of this, so I
left the City of *Canterbury*, and went to *London* in the Stage-Coach; here I
had an odd Scene presented as ever happen'd of its kind.

THERE was in the Stage-Coach a young Woman, and her Maid, she was
sitting in a very melancholly Posture, for she was in the Coach before me,
and sigh'd most dreadfully all the way, and whenever her Maid spoke to
her, she burst out into Tears; I was not long in the Coach with her, but seeing she made such a dismal Figure, I offer'd to Comfort her a little, and
enquir'd into the Occasion of her Affliction, but she would not speak a
Word; but her Maid with a force of crying too, said her Master was dead, at
which Word the Lady burst out again into a Passion of crying, and between
Mistress and Maid, this was all I could get for the Morning part of that
Day: When we came to Dine, I offer'd the Lady, that seeing I suppos'd she
would not Dine with the Company, if she would please to Dine with me, I
would Dine in a separate Room, for the rest of the Company were Foreign-
ers: Her Maid thank'd me in her Mistresses Name, but her Mistress could
eat nothing, and desir'd to be private.

HERE however, I had some Discourse with the Maid, by whom I learn'd that the Lady was Wife to a Captain of a Ship, who was Outward bound to somewhere in the *Streights*,[402] I think it was to *Zant* and *Venice*, that being gone no farther than the *Downs* he was taken sick, and after about ten days Illness had died at *Deal*, that his Wife hearing of his Sickness, had gone to *Deal* to see him, and had come but just time enough to see him die, had stay'd there to bury him, and was now coming to *London*, in a sad disconsolate Condition indeed.

I heartily pitied the young Gentlewoman indeed, and said some things to her in the Coach, to let her know I did so, which she gave no answer to, but in Civility, now and then made a Bow, but never gave me the least Opportunity to see her Face; or so much as to know whether she had a Face, or no; much less to guess what Form of a Face it was; it was Winter time, and the Coach put up at *Rochester*; not going thro' in a Day, as was usual in Summer; and a little before we came to *Rochester*, I told the Lady I understood she had eat nothing to Day, that such a Course would but make her Sick, and doing her Harm could do her deceas'd Husband no good; and therefore I entreated her, that as I was a Stranger, and only offer'd a Civility to her in Order to abate her severely afflicting herself, she would yield so far to matters of Ceremony, let us Sup together as Passengers, for as to the Strangers they did not seem to understand the Custom, or to desire it.

SHE bow'd, but gave no Answer, only after pressing her by Arguments, which she could not deny was very civil and kind; she return'd, that she gave me thanks, but she could not eat; well, Madam, *said I*, do but sit down, tho' you think you cannot eat, perhaps you may eat a Bit; indeed you must eat, or you will destroy yourself at this rate of living, and upon the Road too: In a Word, you will be Sick indeed; I argued with her, the Maid put in, and said, do Madam, pray try to divert yourself a little; I press'd her again, and she bow'd to me very respectively,[403] but still said no, and she could not eat; the Maid continu'd to importune her, and said, dear Madam do, the Gentleman is a civil Gentleman, pray Madam do, and then turning to me said, my Mistress will Sir, I hope, and seem'd pleas'd, and indeed was so.

HOWEVER, I went on to perswade her, and taking no Notice of what her Maid said, that I was a civil Gentleman, I told her, I am a stranger to you Madam; but if I thought you were shye of me on any Account, as to civility, I will send my Supper up to you in your Chamber, and stay below myself; she bow'd then to me twice, and look'd up, which was the first time, and said, she had no Suspicion of that kind, that my offer was so civil, that she was as much ashamed to refuse it, as she should be asham'd to accept it, if she was where she was known; that she thought I was not quite a stranger to her, for she had seen me before; that she would accept my offer, so far as to sit at Table, because I desir'd it, but she could not promise me to eat, and that she hop'd I would take the other as a Constraint upon her, in return to so much kindness.

SHE startled me, when she said she had seen me before, for I had not the least knowledge of her, nor did I remember so much as to have heard of her Name; for I had ask'd her Name of her Maid, and indeed it made me almost Repent my Compliment; for it was many ways essential to me not to be known: However, I could not go back, and besides, if I was known, it was essentially necessary to me to know who it was that knew me, and by what Circumstances; so I went on with my Compliment.

WE came to the Inn, but just before it was Dark, I offer'd to hand my Widow out of the Coach, and she could not decline it, but tho' her Hoods were not then much over her Face, yet being dark, I could see little of her then. I^a waited on her then to the Stair-foot, and led her up the Inn Stairs to a Dining-room, which the Master of the House offer'd to show us, as if for the whole Company; but she declin'd going in there, and said she desir'd rather to go directly to her Chamber, and turning to her Maid, bad her speak to the Inn Keeper to show her her Lodging-room; so I waited on her to the Door, and took my leave telling her I would expect her at Supper.

IN order to Treat her moderately well, and not extravagantly, for I had no thoughts of any thing farther than Civility, which was the Effect of meer Compassion, for the Unhappiness of the most truly disconsolate Woman that I ever met with: *I say*, in order to treat her handsomely, but not extravagantly, I provided what the House afforded, which was a couple of Partridges, and a very good Dish of stew'd Oysters; they brought us up afterward, a Neats[404] Tongue and a Ham, that was almost cut quite down, but we eat none of it, for the other was fully enough for us both; and the Maid made her Supper of the Oysters we had left, which were enough.

I mention this, because it should appear, I did not treat her as a Person I was making any Court to, for I had nothing of that in my Thoughts; but meerly in Pity to the poor Woman, who I saw in a Circumstance that was indeed very unhappy.

WHEN I gave her Maid Notice that Supper was ready, she fetch'd her Mistress, coming in before her, with a Candle in her Hand; and then it was that I saw her Face, and being in her *Disabille*, she had no Hoods over her Eyes, or Black upon her Head,[405] when I was truly surprized, to see one of the most beautiful Faces upon Earth: I saluted her, and led her to the Fireside; the Table tho' spread being too far from the Fire, the Weather being Cold.

SHE was now something Sociable, tho' very grave, and sighing often, on Account of her Circumstances; but she so handsomly govern'd her Grief, yet so artfully made it mingle it self with all her Discourse, that it added exceedingly to her Behaviour, which was every way most exquisitely Genteel: I had a great deal of Discourse with her, and upon many Subjects, and by degrees took her Name; *that is to say*, from her self, as I had before from her Maid, also the Place where she liv'd, *viz.* near *Ratcliff*, or rather *Stepney*, where I ask'd her leave to pay her a Visit, when she thought fit to admit Company, which she seemed to intimate would not be a great while.

IT is a Subject too surfeiting to entertain People with the Beauty of a Person they will never see; let it suffice to tell them she was the most beautiful Creature of her Sex, that I ever saw before, or since; and it cannot be wondered if I was charm'd with her, the very first Moment I see[406] her Face: Her behaviour was likewise a Beauty in itself, and was so extraordinary, that I cannot say I can describe it.

THE next day she was much more free than she was that first Night, and I had so much Conversation as to enter into particulars of things on both sides, also she gave me leave to come and see her House, which however, I did not do under a fortnight, or thereabouts, because I did not know how far she would dispense with the Ceremony, which it was necessary to keep up at the beginning of her Mourning.

HOWEVER I came as a Man that had Business with her, relating to the Ship her Husband was dead out of, and the first time I came was admitted; and in short, the first time I came I made Love to her; she receiv'd that Proposal with disdain, I cannot indeed say she treated me with any disrespect; but she said, she abhorr'd the offer, and would hear no more of it.

HOW I came to make such a Proposal to her, I scarce knew then, tho' it was very much my Intention from the first.

IN the mean time, I enquir'd into her Circumstances, and her Character, and heard nothing but what was very agreeable of them both; and above all, I found she had the Report of the best humoured Lady, and the best bred of all that part of the Town; and now I thought I had found what I had so often wish'd for, to make me happy, and had twice miscarry'd in, and resolv'd not to miss her, if it was possible to obtain her.

IT came indeed, a little into my Thoughts, that I was a marry'd Man, and had a second Wife alive, who tho' she was false to me, and a Whore, yet I was not legally divorc'd from her, and that she was my Wife for all that; but I soon got over that part; for first, as she was a Whore, and the Marquiss had confess'd it to me, I was divorc'd in Law, and I had Power to put her away; but having had the Misfortune of fighting a Duel, and being oblig'd to quit the Country, I could not claim the legal Process, which was my Right, and therefore might conclude my self as much divorc'd, as if it had been actually done, and so that Scruple vanish'd.

I suffer'd now two Months to run, without pressing my Widow any more, only I had kept a strict Watch to find if any one else pretended[407] to her; at the end of two Months I Visited her again, when I found she receiv'd me with more Freedom, and we had no more Sighs, and Sobbs about the last Husband; and tho' she would not let me press my former Proposal, so far as I thought I might have done, yet I found I had leave to come again, and it was the Article of Decency, which she stood upon, as much as any thing; that I was not disagreeable to her, and that my using her so handsomely upon the Road, had given me a great Advantage in her Favour.

I went on gradually with her, and gave her leave to stand off for two Months more; but then I told her the matter of Decency, which was but a Ceremony, was not to stand in Competition with the matter of Affection; and in short, I could not bear any longer delay, but that if she thought fit we might Marry privately, and to cut the Story short, as I did my Court-ship, in about five Months I got her in the Mind, and we were privately Married, and that with so very exact a Concealment, that her Maid that was so Instrumental in it, yet had no Knowledge of it for near a Month more.

I was now not only in my Imagination, but in reality the most happy Creature in the World; as I was so infinitely satisfy'd with my Wife, who was[a] indeed the best humour'd Woman in the World, a most accomplish'd beautiful Creature indeed, perfectly well Bred, and had not one ill Quality about her, and this happiness continu'd without the least Interruption for about six Year.

BUT I, that was to be the most unhappy Fellow alive in the Article of Matrimony, had at last a Disappointment of the worst sort, even here; I had three fine Children by her, and in her time of her lying in with the last, she got some Cold, that she did not in a long time get off and in short she grew very sickly: In being so continually ill, and out of Order, she very unhappily got a Habit of drinking Cordials and hot Liquors; Drink, like the Devil, when it gets hold of any one, tho' but a little, it goes on by little and little to their Destruction; so in my Wife, her Stomach being weak and faint, she first took this Cordial, then that, till in short, she could not live without them, and from a Drop to a Sup, from a Sup to a Dram, from a Dram to a Glass, and so on to Two, till at last, she took in short, to what we call drinking.

As I likened Drink to the Devil, in its gradual Possession of the Habits and Person, so it is yet more like the Devil in its Encroachment on us, where it gets hold of our Sences; in short, my beautiful, good humour'd, modest, well bred Wife, grew a Beast, a Slave to Strong Liquor, and would be drunk at her own Table, nay, in her own Closet by her self; till instead of a well made, fine Shape, she was as Fat as an Hostess;[408] her fine Face bloated and blotch'd, had not so much as the Ruins of the most beautiful Person alive; nothing remain'd but a good Eye, that indeed, she held to the last: In short, she lost her Beauty, her Shape, her Manners, and at last her Virtue; and giving her self up to Drinking, kill'd her self in about a Year and a half, after she first began that cursed Trade; in which Time she twice was exposed in the most scandalous manner, with a Captain of a Ship, who like a Villain, took the Advantage of her being in Drink, and not knowing what she did; but it had this unhappy Effect, that instead of her being asham'd, and repenting of it, when she came to her self, it harden'd her in the Crime, and she grew as void of Modesty at last as of Sobriety.

O! The Power of Intemperance! and how it Encroaches on the best Dispositions in the World; how it comes upon us gradually and insensibly, and what dismal Effects it Works upon our Morals, changing the most Virtuous, regular, well instructed, and well inclin'd Tempers, into worse than Brutal. That was a good Story, whether real or invented, of the Devil tempting a young Man to murder his Father. No, *he said*, that was un-natural. Why, then *says the Devil*, Go and lye with your Mother: No, *says he*, That is abominable. Well, Then, *says the Devil*, If you will do nothing else to oblige me, go and get Drunk; Ay, ay, *says the Fellow*, I'll do that, so he went and made himself Drunk as a Swine; and when he was Drunk, he murdered his Father, and lay with his Mother.[409]

NEVER was a Woman more virtuous, modest, chaste, sober, she never so much as desir'd to drink any thing strong; it was with the greatest entreaty, that I could prevail with her to drink a Glass or two of Wine, and rarely, if ever, above one, or two at a time; even in Company, she had no Inclination to it; not an immodest Word ever came out of her Mouth, nor would she suffer it in any one else, in her Hearing without Resentment and Abhorence: But upon that Weakness, and Illness after her last Lying-In, as above the Nurse press'd her, when ever she found her self faint, and a Sinking of her Spirits, to take this Cordial and that Dram, to keep up her Spirits, till it became necessary even to keep her alive, and gradually increased to a Habit, so that it was no longer her Physick, but her Food; her Appetite sunk and went quite away, and she eat little or nothing, but came at last to such a dreadful Height, that, *as I have said*, she would be Drunk in her own

Dressing Room by Eleven a Clock in the Morning; and in Short, at last was never sober.

IN this Life of Hellish Excess, *as I have said*, She lost all that was before so Valuable in her; and a Villain, if it be proper to call a Man, that was really a Gentleman, by such a Name, who was an intimate Acquaintance coming to pretend a Visit to her, made her and her Maid so Drunk together, that he lay with them both; with the Mistress, the Maid being in the Room, and with the Maid, the Mistress being in the Room; after which, he it seems took the like Liberty with them both, as often as he thought fit, 'till the Wench being with Child, discover'd it for her self, and for her Mistress too: Let any one judge what was my Case now; I that for six Years thought my self the happyest Man alive, was now the most miserable distracted Creature: As to my Wife, I loved her so well, and was so sensible of the Dissaster of her Drinking, being the Occasion of it all, that I could not resent it to such a Degree as I had done in her Predecessor; but I pity'd her heartily; however, I put away all her Servants, and almost lock'd her up; *that is to say*, I set new People over her, who would not suffer any one to come near her, without my Knowledge.

BUT what to do with the Villain, that had thus abused both her and me, *that was the question that remain'd*; to fight him upon equal Terms, I thought, was a little hard; that after a Man had treated me as he had done, he deserv'd no fair Play for his Life, so I resolv'd to wait for him in *Stepney* Fields,[410] and which Way he often came Home pretty late, and Pistol him in the Dark, and if possible, to let him know what I Kill'd him for, before I did it: But when I came to consider of this, it shock'd my Temper too, as well as Principle, and I could not be a Murderer, whatever else I could be, or what ever I was provok'd to be.

HOWEVER, I resolv'd on the other Hand, that I would severely correct him for what he had done, and it was not long before I had an Opportunity; for hearing one Morning that he was walking cross the Fields, from *Stepney* to *Shadwel*, which Way I knew he often went; I waited for his coming Home again, and fairly met him.

I had not many Words with him, but told him, I had long look'd for him; that he knew the Villainy he had been guilty of in my Family, and he could not believe, since he knew also, that I was fully inform'd of it, but that I must be a great Coward as well as a Cuckold, or that I would resent it, and that it was now a very proper Time to call him to an Account for it, and therefore bad him, if he durst show his Face to what he had done, and defend the Name of a Captain of a Man of War, *as they said* he had been, to draw.

He seem'd surpriz'd at the Thing, and began to Parlee, and would lessen the Crime of it; but I told him it was not a time to talk that Way, since he could not deny the Fact; and to lessen the Crime, was to lay it the more upon the Woman, who, I was sure if he had not first debauch'd with Wine, he could never have brought to the rest; and seeing he refused to draw, I knock'd him down with my Cane at one Blow; and I would not strike him again while he lay on the Ground, but waited to see him recover a little, for I saw plainly he was not kill'd; in a few Minutes he came to himself again, and then I took him fast by one Wrist, and can'd him as severely as I was able, and as long as I could hold it, for want of Breath, but forbore his Head, because I was resolv'd he should feel it; in this Condition at last he begg'd for Mercy, but I was Deaf to all Pitty a great while, till he roar'd out like a Boy soundly whipt; then I took his Sword from him, and broke it before his Face, and left him on the Ground, giving him two or three Kicks on the Back-side, and bad him go and take the Law of me, if he thought fit.

I had now as much Satisfaction, as indeed could be taken of a Coward, and had no more to say to him: But as I knew it would make a great Noise about the Town, I immediately remov'd my Family, and that I might be perfectly conceal'd, went into the North of *England*, and liv'd in a little Town called —, not far from *Lancaster*, where I liv'd retir'd, and was no more heard of, for about two Years. My Wife tho' more confin'd than she used to be, and so kept up from the leu'd part; which I believe in the Intervals of her Intemperance, she was truly ashamed of, and abhor'd; yet retain'd the Drinking part, which becoming *as I have said*, necessary for her Subsistance, she soon ruin'd her health, and in about a Year and a half after my Removal into the *North* she died.

Thus I was once more a free Man, and as one would think, should by this time, have been fully satisfy'd that Matrimony was not appointed to be a State of Felicity to me.

I should have mention'd, that the Villain of a Captain, who I had drub'd, *as above*, pretended to make a great Stir about my assaulting him on the High-Way, and that I had fallen upon him with three Ruffians with an Intent to murther him, and this began to obtain Belief among the People in the Neighbourhood: I sent him Word of so much of it as I had heard, and told him I hoped it did not come from his own Mouth, but if it did, I expected he would publickly disown it, he himself declaring he knew it to be false; or else that I should be forced to act the same thing over again, till I had disciplin'd him into better Manners; and that he might be assured, that if he continued to pretend that I had any Body with me when I caned him, I would publish the whole Story in Print, and besides that, would

Cane him again where ever I met him, and as often as I met him, till he thought fit to defend himself with his Sword like a Gentleman.

HE gave me no Answer to this Letter, and the Satisfaction I had for that was, that I gave twenty or thirty Copies of it about among the Neighbours, which made it as publick as if I had printed it, (that is, as to his Acquaintance, and mine) and made him so hiss'd at, and hated, that he was obliged to remove, into some other part of the Town, whither, I did not enquire.

MY Wife being now dead, I knew not what Course to take in the World, and I grew so disconsolate and discouraged, that I was next Door to being distempered, and sometimes indeed, I thought my self a little touch'd in my Head. But it proved nothing but Vapours,[411] and the Vexation of this Affair, and in about a Years time, or there abouts, it wore off again.

I had rambl'd up and down in a most discontented unsettled Posture after this, *I say*, about a Year, and then I consider'd I had three innocent Children, and I could take no Care of them, and that I must either go away and leave them to the wide World, or settle here, and get some Body to look after them, and that better a Mother in-Law, than no Mother, for to live such a wandring Life, it would not do: So I resolved, I would marry as any thing offer'd, tho' it was mean, and the meaner the better; I concluded my next Wife should be only taken as an upper Servant, *that is to say*, a Nurse to my Children, and a House-keeper to my self, and let her be whore or honest Woman, *said I*, as she likes best, I am resolv'd I wont much concern my self about that, for I was now one desperate, that valued not how things went.

IN this careless, and indeed, rash foolish Humour, I talk'd to my self thus; if I Marry an honest Woman, my Children will be taken care of; if she be a Slut and abuses me, as I see every Body does, I'll Kidnap her and send her to *Virginia* to my Plantations there, and there she shall work hard enough, and fare hard enough to keep her Chast, I'll warrant her.

I knew well enough at first, that these were mad, hare-brain'd Notions, and I thought no more of being serious in them, than I thought of being a Man in the Moon: But I know not how it happen'd to me; I reason'd and talk'd to my self in this wild manner so long, that I brought my self to be seriously desperate, *that is*, to resolve upon another Marriage; with all the Suppositions of Unhappiness that could be imagined to fall out.

AND yet even this rash Resolution of my Sences did not come presently to Action, for I was half a Year after this, before I fix'd upon any thing; at last, as he that seeks Mischief, shall certainly find it, so it was with me, there happen'd to be a young, or rather a middle aged Woman in the next Town, which was but half a Mile off, who usually was at my House, and among my Children every Day, when the Weather was tolerable; and tho' she came, but meerly as a Neighbour, and to see us, yet she was always helpful in directing, and ordering things for them, and mighty handy about them, as well before my Wife died as after.

HER Father was one that I employed often to go to *Leverpool*, and sometimes to *Whitehaven*, and do Business for me; for having as it were settled myself in these Northern parts of *England*, I had order'd part of my Effects to be Shipp'd as Occasion of shipping offered to either of those two Towns, to which (the War continuing very sharp) it was safer coming as to Privateers, than about thro' the *Channel* to *London*.

I took a mighty Fancy at last, that this Girl would answer my End, particularly that as I saw she was mighty useful among the Children, so on the other Hand, the Children lov'd her very well, and I resolv'd to love her too; flattering myself mightily, that as I had Married two Gentlewomen, and one Citizen,[412] and they prov'd all three Whores, I should now find what I wanted in an innocent Country Wench.

I took up a World of time in Considering of this Matter: Indeed scarce any of my Matches were done without very mature Consideration; the second was the worst in that Article, but in this I thought of it, I believe, four Months most seriously before I resolv'd, and that very Prudence spoil'd the whole thing; however, at last being resolv'd, I took Mrs. *Margaret* one Day as she pass'd by my Parlour door, call'd her in, and told her I wanted to speak with her; she came readily in, but blush'd mightily, when I bad her sit down, for I bad her sit down in a Chair just by me.

I Us'd no great Ceremony with her, but told her that I had observ'd she had been mighty kind to my Children, and was very tender to them, and that they all lov'd her, and that if she and I could agree about it, I intended to make her their Mother, if she was not engag'd to some Body else; the Girl sat still, and said never a Word, *till I said those Words*, if she was not engag'd to some Body else; however, I took no Notice of it, other than this, look ye *Moggy, said I*, so they call them in the Country, if you have promis'd yourself you must tell me; for we all knew that a young Fellow, a good Clergyman's wicked Son, had hung about her a great while, two or three Year, and made Love to her, but could never get the Girl in the Mind it seems to have him.

SHE knew I was not ignorant of it, and therefore after her first surprise was over, she told me Mr. — had as I knew often come after her, but she had never promis'd him any thing, and had for several Years refus'd him; her Father always telling her that he was a wicked Fellow, and that[a] he would be her Ruin if she had him.

WELL, *Moggy*, then, *says I*, what dost say to me, art thou free to make me a Wife? She blush'd and look'd down upon the Ground, and would not speak a good while, but when I press'd her to tell me, she look'd up, *and said she* suppos'd I was but Jesting with her; well, I got over that, and told her, I was in very good earnest with her, and I took her for a sober, honest, modest Girl, and as, *I said*, one that my Children lov'd mighty well, and I was in earnest with her, if she would give me her Consent, I would give her my Word, that I would have her, and we would be married tomorrow Morning; she look'd up again at that, and smil'd a little, and said no, that was too soon too, to say yes; she hop'd I would give her some time to Consider of it, and to talk with her Father about it.

I told her she needed not much time to consider about it, but however, I would give her till to morrow Morning, which was a great while; by this time I had kiss'd *Moggy* two or three times, and she began to be freer with me, and when I press'd her to Marry me the next Morning, she laugh'd and told me it was not lucky, to be married in her old Cloths.

I stopp'd her Mouth presently with that, and told her she should not be married in her old Cloths, for I would give her some new; *ay, it may be afterwards* says *Moggy*, and laugh'd again: No, just now, *says I*, come along with me *Moggy*; so I carried her up Stairs into my Wive's Room that was, and shew'd her a new Morning Gown of my Wives, that she had never worn above two or three times, and several other fine things; look you there *Moggy, says I*, there's a Wedding Gown for you, give me your Hand now that you will have me to morrow Morning, and as to your Father, you know he is gone to *Liverpool* on my Business, but I will answer for it, he shall not be angry when he comes Home to call his Master Son-in-law, and I ask him no Portion; therefore give me thy Hand for it *Moggy, says I*, very merrily to her, and kiss'd her again, and the Girl gave me her Hand, and very pleasantly too, and I was mightily pleas'd with it, I assure you.

THERE liv'd about three Doors from us, an antient Gentleman, who pass'd for a Doctor of Physick, but who was really a *Romish* Priest in Orders, as there are many in that Part of the Country, and in the Evening I sent to speak with him: He knew that I understood his Profession, and that I had liv'd in Popish Countries, and in a Word, believ'd me a *Roman* too, for I was such Abroad: When he came to me, I told him the occasion, for which I sent for him, and that it was to be to morrow Morning; he readily told me, if I would come, and see him in the Evening, and bring *Moggy* with me, he would Marry us in his own Study, and that it was rather more Private to do it in the Evening, than in the Morning; so I call'd *Moggy* again to me, and told her since she and I had agreed the Matter for to Morrow, it was as well to be done over Night, and told her what the Doctor had said.

Moggy blush'd again, *and said*, she must go Home first, that she could not be ready before to Morrow; look ye *Moggy, says I*, you are my Wife now, and you shall never go away from me a Maid, I know what you mean, you would go Home to shift[413] you: Come *Moggy*, *sayes I*, come along with me again up Stairs, so I carried her to a Chest of Linnen, where was several new shifts of my last Wives, which she had never worn at all, and some that had been worn; there's a clean Smock for you *Moggy*, *says I*, and to Morrow you shall have all the rest: When I had done this, now *Moggy*, *says I*, go and Dress you; so I lock'd her in, and went down Stairs; knock *says I*, when you are Dress'd.

AFTER some time, *Moggy* did not knock, but down she came into my Room, compleatly dress'd, for there were several other things that I bad her take, and the Cloths fitted her, as if they had been made for her; it seems she slipt the Lock back.

WELL *Moggy*, *says I*, now you see you shan't be marry'd in your old Cloaths, so I took her in my Arms, and kiss'd her, and well pleased I was, as ever I was in my Life, or with any thing I ever did in my Life; as soon as it was Dark, *Moggy* slip'd away before hand, as the Doctor and I had agreed, to the old Gentleman's House-keeper, and I came in about half an Hour after, and there we were marry'd in the Doctor's Study, *that is to say*, in his Oratory, or Chapel, a little Room within his Study, and we stay'd and supp'd with him afterward.

WHEN after a short Stay more, I went Home first, because I would send the Children all to Bed, and the other Servants out of the Way, and *Moggy* came some time after, and so we lay together that Night; the next Morning I let all the Family know that *Moggy* was my Wife; and my three Children were rejoyc'd at it to the last Degree: And now I was a marry'd Man a fourth Time; and in short, I was really more happy in this plain country Girl, than with any of all the Wives I had had: She was not Young, being about three and Thirty, but she brought me a Son the first Year; she was very pretty, well shap'd, and of a merry chearful Disposition, but not a Beauty; she was an admirable Family Manager; lov'd my former Children, and used them not at all the worse for having some of her own, in a Word, she made me an excellent Wife; but liv'd with me but four Year, and dy'd of a Hurt she got of a Fall while she was with Child, and in her I had a very great Loss indeed.

AND yet such was my Fate in Wives, that after all the Blushing, and Backwardness of Mrs. *Moggy* at first, Mrs. *Moggy* had, it seems, made a Slip in her younger Days, and was got with Child ten Year before, by a Gentleman of a great Estate in that Country who promised her Marriage, and afterwards deserted her: But as that had happen'd long before I came into the Country, and the Child was dead and forgotten, the People were so good to her, and so kind to me, that hearing I had marry'd her, no Body ever spoke of it, neither did I ever hear of it, or suspect it, till after she was in her Grave, and then it was of small consequence to me one way or other and she was a faithful, virtuous, obliging Wife, to me. I had very severe Affliction indeed, while she lived with me, for the *Small-Pox*, a frightful Distemper in that Country, broke into my Family, and carry'd off three of my Children, and a Maid Servant; so that I had only one of my former Wives, and one by my *Moggy*, the first a Son, the last a Daughter.

WHILE these things were in agitation, came on the Invasion of the Scots, and the Fight at *Preston*,[414] and I have cause to bless the Memory of my *Moggy*, for I was all on Fire on that Side, and just going away with Horse and Arms, to joyn the Lord *Darwentwater*,[415] but *Moggy* begg'd me off, *as I may call it*, and hung about me so, with her Tears and Importunities that I sat still and look'd on, for which I had Reason to be thankful.

I was really a sorrowful Father, and the loss of my Children stuck close to me, but the loss of my Wife stuck closer to me than all the rest, nor was my grief lessen'd, or my kindest Thoughts abated in the least by the Account I heard of her former Miscarriages, seeing they were so long before I knew her, and were not discover'd by me or to me in her life time.

ALL these things put together made me very Comfortless: And now I thought Heaven summon'd me to retire to *Virginia*, the Place, and as I may say, the only Place I had been bless'd at, or had met with any thing that deserv'd the Name of success in, and where indeed my Affairs being in good Hands, the Plantations were encreas'd to such a Degree, that some Years my return here made up eight Hundred Pound, and one Year almost a Thousand, so I resolv'd to leave my native Country once more, and taking my Son with me, and leaving *Moggy*'s Daughter with her Grandfather, I made him my principal Agent, left him considerable in his Hands, for the Maintenance of the Child, and left my Will in his Hand, by which, if I died before I should otherwise Provide for her, I left her 2000*l*. Portion to be paid by my Son out of the Estate I had in *Virginia* and the whole Estate if he died unmarried.

I embark'd for *Virginia*, in the Year ——, at the Town of *Leverpool*, and had a tollerable Voyage thither, only that we met with a Pyrate Ship, in the Latitude of 48 Degrees, who Plunder'd us of every thing they could come at that was for their turn, *that is to say*, Provisions, Ammunition, small Arms and Money; but to give the Rogues their Due, tho' they were the most abandon'd Wretches that were ever seen, they did not use us ill; and as to my Loss, it was not considerable, the Cargo which I had on Board, was in Goods, and was of no use to them; nor could they come at those things without Rumaging the whole Ship, which they did not think worth their while.

I found all my Affairs in very good order at *Virginia*, my Plantations pro-
digiously increas'd, and my Manager, who first inspired me with travelling
Thoughts, and made me Master of any Knowledge worth Naming,
receiv'd me with a transport of Joy, after a Ramble of four and Twenty
Years.

I ought to remember it to the encouragement of all faithful Servants,
that he gave me an Account, which I believe was critically Just, of the
whole Affair of the Plantations, each by themselves; and Ballanc'd in Years,
every Years produce, being fully transmitted; Charges deducted to my
Order at *London*.

I was exceedingly satisfy'd, as I had good Reason indeed with his Management, and with his Management, as much in its degree of his Own. I
can safely say it: He had Improv'd a very large Plantation of his own at the
same time, which he began upon the Foot of the Countries Allowance of
Land, and the Encouragement he had from me.

WHEN he had given me all this pleasing agreeable Account you will not
think it strange, that I had a desire to see the Plantations, and to View all
the Servants, which in both the Works were upwards of three hundred; and
as my Tutor generally bought some every Fleet that came from *England*, I
had the Mortification to see two or three of the *Preston* Gentlemen there,
who being Prisoners of War, were spar'd from the publick Execution, and
sent over for to that Slavery, which to Gentlemen must be worse than
Death.

I do not mention what I did or said, relating to them here, I shall speak
at large of it, when the rest of them came over, which more nearly concern'd me.

BUT one Circumstance occurr'd to me here, that equally surpris'd me,
and terrify'd me to the last degree; looking over all the Servants, as I say
above, and viewing the Plantations narrowly and frequently, I came one
Day by a place where some Women were at Work by themselves: I was
seriously reflecting on the Misery of human Life, when I saw some of those
poor Wretches; thought I, they have perhaps liv'd gay, and pleasantly in
the World, notwithstanding, thro' a variety of Distresses, they may have
been brought to this; and if a Body was to hear the History of some of
them now, it would perhaps be as moving, and as seasonable a Sermon as
any Minister in the Country could Preach.

WHILE I was musing thus, and looking at the Women, on a sudden I
heard a Combustion among other of the Women Servants, who were
almost behind me, in the same Work, and help was call'd loudly for, one of
the Women having swoon'd away; they said she would die immediately if
something was not done to relieve her; I had nothing about me, but a little

Bottle, which we always carried about us there with Rum, to give any Servant a Dram that merited that Favour; so I turn'd my Horse and went up towards the Place; but as the poor Creature was lying flat on the Ground, and the rest of the Women Servants, about her, I did not see her, but gave them the Bottle, and they rubb'd her Temples with it, and with much a do brought her to Life, and gave her a little to Drink; but she could Drink none of it, and was exceeding ill afterwards; so that she was carried to the Infirmary, so they call it in the Religious Houses in *Italy*, where the sick Nuns or Friers, are carried; but here in *Virginia*, I think they should call it the Condemn'd-hole,[416] for it really was only a Place just fit for People to die in, not a Place to be cur'd in.

THE sick Woman refusing to Drink, one of the Women Servants brought me the Bottle again, and I bad them Drink it among them, which had almost set them together by the Ears for the Liquor, there being not enough to give every one a Sup.

I went home to my House immediately, and reflecting on the miserable Provision was wont to be made for poor Servants, when they were sick, I inquir'd of my Manager, if it was so still? *he said*, he believ'd mine was better than any in the Country; but he confess'd it was but sad Lodging; however, *he said*, he would go and look after it immediately, and see how it was.

HE came to me again, about an Hour after, and told me the Woman was very ill, and frighted with her Condition, that she seem'd to be very Penitent, for some things in her past Life, which lay heavy upon her Mind, believing she should die; that she ask'd him, if there was no Minister to Comfort poor dying Servants; and he told her, that she knew they had no Minister nearer than such a Place, but that if she liv'd till Morning, he should be sent for; he told me also, that he had remov'd her into a Room where their chief Workman us'd to Lodge; that he had given her a pair of Sheets, and every thing he could, that he thought she wanted, and had appointed another Woman Servant to tend her, and sit up with her.

WELL, *says I*, that's well, for I cannot bear to have poor Creatures lye and perish, by the meer Hardship of the Place they are in, when they are Sick, and want help; besides, *said I*, some of those unfortunate Creatures, they call Convicts, may be People that have been tenderly brought up: Really[a] Sir, *says he*, this poor Creature I always said had something of a Gentlewoman in her, I could see it by her Behaviour, and I have heard the other Women say, that she liv'd very great once, and that she had fifteen Hundred Pound to her Portion, and I dare say she has been a handsome Woman in her time, and she has a Hand as fine as a Ladies now; tho' it be Tanned with the Weather; I dare say she was never brought up to Labour as she does here, and she says to the rest that it will kill her.

TRULY, *says I*, it may be so, and that may be the Reason that she faints under it; and, *I added*, is there nothing you can put her to within Doors, that may not be so Laborious, and expose her to so much Heat and Cold; he told me yes, there was; he could set her to be the House-keeper, for the Woman that lately was such, was out of her Time, and was married and turn'd Planter. Why then let her have it, said I, if she Recovers, and in the mean time go, *said I*, and tell her so, perhaps the Comfort of it may help Restore her.

HE did so, and with that, taking good care of her, and giving her good warm Dyet, the Woman recover'd, and in a little time was Abroad again, for it was the meer Weight of Labour and being expos'd to hard Lodging, and mean Dyet, to one so tenderly bred, that struck her, and she fainted at her Work.

WHEN she was made House-Keeper, she was quite another Body; she put all the Houshold in such excellent Order, and manag'd their Provisions so well, that my Tutor admir'd her Conduct, and would be every now and then speaking of her to me; that she was an excellent Manager; I'll warrant, *says he*, she has been Bred a Gentlewoman, and she has been a fine Woman in her time too: In a Word, he said so many good things of her, that I had a mind to see her; so one Day I took occasion to go to the Plantation House, as they call'd it and into a Parlour always reserv'd for the Master of the Plantation; there she had Opportunity to see me before I could see her, and as soon as she had seen me, she knew me; but indeed had I seen her an Hundred times, I should not have known her; she was it seems in the greatest Confusion, aud Surprize at seeing who I was, that it was possible for any one to be; and when I order'd my Manager to bring her into the Room, he found her crying, and beg'd him to excuse her, that she was frighted, and should die away, if she came near me.

I NOT imagining any thing, but that the poor Creature was afraid of me, *for Masters in* Virginia *are terrible things*; bad him tell her she need to be under no Concern at my calling for her, for it was not for any hurt, nor any Displeasure; but that I had some Orders to give her; so having as he thought encourag'd her, *tho' her surprize was of another kind*, he brought her in; when she came in, she held a Handkerchief in her Hand, wiping her Eyes, as if she had cry'd. Mrs.ª House-keeper, *said I*, speaking chearfully to her, don't be concern'd at my sending for you, I have had a very good Account of your Management, and I call'd for you, to let you know I am very well pleas'd with it; and if it falls in my way to do you any good, if your Circumstances will allow it, I may be willing enough to help you out of your Misery.

SHE made low Curtisies, but said nothing, however, she was so far encourag'd that she took her Hand from her Face, and I saw her Face fully, and I believe she did it, desiring I should discover who she was, but I really knew nothing of her any more, than if I had never seen her in my Life; but went on as I thought to encourage her as I us'd to do with any that I saw deserv'd it.

IN the mean time my Tutor, who was in the Room went out on some Business or other, I know not what; as soon as he was gone, she burst out into a Passion, and falling down on her Knees just before me, O! Sir, *says she*, I see you don't know me, be merciful to me, I am your miserable divorc'd Wife!

I WAS astonish'd, I was frighted, I trembled like one in an Ague, I was Speechless; in a Word, I was ready to sink, and she fell flat on her Face, and lay there, as if she had been dead; I was Speechless, *I say*, as a Stone, I had only Presence of Mind enough to step to the Door, and fasten it, that my Tutor might not come in: Then going back to her, I took her up, and spoke comfortably to her, and told her, I no more knew her, than if I had never seen her.

O! Sir, *said she*, Afflictions are dreadful Things, such as I have suffer'd have been enough to alter my Countenance; but forgive *said she*, for God's sake the Injuries I have done you! I have paid dear for all my wickedness, and 'tis just, 'tis righteous that God should bring me to your Foot, to ask you Pardon for all my brutish doings: Forgive me Sir, *said she*, I beseech you, and let me be your Slave or Servant for it as long as I live; 'tis all I ask, and with those Words, she fell upon her Knees again, and cry'd so vehemently, that it was impossible for her to stop it, or to speak a Word more: I took her up again, made her sit down, desir'd her to Compose herself, and to hear what I was going to say, tho' indeed it touch'd me so sensibly, I was hardly able to speak any more then she was.

FIRST, I told her it was such a surprize to me, that I was not able to say much to her, *and indeed the Tears ran down my Face almost as fast as they did on hers*, I told her that I should only tell her now, that as no Body had yet known any thing that had pass'd, so it was absolutely necessary, not a Word of it should be known, that it should not be the worse for her, that she was thus thrown into my Hands again; but that I could do nothing for her, if it was known, and therefore that her future good, or ill Fortune would depend upon her entire concealing it; that as my Manager would come in again presently, she should go back to her part of the House, and go on in the Business, as she did before; that I would come to her, and talk more at large with her in a Day or two; so she retir'd, after assuring me that not a word of it should go out of her Mouth, and indeed she was willing to retire before my Tutor came again, that he might not see the Agony she was in.

I WAS so perplex'd about this surprizing Incident, that I hardly knew what I did, or said all that Night, nor was I come to any settled Resolution in the Morning, what Course to take in it: However, in the^a Morning I call'd my Tutor, and told him that I had been exceedingly concern'd about the poor distress'd Creature, the House-Keeper; that I had heard some of her Story, which was very dismal; that she had been in very good Circumstances, and was bred very well, and that I was glad he had remov'd her Out of the Field into the House, but still she was almost naked, and that I would have him go to the Warehouse, and give her some Linnen; especially Head Cloaths, and all sorts of small things, such as Hoods, Gloves, Stockings, Shoes, Petty-Coats, &c. and to let her chuse for her self; also, a Morning Gown of Callico, and a Mantua⁴¹⁷ of a better kind of Callico, *that is to say,* to new Cloath her, which he did: But brought me Word, that he found her all in Tears, and that she had cry'd all Night long, and in short, that he believ'd, she would indeed cry her self to Death; that all the while she was receiving the things he gave her, she cry'd; that now and then she would struggle with, and stop it, but that then upon another Word speaking, she would burst out again, so that it griev'd every Body that saw her.

I WAS really affected with her Case very much, but struggled hard with my self, to hide it, and turn'd the Discourse to something else; in the mean time, tho' I did not go to her the next Day, nor till the third Day, yet I study'd Day and Night, how to Act, and what I should do in this remarkable Case.

WHEN I came to the House which was the third Day, she came into the Room I was in, cloath'd all over with my Things, which I had ordered her, and told me she thank'd God, she was now my Servant again, and wore my Livery, thank'd me for the Cloaths I had sent her; and said it was much more than she had deserv'd from me.

I then entered into Discourses with her, *no Body being present but our selves,* and first, *I told her,* She should name no more of the unkind things that had past, for she had humbled herself more than enough on that Subject, and I would never reproach her with any thing that was past; I found that she had been the deepest sufferer by far. I^b told her it was impossible for me in my present Circumstances to receive her there as a Wife, who came over as a Convict, neither did she know so little, as to desire it. But, *I told her,* I might be Instrumental to put an End to her Misfortunes in the World, and especially to the miserable part of it, which was her present Load, provided she could effectually keep her own Council, and never let the particulars come out of her Mouth, and that from the Day she did, she might date her irrecoverable Ruin.

SHE was as sensible of the Necessity of that Part, as I was, and told me all she could claim of me, would be only to deliver her from her present Calamity, that she was not able to support, and that then if I pleased, she might live such a Life, as that she might apply the residue of what time she should have, wholly to Repentance; that she was willing to do the meanest Offices in the World for me; and tho' she should rejoyce to hear that I would forgive her former Life, yet that she would not look any higher than to be my Servant, as long as she liv'd, and in the mean time, I might be satisfy'd she would not let any Creature so much as know that I had ever seen her before.

I ASK'D her, if she was willing to let me into any Part of the History of her Life, since she and I Parted, but I did not Insist upon it, otherwise, than as she thought convenient; *she said*, as her Breach with me began first in Folly, and ended in Sin, so her whole Life afterward, was a continu'd Series of Callamity, Sin and Sorrow, Sin and Shame, and at last Misery; that she was deluded into Gay Company, and to an expensive way of Living, which betray'd her to several wicked Courses to support the Expences of it; that after a thousand Distresses and Difficulties, being not able to maintain her self, she was reduced to extreme Poverty.

THAT she would many Times have humbled her self to me in the lowest and most submissive manner in the World, being sincerely Penitent for her first Crime, but that she could never hear of me, nor which way I was gone; that she was by that Means so abandon'd, that she wanted Bread, and those Wants and Distresses brought her into bad Company of another Kind, and that she fell in among a Gang of Thieves, with whom she Herded[418] for some time, and got Money enough a great while, but under the greatest Dread and Terror imaginable, being in the constant Fear of coming to Shame; that afterwards, what she fear'd, was come upon her, and for a very triffling Attempt, in which she was not Principal, but accidentally concern'd, She was sent to this Place: She told me, her Life was such a Collection of various Fortunes, up and down, in Plenty, and in Misery; in Prison, and at Liberty; at Ease, and in Torment; that it would take up a great many Days to give me a History of it, that I was come to see the End of it, as I had seen the best part of the Beginning, that I knew she was brought up tenderly, and far'd[a] delicately, but that now she was with the Prodigal, brought to desire Husks with Swine and even to want that Supply:[419] Her Tears flow'd so Strongly upon this Discourse, that they frequently interrupted her, so that she could not go on without Difficulty;

and at last could not go on at all, so I told her, I would excuse her telling any more of her Story at that Time; that I saw it was but a renewing of her Grief, and that I would rather Contribute to her forgetting what was past, and desir'd her to say no more of it, so I broke off that Part.

IN the mean time, I told her, since Providence had thus cast her upon my Hands again, I would take Care that she should not want, and that she should not live hardly neither, tho' I could go no farther at present; and thus we parted for that Time; and she continu'd in the Business of House keeper; only, that to ease her, I gave her an Assistant, and tho' I would not have it call'd so, it was neither more nor less than a Servant to wait on her, and do every thing for her, and told her too,[a] that it was so.

AFTER she had been some time in this Place, she recover'd her Spirits, and grew chearful; her fallen Flesh plump'd up, and the sunk and hollow parts fill'd again, so that she began to recover something of that Brightness, and Charming Countenance, which was once so very agreeable to me; and sometimes I could not help having warm Desires towards her, and of taking her into her first Station again; but there were many Difficulties occur'd, which I could not get over a great while.

BUT in the mean time an other odd Accident happen'd, which put me to a very great Difficulty, and more than I could have thought such a thing could be capable of; my Tutor, a Man of Wit and Learning, and full of generous Principles, who was at first mov'd with Compassion for the Misery of this Gentlewoman, and even then, thought there were some things more than Common in her, as I have hinted: Now, when, as I say, she was recover'd, and her sprightly Temper restor'd, and comforted, he was charm'd so with her Conversation, that in short, he fell in Love with her.

I hinted in my former Account of her, that she had a Charming Tongue, was Mistress of abundance of Wit, that she sung incomparibly fine, and was perfectly well Bred, these all remained with her still, and made her a very agreeable Person; and in short, he came to me one Evening, and told me, that he came to ask my Leave to let him marry the House-keeper.

I WAS exceedingly perplex'd at this Proposal but however, I gave him no Room to perceive that; I told him, I hop'd he had consider'd well of it, before he brought it so far as to offer it to me, and suppos'd that he had agreed that Point so; that I had no Consent to give, but as she had almost four Year of her Time to Serve.

HE answer'd no, he paid such a regard to me, that he would not so much as take one step in such a thing without my Knowledge, and assur'd me, he had not so much as mentioned it to her; I knew not what answer indeed to make to him, but at last I resolv'd to put it off from myself to her, because then I should have opportunity to talk with her before hand; so I told him he was[a] perfectly free to act in the matter as he thought fit; that I could not say either, one thing or another to it, neither had I any right to meddle in it; as to her serving out her time with me, that was a Trifle, and not worth Naming; but I hop'd he would consider well every Circumstances before he entered upon such an Affair as that.

HE told me he had fully consider'd it already, and that he was resolv'd, seeing I was not against it, to have her whatever came of it, for he believ'd he should be the happiest Man alive with her; then he run on in his Character of her, how clever a Woman she was, in the management of all manner of Business; how admirable in Conversation[b] she was; what a Wit, what a Memory, what a vast share of Knowledge, and the like; all which I knew to be the Truth, and yet short of her just Character too; for as she was all that formerly, when she was mine, she was vastly improv'd in the School of Affliction, and was all the bright Part, with a vast Addition of Temper, Prudence, Judgment, and all that she formerly wanted.

I HAD not much Patience as you may well imagine, till I saw my honest House-keeper to communicate this Secret to her, and to see what Course she would steer on so nice[420] an Occasion; but I was suddenly taken so ill with a Cold, which held for two Days, that I could not stir out of Doors and in this time the matter was all done, and over, for my Tutor had gone the same Night, and made his attack, but was coldly receiv'd at first, which very much surpris'd him, for he made no doubt to have her consent at first Word; however, the next Day he came again, and again the third Day, when finding he was in earnest, and yet that she could not think of any thing of that kind, she told him in few Words that she thought herself greatly oblig'd to him for such a Testimony of his Respect to her, and should have embrac'd it willingly, as any Body would suppose one in her Circumstances should do, but that she would not abuse him so much; for that she must acknowledge to him, she was under Obligations that prevented her, that was, in short, that she was a married Woman, and had a Husband alive.

THIS was so sincere, but so Effectual an Answer, that he could have no room to reply one Word to it; but that he was very sorry, and that it was a very great Affliction to him, and as a great Disappointment as ever he met with.

THE next Day after he had receiv'd this repulse I came to the Plantation House, and sending for the House-keeper, I began with her, and told her that I understood she would have a very advantageous Proposal made to her, and that I would have her Consider well of it, and then told her what my Tutor had said to me.

SHE immediately fell a crying, at which I seem'd to wonder very much, O! Sir, *says she*, how can you Name such a thing to me? I told her that I had been married myself since I parted from her: Yes Sir, *says she*, but the Case alters, the Crime being on my Side, I ought not to Marry; but, *says she*, that is not the Reason at all, but I cannot do it; I pretended to press her to it, (tho' not sincerely I must acknowledge, for my heart had turned toward her for some time, and I had fully forgiven her in my Mind all her former Conduct) but, I say, I seem'd to press her to it, at which she burst out in a Passion, no, no, *says she*, let me be your Slave rather than the best Man's Wife in the World: I reason'd with her upon her Circumstances, and how such a Marriage would restore her to a State of Ease and Plenty, and none in the World might ever know or suspect who or what she had been, but she could not bear it; but with Tears again raising her Voice, that I was affraid she would be heard, I beseech you, *says she*, do not speak it any more, I was once yours, and I will never belong to any Man else in the World; let me be as I am, or any thing else you please to make me, but not a Wife, to any Man alive but yourself.

I was so mov'd with the Passion she was in at speaking this, that I knew not what I said or did for sometime; at length, I said to her, it is great pity, you had not long ago been as sincere as you are now, it had been better for us both; however, as it is, you shall not be forc'd to any thing against your Mind; nor shall you be the worse treated for refusing. But how will you put him off? no doubt he expects you will receive his Proposal, as an Advantage, and as he sees no farther into your Circumstances, so it is. O, Sir, *says she*, I have done all that already; he has his Answer, and is fully satisfy'd; he will never trouble you any more on that Head, and then she told me what answer she had given him.

FROM that minute I resolv'd that I would certainly take her again to be my Wife as before, I thought she had fully made me amends for her former ill Conduct, and she deserv'd to be forgiven; and so indeed she did, if ever Woman did, considering also, what dreadful Pennance she had undergone, and how long she had liv'd in Misery and Distress; and that Providence had, as it were cast her upon me again, and above all, had given her such an Affection to me, and so resolv'd a Mind that she could refuse so handsome an offer of Deliverance, rather than be farther separated from me.

As I resolved this in my Mind, so I thought it was cruel to conceal it any longer from her; nor indeed, could I contain my self any longer, but I took her in my Arms; well, *says I*, you have given me such a Testimony of Affection in this, that I can no longer withstand; I forgive you all that ever was between us on this Account, and since you will be no Body's but mine, you shall be mine again, as you were at first.

BUT this was too much for her the other way, and now she was so far overcome with my yielding to her, that had she not got Vent to her Passion by the most Vehement Crying, she must have dy'd in my Arms, and I was forc'd to let her go, and set her down in a Chair, where she cry'd for a Quarter of an Hour, before she could speak a Word.

WHEN she was come to her self enough to talk again, I told her we must consider of a Method how to bring this to pass; and that it must not be done by publishing there, that she was my Wife before, for that would expose us both, but that I would openly marry her again; this she agreed was very rational, and accordingly, about two Months after, we were marry'd again, and no Man in the World ever enjoy'd a better Wife, or liv'd more happy than we both did for several Years after.

AND now I began to think my Fortunes were settled for this World, and I had nothing before me, but to finish a Life of infinite Variety, such as mine had been with a comfortable Retreat, being both made wiser by our Sufferings and Difficulties, and able to judge for our selves, what kind of Life would be best adapted to our present Circumstances, and in what Station we might look upon our selves to be most compleatly happy.

BUT Man is a short sighted Creature at best, and in nothing more than in that of fixing his own Felicity; or, *as we may say*, choosing for himself: One would have thought, and so my Wife often suggested to me, that the State of Life that I was now in, was as perfectly calculated to make a Man compleatly happy, as any private Station in the World could be: We had an Estate more than sufficient, and daily encreasing, for the supporting any State or Figure that in that Place we could propose to our selves, or even desire to live in: We had every thing that was Pleasant and agreeable, without the least Mortification in any Circumstances of it; every sweet thing, and nothing to embitter it; every Good, and no mixture of Evil with it; nor any Gap open, where we could have the least apprehensions of any Evil breaking out upon us; nor indeed, was it easie for either of us in our most phlegmatick melancholly Notions, to have the least Imagination how any thing dissastrous could happen to us in the common Course of Things, unless something should befall us out of the ordinary way of Providence, or of its actings in the World.

BUT an unseen Mine blew up all this apparent Tranquility at once, and tho' it did not remove my Affairs there from me, yet it effectually remov'd me from them, and sent me a wandring into the World again; a Condition full of Hazards, and always attended with Circumstances dangerous to Mankind, while he is left to choose his own Fortunes, and be guided by his own short sighted Measures.

I must now return to a Circumstance of my History, which had been past for some Time, and which relates to my Conduct, while I was last in *England*.

I mention'd how my faithful Wife *Moggy*, with her Tears, and her Entreaties had prevail'd with me not to play the Mad-man, and openly joyn in the Rebellion with the late Lord *Derwent-water*, and his Party, when they enter'd *Lancashire*; and thereby, *as I may say*, sav'd my Life. But my Curiosity prevail'd so much at last, that I gave her the Slip when they came to *Preston*, and at least thought I would go and look at them, and see what they were likely to come to.

MY former Wife's importunities, *as above*, had indeed prevail'd with me from publickly embarking in that Enterprise and joyning openly with them in Arms; and by this, as I have observ'd, she sav'd my Life to be sure, because I had then publickly espoused the Rebellion, and had been known to have been among them, which might have been as fatal to me afterwards, tho' I had not been taken in the Action, as if I had.

BUT when they advanc'd, and came nearer to us to *Preston*, and there appear'd a greater Spirit among the People in their Favour, my old Doctor, who I had mention'd before, who was a *Romish* Priest, and had married us, inspir'd me with new Zeal, and gave me no rest, till he oblig'd me with only a good Horse, and Arms to joyn them the Day before they enter'd *Preston*, he himself venturing in the same Posture with me.

I WAS not so publick here, as to be very well known, at least by any one that had Knowledge of me in the Country where I liv'd; and this was indeed my safety afterward, as you will soon hear; but yet I was known too among the Men, especially, among the *Scots*, with some of whom I had been acquainted in foreign Service; with these I was particularly Conversant, and passing for a *French* Officer, I talk'd to them of making a select Detachment to defend the pass between *Preston*, and the River and Bridge; upon maintaining which, as I insisted, depended the safety of the whole Party.

IT was with some warmth that I spoke of that Affair, and as I pass'd among them, *I say*, for a *French* Officer, and a Man of Experience, it caus'd several Debates among them; but the hint was not follow'd, as is well known; and from that Moment I gave them all up as lost, and meditated nothing but how to escape from them, which I effected the Night before they were surrounded by the Royal Cavalry: I did not do this without great difficulty, swimming the River *Ribble*, at a Place, where tho' I got well over, yet I could not for a long while get to a Place where my Horse cou'd land himself, *that is to say*, where the Ground was firm enough for him to take the Land; however, at length I got on shoar, and riding very hard came the next Evening in sight of my own Dwelling; here after lying by in a Wood till the Depth of Night, I shot my Horse in a little kind of a Gravel-pit, or Marl-pit,[421] where I soon cover'd him with Earth for the present; and marching all alone, I came about two in the Morning to my House, where my Wife surpriz'd with Joy,[a] and yet terribly Frighted, let me in, and then I took immediate Measures to secure myself upon whatever incident might happen, but which as things were ordered, I had no need to make use of, for the Rebels being intirely defeated, and either all killed, or taken Prisoners. I was not known by any Body in the County to have been among them; no, nor so much as suspected, and thus I made a narrow Escape from the most dangerous Action, and most foolishly embark'd in, of any that I had ever been engag'd in before.

IT was very lucky to me, that I killed and bury'd my horse, for he would have been taken two Days after, and would to be sure have been known by those who had seen me upon him at *Preston*; but now, as none knew I had been abroad, nor any such Circumstance could discover me; I kept close, and as my Excursion had been short, and I had not been miss'd by any of my Neighbours, if any Body came to speak with me, behold, I was at Home.

HOWEVER, I was not thoroughly easy in my Mind, and secretly wish'd I was in my own Dominions in *Virginia*, to which, in a little time, other Circumstances concurring, I made Preparations to remove with my whole Family.

IN the mean time, *as above*, the Action at *Preston* happen'd, and the Miserable People surrender'd to the King's Troops; some were executed for Examples, as in such Cases is usual; and the Government extending Mercy to the Multitude; they were kept in *Chester* Castle, and other places a considerable time, till they were disposed of, some one Way, some another, as we shall hear.

SEVERAL hundreds of them after this, were at their own Request transported, *as tis vulgarly Express'd*, to the Plantations, *that is to say*, sent to *Virginia*, and other *British* Collonies, to be sold after the usual manner of condemn'd Criminals, or, *as we call them there*, Convicts, to serve a limited Time in the Country, and then be made Freemen again; some of these I have spoken of above; but now to my no little Uneasiness, I found, after I had been there some time, two Ships arrived with more of these People in the same River where all my Plantations lay.

I no sooner heard of it, but the first Step I took was, to resolve to let none of them be bought into my Work, or to any of my Plantations; and this I did, pretending that I would not make Slaves every Day of unfortunate Gentlemen, who fell into that Condition, for their Zeal to their Party only, and the like: But the true Reason was, that I expected several of them would know me, and might perhaps betray me, and make it publick, that I was one of the same sort, but had made my Escape, and so I might be brought into Trouble; and if I came off with my Life, might have all my Effects seiz'd on, and be reduc'd to Misery and Poverty again at once, all which I thought I had done enough to deserve.

THIS was a just Caution, but as I found quickly, was not a sufficient one, as my Circumstances stood, for my Safety; for tho' I bought none of these poor Men my self, yet several of my Neighbours did, and there was scarce a Plantation near me, but had some of them, more or less among them; So that in a Word, I could not peep abroad hardly, but I was in Danger to be seen and known too, by some or other of them.

I may be allow'd to say, that this was a very uneasy Life to me, and such, that in short, I found my self utterly unable to bear; for I was now reduced from a great Man, a Magistrate, a Governor, or Master of three great Plantations, and having three or four Hundred Servants at my Command, to be a poor self condemn'd Rebel, and durst not shew my Face; and that I might with the same safety, or rather more, have skulk'd about in *Lancashire*, where I was; or gone up to *London*, and conceal'd my self there, till things had been over; but now the Danger was come Home to me, even to my Door, and I expected nothing, but to be inform'd against every Day, be taken up, and sent to *England* in Irons, and have all my Plantations seiz'd on, as a forfeited Estate to the Crown.

I had but one hope of Safety to trust to, and that was, that having been so little a while among them; done nothing for them; and passing for a Stranger, they never knew my Name, but only I was call'd the *French* Colonel, or the *French* Officer, or the *French* Gentleman, by most, if not, by all the People there; and as for the Doctor that went with me, he had found Means to escape too, tho' not the same way that I did, finding the Cause not like to be supported and that the King's Troops were gathering on all sides round them like a Cloud.

BUT to return to my self, this was no Satisfaction to me, and what to do, I really knew not; for I was more at a Loss how to Shift in such a distress'd Case as this, now it lay so close to me, than ever I was in any other Difficulty of my Life. The first thing I did was to come Home, and make a Confidence of the whole Affair to my Wife; and tho' I did it generously, without Conditions, yet I did not do it, without first telling her, how I was now going to put my Life into her Hands, that she might have it in her Power to pay me Home, for all that she might think had been hard in my former Usage of her; and that in short, it would be in her Power to deliver me up into the Hands of my Enemies; but that I would trust her Generosity, as well as her renew'd Affection, and put all upon her Fidelity; and without any more Precaution, I open'd the whole thing to her, and particularly, the Danger I was now in.

A faithful Counsellor is Life from the Dead, gives courage where the Heart is sinking, and raises the Mind to a proper use of Means; and such she was to me indeed, upon every Step of this Affair; and it was by her Direction that I took every Step that follow'd for the extricating my self out of this Labrinth.

COME, come, my Dear, *says she*, if this be all, there is no room for any such Disconsolate doings as your fears run you upon; for I was immediately for selling off my Plantations, and all my Stock, and embarking myself forthwith, and to get to *Maderas*,[422] or to any Place out of the King's Dominions.

BUT my Wife was quite of another Opinion, and encouraging me on another Account, propos'd two Things, either my Freighting a Sloop with Provisions to the *West-Indies*, and so taking Passage from thence to *London*, or letting her go away directly for *England*, and endeavour to obtain the King's Pardon whatever it might cost.

I inclin'd to the last Proposal, for tho' I was unhappily Prejudic'd in favour of a wrong Interest, yet I had always a Secret, and right Notion of the Clemency, and merciful Disposition of his Majesty, and had I been in *England*, should I believe have been easily perswaded to have thrown myself at his Foot.

BUT going to *England*, as I was Circumstanced,[a] must have been a publick Action, and I must have made all the usual Preparations for it, must have appear'd in Publick, have staid till the Crop was ready, and gone away in Form, and State, as usual; or have acted as if something extraordinary was the Matter, and have fill'd the Heads of People there with innumerable Suggestions of they knew not what.

BUT my Wife made all this easie to me, from her own Invention; for without acquainting me with any thing, she comes merrily to me one Morning before I was up; My dear, *says she*, I am very sorry to hear that you are not very well, this Morning; I have order'd *Pennico*, that was a young *Negro* Girl, which I had given her, to make you a Fire in your Chamber, and pray lye still where you are a while, till 'tis done; at the same instant, the little *Negro* came in with Wood, and a pair of Bellows, &c. to kindle the Fire, and my Wife not giving me time to reply, Whispers close to my Ear to lye still, and say nothing till she came up again to me.

I WAS thoroughly frighted, that you may be sure of, and thought of nothing, but of being discover'd, betray'd, carried to *England*, hang'd, quarter'd, and all that was terrible, and my very Heart sunk within me; she perceiv'd my Disorder, and turn'd back, assuring me there was no Harm, desir'd me to be easie, and she would come back again presently, and give me satisfaction in every particular that I could desire; so I compos'd myself a while as well as I could; but it was but a little while that I could bear it, and I sent *Pennico* down Stairs to find out her Mistress, and tell her I was very Ill, and must speak with her immediately, and the Girl was scarce out of the Room before I jump'd out of Bed, and began to dress me, that I might be ready for all Events.

MY Wife was as good as her Word, and was coming up as the Girl was coming down; I see, *says she*, you want Patience, but pray do not want Government of yourself, but take that Skreen[423] before your Face, and go to the Window, and see if you know any of those *Scotsmen*, that are in the Yard, for there are seven or eight of them, come about some Business to your Clerk.

I went and look'd through the Skreen, and saw the Faces of them all distinctly, but could make nothing of them, other than that they were *Scotsmen*, which it was easie to discern; however, it was no satisfaction to me that I knew not their Faces, for they might know mine for all that, according to the old *English* Proverb, *that more knows* Tom *Fool, than* Tom *Fool knows*;[424] so I kept close in my Chamber, till I understood they were all gone.

AFTER this, my Wife caus'd it to be given out in the House, that I was not well, and when this not being well had lasted three or four Days, I had my Leg wrap'd up in a great piece of Flannel, and laid upon a Stool, and there I was lame of the Gout; and this serv'd for about six Weeks, when my Wife told me she had given it out, that my Gout was rather Rheumatick, than a settled Gout, and that I was resolv'd to take one of my own Sloops, and go away to *Nevis* or *Antegoa*,[425] and use the Hot Baths there for my Cure.

ALL this was very well, and I approv'd my Wife's contrivance, as admirably good, both to keep me within Doors, eight or ten Weeks at first, and to convey me away afterwards without any extraordinary Bustle to be made about it; but still I did not know what it all tended to, and what the Design of it all was; but as my Wife desir'd me to leave that to her, so I readily did, and she carried it all on with a Prudence not to be disputed; and after she had wrapt my Legs in Flannel almost three Months, she came and told me the Sloop was ready; and all the Goods put on Board: And now, my Dear, *says she*, I come to tell you all the rest of my Design; for added she, I hope you will not think I am going to kidnap you, and transport you from *Virginia* as other People are transported to it; or, that I am going to get you sent away, and leave myself in Possession of your Estate; But you shall find me the same faithful humble Creature, which I should have been, if I had been still your Slave, and not had any Hopes of being your Wife; and that in all my Scheme which I have laid for your Safety, in this new Exigence, I have not proposed your going one Step, but where I shall go, and be always with you, to assist, and serve you on all Occasions, and to take my Portion with you, of what kind soever our Lot may be.

THIS was so generous, and so handsome a Declaration of her Fidelity, and so great a Token too of the Goodness of her Judgment, in considering of the Things which were before her, and of what my present Circumstances called for, that from that time forward, I gave my self cheerfully up to her Management, without any Hessitation in the least, and in about ten Days Preparation, we embark'd in a large Sloop of my own of about Sixty Ton.

I should have mention'd here, that I had still my faithful Tutor, (as I called him) at the Head of my Affairs, and as he knew who to Correspond with, and how to mannage the Correspondence in *England*, we left all that part to him, as I had done before; and I did this with a full Satisfaction in his Ability, as well as in his Integrity; it is true, he had been a little sha-green'd [426] in that Affair of my Wife, who, *as I hinted before*, had marry'd me, after telling him, in Answer to his Solicitations, that she had a Husband alive.

NOW, tho' this was litterally true, yet as it was a Secret not fit to be open'd to him, I was obliged to put him off with other Reasons, as well as I could, perhaps not much to the Purpose, and perhaps, not much to his Satisfaction; so that I reckon'd, he look'd on himself, as not very kindly used several Ways.

BUT he began to get over it, and to be easy, especially at our going away, when he found that the Trust of every Thing was still left in his Hands, as it was before.

WHEN my Wife had thus communicated every thing of the Voyage to me, and we began to be ready to go off, she came to me one Morning, and with her usual Chearfulness told me, she now came to tell me the rest of her Measures, for the Compleating my Deliverance; and this was, that while we made this Trip, *as she call'd it*, to the hot Springs at *Nevis*, She would write to a particular Friend at *London*, who she could depend upon, to try to get a Pardon for a Person on Account of the late Rebellion, with all the Circumstances which my case was attended with, *viz.* of having acted nothing among them but being three Days in the Place; and while we were thus absent, she did not question, but to have an Answer, which she would direct to come so many Ways, that we would be sure to have the first of it, as soon as it was possible the Vessels could go and come; and in the mean time, the Expence should be very small, for she would have an Answer to the grand Question first, Whether it could be obtain'd or no, and then an account of the Expence of it, that so I might Judge for my self, whether I would Part with the needful Sum, or no, before any Money was Disburss'd on my Account.

I could not but be thoroughly satisfy'd with her Contrivance in this particular, and I had nothing to add to it, but that I would not have her limit her Friend so strictly, but that if he saw the way clear, and that he was sure to obtain it, he should go thorough Stitch with it, if within the Expence of two, or three, or four Hundred Pounds, and that upon Advice of its being practicable, he should have Bills payable by such a Person on Delivery of the Warrant for the thing.

To fortifie this I enclos'd in her Packet a Letter to one of my Correspondents, who I could more particularly Trust, with a Credit for the Money, on such, and such Conditions; but the Honesty and Integrity of my Wife's Correspondent was such, as prevented all the Expence, and yet I had the wish'd for Security as if it had been all paid, as you shall hear presently.

ALL these things being fix'd to our Minds, and all things left behind in good Posture of Settlement as usual, we embark'd together, and put to Sea, having the opportunity of an *Englishman* of War being on the Coast in pursuit of the Pyrates, and who was just then standing away towards the Gulph of *Florida*,[427] and told us he would see us safe, as far as *New Providence*, or the *Bahama Islands*.

AND now having fair Weather, and a pleasant Voyage, and my Flannels taken off of my Legs, I must hint[428] a little, what Cargo I had with me; for as my Circumstances were very good in that Country, so I did not go such a Voyage as this, and with a particular reserve of Fortunes whatever might afterwards happen, without a sufficient Cargo, for our Support, and whatever Exigence might happen.

OUR Sloop, *as I said*, was of about 60 or 70 Ton, and as Tobacco, which is the general Produce of the Country was no Merchandize at *Nevis*, *that is to say*, for a great Quantity; so we carried very little, but loaded the Sloop with Corn, Pease, Meal and some Barrels of Pork, and an excellent Cargo it was; most of it being the Produce of my own Plantation; we took also a considerable Sum of Money with us in *Spanish* Gold, which was as above, not for Trade, but for all Events; I also order'd another Sloop to be hir'd, and to be sent after me loaden with the same Goods, as soon as they should have Advice from me that I was safe arriv'd.

WE came to the Latitude of the *Island* of *Antegoa*, which was very near to that of *Nevis*, whether we intended to go, on the 18th Day after our passing the Capes of *Virginia*; but had no sight of the *Island*, only our Master said he was very sure if he stood the same Course as he then was, and the Gale held, I say he told me, he was sure he should make the *Island* in less than five Hours Sail; so he stood on fair for the *Islands*: However, his Account had fail'd him, for we held on all the Evening, made no Land, and likewise all Night; when in the Gray of the Morning we discover'd from the Topmast-head, a Brigantine,[429] and a Sloop making Sail after us, at the distance of about six Leagues, fair Weather, and the Wind fresh at S.E.

OUR Master soon understood what they were, and came down into the Cabbin to me, to let me know it; I was much surpriz'd you may be sure at the Danger, but my poor Wife took me off of all the Concern for myself to take care of her, for she was frighted to that degree, that I thought we should not have been able to keep Life in her.

WHILE we were thus under the first Hurry, and Surprize of the thing, suddenly another Noise from the Deck call'd us up to look out, and that was *Land, Land*; the Master, and I, (for by this time I had gotten out of my Cabbin) run upon the Deck, and there we saw the state of our Case very plain; the two Rogues that stood after us, laid on all the Canvas they could carry, and crowded[430] after us a main; but at the distance, as I have said, of about six Leagues, rather more than less; on the other Hand, the Land discover'd lay about nine Leagues right a Head; so that if the Pyrates could get of us, so as to sail three Foot for our two, it was evident they would be up with us, before we could make the *Island*, if not, we should escape them, and get in; but even then we had no great hope to do any more, than run the Ship a Shoar to save our Lives, and so standing our Vessel, spoil both Sloop and Cargo.

WHEN we were making this Calculation, our Master came in chearfully, and told me he had crowded on more Sail, and found the Sloop carried it very well, and that he did not find the Rogues gain'd much upon us, and that especially, if one of them did not, that was the Sloop; he found he could go away from the Brigantine, as he pleas'd. Thus we gave them what they call a steern Chase,[431] and they work'd hard to come up with us, till towards Noon, when on a sudden they both stood away, and gave us over, to our great satisfaction, you may be sure.

WE did not it seems so easily see the Occasion of our Deliverance, as the Pyrate did, for while we went spooning[432] away large with the Wind, for one of the *Islands*, *with those two Spurs in our Heels*; that is, with these two Thieves at our Sterns: There lay an *Englishman* of War in the Road[433] of *Nevis*, which was the other *Island* from whence they spy'd the Pyrates, tho' the Land lying between, we could not see them.

AS the Man of War discover'd them, she immediately slip'd her Cable, and put herself under Sail in Chase of the Rogues, and they as soon persu'd her, and being to Windward, put themselves upon a Wind to escape her; and thus we were deliver'd, and in about an Hour more, we knew who was our Deliverer, seeing the Man of War stretch a Head clear of the *Island*, and stand directly after the Pyrates, who now crowded from us, as fast as they crowded after us before, and thus we got safe into *Antegoa*, after the terrible apprehension we had been in of being taken; our Apprehensions of being taken now, were much more than they would have been on Board a loaden Ship, from, or to *London*, where the most they ordinarily do, is to rifle the Ship, take what is Valuable, and Portable, and let her go; but ours being but a Sloop, and all our Loading being good Provisions, such as they wanted to be sure, for their Ships Store, they would certainly have carried us away, Ship and all; taken out the Cargo, and the Men; and perhaps, have set the Sloop on Fire; so that as to our Cargo of Gold it had been inevitably lost, and we hurry'd away, no Body knows where, and us'd as such barbarous Fellows are wont to use such innocent People as fall into their Hands.

BUT we were now out of their Hands, and had the satisfaction a few Days after, to hear that the Man of War pursu'd them so close, notwithstanding they chang'd their Course in the Night, that the next Day they were oblig'd to separate, and shift for themselves; so the Man of War took one of them, namely, the Brigantine, and carried her into *Jamaica*, but the other (*viz.*) the Sloop, made her escape.

BEING arriv'd here, we presently dispos'd of our Cargo, and at a tolerable good Price and now the Question was, what I should do next? I look'd upon myself to be safe here from the Fears I had been under of being discover'd as a Rebel, and so indeed I was, but having been now absent five Months, and having sent the Sloop back with a Cargo of Rum, and Molasses, such as I knew was wanting in my Plantations, I receiv'd the same Vessel back in return loaden as at first with Provisions.

WITH this Cargo my Wife receiv'd a Packet from *London*, from the Person, who she had employ'd, *as above*, to Solicit a Pardon, and who very honestly wrote to her, that he would not be so unjust to her Friend, whoever he was, as to put him to any Expence for a private Sollicitation, for that he was very well assur'd that his Majesty had resolv'd, from his own native Disposition to acts of Clemency and Mercy to his Subjects, to grant a general Pardon, with some few Exceptions to Persons extraordinary, and he hop'd her Friend was none of the extraordinary Persons to be excepted.

THIS was a kind of Life from the Dead to us both, and it was resolv'd that my Wife should go back in the Sloop directly to *Virginia*, where she should wait the good News from *England*, and should send me an Account of it as soon as she receiv'd it.

ACCORDINGLY she went back, and came safe with the Sloop and Cargo to our Plantation, from whence after above four Months more Expectation, behold! the Sloop came to me again but empty, and gutted of all her

Cargo, except about 100 Sacks of unground Malt, which the Pyrates (not knowing how to Brew) knew not what to do with, and so had left in her: However, to my infinite satisfaction, there was a Packet of Letters from my Wife, with another to her from *England*, as well one from her Friend, as one from my own Correspondent; both of them intimating that the King had sign'd an Act of Grace,[434] *that is to say*, a General Free Pardon, and sent me Copies of the Act, wherein it was manifest I was fully included.

AND here let me hint, that having now as it were receiv'd my Life at the Hands of King *GEORGE*,[435] and in a manner so satisfying as it was to me, it made a generous Convert of me, and I became sincerely given in[436] to the Interest of King *GEORGE*; and this from a Principle of Gratitude, and a Sense of my Obligation to his Majesty for my Life; and it has continu'd ever since, and will certainly remain with me as long as any Sense of Honour, and of the Debt of Gratitude remains with me: I mention this to hint how far in such Cases Justice, and Duty to our selves commands us; namely, that to those who graciously give us our Lives, when it is in their Power to take them away; those Lives are a Debt ever after, and ought to be set apart for their Service, and Interest as long as any of the Powers of Life remain; for Gratitude is a Debt that never ceases while the Benefit receiv'd remains,[437] and if my Prince has given me my Life, I can never pay the Debt fully, unless such a Circumstance as this should happen, that the Prince's Life should be in my Power, and I as generously preserv'd it; and yet neither would the Obligation be paid then, because the Cases would differ thus, that my preserving the Life of my Prince was my natural Duty, whereas the Prince on his Side (my Life being forfeited to him) had no Motive but meer Clemency, and Beneficence.

PERHAPS this Principle may not please all that read it; but as I have resolv'd to guide my Actions in things of such a Nature by the Rules of strict Vertue and Principles of Honour; so I must lay it down as a Rule of Honour, that a Man having once forfeited his Life to the Justice of his Prince, and to the Laws of his Country, and receiving it back as a Bounty from the Grace of his Soveraign; such a Man can never lift up his Hand again against that Prince, without a forfeiture of his Vertue, and an irreparable Breach of his Honour and Duty, and deserves no Pardon after it, either from God or Man; but all this is a Digression, I leave it as a Sketch of the Laws of Honour, printed by the Laws of Nature in the Breast of a Soldier, or a Man of Honour, and which I believe all impartial Persons who understand what Honour means, will Subscribe to.

BUT I return now to my present Circumstances; my Wife was gone, and with her, all my good Fortune, and Success in Business seem'd to have forsaken me; and I had another Scene of Misery to go thro', after I had thought that all my Misfortunes were over, and at an End.

MY Sloop as I have told you arriv'd, but having met with a Pyrate Rogue, in the Gulph of *Florida*, they took her first, then finding her Cargo to be all Eatables, which they always want, they gutted her of all her Loading, except, *as I have said*, about 100 Sacks of *Malt*, which they really knew not what to do with; and which was still worse, they took away all the Men, except the Master and two Boys, who they left on Board, just to run the Vessel into *Antegoa* where they said they were Bound.

BUT the most valuable Part of my Cargo, *viz.* a Packet of Letters from *England*, those they left to my inexpressible Comfort and Satisfaction; and particularly, that by those, I saw my Way open to return to my Wife, and to my Plantations, from which I promised my self never to wander any more.

IN order to this, I now embark'd my self, and all my Effects on board the Sloop, resolving to Sail Directly to the Capes of *Virginia*; my Capt. beating it up[438] to reach the *Bahama* Channel,[439] had not been two Days at Sea, but we were over-taken with a violent Storm, which drove us so far upon the Coast of *Florida*, as that we twice struck upon the Shore, and had we struck a third time, we had been inevitably lost. A Day or two after that, the Storm abating a little, we kept the Sea, but found that the Wind blowing so strong against our passing the Gulph, and the Sea going so high, we could not hold it any longer; so we were forced to bear away, and make what shift we could; in which distress, the fifth Day after, we made Land, but found it to be Cape — the *North West* part of the Isle of *Cuba*: Here we found ourselves under a Necessity to run in under the Land for Shelter, tho' we had not come to an Anchor, so that we had not touch'd the King of *Spain*'s Territories at all. However in the Morning we were surrounded with five *Spanish* Barks, or Boats, such as they call *Barco Longos*,[440] full of Men; who instantly boarded us, took us, and carry'd us into the *Havana*, the most considerable Port belonging to the *Spaniards* in that Part of the World.

HERE the Sloop was immediately Seiz'd, and in Consequence plundred, as any one that knows the *Spaniards*, especially in that Country, will easily guess; our Men were made Prisoners and sent to the common Goal,[441] and as for my self, and the Captain, we were carry'd before the *Alcade*[442] Major, or Intendant[443] of the Place as Criminals.

I spoke *Spanish* very well, having serv'd under the King of *Spain* in *Italy*, and it stood me in good stead at this time, for I so effectually argued the Injustice of their Treatment of me, that the Governor, or what I ought to call him, frankly own'd they ought not to have stopp'd me, seeing I was in the open Sea, persuing my Voyage and offer'd no Offence to any Body, and had not landed or offer'd to land upon any Part of his *Catholick* Majesty's Dominions, 'till I was brought in as a Prisoner.

IT was a great Favour, that I could obtain thus much, but I found it easier to obtain an Acknowledgement that I had receiv'd Wrong, than to get any Satisfaction for that Wrong, and much less was there any Hope or Prospect of Restitution: And I was let know, that I was to wait, till an Account could be sent to the Viceroy of *Mexico*, and Orders could be received back from him, how to act in the Affair.

I could easily foresee what all this tended to, namely to a Confiscation of the Ship and Goods, by the ordinary Process at the Place; and that my being left to the Decision of the Viceroy of *Mexico*, was but a pretended Representation of things to him from the Corregidore[444] or Judge of the Place.

HOWEVER, I had no Remedy but the old insignificant thing call'd Patience; and this I was better furnish'd with, because I did not so much value the Loss as I made them believe I did; my greatest Apprehensions were, that they would detain me, and keep me as a Prisoner for Life, and perhaps send me to their Mines in *Peru*, as they have done many, and pretended to do to all that come on Shore in their Dominions, how great soever the Distresses may have been which have brought them thither, and which has been the Reason why others who have been forc'd on Shore, have committed all manner of Violence upon the *Spaniards* in their turn; resolving, however Dear they sold their Lives, not to fall into their Hands.

BUT I got better Quarter among them, than that too; which was, *as I have said*, much of it owing to my speaking *Spanish*, and to my telling them how I had fought in so many Occassions in the Quarrel of his *Catholick* Majesty,[445] in *Italy*, and by great good Chance, I had the King of *France's* Commission for Lieutenant Colonel, in the *Irish* Brigade in my Pocket, where it was mention'd, that the said Brigade was then serving in the Armies of *France*, under the Orders of his *Catholick* Majesty in *Italy*.

I fail'd not to talk up the Gallantry and personal Bravery of his Catholick Majesty on all Occasions, and particularly in many Battles where by the Way, his Majesty had never been at all, and in some, where I had never been my self; but I found I talk'd to People who knew nothing of the Matter, and so any thing went down with them, if it did but praise the King of *Spain*, and talk big of the *Spanish* Cavalry, of which, God knows, there was not one Regiment in the Army, at least while I was there.

HOWEVER, this way of managing my self, obtain'd me the Liberty of the Place, upon my Parole, that I would not attempt an Escape; and I obtain'd also, which was a great Favour, to have 200 Pieces of Eight allow'd me out of the Sale of my Cargo, for Subsistance, till I could Negotiate my Affairs at *Mexico*; as for my Men they were maintain'd as Prisoners, at the publick Charge.

WELL, after several Months Solicitation and Attendance, all I could obtain was, the Satisfaction of seeing my Ship and Cargo confiscated, and my poor Sailors in a fair way to be sent to the Mines: The last I begg'd off, upon Condition of paying 300 Pieces of Eight for their Ransom, and having them set on Shore at *Antegoa*, and my self to remain Hostage for the Payment of the said 300 Pieces of Eight, and for 200 Pieces of Eight, which I had already had, and for 500 Pieces of Eight more for my own Ransom, if upon a Return from *Mexico*, the Sentence of Confiscation, *as above*, should be confirm'd by the Vice-roy.

THESE were hard Articles indeed, but I was forced to submitt to them: Nor as my Circumstances were above all such Matters as these, as to Substance, did I lay it much to Heart; the greatest Difficulty that lay in my Way was that I knew not how to correspond with my Friends in any part of the World, or which way to supply my self with Necessaries, or with Money for the payment I had agreed to: The *Spaniards* being so Tenacious of their Ports, that they allowed no Body to come on Shore, or, indeed, near the Shore, from any Part of the World, *upon Pain of Seizure and Confiscation, as had been my Case already.*

UPON this Difficulty I began to Reason with the Corregidore, and tell him, that he put things upon us, that were impossible, and that were Inconsistent with the Customs of Nations, that if a Man was a Prisoner at *Algiers*, they would allow him to write to his Friends to pay his Ransom, and would admit the Person that brought it to come and go free, as a Publick Person, and if they did not, no Treaty could be cary'd on for the Ransom of a Slave, nor the Conditions be perform'd when they were agreed upon.

I brought it then down to my own Case, and desired to know, upon Supposition, that I might within the Time limitted in that Agreement, have the Sums of Money ready for the Ransom, of my Men, and of my Self, how I should obtain to have Notice given me of it? Or, how it should be brought, seeing the very Persons bringing that Notice, or afterwards presuming to bring the Money, might be liable to be seiz'd and confiscated, as I had been, and the Money itself be taken as a second Prize, without redeeming the first.

THO' this was so reasonable a Request, that it could not be withstood, in point of Argument, yet the *Spaniard* shrunk his Head into his Shoulders, *and said*, they had not Power sufficient to act in such a Case; that the King's Laws were so severe against the suffering any Strangers to set their

Foot on his *Catholick* Majesty's Dominions in *America*, and they could not dispence with the least Title of them, without a particular Assiento,[446] *as they called it*, from the Consulado, or Chamber of Commerce at *Sevelle*; or, a Command under the Hand and Seal of the Viceroy of *Mexico*.

HOW Senior Corregidore! *said I*, with some Warmth, and as it were with Astonishment, have you not Authority enough to sign a Passport for an Agent, or Ambassador, to come on Shore here, from any of the King of *Great Britain*'s Governours in these Parts, under a white Flag, or Flag of Truce, to speak with the Governour of this Place, or with any other Person in the King's Name, on the Subject of such Business as the Governour may have to Communicate? why said I,[a] if you cannot do that, you cannot Act according to the Law of Nations.

HE shook his Head, but still said no, he could not do even so much as that; but here one of the Military Governours put in and oppos'd him, and they two differ'd warmly; the first insisting that their Orders were deffi- cient in that particular; but the other said, that as they were bound up to them, it could not be in their Power to Act otherwise, and that they was answerable for the ill Consequences.

WELL then, says the Governour to the Corregidore, now you have kept this *Englishman* as Hostage for the Ransom of the Men, that you have dis- miss'd; suppose he tells you, the Money is ready, either at such, or such, or such a Place; How shall be bring it hither? you will take all the People Pris- oners that offer to bring it; What must he do? if you say you will send and fetch it, What Security shall he have, that he shall have his Liberty, when it is paid you? and why should he trust you so far, as to pay the Money, and yet remain here a Prisoner.

THIS carried so much Reason with it, that the Corregidore knew not what to say; but that so was the Law, and he could Act no otherwise, but by the very Letter of it; and here each was so positive, that nothing could determine it, but another Express to be sent to the Viceroy of *Mexico*.

UPON this, the Governour was so kind, as to say he would get me a Passport for any Body that should bring the Money, and any Vessel they were in by his own Authority, and for their safe returning, and taking me with them, provided I would answer for it, that they should bring no *Euro- pean*, or other Goods whatever with them, and should not set Foot on Shoar without his express Permission; and provided he did not receive Orders to the contrary, in the mean time from any superior Hand, and that even in such a Case, they should have liberty to go back freely from whence they came, under the Protection of a white Flag.

I Bow'd very respectively[447] to the Governour, in Token of my acknowl- edging his Justice, and then presented my humble Petition to him, that he would allow my Men to take their own Sloop, that it should be rated at a certain Value, and I would be oblig'd they should bring Specie[448] on Board with them, and that they should either pay it for the Sloop or leave the Sloop again.

THEN he enquired to what Country I would send them for so much Money, and if I could assure him of the Payment; and when he understood it was no farther than to *Virginia*, he seem'd very easie, and to satisfie the Corregidore, who still stood off, adhering with a true *Spanish* stiffness to the Letter of the Law; the said Governour calls out to me, Seignior, *says he*, I shall make all this matter easie to you, if you agree to my Proposal; your Men shall have the Sloop, on Condition you shall be my Hostage for her return; but they shall not take her as your Sloop, tho' she shall in the Effect be yours, on the Payment of the Money; but you shall take two of my Men on Board with you upon your Parole, for their safe return, and when she returns, she shall carry his Catholick Majesty's Colours, and to be enter'd as one of the Sloops belonging to the *Havana*; one of the *Spaniards* to be Commander, and to be call'd by such a Name as he should appoint.

THIS the Corregidore came into immediately, and said, this was within the Letter of the King's Commanderie[449] or Precept, upon Condition, however, that she should bring no *European* Goods on Board. I desir'd it might be put in other Words; namely, that she should bring no *European* Goods on Shoar: It cost two days Debate between those two, whether it should pass; that no *European* Goods should be brought in the Ship, or brought on Shoar; but having found means to intimate that I meant not to Trade there; but would not be tyed from bringing a small Present to a certain Person in acknowledgement of favours, *I say*, after I had found Room to Place such a hint Right, where it should be Plac'd, I found it was all made easie to me, and it was all agreed presently, that after the Ransom was paid, and the Ship also bought, it was but reasonable, that I should have liberty to Trade to any other Country, not in the Dominions of the King of *Spain*'s, so to make up my Losses; and that it would be hard to oblige my Men to bring away the Vessel light, and so lose the Voyage, and add so much to our former Misfortunes; that so long as no Goods were brought on Shore in the Country belonging to his Catholick Majesty's Dominions which was all that they had to Defend, that the rest was no business of theirs.

NOW I began to see my way thro' this unhappy Business, and to find that as Money would bring me out of it, so Money would bring it to turn to a good Account another way; wherefore I sent the Sloop away under *Spanish* Colours, and call'd her the *Nuestra Segniora de la Val de Grace*, commanded by Segnior *Giraldo de Nesma*, one of the two *Spaniards*.

WITH the Sloop I sent Letters to my Wife and to my chief Manager with Orders to Load her back, as I there directed (*viz.*) That she should have 200 Barrels of Flower,[450] 50 Barrels of Peas, and to answer my other Views, I ordered 100 Bales to be made up of all sorts of *European* Goods, such as not my own Ware-houses only would supply, but such as they could be supply'd with in other Warehouses, where I knew they had Credit for any thing.

IN this Cargo I directed all the richest, and most valuable *English* Goods, they had, or could get, whether Linnen, Woollen or Silk, to be made up; the Courser[451] things, such as we use in *Virginia*, for Clothing of Servants, such I ordered to be left behind, for the use of the Plantation: In less than seven Weeks time the Sloop return'd, and I that fail'd not every Day to look out for her on the Strand, was the first that spy'd her at Sea at a distance, and knew her by her Sails, but afterwards more particularly by her Signals.

WHEN she return'd, she came into the Road[452] with her *Spanish* Antient[453] flying, and came to an Anchor, as directed; but I that had seen her some Hours before, went directly to the Governour, and gave him an Account of her being come, and fain I would have obtain'd the Favour to have his Excellence, *as I call'd him*, go on Board in Person, that he might see how well his Orders were executed, but he declin'd that; saying he could not justifie going off of the *Island*, which was, in short, to go out of his Command of the Fort, which he could not re-assume without a new Commission from the King's own Hand.

THEN I ask'd leave to go on Board myself, which he granted me, and I brought on shoar with me the full Sum in Gold, which I had condition'd to pay for the Ransom, both of my Men and myself, and for the Purchase of the Sloop; and as I obtain'd leave to Land in a different Place, so my Governour sent his Son with six Soldiers to receive, and convey me with the Money to the Castle, where he Commanded; and therein to his own House: I had made up the Money in heavy Parcels, as if it had been all Silver; and gave it to two of my Men, who belong'd to the Sloop, with Orders to them, that they should make it seem by their carrying it to be much heavier than it was; this was done to conceal three Parcels of Goods, which I had pack'd up with the Money to make a Present to the Governour as I intended.

WHEN the Money was carried in, and laid down on a Table, my Governour order'd the Men to withdraw, and I gave the Soldiers each of them a Peice of Eight to Drink, for which they were very thankful, and the Governour seem'd well pleas'd with it also: Then I ask'd him pleasantly if he would please to receive the Money, he said, no, he would not receive it, but in presence of the Corregidore, and the other People concern'd; then I beg'd his Excellency, *as I call'd him*, give me leave to open the Parcels in his Presence, for that I would do myself the Honour to acknowledge his Favours in the best manner I could.

HE told me, no, he could not see any thing be brought on Shoar, but the Money, but if I had brought any thing on Shoar for my own use, he would not be so strict to enquire into that, so I might do what I pleas'd myself.

UPON that I went into the Place, shut my self in, and having open'd all things and placed them to my Mind: There was five little Parcels, as follows,

1. 2. A piece of 20 Yards fine *English* Broad-Cloth, 5 yds Black, 5 yds Crimson in one Parcel, and the rest of fine Mixtures in another Parcel.
3. A piece of 30 Ells[454] fine[a] *Holland* Linnen.
4. A Piece of 18 yds fine *English* brocaded Silk.
5. A Piece of black *Colchester* Bays.[455]

AFTER I had plac'd these by themselves, I found means with some seeming difficulties, and much Grimace,[456] to bring him to know that this was intended for a Present to himself: After all that Part was over, and he had seem'd to accept them, signified, after walking a hundred Turns and more in the Room by them, by throwing his Hat which was under his Arm, upon them, and making a very stiff Bow, *I say*, after this, he seem'd to take his leave of me, for a while, and I waited in an Outer-Room; when I was call'd in again, I found that he had look'd over all the particulars, and caus'd them to be remov'd out of the Place.

BUT when I came again, I found him quite another Man; he thank'd me for my Present, told me it was a Present fit to be given to a Viceroy of *Mexico*, rather than to a meer Governour of a Fort, that he had done me no Services suitable to such a Return, but that he would see if he could not oblige me farther before I left the Place.

AFTER our Compliments were over, I obtain'd to have the Corregidore sent for, who accordingly came, and in his Presence the Money stipulated for the Ransome of the Ship, and of the Men was paid.

BUT here the Corregidore shew'd that he would be as severely just on my Side, as on theirs, for he would not admit the Money as a Ransom for us as Prisoners, but as a deposite for so much as we were to be Ransom'd for, if the Sentence for our being made Prisoners should be confirm'd.

AND then the Governour and Corregidore joyning together sent a Representation of the whole Affair, at least we were told so, to the Viceroy of *Mexico*, and it was privately hinted to me, that I would do well to stay for the Return of the *Aviso*,[457] that is a Boat which they send over the *Bay* to *Vera Cruz*, with an Express to *Mexico*, whose return is generally perform'd in two Months.

I WAS not unwilling to stay, having secret Hints given me, that I should find some way, to go with my Sloop towards *Vera Cruz* myself, where I might have an occasion to Trade privately, for the Cargo which I had on Board; but it came about a nearer way, for about two Days after this Money being deposited, *as above*, the Governours Son invited himself on Board my Sloop, where I told him I would be very glad to see him, and whether at the same time he brought with him three considerable Merchants *Spaniards*, Two of them not Inhabitants of the Place.

WHEN they were on Board, they were very Merry and Pleasant, and I treated them so much to their satisfaction, that in short, they were not very well able to go on Shoar for that Night, but were content to take a Nap on some Carpets, which I caus'd to be spread for them; and that the Governour's Son might think himself well us'd, I brought him a very good Silk Night-Gown, with a Crimson Velvet Cap to lye down in, and in the Morning desir'd him to accept of them for his use, which he took very kindly.

DURING that merry Evening one of the Merchants not so touch'd with Drink as the young Gentleman, nor so, as not to mind what it was he came about, takes an occasion to withdraw out of the Great Cabbin, and enter into a Parlee with the Master of the Sloop, in order to Trade for what *European* Goods we had on Board; the Master took the Hint, and gave me Notice of what had pass'd, and I gave him Instructions what to say, and what to do, according to which Instructions they made but few Words for about 5000 Peices of Eight's, and carried the Goods away themselves, and at their own hazards.

THIS was very agreeable to me, for now I began to see I should lick my self whole,[458] by the Sale of this Cargo, and should make my self full amends of *Jack Spaniard*, for all the injuries he had done me in the first of these things; with this View I gave my Master, or Captain of the Sloop Instructions for Sale of all the rest of the Goods, and left him to manage by himself, which he did so well, that he sold the whole Cargo the next Day to the three *Spaniards*, with this additional Circumstance, that they desir'd the Sloop might carry the Goods, as they were on Board, to such Part of the *Terra Firma*, as they should appoint between the *Honduras* and the Coast of *La Vera Cruz*.

IT was difficult for me to make good this Part of the Bargain, but finding the Price agreed for, would very well answer the Voyage, I consented; but then how to send the Sloop away, and remain among the *Spaniards*, when I was now a clear Man, this was a difficulty too, as it was also to go away, and not wait for a favourable Answer from the Viceroy of *Mexico*, to the Representation of the Governor and the Corregidore; however at last, I resolv'd to go in the Sloop fall out what would, so I went to the Governor and represented to him, that being now to expect a favourable Answer from *Mexico*, it would be a great Loss to me to keep the Sloop there all the while, and I desir'd his leave for me to go with the Sloop to *Antegoa*, to sell and dispose of the Cargo, which He well knew I was oblig'd not to bring on shoar there at the *Havana*, and which would be in Danger of being spoil'd by lying so long on Board.

THIS I obtain'd readily with License to come again into the Road, and (for myself only) to come on shoar, in order to hear the Viceroy's pleasure in my Case, which was depending.[459]

HAVING thus obtain'd a License at, or Passport for the Sloop and myself, I put to Sea with the three *Spanish* Merchants on Board with me; they told me, they did not live at the *Havana*, but it seems one of them did; and some rich Merchants of the *Havana*, or of the Parts thereabouts in the same *Island* were concern'd with them, for they brought on Board that Night we put to Sea a great Sum of Money in Peices of Eight, and as I understood afterwards that these Merchants bought the Cargo of me, and tho' they gave me a very great Price for every thing, yet that they sold them again to the Merchants, who they procur'd on the Coast of *La Vera Cruz*, at a prodigious Advantage; so that they got above a Hundred *per Cent* after I had gain'd very sufficiently before.

WE sail'd from the *Havana* directly for *Vera Cruz*: I scrupl'd venturing into the Port at first, and was very uneasie, least I should have another *Spanish* Trick put upon me; but as we sail'd under *Spanish* Colours, they shew'd us such Authentick Papers from the proper Officers, that there was no room to fear any thing.

HOWEVER, when we came in sight of the *Spanish* Coast, I found that they had a secret clandestine Trade to carry on, which tho' it was Secret, yet they knew the way of it so well, that it was but a meer Road to them. The Case was this, we stood in close under shoar in the Night, about six Leagues to the North of the Port, where two of the Three Merchants went on shoar in the Boat, and in three Hours, or thereabouts they came on shoar again with five Canoes, and seven or eight Merchants more with them, and as soon as they were on Board we stood off to Sea, so that by Day-light we were quite out of sight of Land.

I ought to have mention'd before, that as soon as we were put out to Sea from the *Havana*, and during our Voyage into the Gulph of *Mexico*, which was eight Days, we Rumag'd the whole Cargo, and opening every Bale, as far as the *Spanish* Merchants desired, we Traffick'd with them for the whole Cargo, except the Barrels of Flower and Peas.

THIS Cargo was considerable in itself, for my Wife's account, or Invoyce drawn out by my Tutor, and Manager, amounted to 2684*l.* 10*s.* and I sold the whole, including what had been sold in the Evening, when they were on Board first, *as I have said*, for 38593 Peices of Eight, and they allow'd me 1200 Peices of Eight for the Freight of the Sloop, and made my Master and the Seamen very handsome Presents besides, and they were well able to do this too, as you shall hear presently.

AFTER we were gotten out of Sight of Land, the *Spaniards* fell to their Traffick, and our three Merchants open'd their Shop, *as they might say*, for it was their Shop; as to me, I had nothing to do with it, or with their Goods; they drove their Bargain in a few Hours, and at Night we stood in again for the Shore, when the five Canoes carry'd a great part of the Goods on Shore, and brought the Money back in Specie, as well for that they carry'd, as for all the rest, and at their Second Voyage carry'd all away clear, leaving me nothing on Board, but my Barrels of Flower and Peas, which they bad[460] me Money for too, but not so much as I expected.

HERE, I found that my *Spanish* Merchants made above 70000 Peices of Eight of the Cargo I had sold them; upon which, I had a great Mind to be acquainted with those Merchants on the *Terra Ferma*, who were the last Customers, for it presently occurr'd to me, that I could easily go with a Sloop from *Virginia*, and taking a Cargo directed on purpose from *England*, of about five or six thousand Pound, I might easily make four of one; with this View, I began to make a kind of an Acquaintance with the *Spaniards* which came in the Canoes, and we became so intimate, that at last, with the Consent of the three *Spaniards* of the *Havana*, I accepted an invitation on Shore to their House, which was a little Villa, or rather Plantation, where they had an *Ingenio, that is to say,* a Sugar-house, or Sugar Work, and there they treated us like Princes.

I took Occasion, at this Invitation, to say, that if I knew how to find my Way thither again, I could visit them once or twice a Year, very much to their Advantage, and mine too; one of the *Spaniards* took the Hint; and taking me into a Room by my self: Seignior, *says he,* if you have any Thoughts of coming to this Place again, I shall give you such Directions as you shall be sure not to mistake, and upon either coming on Shoar in the Night, and coming up to this Place; or, upon making the Signals which we shall give you, we will not fail to come off to you, and bring Money enough for any *Cargaison, so they call it,*[461] that you shall bring.

I took all their Directions, took their Paroles of Honour for my Safety, and without taking any Notice to my first three Merchants, laid up all the rest in my most secret Thoughts, resolving to visit them again in as short a time as I could; and thus, having in about five Days finished all our Merchandizing, we stood off to Sea, and made for the Island of *Cuba*, where I set my three *Spaniards* a Shore, with all their Treasure, to their Hearts Content, and made the best of my way to *Antegoa*; where, with all the Dispatch I could, I sold my 200 Barrels of Flower; which, however, had suffer'd a little, by the length of the Voyage; and having laden the Sloop with Rum, Molasses, and Sugar, I set Sail again for the *Havana*.

I was now uneasy, indeed, for Fear of the Pyrates, for I was a rich Ship, having besides Goods, near 40000 Pieces of Eight in Silver.

WHEN I came back to the *Havana*, I went on Shore, to wait on the Governour, and the Corregidore, and to hear what Return was had from the Viceroy, and had the good Fortune to know that the Viceroy had dissallow'd that part of the Sentence which condemn'd us as Prisoners, and put a Ransom on us, which he insisted could not be, but in time of open War; but as to the Confiscation, he deferr'd it to the Chamber or Council of Commerce at *Sevil*; and the Appeal to the King if such be preferr'd.

THIS was in some Measure a very good piece of Justice in the Viceroy; for as we had not been on Shore, we could not legally be imprisoned; and for the rest, I believe, if I would have given my self the Trouble, to have gone to old *Spain*, and have preferr'd my Claim to both the Ship, and the Cargo, I had recover'd them also.

HOWEVER, as it was, I was now a free Man, without Ransom, and my Men were also free, so that all the Money which I had deposited, *as above*, was return'd me; and thus I took my Leave of the *Havana*, and made the best of my way for *Virginia*, where I arriv'd, after a Year and a half Absence, and notwithstanding all my Losses, came Home above 4000 Pieces of Eight richer than I went out.

AS to the old Affair, about the *Preston* Prisoners, that was quite at an End, for the general Pardon, past in Parliament, made me perfectly easy, and I took no more Thought about that Part: I might here very usefully observe, how necessary and inseperable a Companion, Fear is to Guilt; it was but a few Months that the Face of a Poor *Preston* Transport, would have frighted me out of my Wits; to avoid them, I fain'd my self Sick, and wrapt my Legs in Flannel, as if I had the Gout; whereas now, they were no more Surprize to me, nor was I any more uneasy to see them, than I was to see any other of the Servants of the Plantations.

AND that which was more particular than all, was, that tho' before I fancied every one of them would know me, and remember me, and consequently betray and accuse me; now, tho' I was frequently among them, and saw most of them, and if not all of them, one time or other; nay, tho' I remember'd several of their Faces, and even some of their Names, yet there was not a Man of them, that ever took the least notice of me, or of having known or seen me before.

IT would have been a singular Satisfaction to me, if I could have known so much as this of them before, and had saved me all the Fatiegue, Hazard, and Misfortune that befel me afterwards; but Man, a short sighted Creature, sees so little before him, that he can neither anticipate his Joys, nor prevent his Disasters, be they at ever so little a Distance from him.

I had now my Head full of my *West-India* Project, and I began to make Provision for it accordingly; I had a full Account of what *European* Goods were most acceptable in *New Spain*, and to add to my Speed, I knew that the *Spaniards* were in great want of *European* Goods; the Galleons from *Old Spain* having been delay'd, to an unusual length of Time, for the two Years before: Upon this Account, having not time, as I thought, to send to *England* for a Cargo of such Goods as were most proper; I resolv'd to load my Sloop with Tobacco, and with Rum, the last I brought from *Antegoa*, and go away to *Boston* in *New England*, and to *New York*, and see if I could pick up a Cargo to my Mind.

ACCORDINGLY, I took 20000 Pieces of Eight in Money, and my Sloop laden, *as above*, and taking my Wife with me, we went away; it was an odd and new Thing at *New-England*, to have such a Quantity of Goods bought up there by a Sloop from *Virginia*, and especially to be pay'd for in ready Money, as I did for most of my Goods; and this set all the Trading Heads upon the Stretch, to enquire what, and who I was; to which, they had an immediate and direct Answer, that I was a very considerable Planter in *Virginia*, and that was all any of my Men on Board the Sloop could tell of me, and enough too.

WELL, it was the Cause of much Speculation among them, as I heard at second and third Hands; some said, he is certainly going to *Jamaica*; others said, he is going to Trade with the *Spaniards*; others, that he is going to the *South-Sea*, and turn half Merchant, half Pyrate on the Coast of *Chily* and *Peru*; some one thing, some another, as the *Men-Gossips* found their Imaginations directed: But we went on with our Business, and lay'd out 12000 Pieces of Eight, besides our Cargo of Rum and Tobacco, and went from thence to *New York*, where we lay'd out the rest.

THE chief of the Cargo we bought here, was fine *English* Broad Cloath, Serges, Drugets,[462] *Norwich* Stuffs, Bays, Says,[463] and all kinds of Woollen Manufactures, as also Linnen of all Sorts, a very great quantity, and near a thousand Pounds in fine Silks of several Sorts.

BEING thus Freighted, I came back safe to *Virginia*, and with very little Addition to my Cargo, began to prepare for my *West-India* Voyage.

I should have mention'd, that I had built up on my Sloop, and raised her a little so that I had made her carry Twelve Guns, and fitted her up for Defence, for I thought she should not be attack'd and Boarded by a few *Spanish* Barco Longos,[464] as she was before; and I found the Benefit of it afterwards, as you shall hear.

WE set sail the beginning of *August*, and as I had twice been attack'd by Pyrates in passing the Gulph of *Florida*, or among the *Bahama* Islands, I resolv'd, tho' it was farther about, to stand off to Sea, and so keep as I believ'd it would be, out of the way of them.

WE pass'd the Tropick, as near as we could guess, just where the famous Sir *William Phipps*[465] fish'd up the Silver from the *Spanish* Plate Wreck, and standing in between the Islands, kept our Course W. by S. keeping under the *Isle* of *Cuba*, and so running away Trade, as they call it,[466] into the Great Gulph of *Mexico*, leaving the Island of *Jamaica* to the S. and S. E. by this means avoiding, as I thought, all the *Spaniards* of *Cuba*, or the *Havana*.

AS we pass'd the West Point of *Cuba*, three *Spanish* Boats came off to Board us, as they had done before, on the other Side of the Island; but they found themselves mistaken, we were too many for them, for we run out our Guns, which they not did perceive before, and firing three or four Shot at them, they retir'd.

THE next Morning they appear'd again, being five large Boats, and a Bark, and gave us Chase; but we then spread our *Spanish* Colours and brought to[a] to Fight them, at which they retir'd, so we escap'd this Danger by the addition of Force which we had made to our Vessel.

WE now had a fair run for our Port, and as I had taken very good Directions, I stood away to the North of St. *John d' Ulva*,[467] and then running in for the shoar found the Place appointed exactly, and going on shoar, I sent the Master of my Sloop directly to the Ingenio, where he found the *Spanish* Merchant at his House, and where he dwelt like a little Sovereign Prince, who welcom'd him, and understanding that I was in a particular Boat at the *Creek*, as appointed, he came immediately with him, and bringing another *Spaniard* from a *Villa* not far off, in about four Hours they were with me.

THEY would have perswaded me to go up to their Houses, and have staid there till the next Night, ordering the Sloop to stand off as usual but I would not consent to let the Sloop go to Sea, without me, so we went on Board directly, and as the Night was almost run, stood off to Sea, so by Day-break we were quite out of Sight of Land.

HERE we began, *as I said* before, to open Shop, and I found the *Spaniards* were extreamly surpriz'd at seeing such a Cargo, I mean so large; for in short, they had cared not if it had been four times as much: They soon ran thro' the Contents of all the Bales we open'd that Night, and with very little Dispute about the Price they approv'd, and accepted all that I show'd them; but as they said they had not Money for any greater Parcel, they agreed to go on shoar the next Evening for more Mony.

HOWEVER, we spent the remainder of the Night in looking over, and making Inventories, or Invoyces of the rest of the Cargo, that so they might see the Goods, know the Value, and know what more Money they had to bring.

ACCORDINGLY, in the Evening we stood in for the shoar, and they carried part of the Cargo with them, borrowing the Sloops Boat to assist them, and after they had lodg'd, and Landed the Goods, they came on Board again, bringing three of the other Merchants with them, who were concern'd before, and Money enough to clear the whole Ship, ay, and Ship and all, if I had been willing to sell her.

To give them their Due, they dealt with me like Men of Honour; they were indeed sensible that they bought every thing much Cheaper of me, than they did before of the three Merchants of the *Havana*; these Merchants having been as it were the Hucksters, [468] and bought them first of me, and then advanc'd, as I have said, above 100 *per Cent* upon the Price they gave me; but yet at the same time I advanc'd in the Price much more now, than I did before to the said *Spaniards*, nor was it without Reason, because of the length, and risque of the Voyage, both out and home, which now lay wholly upon me.

IN short, I sold the whole Cargo to them, and for which I receiv'd near two Hundred Thousand Pieces of Eight in Money, besides which, when they came on Board the second time they brought all their Boats loaden with fresh Provisions, Hogs, Sheep, Fowls, Sweetmeats, &c. enough for my whole Voyage, all which they made a Present to me of, and thus we finish'd our Traffick to our mutal Satisfaction, and parted with Promises of farther Commerce, and with assurances on their part of all acts of Friendship, and Assistance that I could desire, if any Disaster should befal me in any of these Adventures; as indeed was not improbable, considering the strictness and severity of their Customs, in Case any People were taken Trading upon their Coast.

I immediately call'd a Council with my little Crew, which way we should go back; the Mate was for beating it up to Windward,[469] and getting up to *Jamaica*, but as we were too rich to run any Risques, and were to take the best Course to get safe Home, I thought, and so did the Master of the Sloop, that our best way was to Coast about the Bay, and keeping the shoar of *Florida* on Board,[470] make the shortest Course to the Gulph, and so make for the Coast of *Carolina*, and to put in there into the first Port we could, and wait for any *Englishmen* of War that might be on the Coast to secure us to the *Capes*.

THIS was the best Course we could take, and prov'd very safe to us, excepting that about the Cape of *Florida*, and on the Coast in the Gulph, till we came the height of St. *Augustine*,[471] we were several times visited with the *Spaniards* Barco Longos, and small Barks, in hope of making a Prize of us; but carrying *Spanish* Colours, deceiv'd most of them, and a good Tire[472] of Guns kept the rest at a distance; so that we came safe, tho' once or twice in Danger of being run on shoar by a Storm of Wind; I say we came safe into *Charles* River in *Carolina*.

FROM hence I found means to send a Letter home, with an Account to my Wife of my good Success and having an Account that the Coast was clear of Pyrates, tho' there were no Men of War in the Place, I ventur'd forward; and in short, got safe into the Bay of *Chesapeak*, that is to say, within the Capes of *Virginia*, and in a few days more to my own House, having been absent three Months, and four days.

NEVER did any Vessel on this side the World make a better Voyage in so short a time, than I made in this Sloop, for by the most moderate Computation, I clear'd in these three Months five and Twenty Thousand Pounds Sterling in ready Money, all the Charges of the Voyage to *New-England* also being reckon'd up.

NOW was my time to have sat still contented with what I had got, if it was in the power of Man to know when his good Fortune was at the highest; and more, my prudent Wife gave it as her Opinion, that I should sit down satisfy'd, and push the Affair no farther, and earnestly persuaded me to do so; but I that had a Door open, as I thought to immense Treasure, that had found the way to have a Stream of the Golden Rivers of *Mexico* flow into my Plantation of *Virginia*, and saw no hazards, more then what was common to all such things in the Prosecution; *I say* to me, these things look'd with another Face, and I Dream'd of nothing but Millions and Hundred of Thousands; so contrary to all moderate Measures, I push'd on for another Voyage, and laid up a Stock of all sorts of Goods that I could get together proper for the Trade; I did not indeed go again to *New England*, for I had by this time a very good Cargo come from *England*, pursuant to a Commission I had sent several Months before; so that in short, my Cargo, according to the Invoyce now made up, amounted to above ten Thousand Pounds Sterling first Cost, and was a Cargo so sorted, and so well bought, that I expected to have advanc'd upon them much more in proportion than I had done in the Cargo before.

WITH these Expectations, we began our second Voyage, in *April*, being about five Months after our Return from the First; we had not indeed the same good Speed, even in our Beginning, as we had at first, for tho' we stood off to Sea about 60 Leagues, in order to be out of the Way of the Pyrates, yet we had not been above five Days at Sea, but we were visited and rifled by two Pyrate Barks, who being Bound to the *Northward, that is to say,* the Banks of *Newfoundland,* took away all our Provisions, and all our Ammunition, and small Arms, and left us very ill provided to persue our Voyage; and it being so near Home, we thought it advisable to come about, and stand in for the Capes again, to restore our Condition, and furnish our selves with Stores of all Kinds for our Voyage; this took us up about 10 Days, and we put to Sea again; as for our Cargo, the Pyrates did not meddle with it, being all Bale Goods, which they had no present Use for, and knew not what to do with, if they had them.

WE met with no other Adventure, worth naming, till by the same Course that we had steer'd before, we came into the Gulph of *Mexico,* and the first Misfortune we met with here, was, that on the Back of *Cuba,* crossing towards the Point of the *Terra Ferma,* on the Coast of *Jucatan,* we had Sight of the Flota of *New Spain, that is,* of the Ships which come from *Carthagena* or *Porto Bello,* and go to the *Havana,* in order to persue their Voyage to *Europe.*

THEY had with them one *Spanish* Man of War, and three Frigats; two of the Frigats gave us Chase, but it being just at the shutting in of the Day, we soon lost Sight of them, and standing to the *North cross* the Bay of *Mexico,* as if we were going to the Mouth of *Missisipi,* they lost us quite, and in a few Days more we made the bottom of the Bay, being the Port we were bound for.

WE stood in as usual, in the Night, and gave Notice to our Friends, but in stead of their former Readiness to come on Board, they gave us Notice, that we had been seen in the Bay, and that Notice of us was given at *Vera Cruz,* and at other Places, and that several Frigats were in Quest of us, and that three more would be Cruising the next Morning in search for us.

WE could not conceive how this could be; but we were afterwards told, that those three Frigats, having lost Sight of us in the Night, had made in for the Shore, and had given the Allarm of us, as of Privateers.

BE that as it would, we had nothing to do, but to Consider what Course to take immediately; the *Spanish* Merchants Advice was very good if we had taken it, namely, to have unladen as many of our Bails as we could that very Night, by the help of our Boat and their *Canoes,* and to make the best of our Way in the Morning, to the *North* of the Gulph, and take our Fate.

THIS my Skipper, or Master, thought very well of, but when we began to put it in Execution, we were so confus'd, and in such a Hurry, being not resolv'd what Course to take, that we could not get out above sixteen Bales of all sorts of Goods, before it began to be too light, and we behov'd to set Sail; at last, the Master propos'd a Medium,[473] which was that I should go on Shore in the next Boat, in which was five Bales of Goods more, and that I should stay on shoar, if the *Spanish* Merchants would undertake to conceal me, and let them go to Sea, and take their Chance.

THE *Spanish* Merchants readily undertook to protect me, especially it being so easie to have me pass for a natural *Spaniard*, and so they took me on shoar with 21 Bales of my Goods, and the Sloop stood off to Sea; if they met with any Enemies, they were to stand in for the shoar the next Night, and we fail'd not to look well out for them, but to no purpose, for the next Day they were discover'd and Chased by two *Spanish* Fregates; they stood from them, and the Sloop being an excellent Sailor gain'd so much that they would certainly have been clear of them when Night came on, but a small Picaroon[474] of a Sloop kept them Company in spight of all they could do, and two or three times offer'd to Engage them, thereby to give time to the rest to come up, but the Sloop kept her way, and gave them a Chase of three Days and Nights, having a fresh Gale of Wind, at South West, till she made the *Rio Grand*,[475] or as the *French* call it the *Missisipi*, and there finding no remedy, they run the Vessel on shoar, not far from the Fort, which the *Spaniards* call *Pensacola*, Garrison'd at that time with *French*; our Men would have enter'd the River as a Port, but having no Pilot, and the Current of the River being strong against them, the Sloop run on shoar, and the Men shifted as well as they could in their Boats.

I was now in a very odd Condition indeed, my Circumstances were in one Sense indeed very happy; Namely, that I was in the Hands of my Friends, for such really they were, and so faithful, that no Men could have been more careful of their own Safety than were they of mine, and that which added to the comfort of my new Condition, was the produce of my Goods, which were gotten on shoar by their own Advice and Direction, which was a Fund sufficient to Maintain me with them as long as I could be suppos'd to stay there; and, if not, the first Merchant to whose House I went, assur'd me, that he would give me Credit for twenty Thousand Pieces of Eight, if I had occasion for it.

MY greatest Affliction was, that I knew not how to convey News to my Wife, of my present Condition, and how among the many Misfortunes of the Voyage I was yet safe, and in good Hands.

BUT there was no remedy for this Part, but the great universal Cure of all incurable Sorrows, (*viz.*) Patience, and indeed I had a great deal of Reason, not for Patience only, but Thankfulness, if I had known the Circumstances, which I should have been reduc'd to, if I had fallen into the Hands of the *Spaniards*; the best of which that I could reasonably have expected, had been, to have been sent to the Mines, or which was ten Thousand times worse, the Inquisition;[476] or if I had escap'd the *Spaniards*, as my Men in the Sloop did, the Hardships they were expos'd to, the Dangers they were in, and the Miseries they suffered, were still worse, in wandering among Savages, and the more Savage *French*, who plunder'd and strip'd them, instead of relieving, and supplying them in their long wilderness Journey over the Mountains, till they reach'd the S.W. parts of South *Carolina*. A Journey, which indeed deserves to have an Account to be given of it by itself; *I say*, all these things had I known of them would have let me see that I had a great deal of Reason, not only to be Patient, under my present Circumstances but satisfy'd, and thankful.

HERE, *as I said*, my Patron the Merchant entertain'd me like a Prince, he made my safety his peculiar Care, and while we were in any Expectation of the Sloop being taken, and brought into *Vera Cruz*, he kept me retired at a little House in a Wood, where he kept a fine *Avery* of all sorts of *American* Birds, and out of which he Yearly sent some as Presents to his Friends in old *Spain*.

THIS Retreat was necessary, least if the Sloop should be taken, and brought into *Vera Cruz*, and the Men be brought in Prisoners, they should be tempted to give an Account of me as their Super Cargo,[477] or Merchant, and where both I and the 21 Bales of Goods were set on shoar; as for the Goods he made sure Work with them, for they were all open'd, taken out of the Bales, and separated, and being mix'd with other *European* Goods, which came by the Galeons, were made up in new Package, and sent to *Mexico* in several Parcels, some to one Merchant, some to another; so that it was impossible to have found them out, even if they had had Information of them.

IN this Posture, and in Apprehension of some bad News of the Sloop, I remain'd at the Villa, or House in the Vale, for so they call'd it, about five Weeks; I had two *Negroes* appointed to wait on me, one of which was my Purveyor,[a] or my Cook, the other my Valet; and my Friend, the Master of all came constantly every Evening to Visit, and Sup with me, when we walk'd out together into the *Avery*, which was of its kind, the most beautiful thing that ever I saw in the World.

AFTER above five Weeks retreat of this kind, he had good Intelligence of the Fate of the Sloop, (*viz.*) that the two Fregates, and a Sloop had Chas'd her till she ran on Ground near the Fort of *Pensacola*, that they saw her strand'd and broke in pieces by the force of the Waves, the Men making their escape in their Boat. This News was brought it seems by the said Fregates to *La Vera Cruz*, where my Friend went on purpose to be fully inform'd, and receiv'd the Account from one of the Captains of the Fregates, and discours'd with him at large about it.

I was better pleas'd with the loss of the Sloop, and all my Cargo, the Men being got a Shoar, and escaping, than I should have been with the saving the whole Cargo, if the Men had fallen into the Hands of the *Spaniards*, for now I was safe, whereas then it being suppos'd they would have been forc'd to some discovery about me, I must have fled, and should have found it very difficult to have made my Escape, even with all that my Friends could have done for me too.

BUT now I was perfectly easie, and my Friend, who thought confining me at the House in the Vale no longer needful, brought me publickly home to his dwelling House, as a Merchant come from old *Spain*, by the last Galeons, and who having been at *Mexico* was come to reside with him.

HERE I was dress'd like a *Spaniard* of the better sort, had three *Negroes* to attend me, and was call'd *Don Ferdinand de Villa Moresa*, in *Castilia Veja*, *that is to say*, in *Old Castile*.

HERE I had nothing to do but to walk about, and ride out into the Woods, and come home again to enjoy the pleasantest, and most agreeable Retirement in the World; for certainly no Men in the World live in such splendor, and wallow in such immense Treasures, as the Merchants of this Place.

THEY live, *as I have said*, in a Kind of Country Retreat at their *Villa's*, or, as we would call them, in *Virginia*, their Plantations, *and as they do call them*, their *Ingenio's*, where they make their Indigo, and their Sugars: but they have also Houses, and Ware-houses, at *Vera Cruz*, where they go twice a Year, when the Galeons arrive from *Old Spain*; and when those Galeons relade for their return; and it was surprising to me, when I went to *la Vera Cruz* with them, to see what prodigious Consignments they had from their Correspondents in *Old Spain*, and with what Dispatch they mannag'd them; for no sooner were the Cases, Packs, and Bales of *European* Goods brought into their Ware-houses, but they were open'd, and repack'd by Porters, and Packers of their own, *that is to say*, Negroes, and *Indian*[478] Servants; and being made up into new Bales, and separate Parcels were all dispatch'd again, by Horses, for *Mexico*, and directed to their several Merchants there; and the remainder carry'd home, *as above*, to the *Ingenio*, where they liv'd, which was near 30 *English* Miles from *Vera Cruz*, so that in about 20 Days, their Ware houses were again entirely free, at *la Vera Cruz*, all their Business was over there; and they, and all their Servants retir'd; for they stay'd no longer there than needs must, because of the unhealthiness of the Air.

AFTER the Goods were thus dispatch'd, it was equally Surprizing, to see how soon, and with what Exactness, the Merchants of *Mexico*, to whom those Cargoes were separately Consign'd, made the Return, and how it came all in Silver, or in Gold; so that their Ware houses, in a few Months, were piled up, even to the Ceiling, with Chests of Pieces of Eight, and with Bars of Silver.

IT is impossible to describe in the narrow Compass of this Work, with what Exactness, and Order, and yet, with how little Hurry, and not the least Confusion, every thing was done; and how soon a Weight of Business of such Importance and Value, was negotiated and finish'd, the Goods repack'd, Invoyces made, and every thing dispatch'd and gone; so that in about five Weeks, all the Goods they had receiv'd from *Europe* by the Galeons were disposed of, and entered in their Journals, to the proper Account of the Merchant, to whom they were respectively consign'd; from thence they had Book-keepers, who drew out the Invoyces, and wrote the Letters, which the Merchant himself only read over, and Sign'd, and then other Hands copy'd all again, into other Books.

I can give no Estimate of the Value of the several Consignments they receiv'd by that Flota; but I remember, that when the Galeons went back, they Ship'd on Board, at several Times, one Million three hundred Thousand Pieces of Eight, in Specie, besides 180 Bales or Bags of Cochoneal,[479] and about 300 Bales of Indigo; but they were so Modest, *that they said*, this was for themselves, and their Friends; *that is to say*, the several Merchants of *Mexico*, consign'd large Quantities of Bullion to them, to Ship on Board, and consign according to their Order; but then I know also, that for all that, they were allow'd Commission, so that their Gain, was very considerable, even that way also.

I had been with them at *la Vera Cruz*, and came back again before we came to an Account for the Goods which I had brought on Shore, in the 21 Bales; which by the Account we brought them to, leaving the Price[a] of every thing to be govern'd by our last Market, amounted to 8570 Pieces of Eight, all which Money, my Friend, *for so I must now call him*, brought me in Specie, and caused his *Negroes* to pile them up in one Corner of my Apartment; so that I was indeed, still very Rich, all things consider'd.

THERE was a Bale which I had caused to be pack'd up on purpose in *Virginia*, and which indeed I had written for from *England*, being chiefly of Fine *English* Broad Cloaths, Silk, Silk-Druggets, and fine Stuffs of several Kinds, with some very fine Hollands, which I set a part for Presents, as I should find Occasion; and as what ever Hurry I was in, at carrying the 21 Bales of Goods on Shore, I did not forget to let this Bale be one of them, so when we came to a Sale for the Rest, I told them, that was a Pack with

Cloaths and Necessaries for my own Wearing and Use, and so desired it might not be open'd with the rest; which was accordingly observ'd, and that Bale, or Pack was brought into my Apartment.

THIS Bale was in general made up of several smaller Bales, which I had directed, so that I might have Room to make Presents, equally sorted as the Circumstance might direct me: However, they were all considerable, and I reckon'd the whole Bale cost me near 200*l. Sterling*, in *England*; and tho' my present Circumstances requir'd some Limits to my Bounty, in making Presents, yet the Obligation I was under, being so much the greater, especially, to this one friendly Generous *Spaniard*, I thought I could not do better than by opening two of the smaller Bales joyn them together, and make my Gift something suitable to the Benefactor, and to the Respect he had shewn me; accordingly, I took two Bales, and laying the Goods together; the Contents were as follows.

TWO Pieces of fine *English* broad Cloth, the finest that could be got in *London*, divided as was that which I gave to the Governor at the *Havana*, into fine Crimson in Grain, fine light Mixtures, and fine Black.

FOUR Pieces of fine *Holland*, of 7*s.* to 8*s. per* Ell in *London*.

TWELVE Pieces of fine Silk Drugget, and *du Roys*,[480] for Men's Ware.

SIX Peices of Broad Silks, 2 Damasks, 2 Brocaded Silks, and 2 Mantuas.

WITH a Box of Ribbons, and a Box of Lace, the last Cost about 40*l. Sterling*, in *England*.

THIS handsome Parcel I laid open in my Appartment, and brought him up Stairs one Morning, on Pretence to drink *Chocolate* with me, which he ordinarily did; when as we drank *Chocolate*, and was merry, *I said to him*, tho I had sold him almost all my Cargo, and taken his Money; yet the Truth was, that I ought not to have sold them to him, but to have lay'd them all at his Feet, for that it was to his Direction I ow'd the having any thing sav'd at all.

HE smil'd, and with a great deal of Friendship in his Face, *told me*, that not to have paid me for them, would have been to have plunder'd a Ship-wreck, which had been worse than to have robb'd an Hospital.

AT last I told him, I had two Requests to make to him, which must not be deny'd, *I told him*, I had a small present to make to him, which I would give him a Reason why he should not refuse to accept: And the second Request I would make after the First was granted. He said he would have accepted any Present from me, if I had not been under a Dissaster, but as it was, it would be cruel and ungenerous. But, *I told him*, he was oblig'd to hear my Reason for his accepting it: *Then I told him*, that this Parcel was made up for him by Name, by my Wife, and I, in *Virginia*, and his Name set on the Marks of the Bale, and accordingly, I shew'd him the Marks, which was indeed, on one of the Bales, but I had doubled it now, *as above*, so that I told him these were his Own proper Goods; and in short, I press'd him so to receive them, that he made a Bow, and I said no more, but order'd my *Negro*, *that is to say*, his *Negro* that waited on me, to carry them all except the two Boxes into his Apartments, but would not let him see the Particulars, till they were all carry'd away.

AFTER he was gone, about a Quarter of an Hour, he came in raving, and almost swearing, and in a great Passion, but I could easily see, he was exceedingly pleased; and told me, had he known the Particulars, he would never have suffer'd them to have gone, as he did, and at last used the very same Compliment, that the Governour at the *Havana* used, *viz.* that it was a Present, fit for a Viceroy of *Mexico*, rather than for him.

WHEN he had done, *he then told me*, he remember'd I had two Requests to him, and that one was not to be told till after the first was granted, and he hoped now, I had something to ask of him, that was equal to the Obligation I had lay'd upon him.

I told him, I knew it was not the Custom in *Spain*, for a Stranger to make Presents to the Ladies; and that I would not in the least doubt, but that whatever the Ladies of his Family requir'd, as proper for their Use, he would appropriate to them as he thought fit. But that there was two little Boxes in the Parcel, which my Wife, with her own Hand had directed to the Ladies; and I beg'd he would be pleas'd with his own Hand to give them in my Wife's Name as directed; that I was only the Messenger, but that I could not be honest, if I did not discharge the Trust repos'd myself of.

THESE were the two Boxes of Ribbands, and Lace, which knowing the nicety of the Ladies in *Spain*, or rather of the *Spaniards* about their Women I had made my Wife pack up, and direct with her own hand, *as I have said*.

HE smil'd, and told me it was true, the *Spaniards* did not ordinarily admit so much Freedom among the Women, as other Nations; but he hop'd, *he said*, I would not think the *Spaniards* thought all their Women Whores, or that all *Spaniards* were jealous of their Wive's: That as to my Present, since he had agreed to accept of it; I should have the Directing of what Part I pleas'd to his Wife and Daughters; for he had three Daughters.

HERE I strain'd Courtisies[481] again, and told him by No means, I would direct nothing of that kind, I only beg'd that he would with his own Hand present to his *Donna*, or Lady, the Present design'd them by my Wife, and that he would Present it in her Name now living in *Virginia*. He was extreamly pleas'd with the nicety I us'd; and I saw him Present it to her accordingly, and could see at the opening of it, that she was extreamly pleas'd with the Present it self, as indeed, she might very well be, for in that Country it was worth a very considerable Sum of Money.

THO' I was us'd with an uncommon Friendship before, and nothing could well be desir'd more, yet the grateful Sense I shew'd of it, in the Magnificence of this Present was not lost, and the whole Family appear'd sensible of it; so that I must allow that Presents, where they can be made in such a manner, are not without their influence, where the Persons were not at all Mercenary, either before or after.

I had here now a most happy, and comfortable Retreat, tho' it was a kind of an Exile; here I enjoy'd every thing I could think of, that was agree-able and pleasant, except only a Liberty of going home, which for that Reason perhaps, was the only thing I desir'd in the World; for the grief of one absent Comfort is oftentimes capable of imbittering all the other Enjoyments in the World.

HERE I enjoy'd the Moments which I had never before known how to employ. I mean, that here I learn'd to look back upon a long ill-spent Life, bless'd with infinite Advantage, which I had no Heart given me till now to make use of, and here I found just Reflections were the utmost Felicity of human Life.

HERE I wrote these Memoirs, having to add to the Pleasure of looking back with due Reflections, the Benefit of a violent Fit of the Gout, which as it is allow'd by most People, clears the Head, restores the Memory, and Qualifies us to make the most, and just, and useful Remarks upon our own Actions.

PERHAPS, when I wrote these things down, I did not foresee that the Writings of our own Stories would be so much the Fashion in *England*, or so agreeable to others to read, as I find Custom, and the Humour of the Times has caus'd it to be; if any one that reads my Story, pleases to make the same just Reflections, which I acknowledge, I ought to have made, he will reap the benefit of my Misfortunes, perhaps, more than I have done myself; 'tis evident by the long Series of Changes, and Turns, which have appear'd in the narrow Compass of one private mean Person's Life, that the History of Men's Lives may be many ways made Useful, and Instructing to those who read them, if moral and religious Improvement, and Reflections are made by those that write them.

THERE remains many things in the Course of this unhappy Life of mine, tho' I have left so little a part of it to speak of, that are worth giving a large, and distinct Account of, and which give Room for just Reflections of a Kind which I have not made yet; particularly, I think it just to add how in collecting the various Changes, and Turns of my Affairs, I saw clearer than ever I had done before, how an invisible over-ruling Power, a Hand influenced from above, Governs all our Actions of every Kind, limits all our Designs, and orders the Events of every Thing relating to us.

AND from this Observation it necessarily occurr'd to me, how just it was, that we should pay the homage of all Events to him; that as he guided, and had even made the Chain of Causes, and Consequences, which Nature in general strictly obey'd, so to him should be given the Honour of all Events, the Consequences of those Causes, as the first Mover, and Maker of all Things.

I WHO had hitherto liv'd, as might be truly said, *without God in the World*,[482] began now to see farther into all those Things, than I had ever yet been capable of before, and this brought me at last to look with shame and blushes, upon such a Course of Wickedness, as I had gone through in the World: I had been bred indeed to nothing of either religious, or moral Knowledge; what I gain'd of either, was first by the little time of civil Life, which I liv'd in *Scotland*, where my abhorrence of the wickedness of my Captain and Comrade, and some sober religious Company I fell into, first gave me some Knowledge of Good and Evil, and shew'd me the Beauty of a sober religious Life, tho' with my leaving that Country, it soon left me too; or secondly, the modest Hints, and just Reflections of my Steward, who I call'd my Tutor, who was a Man of sincere Religion, good Principles, and a real true Penitent for his past Miscarriages: O! had I with him sincerely repented of what was pass'd, I had not for 24 Year together liv'd a Life of levity, and profligate Wickedness after it.

BUT here I had, *as I said*, leisure to reflect, and to repent, to call to mind things pass'd, and with a just Detestation, learn as *Job* says, *to abhor my self in Dust and Ashes*.[483]

IT is with this Temper that I have written my Story, I would have all that design to read it, prepare to do so with the Temper of Penitents; and remember with how much Advantage they may make their penitent reflections at Home, under the merciful Dispositions of Providence in Peace, Plenty, and Ease, rather than Abroad under the Discipline of a Transported Criminal as my Wife and my Tutor, or under the Miseries and Distresses of a Shipwreck'd wanderer, as my Skipper or Captain of the Sloop, who as I hear dyed a very great Penitent, labouring in the Deserts and Mountains to find his way home to *Virginia*, by the way of *Carolina*, whether[484] the rest of the Crew reached after infinite Dangers and Hardships; or in Exile, however favourably circumstantiated as mine, in absence from my Family, and for some time in no probable View of ever seeing them any more.

SUCH I say, may repent with Advantage, but how few are they that seriously look in, till their way is hedg'd up, and they have no other way to look?

HERE, *I say,* I had Leisure to Repent; how far it pleases God to give the Grace of Repentance where he gives the Opportunity of it, is not for me to say of myself, it is sufficient that I recommend it to all that read this Story, that when they find their Lives come up in any degree to any Similitude of Cases, they will enquire by me, and ask themselves, Is not this the time to Repent? perhaps the Answer may touch them.

I have only to add to what was then written, that my kind Friend the *Spaniard* finding no other Method presented for conveying me to my home, that is to say, to *Virginia,* got a License for me to come in the next Galeons, as a *Spanish* Merchant to *Cadiz,* where I arriv'd safe with all my Treasure, for he suffer'd me to be at no Expences in his House; and from *Cadiz,* I soon got Passage on Board an *English* Merchant Ship for *London,* from whence I sent an Account of my Adventures to my Wife, and where in about five Months more, she came over to me, leaving with full satisfaction the Management of all our Affairs in *Virginia,* in the same faithful Hands as before.

EXPLANATORY NOTES

Col. Jacque was advertised as published 'this day' in the *Post Boy* for 18–20 December and *Mist's Weekly Journal* for 22 December 1722.

page
31 1 *capable of so many Improvements*: offering scope for so many moral lessons.

2 *publick Schools, and Charities*: elementary schools erected and maintained in various parishes by the voluntary contributions of the inhabitants. They taught poor children to read and write and offered other necessary parts of education and were usually maintained by religious organisations, often providing clothing and education to students freely, or at little charge.

3 *docible*: apt to be taught, submissive to teaching and training.

4 *Necessity*: poverty and deprivation.

32 5 *like the Prodigal*: See Luke 15:11–32 for the parable of the prodigal son.

6 *his Latter End be better than his Beginning*: see Job 8:7: 'Though thy beginning was small, yet thy latter end should greatly increase'.

33 7 *a Checquer Work of Nature*: A chessboard was originally known as a 'checquer' (or 'checker'), and so anything marked like a chessboard, with crossing colours, was said to be 'chequered'. Hence, figuratively, 'checquer-work' is 'anything chequered or diversified with contrasting characters' (*OED*). Defoe was fond of the phrase. In the Preface to volume 8 of his *Review* he described his own life as a 'Life of Wonders', saying that 'the same Checquer-Work of Fortune attends me still'. In *Robinson Crusoe*, Robinson exclaims, 'How strange a Chequer Work of Providence is the Life of Man'; see *The Novels of Daniel Defoe*, Vol. 1, ed. W. R. Owens, p. 172.

34 8 *Son of shame*: son born out of wedlock.

9 *Goodman's-fields*: in 1722 a square open ground bordered by trees, north-east of the Tower of London, and south of the area between Aldgate, Whitechapel and the Royal Mint. Jack would therefore have grown up in the westernmost extremity of what is today's Stepney district.

page
34   10 *Tarpawlin*: or tarpaulin, an old term for a common sailor.

11 *Press-Smack*: a boat used to press or compulsorily enlist men into the navy.

12 *Bas—ds*: bastards.

35   13 *meer*: mere.

14 *Carman*: man who drives a cart, a carter, and therefore considered to belong to a low social class.

15 *generous*: gentlemanly.

16 *rove*: ramble (in search of mischief).

17 *Off-hand-Wit*: extempore wit.

36   18 *Glass-Bottle House*: In 1549 glass blowers from Venice had come to work in London, and by the end of the seventeenth century there were about twenty-four glasshouses in and around London. Their former presence is still remembered in names such as Glasshouse Street, Glasshouse Yard, and Glasshouse Walk. In Defoe's time there was a Glass House in Glass House Yard, east of The Minories and immediately south of Goodman's Yard, near Goodman's Fields; this could well have been the location of one of Jack's night-time dwellings.

19 *Black-Guard Boy*: a boy of the streets who moved between shoe-blacking work and criminal activity.

20 *Sirrah*: a term of address used to men and boys expressing contempt, reprimand or assumption of authority on the part of the speaker; sometimes employed less seriously in addressing children.

37   21 *I lay'd up all these things in my Heart*: This phrase is found in Deuteronomy 11:18, 'Therefore shall ye lay up these my words in your heart', and in Job 22:22, 'lay up his words in thine heart', but the allusion is almost certainly to the account in Luke 1:66 of the impression made on people by the young John the Baptist: 'And all they that heard [these sayings about John] laid them up in their hearts, saying, What manner of child shall this be!'

22 *the Gloucester Frigat ... Duke of York*: On 6 May 1682, this frigate, with the Duke of York and his friends aboard, broke up and sank on Yarmouth Sands off the Norfolk coast. The date of the event means that Jack was born around 1672.

23 *Rosemary-Lane ... Ratcliff*: Rosemary Lane (now Royal Mint Street) ran eastward, south of Goodman's Fields, from The Minories, along today's Cable Street as far as Glass House Fields, a street still running between Cable Street and The Highway (formerly Ratcliff Highway). Ratcliff is an area nearby, just south of Stepney, adjoining Limehouse around White Horse Lane, north of Commercial Road.

24 *Errant*: arrant.

25 *ask a Man for his Purse*: i.e. become a highwayman.

38   26 *Watch-houses ... Bulk-heads*: A watch-house was a station inhabited by municipal nightwatchmen, the chief constable each night sitting to receive and detain in custody until the morning any disorderly persons brought in by the watchmen. A bulkhead was the roof of a bulk or stall, a kind of framework projecting from the front of a shop.

27 *Ash-holes, and Nealing-Arches*: The furnaces used to heat and make glass within a glassworks or glasshouse left behind piles of hot ash which homeless characters such as Jack slept on to keep themselves warm. For 'nealing' see note 45 below.

39   28 *the Dutch War*: the war of France and England against the Dutch in 1672.

29 *Maestricht*: The French took the city of Maastricht (in modern-day Holland) in battle in June 1673.

30 *Tars*: short-hand term for common sailors, a contraction of tarpawlin (see note 10 above). Such sailors were also sometimes known as jacktars.

31 *the Wars in Oliver's time ... King Charles the first*: Jack refers to the battles that took place in the period of the English civil wars 1642–51, when Oliver Cromwell led his Puritan forces against those of the monarchy. Cromwell's Commonwealth or republic was established soon after the execution of King Charles I in 1649.

32 *Newgate*: Newgate prison was the main prison in London, located at the corner of Newgate Street and Old Bailey just inside the City of London. The prison was extended and rebuilt many times, remaining in use for over 700 years, from 1188 to 1902.

33 *Bridewell*: house of correction, established in the former palace at Bridewell in the City of London in 1556. After 1609 each English county was required to have such houses of correction (generically known as the 'Bridewell') where thieves, beggars and other petty criminals were put to hard labour or punished in an attempt to reform their criminal tendencies.

40   34 *Sir William Turner*: Sir William Turner (1615–92) made his fortune in London as a merchant tailor, was knighted by King Charles II in recognition of his many public works and in 1668 became the City's lord mayor for a term. Praised for his abilities as a manager, his services were called on after the Great Fire of London to work with Christopher Wren and the Crown in the rebuilding of the city.

35 *Bartholomew Fair*: Located about 1 km north of St Paul's at Smithfield, adjacent to the still-standing Bart's hospital, this was from 1133 to 1855 one of London's pre-eminent summer fairs. It was both a trading event for cloth and other goods and a pleasure fair, the four-day event drawing crowds from all classes of London society.

41   36 *Purchase*: goods obtained by theft or force.

page
41   37 *Jackpudding*: a buffoon or clown.

38 *China Orange*: 'the sweet orange of commerce (*Citrus Aurantium*), originally brought from China' (*OED*).

39 *Ribband Purse*: purse closed up with a ribbon.

40 *A Joynted Baby*: a doll with jointed arms and legs.

42   41 *Handkercher*: handkerchief.

42 *Rag-Fair*: a market for the sale of old clothes, held at Rosemary Lane
(see note 23 above). It had disappeared by the beginning of the twenti-
eth century.

43 *a boiling Cook's*: an eating house specialising in serving boiled meats.

43   44 *Box*: 'a compartment partitioned off in the public room of a coffee-
house or tavern' (*OED*).

45 *Neal*: i.e. anneal, the process of toughening glass by exposing it to
slowly diminishing heat.

46 *Bagnio*: in Defoe's time a kind of bathing house with hot baths.

47 *Nova Zembla*: or Novaya Zemlya, an island in the Russian Arctic sepa-
rating the Barents Sea from the Kara Sea.

48 *a Tester*: colloquial or slang term for a sixpence.

49 *a Society Lodging*: a lodging shared by a 'society' of thieves.

44   50 *Address*: 'general preparedness ... adroitness' (*OED*).

51 *Bills*: goldsmith's notes.

52 *Principal*: in this (quasi-legal) sense, 'a person ... either as the actual
perpetrator ... or as present, aiding and abetting, at the commission of
it' (as opposed to an accessory) (*OED*).

53 *go Thro'-Stitch*: see a difficult action through to the end.

45   54 *Duck'd or Pump'd*: ducked in a pond or soaked under a parish pump.

55 *Capital*: punishable by death.

56 *Goldsmith*: a worker in gold; one who fashions gold into jewels, orna-
ments, articles of plate, etc. Down to the eighteenth century
goldsmiths were also tradesmen and frequently acted as bankers.

57 *Period*: end.

58 *long room at the Custom-house*: the public lobby where customs due were
paid. In London the Custom House was located on the river at Lower
Thames Street, near the Tower.

46   59 *pretend*: claim.

60 *Cocquets*: or cockets, documents sealed by the officers of the custom
house, and delivered to merchants as a certificate that their merchandise had been duly entered and that duty had been paid.

61 *put that up*: hide that.

62 *Lug out*: show him what he was hiding.

63 *Sir Stephen Evans*: Sir Stephen Evance (1654/5–1712) was a prominent
goldsmith and entrepreneur of London, and governor of the Hudson's
Bay Company. An important lender of money to the Crown, he was

appointed the king's jeweller, and commissioner of excise and wine licences. Following an unsuccessful business venture to insure merchants, he went bankrupt in 1712 and committed suicide.

46 64 *accepted*: A bill of exchange has to be 'accepted' by the 'drawee', i.e. the person or firm etc. on which it is drawn.

65 *Lombard-street*: a street adjacent to the Bank of England, historically the London home for money lenders and until the 1980s where most UK-based banks had their head offices.

66 *enquir'd the Name out*: made sure in whose name the bill was.

47 67 *Cole-Harbour*: i.e. Coldharbour, on the north bank of the Thames, formerly a residence but rebuilt after the Great Fire and used by the Watermen's Company as their Hall.

68 *St. Mary Overs Stairs*: i.e. the landing steps at St Mary Overie (St Mary over the water), the parish church of St Saviour, Southwark.

69 *St. George's-Fields*: Now built over, St George's Fields in the seventeenth century was an extensive open space between Southwark and Lambeth. It took its name from the nearby church of St George the Martyr.

70 *Old*: crafty and experienced.

48 71 *I had never heard*: I would never have heard.

72 *give him that for Handsel*: that is, give him something to mark an auspicious beginning of their enterprise together.

73 *a foul Clout*: a worthless piece of cloth or rag. The sense seems to be that people who are owed sums that they cannot manage to collect ('get in') say 'I would be glad to have it, even if wrapped in a filthy rag'.

74 *in the Kennel*: in street-gutter water.

49 75 *down Bed*: luxurious feather-bed.

76 *the Cares of this Life, and the deceitfulness of Riches*: see Mark 4:19, where Jesus is explaining the moral of the parable of the sower to his disciples: 'And the cares of this world, and the deceitfulness of riches, and the lusts of other things entering in, choke the word, and it becometh unfruitful'. (See also Matthew 13:22.)

77 *Blind Beggars at Bednal-Green*: an inn at Bethnal Green, named after a Tudor ballad where the blind beggar of the song is reputed to have begged. Today's Blind Beggar public house at the corner of Cambridge Heath Road and Mile End Road could occupy the site of the original inn, since the district of Bethnal Green extended further south in Defoe's day than it does today.

50 78 *told it*: counted it.

79 *savourly*: vehemently, bitterly.

51 80 *Joy is as Extravagant as Grief*: Defoe often quoted a line from a poem of 1672 by Robert Wild, 'For sudden Joys, like Griefs, confound at first'. See *Robinson Crusoe*, in *The Novels*, Vol. 1, p. 91 (and n. 187, p. 299). In the *Farther Adventures of Robinson Crusoe*, Crusoe discusses at some

length the wild psychological effects of 'sudden joy' as exhibited by a French crew and passengers rescued by Crusoe from their burning ship; *The Novels*, Vol. 2, ed. W. R. Owens, pp. 17–19.

51   81 *Chandler's Shop*: A chandler was generally a maker and supplier of candles, but sometimes also a retailer of groceries, as in this case.

       82 *a Broker's Shop*: A broker was a dealer in second-hand furniture and clothes; also sometimes a pawnbroker.

       83 *Huffed at*: treated with arrogance or contempt.

52   84 *tite*: variant spelling of 'tight', in this case meaning a neat fit of clothes.

       85 *Fob*: a small pocket in the waistband.

       86 *the Church-yard*: most likely referring to Whitechapel Church Yard, the site of St Mary Church, located on the south side of White Chapel Street, at the western end of today's Whitechapel Road.

       87 *hall'd*: hauled.

       88 *the Commissioners*: the officers of the Customs.

53   89 *Fact*: deed, i.e. misdemeanour.

       90 *Mittimus*: a warrant issued by a justice of the peace committing a person to custody.

54   91 *ROBIN*: This is in fact the character later named Will, and 'Robin' is evidently a slip on Defoe's part.

55   92 *Standish*: 'a stand containing ink, pens and other writing materials and accessories; an inkstand; also, an inkpot' (*OED*).

57   93 *Tower-Street*: a street to the west of the Tower of London, today's Great Tower Street. The Custom House was just south of Tower Street, on (nowadays Lower) Thames Street, very close to the river, therefore the walk from it to the custom house clerk's house would be but a short one.

58   94 *tell*: count.

60   95 *be starv'd*: die.

61   96 *who wanted every thing*: who was in want of everything (a play of words on the two senses of 'want').

62   97 *stands to Courtisie*: must depend on his associates' goodwill.

63   98 *hankered about*: hung about (to 'hanker' is to linger or loiter about with longing or expectation).

       99 *Bait*: meal, food or refreshment.

     100 *Billingsgate*: in Defoe's time a fish market on the north bank of the River Thames next to Billingsgate Dock, between London Bridge and Custom House Key.

     101 *Crimps*: those employed to load or unload coal ships.

     102 *the Gun-Tavern*: possibly near Gun Wharf, located on the south bank of the River Thames opposite Billingsgate, easily accessible to Jack by crossing the nearby London Bridge.

64   103   *St Mary axe*: The street, running between Leadenhall Street and Houndsditch, took its name from the ancient church of St Mary Axe, which was suppressed in 1560. (The 'Axe' of the dedication was one of the three axes reputed to have been used by Attila the Hun in the slaughter of St Ursula and her 11,000 virgins. It was kept in the church.)

104   *old Bedlam*: The site of the original Bethlehem Royal Hospital (known as Bedlam) was an ancient priory outside Bishopsgate.

105   *where now the Great Hospital stands*: In 1675–6, Bethlehem Royal Hospital was moved to a splendid new building in Moorfields, designed by Robert Hooke.

106   *Jobb*: robbery, in thieves' slang.

107   *Hallow*: halloo.

108   *old Thirteen-pence-halfpenny ... Four-pence-half-penny's*: The 'thirteen-pence-halfpenny piece' was the name by which the Scottish mark (a coin worth 13*s.* 4*d.* in Scots money) was known in the seventeenth century. 'Piece' was the name popularly applied to the guinea, hence 'half-piece', 'quarter-piece'. The 'ninepence' was a coin worth nine pennies, often applied in the seventeenth century to the Irish shilling, and the 'fourpence-halfpenny' was similarly applied to the Irish sixpence.

66   109   *like the Cock in the Fable*: In Aesop's fable, the cock who found a precious stone among the straw declared that he would rather have found barley-corn. The phrase 'a barley-corn is better than a diamond to a cock' became proverbial.

110   *Sir Henry Furness's*: Sir Henry Furnese (1658–1712) made his fortune in the stocking trade and was one of the original directors of the Bank of England. Defoe satirised him in *Reformation of Manners* (1702), ll. 149–81; see *Satire, Fantasy and Writings on the Supernatural by Daniel Defoe* (8 vols, London, 2003–5), Vol. 1, ed. W. R. Owens, pp. 161–2.

111   *Temple-bar*: Temple Bar marked the dividing-line between the City and Westminster.

67   112   *the King's-Head-Tavern*: a famous tavern in Fleet Street, dating from the time of Henry VIII. It was demolished in 1799 when Chancery Lane was widened.

113   *Crying it*: getting the town-crier to proclaim the theft.

68   114   *an Artist*: one highly skilled in his craft – in this case, robbery.

69   115   *lissen*: variant spelling of listen.

70   116   *Sir Henry Furness's*: see note 110 above.

117   *Sir Charles Duncomb's*: Sir Charles Duncombe (1648–1711) was an immensely rich goldsmith, banker and Tory MP. He was previously satirised by Defoe in *The True-Born Englishman* (1700); see *Satire, Fantasy and Writings on the Supernatural*, Vol. 1, pp. 113–17.

page

70   118 *Endorst off*: endorsed (presumably as 'pay to bearer') in favour of another recipient.

       119 *J. Tassell*: A John Tassel operated as a goldsmith in London between 1670 and 1692; see *Jackson's Silver & Gold Marks of England, Scotland & Ireland*, 3rd edn, ed. Ian Pickford (Woodbridge, Suffolk, 1989), p. 244.

       120 *Sir Francis Child*: Sir Francis Child (1642–1713) was a very wealthy goldsmith-banker in London, jeweller to the king, and lent large sums of money to the government. A freeman of the City of London, in 1689 he became an alderman, served as sheriff of London in 1691 and in 1699 was its lord mayor.

       121 *Stewart*: unidentified.

71   122 *told out*: counted out (see note 78 above).

72   123 *the Exchange*: the New Exchange, in the Strand.

73   124 *while*: until.

       125 *the Cloyster-Gate in Smithfield*: The Cloisters was an area of ill repute in Smithfield. See *The Observator* for 21 August 1703: 'they'd Raffle with the Punks in the *Cloysters*'.

74   126 *Hits*: robberies.

75   127 *Sir John Sweetapple*: Sir John Sweetapple, a Lombard Street banker, became sheriff of London in 1694. He was knighted later the same year, and went bankrupt in 1701. He is almost certainly the '*S----ple*' satirised in Defoe's *Reformation of Manners*, ll. 181–215; see *Satire, Fantasy and Writings on the Supernatural*, Vol. 1, p. 162.

76   128 *Push-pin*: a child's game in which each player pushes his or her pin with the object of crossing another player's.

77   129 *such an hateful Practice*: The evil of profane swearing was a constant theme of Defoe's writing. See, for example, his *Essay upon Projects* (1697), in *Political and Economic Writings* (London, 2000), Vol. 8, ed. W. R. Owens, pp. 111–14, 280–1; *The Family Instructor, Volume II* (1718), in *The Religious and Didactic Writings of Daniel Defoe* (10 vols, London, 2006–7), Vol. 2, ed. P. N. Furbank, pp. 182–241 (and see also Introduction to Vol. 1, ed. P. N. Furbank, pp. 23–4).

       130 *small Beer*: beer low in alcoholic strength.

78   131 *the Word took with me*: i.e. the word 'gentleman' appealed to me.

       132 *Pindar of Wakefield*: the site of Pindar of Wakefield's fort, near Gray's Inn Lane, built by Parliament during the Civil War. Pindar was a semi-legendary folk hero.

       133 *Pancrass Church*: that is to say, what is known today as St Pancras Old Church, one of the oldest churches in Britain, which still stands in Pancras Road, behind today's Kings Cross in north London.

       134 *shoot Flying*: i.e. rob unwary victims of their money.

       135 *Doctor of Physick*: physician.

79   136 *Plaister-box*: box of plasters for the treatment of wounds, etc.

79 137 *presently*: immediately.

    138 *jog'd*: jogged.

    139 *Tottenham-Court*: located near what is today's Tottenham Court Road, north of Oxford Street.

80 140 *High-Park-Gate*: i.e. Hyde Park Gate.

    141 *Punk*: prostitute.

    142 *Spring-Garden*: pleasure gardens, adjacent to Cockspur Street, laid out at the beginning of the seventeenth century.

    143 *Beaufort-House*: also known as Chelsea House, built in 1521 and Sir Thomas More's residence for a period. It was demolished in 1740.

81 144 *Copper*: vessel made of copper.

83 145 *upon the Scout*: on the look-out for booty.

    146 *Hownslow*: or Hounslow, a town on the Great West Road about 7 km south-west of Charing Cross, in Defoe's day a main stop on the coaching route to the west.

    147 *from Chertsy ... a boat to London*: Chertsey, Kingston and Mortlake were and are all towns located on the banks of the River Thames, west of London.

    148 *Comerades*: variant spelling of comrades.

84 149 *hal'd*: hauled.

    150 *hale*: haul.

85 151 *Headborough*: a parish officer whose functions were the same as those of a petty constable.

    152 *Peach'd*: incriminated (i.e. betrayed).

86 153 *whether*: whither.

    154 *blown*: known to be a malefactor.

    155 *Cloth-fair*: a street off West Smithfield, originally the site of a fair specialising in the sale of cloth and woollen products.

    156 *GOOD TOWER STANDARD*: the code word is evidently an imaginary hallmark.

88 157 *Galloon*: a kind of narrow, close-woven ribbon or braid, of gold, silver or silk thread, used for trimming articles of apparel; a trimming of this material.

    158 *Edg'd*: 'having a border (of ornamental work)' (*OED*). Defoe's usage here is the only one cited in *OED* as applied to a hat.

    159 *Cring'd*: bowed servilely.

    160 *Country*: i.e. county.

89 161 *Suit of Mourning*: set of mourning garments.

    162 *shift*: change.

    163 *Rag-Fair*: see note 42 above.

90 164 *Sir Name*: variant spelling of surname.

92 165 *discover'd*: revealed or disclosed.

page

93 166 *good Husbands*: to husband well here means to manage with thrift and prudence; to use, spend or apply economically.

95 167 *fast enough*: safely in custody.

168 *told*: see note 78 above.

96 169 *lissening*: see note 115 above.

170 *Crown*: a crown represented five shillings.

97 171 *hear in its Order*: see above, pp. 170–1.

98 172 *hangs*: ties up.

173 *rod*: rode.

174 *upon the Spur*: hastily.

99 175 *St. Edmunds-Bury*: i.e. Bury St Edmunds.

100 176 *Politick*: cunning.

177 *Parl'd*: talked.

178 *The Man*: presumably the innkeeper of the other inn in Bourn-Bridge.

101 179 *the Divel's-Ditch*: now known as Devil's Dyke.

102 180 *ventrous*: variant spelling of venturous.

181 *Mountebank*: an itinerant quack (with a crowd round him).

182 *a Peice of new Holland, of eight or nine Ells*: Holland is here a linen fabric, originally named Holland cloth, after the province of Holland in the Netherlands; an ell was a measure of length (now archaic) varying from European country to country, but in England being 1.15 m.

183 *Stuff*: woollen material (as opposed to silk).

184 *Pranks*: wicked deeds.

103 185 *Physick*: see note 135 above.

186 *and but you have Reason*: The wording here is obscure, but perhaps the sense is 'and although you have reason'.

187 *accidentally comparing the Roads*: happened to be discussing the various routes.

104 188 *amus'd*: bewildered.

105 189 *a Ford a little below Kelso ... opposite to the Town*: In his *Tour thro' the Whole Island of Great Britain*, Defoe noted that there was great need of a bridge over the Tweed at Kelso: 'at present they have a Ferry just at the Town, and a good Ford through the River, a little below it; but, though I call it a good Ford, and so it is when the Water is low, yet ... the *Tweed* is so dangerous a River, and rises sometimes so suddenly, that ... it is not very strange to them at *Kelso*, to hear of frequent Disasters, in the Passage, both to Men and Cattle'; see *Writings on Travel, Discovery and History by Daniel Defoe* (8 vols, London, 2001–2), Vol. 3, ed. John McVeagh, p. 218

190 *Woller-haugh-head*: In the *Tour*, Defoe writes that 'our Guide carry'd us not to the Town of *Wooller*, where we were before, but to a single House, which they call *Wooller Haugh-head*, and is a very good Inn'; in ibid., p. 221.

191 *doubted*: suspected.

192 *the Capital City*: i.e. Edinburgh.

page

105 193 *Plads*: plaids (outer garments worn in Scotland).

106 194 *course*: rough.

195 *Lauderdale*: see Defoe's *Tour*: 'we pass'd through *Lauderdale*, a long Valley on both Sides the little River *Lauder*, from whence the House of *Maitland*, Earls first, and at last Duke of *Lauderdale*, took their Title'; in *Writings on Travel, Discovery and History*, Vol. 3, p. 221.

196 *he had a Proverb in his Favour*: The usual form of the proverb is 'He that is born to be hanged shall never be drowned'.

197 *Mercart-Cross*: i.e. the Market Cross, 'where all their Proclamations and publick Acts are read and publish'd by Sound of Trumpet. Here is the great Parade, where, every Day, the Gentlemen meet for Business or News, as at an Exchange' (*Tour*, in *Writings on Travel, Discovery and History*, Vol. 3, p. 171).

107 198 *the famous place, call'd Bridewell*: as mentioned in note 33 above, London's 'house of correction'.

199 *the City Hangman*: The public hangman in Edinburgh was responsible not only for executions, but for the imprisonment of criminals and the carrying out of sentences involving scourging or whipping. See Robert Chambers, *Domestic Annals of Scotland from the Reformation to the Revolution* (2 vols, 2nd edn, Edinburgh and London, 1859), Vol. 2, p. 345, for an account of a woman sentenced in 1671 'to be scourged by the hangman from [the Market Cross] to the Nether Bow'. In 1684 the then hangman lashed a victim so severely that he was deprived of his post and punished (ibid., Vol. 2, p. 461).

200 *Mercery and Millenary Goods*: respectively, fabrics and articles of female clothing, especially hats (the modern spelling is 'millinery').

201 *spight*: spite.

108 202 *whether*: whither.

109 203 *I could not Write or Read*: Defoe has evidently forgotten Jack's earlier claim that he could read and write before the age of ten; see pp. 35–6 above.

204 *Farmers of the Customs*: collectors of customs dues.

205 *Mis-applications*: malversations, corrupt behaviour or administration in a position of trust.

206 *Raparee*: Irish irregular soldiers and pikemen were known as 'rapparees'. (See the title of Defoe's first poem, *A New Discovery of an Old Intreague: A Satyr ... Calculated to the Nativity of the Rapparree Plott* (1691).)

207 *Regiment of Douglas*: A 'regiment de Douglas' existed in Scotland from the mid-1640s, and was one of several that operated in France and the Low Countries.

110 208 *a private Centinel*: (or sentinel) a private soldier.

111 209 *a Colours*: a place as a commissioned officer.

112 210 *shot in*: closed in, shut in. The spelling 'shot' may be a misprint, but this was a dialect form of shut.

211 *Haddingtown*: i.e. Haddington.

212 *Mounting*: equipment.

page

113　213　*Glass-houses*: The Henzell and Tyzack families owned eleven houses in Newcastle for the manufacture of glass.

　　214　*Shields*: i.e. South Shields, at the mouth of the Tyne.

　　215　*whether*: whither.

114　216　*Sneaker*: small bowl.

　　217　*Jack*: rotary roasting spit.

115　218　*Boatson*: i.e. boatswain.

　　219　*Hurry*: commotion.

　　220　*Trappan'd*: trepanned, lured into a trap.

117　221　*Geers*: i.e. gear, rigging.

　　222　*Cat-a-nine-tales*: The 'cat-a-nine-tales' (more correctly 'tails') was a short-handled whip with nine leather straps, used to punish wrongdoers aboard ship.

　　223　*Whipp'd and Pickl'd*: Flogged men had salt or vinegar applied to their backs, so as to ensure that they recovered from the punishment. See *A New Voyage Round the World*: 'tho' Pickling, that is to say, throwing Salt and Vinegar on the Back after the whipping be cruel enough, as to the Pain it is to the Patient, yet 'tis certainly the Way to prevent Mortification, and causes it to heal again with the more Ease'; *The Novels*, Vol. 10, ed. John McVeagh, p. 85.

118　224　*took up the air of what my Habit did not agree with*: assumed a haughtiness not to be expected from someone in such shabby clothes.

119　225　*Potomack*: The Potomac river marked the boundary between Maryland and West Virginia.

　　226　*the five Years Servitude*: Jack, of course, was not transported as a convict, for whom the more usual term would have been seven or fourteen years, or life.

　　227　*Land ... for myself*: One source for the kind of indentured labour in seventeenth-century Maryland that Jack describes specifies that a servant was to work at whatever his master 'shall there imploy him, according to the custome of the Country'. At the completion of the 'said term' of labour, a master was obliged to give his indentured servant 'one whole years provision of Corne, and fifty acres of Land, according to the order of the Country'. See Russell R. Menard and Lois Green Carr, 'The Lords Baltimore and the Colonization of Maryland', in David B. Quinn (ed.), *Early Maryland in a Wider World* (Detroit, 1982), p. 204.

120　228　*Sasquehanuagh*: i.e. Susquehanna.

121　229　*gaged*: engaged.

　　230　*Transported Fellons*: Magistrates had the power to transport felons 'beyond the seas' from 1597, but mass, systematic transportation began in 1718, with the passing of the Transportation Act. This made transportation a punishment in its own right, rather than a condition of judicial pardons.

　　231　*burnt in the Hand*: Offenders convicted of a capital crime, but who escaped the death penalty, were branded with a hot iron. Anyone caught reoffending after having been branded would almost certainly receive the death penalty.

121 232 *in a kind of State*: ceremoniously.

125 233 *Listed*: enlisted.

126 234 *whether*: whither.

127 235 *upon the Foot*: to the sum or total (of an account).

128 236 *Cruelty ... in Whipping the Negro Slaves*: The most common punishment meted out to slaves was whipping to the bare back, but 'some masters escalated the punishment beyond whipping to include branding on the face, lopping off an ear, slitting the nose, and cutting the hamstrings or severing the foot'. Under the Barbadian slave code, systematised in 1661, a slave owner had the right to whip, torture, maim, castrate and even destroy a slave's property. See Alan Taylor, *American Colonies* (London and New York, 2001), pp. 213, 330.

    237 *a Rod of Iron ... as the Scripture calls it*: There are three references to ruling 'with a rod of iron' in Revelation 2:27, 12:5 and 19:15. In the Old Testament, King Rehoboam tells the people 'I will chastise you with scorpions'; 1 Kings 12:11, 14; 2 Chronicles 10:11, 14.

129 238 *Rod*: rode.

130 239 *Hand-spike*: 'a wooden bar, used as a lever or crow, chiefly on shipboard or artillery service' (*OED*).

    240 *striking up the Negroes Heels*: kicking the negro's feet from under him.

132 241 *lay that Sin to my Charge*: see the words of Stephen as he is being stoned: 'Lord, lay not this sin to their charge', Acts 7:60.

133 242 *like Noah*: see Genesis 9:20–1, where Noah, having planted a vineyard, 'drank of the wine, and was drunken'.

134 243 *Whipp'd and Pickl'd*: see note 223 above.

    244 *Pranks*: see note 184 above.

    245 *muchee sorree*: In *The Farther Adventures of Robinson Crusoe*, Crusoe notes that when natives of Africa learn to speak English, 'they always add two E's at the End of the Words where we use one, and place the Accent upon them, as *makéé takéé*, and the like'. In his note on this passage, W. R. Owens cites an account, first published in Samuel Purchas, *Purchas His Pilgrimes* (1625), of the way native Dominicans pronounced English words: 'to all words ending in a consonant they always set the second vowel, as for chinne, they say chin-ne, so making most of the monasillables, dissillables'; see *The Novels*, Vol. 2, pp. 122–3, 231, n. 182.

    246 *Gratitude is the Product of generous Principles*: For Defoe, gratitude was the greatest of the social virtues. It is, he writes in the *Review* for 26 March 1706, 'a Debt of Honour, and every Honest Man, is more bound by one Act of Generosity than ten Injuries'. Here, however, it is difficult not to feel that there is something morally distasteful about the way in

page

which Jack 'buys' Mouchat's gratitude by first terrifying him with the threat of inhuman punishment and then pretending to have obtained a pardon for him from the plantation owner. Even worse is Jack's manipulation of Mouchat's feelings, when he circulates the fiction that he (Jack) is to be dismissed and hanged for some unspecified offence, with the result that Mouchat asks if he can be hanged in Jack's place. For a discussion of Defoe's ideas about gratitude, see Maximillian E. Novak, *Defoe and the Nature of Man* (London, 1963), pp. 113–28.

136 247 *ingenious Spirit*: man of intelligent ideas.

137 248 *Potuxent River*: This river flows through the eastern shore of Maryland into Chesapeake Bay.

139 249 *stupid*: stupified.

141 250 *undocible*: unteachable.

251 *the English Proverb ... Cut your Throat*: This is an ancient proverb, sometimes in the form 'Save a thief from the gallows and he will hate (or never love) you'. Defoe's usage here is the latest cited in *The Oxford Dictionary of English Proverbs*, 3rd edn, rev. F. P. Wilson (Oxford, 1970).

143 252 *Trapann'd*: see note 220 above.

253 *Buy your Liberty of me*: Felons with sufficient money could buy their liberty on arrival in America by paying the merchant the price they would have fetched if sold.

254 *a Certificate ... for five Years*: Under the terms of the Transportation Act, merchants were required to provide bonds and landing certificates to ensure that transports reached their destination.

255 *strain'd Courtisies*: competed in politeness.

144 256 *less Cruel ... as they do in those*: see Introduction above, p. 12.

257 *I continu'd in this Station between five and six Year after this*: Jack must therefore be about 27 at this point in his history.

145 258 *unluckly*: an obsolete form of 'unlucky'. The latest usage cited in *OED* is from 1678.

259 *the Country Bounty ... Plant for myself*: see note 227 above.

260 *the Lord Proprietor*: Virginia and Maryland were organised on the 'proprietorial' system, the territory legally belonging to a 'proprietor' who held it directly from the Crown.

146 261 *bare Walls make giddy Hussy's*: a seventeenth-century proverb, sometimes using the phrase 'gadding housewives'.

262 *Trappan'd*: see note 220 above.

147 263 *Rated*: fixed, settled.

264 *naked*: i.e. starting out, without funds.

265 *cure*: clear.

266 *Husband*: cultivator, farmer, husbandman.

page
147 267 *Condemn'd-Hole in Newgate*: Prisoners awaiting execution in Newgate were kept in the Condemned Hold, a stone chamber underneath the keeper's house.

148 268 *good Forwardness*: a good state of cultivation.

269 *under the Hatches*: in trouble.

149 270 *an Honest Man*: The meaning is akin to the French *honnête homme*, i.e. a decent and respectworthy man.

150 271 *be fire in my Flax*: wreak havoc upon me.

272 *as a Moth to consume*: There is perhaps an allusion here to Christ's injunction in the Sermon on the Mount, 'Lay not up for yourselves treasures upon earth, where moth and rust doth corrupt' (Matthew 6:19; Luke 12:33).

273 *expect*: await.

274 *Livy's Roman History ... Conquest of Mexico*: The references here are (most likely) to the history of Rome by Titus Livius (59 BC–AD 17), Richard Knolles's *The Turkish History*, ed. Paul Rycaut (3 vols, 1687–1700), John Speed's *Historie of Great Britaine* (1611), Famianus Strada's *De Bello Belgico* (1632–47) and Bartolomeo de las Casas's *Brevisima Relacion de la Destruycion de las Indias* (1552). There is evidence that Defoe knew all of these works. It is uncertain which history of Gustavus Adolphus is being referred to, for Gustavus was a particular hero of Defoe's and he would have read a great deal about him.

275 *meer*: mere.

151 276 *In this Posture I went on for 12 Year*: by his own accounting, Jack is therefore now 42.

152 277 *gone ... into their own Country*: Vincent Brown cites one seventeenth-century chronicler of slave society in Barbados as stating that Africans 'believe in a Resurrection, and that they shall go into their own Country again, and have their youth renewed'. See Vincent Brown, *The Reaper's Garden: Death and Power in the World of Atlantic Slavery* (Cambridge, Massachusetts, 2008), p. 133.

153 278 *renovare dolorem*: an allusion to Aeneas's words to Dido in line 3 of Virgil's *Aeneid*: 'Infandum, regina, iubes renovare dolorem' ('Too deep for words, O Queen, is the grief you bid me renew').

279 *to be reduc'd to Necessity is to be wicked*: see note 281 below.

154 280 *Lord's Prayer ... into Temptation*: see Matthew 6:13; Luke 11:4.

281 *Solomon's or Agar's Prayer: Give me not Poverty, least I Steal*: In the Proverbs of Solomon, Agur prays 'give me neither poverty nor riches; feed me with food convenient for me: Lest I be full, and deny thee, and say, Who is the Lord? Or lest I be poor, and steal, and take the name of my God in vain' (Proverbs 30:8, 9). Defoe frequently quotes or alludes to this text; see, for example, the *Review*, 5 March 1706; *Robinson Crusoe* (1719), in *The Novels*, Vol. 1, p. 58; *Serious Reflections* (1720), in ibid.,

Vol. 3, ed. G. A. Starr, p. 80; *Moll Flanders*, in ibid., Vol. 6, ed. Liz Bellamy, p. 163. For a discussion of 'the problem of necessity in Defoe's fiction', see Novak, *Defoe and the Nature of Man*, pp. 65–88.

155 282 *Lord! Whatsoever Sorrows ... my Subjection True*: source untraced; perhaps by Defoe himself.

156 283 *Fact*: see note 89 above.

284 *within Benefit of Clergy*: In the case of minor crimes, the ancient privilege of the clergy and the literate not to be judged by a secular court still existed.

157 285 *Shooters hill*: a steep, thickly wooded hill south of London, notorious as a haunt for highwaymen. There was a gallows at the bottom, and on the summit a gibbet where bodies of those executed were displayed.

159 286 *I was now more than Thirty Year old*: In general terms this is correct but, as pointed out in note 276 above, Jack is 42, according to his own computation.

160 287 *nor, so much as like the Pharisee had said, one God I thank thee*: i.e. he had not said a single 'God I thank thee'. See Luke 18:11.

288 *That not a Hair ... without his Permission*: see 1 Kings 1: 52.

289 *the Words of the Eunuch ... some one Guide me*: see Acts 8:27–40, esp. 31.

161 290 *the great War ... Powers of Europe*: Jack is referring to the War of the League of Augsburg, 1688–97.

162 291 *Certificate of his Transportation*: see note 254 above.

292 *only, that I did not assist him ... as a Servant*: The sense here is obscure, and it may be that some words have been set in the wrong place. A possible reading is: 'only, that I did not assist him to enter upon Planting for himself as I was assisted, neither was I upon the Spot to do it, any farther than, as *I say*, by making him an Overseer, which was only a present Ease and Deliverance to him from the hard Labour, and Fare, which he endured as a Servant; but [t]his Man's Diligence and honest Application, even unassisted, deliver'd himself.'

163 293 *go voluntarily over to those Countries*: The labour force in the earlier days of the American colonies took the form of voluntary indentured servitude, whether on the part of whites or blacks; when the terms of indentures were up, such workers could establish themselves as free labour.

294 *Hogsheads*: large casks for transporting various articles, usually molasses, tobacco and beer.

295 *Correspondent*: mercantile associate.

296 *sour*: disagreeable.

297 *beaten up*: In nautical usage, to 'beat up' is to sail against the wind.

164 298 *an excellent Sea Artist*: a master of the art of navigation.

299 *Wake*: course, or general line of direction (of a ship).

300 *Cape de Verd Islands*: i.e. the Cape Verde Islands, a group of islands in the Atlantic about 560 km west of Cape Verde in Senegal.

page

164 301 *Pico Teneriffe ... Islands*: Teneriffe is the largest of the Canary Islands. It is the site of the volcanic Pico de Teide, which rises to about 4,000 m.

302 *the Soundings*: A sounding is a place at sea where it is possible to reach the bottom with the ordinary deep-sea lead.

303 *keep a larger Offing*: To keep, or make, 'a good offing' is to lay a course that keeps a ship well clear of land so as to avoid any hazards.

165 304 *St. Malo's*: St Malo, a port on the northern coast of Brittany.

305 *the Cruiser ... the Ship I was in*: i.e. the French privateer, and the ship he *had* been in.

306 *Rover*: pirate, or privateer. (The word 'rover' comes from the Dutch word for pirate, *zee-rover*, literally sea-robber.)

307 *made a Sail*: saw a ship.

308 *St Georges Channel*: the channel between southern Ireland and Wales.

309 *the Round-Top*: the platform (formerly circular) about a ship's masthead.

310 *Hurry and Clutter*: excitement and confusion.

166 311 *by the time ... prepar'd to Fight*: The meaning of this passage seems to be as follows: 'by the time I was turn'd out I could perceive they [the crew of the French cruiser, aboard which Jack now is] had all their Sails bent, and full, having begun to Chace, and [were] making great way; on the other Hand, it was Evident the Ship [the large English ship coming from Jamaica] saw them too, and knew what they were, and to avoid them, stretch'd away with all the Canvas they could lay on, for the Coast of *Ireland*, to run in there for Harbour.

'Our Privateer [the French cruiser], it was plain, infinitely outsail'd her, running two Foot for her one, and towards Evening came up with them [the large English ship]; had they been able to have held it but six Hours longer, they would have got into *Limerick* River, or somewhere under Shore, so that we [the French] should not have ventured upon them, but we came up with them, and the Captain [of the large English ship] when he see [saw] there was no Remedy, bravely brought to, and prepar'd to Fight.'

312 *Hause*: (or hawse) 'the space between the head of a vessel at anchor and the anchors, or a little beyond the anchors, *esp.* in phr. *athwart the hawse*' (*OED*).

313 *Tire*: tier or row.

314 *Missen-Mast and Bole-sprit*: mizzen mast and bowsprit.

315 *oblig'd to Strike*: forced to surrender.

167 316 *pieces of Eight*: the old Spanish silver *peso* or 'dollar' of eight *reals*.

317 *Hhds*: i.e. hogsheads (see note 294 above).

318 *Indico*: or indigo, substance obtained in the form of a blue powder from plants of the genus indigofera, and largely used as a blue dye.

319 *Piemento*: allspice, the dried aromatic berries of the pimento tree.

320 *Succads*: fruits preserved in sugar, either candied or in syrup.

page

168 321 *the Streights*: the Straits of Gibraltar.

322 *Ushant*: town on the tip of the Brittany peninsula.

323 *Diep*: i.e. Dieppe.

324 *Dinant*: i.e. Dinan, an ancient township on the Rance, 22 km south of St Malo.

169 325 *Bilk'd*: cheated.

326 *Intendant*: 'The functionary who formerly administered a French province, according to the system introduced under Richelieu in the seventeenth century, called also *intendant of justice, police, and finances*' (*OED*).

170 327 *The Prince of Orange had been made King of England*: William accepted the Crown of England, with Mary as his Queen, on 13 February 1689.

328 *Hhds*: see note 317 above.

171 329 *the Greve*: (more properly *Grève*, meaning beach, or strand) the place of execution in Paris, on the banks of the Seine.

172 330 *the French-Church*: According to a note in *The Diary of Samuel Pepys*, ed. R. Latham and W. Matthews (11 vols, London, 1970–83), Vol. 3, p. 207, the congregation of the French Calvinist church moved in 1661 to the chapel of the Savoy Hospital. Both this and the other French church in Threadneedle Street were favourite resorts for Londoners anxious to improve their French.

331 *owing me a Spleen*: having a grudge against me.

332 *Circle*: the enchanted circle supposedly made by a sorcerer or witch.

173 333 *rally*: speak sarcastically about.

174 334 *Politicks*: intriguing machinations.

175 335 *Posture Mistress*: an instructor in deportment.

336 *Work*: i.e. needlework.

176 337 *discover'd myself*: revealed my feelings.

338 *gone abroad*: gone out.

339 *rallyed*: bickered playfully.

177 340 *the grand Parlee*: the great debate.

341 *Treating of*: coming to an agreement about.

342 *Play*: i.e. cards.

343 *Rallery*: variant spelling of raillery.

178 344 *breaking upon the Wheel*: a form of penal torture and execution, the first stage of which was spreadeagling the victim's body on a wheel and dislocating his limbs.

345 *a Box and Dice*: serious gambling.

346 *Rattle*: a torrent of angry words, altercation, row.

347 *Figures*: expenses.

348 *drop her Burthen with me*: Jack's wife seems to mean that she will give birth to her child in his house, but if he is subsequently unhappy with

what he may consider to be her unrestrained lifestyle following this time, she will find this intolerable, and therefore leave him.

180 349 *out-cry*: auction.

     350 *pass'd the Rubicon*: The Rubicon was a small river separating Italy and Cisalpine Gaul. When Caesar crossed it he passed beyond the limits of his province and became an invader. 'Passing the Rubicon' has thus come to mean taking an irrevocable step.

181 351 *which I refus'd to accept*: i.e. which he refused to be drawn upon for, or, in technical language, to 'accept'.

     352 *Sued her in the Ecclesiastick Court, in order to obtain a Divorce*: According to Canon Law, as administered by ecclesiastical courts, divorce *a mensa et thoro*, i.e. legal separation, could be granted and if on grounds of adultery was permanent.

     353 *Debts, which I should be oblig'd to Pay*: Although on marriage a husband acquired control of all his wife's personal property, he also became legally responsible for all her debts. See Lawrence Stone, *The Family, Sex and Marriage in England 1500–1800* (1977; Harmondsworth, 1979), p. 136.

185 354 *Cry her down*: condemn her publicly.

188 355 *Regiment of Dillon*: Arthur Dillon (1670–1733), an Irish gentleman, raised a regiment to fight for Louis XIV.

     356 *Commanded into Italy*: The conflict between the French and the Imperialists in northern Italy in 1701, in which Jack serves on the French side, was the prelude to the War of the Spanish Succession.

     357 *the Famous Attack upon Cremona*: This was Prince Eugene's raid on Cremona on 17 February 1702, in which the French marshal Villeroi was captured.

     358 *in the Millanese*: The 'Millanese' was the name given to the territory of the old duchy of Milan.

     359 *Germans*: i.e. Austrians.

     360 *Common-Shoar*: sewer.

     361 *the Mareschal Duke de Villeroy*: François de Neuville, Duc de Villeroi (1644–1730), marshal of France.

     362 *Philip de Comines*: the French statesman and memorialist Philippe de Commynes (1447–1511), whose *Mémoires* (1489–98) are an important source for the history of France in the later fifteenth century.

     363 *the Count de Charolois*: Charles the Bold, Comte de Charolais and Duke of Burgundy (1433–77). The battle of Monteleri took place in 1465.

189 364 *a Breviat*: i.e. a brevet, an official Army document conferring rank on an officer.

     365 *Alexandria*: present-day Alessandria, a city of the Marengo plain in northern Italy, situated on the south bank of the River Tanaro.

     366 *Ports*: By 'ports' Jack perhaps means 'gates' (*portes* in French).

page

189 367 *Pistols*: A *pistole* was a Spanish gold coin, equivalent to the French *louis*.

      368 *Prince Vaudemont*: Charles Henri de Lorraine, Prince de Vaudemont (1643–1723).

190 369 *King Philip*: Philip V, grandson of Louis XIV, had been king of Spain since 1700.

      370 *Count de Tesse*: René III de Froulay, Comte de Tessé (1650–1725), marshal of France.

      371 *Duke de Vandosme*: Louis Joseph, Duc de Vendôme (1654–1712), marshal of France.

      372 *Prince Eugene of Savoy*: Eugene, Prince of Savoy (1663–1736). He was commander-in-chief of the Imperial forces during the War of the Spanish Succession, collaborating closely with Marlborough.

      373 *Carpi, July 1701*: The engagement took place on 9 July 1701.

      374 *Monsieur Catinate*: Nicholas de Catinat (1637–1712), marshal of France. He had occupied Mantua and the valley of the Po.

191 375 *Chiar*: i.e. Chiari (20 km west of Brescia).

      376 *a party War*: a guerrilla war.

      377 *Duke of Savoy*: Victor Amadeus II (1666–1732), ruler of the duchy of Savoy. (In 1703 he would transfer his allegiance from France to the Allies.)

192 378 *Prince Commercy*: Charles Henry de Lorraine-Vaudemont (1649–1723).

193 379 *shifting every one*: everyone looking after themselves.

195 380 *Monsieur Pracontal*: unidentified.

      381 *in Batalia*: (battalia) in marching order or order of battle.

      382 *General Visconti*: unidentified.

196 383 *General Herbeville*: unidentified.

197 384 *Marquis de Crequi*: François Créquy de Blanchefort (1662–1702), marshal of France.

198 385 *Cartel*: agreed code (for the treatment and exchange of prisoners-of-war).

199 386 *Chartel*: cartel (see previous note).

      387 *the Chevalier de St. George*: the French name for the Old Pretender.

200 388 *Sir George Bing*: Admiral Sir George Byng (1668–1733).

      389 *keeping that Shore on Board*: following that shore.

201 390 *Jealousie, as the wise Man says, is the wrath of a Man*: see Proverbs 6:34: 'Jealousy is the rage of a man'.

      391 *so good a Hussy*: so prudent a 'husband' or manager.

202 392 *tho' she had been*: even if she had been.

      393 *Affronting*: confronting.

      394 *Hem'd*: came uttering discreet rebukes.

205 395 *alle*: (French) *allez* ('go').

      396 *Deux Ponts*: or Zweibrucken, a German town in the *Land* of Rhineland Palatinate.

page
207 397 *easiest*: without anxiety.

398 *it is not good for Man to be alone*: see Genesis 2:18.

399 *Canterbury*: a town which had welcomed French refugees since the time of Elizabeth I.

208 400 *Incog.*: i.e. incognito, unobtrusively, without drawing attention to himself.

401 *Walloons*: French-speaking inhabitants of Belgium.

209 402 *in the Streights*: through the Straits of Gibraltar.

403 *respectively*: respectfully, courteously.

210 404 *Neats*: ox's.

405 *Hoods over her Eyes, or Black upon her Head*: having exchanged her travelling attire for more informal wear, it appears that Jack's female companion has removed both the hooded garment previously hiding her face, as well as her mourning headgear.

406 *see*: i.e. saw.

212 407 *pretended*: laid claim.

213 408 *Hostess*: mistress of an inn.

409 *That was a good Story … lay with his Mother*: As Everett Zimmerman has suggested, this is a version of the Oedipus myth; see his *Defoe and the Novel* (Berkeley, California, and London, 1975), p. 148.

214 410 *Stepney Fields*: The peninsula on the north bank of the Thames opposite Greenwich, now known as the Isle of Dogs, was formerly known as Stepney Marsh, which is presumably what Jack is referring to here.

216 411 *Vapours*: morbid imaginings.

217 412 *one Citizen*: Jack is presumably referring to the daughter of the burgher of Trent (see p. 198 above).

219 413 *shift*: dress.

220 414 *the invasion of the Scots, and the Fight at Preston*: On 6 September 1715 the Earl of Mar raised the standard of rebellion against England at Braemar, being supported by a small force of gentry on the border and an English force in Lancashire recruited by the Northumberland MP Thomas Forster. The rebellion was crippled by the lack of help from France, and by 3 November Forster's troops had surrendered at Preston, and on the same day Mar was defeated at Sherrifmuir. The Pretender arrived in Scotland just before Christmas, but too late to redeem the situation.

415 *Lord Darwentwater*: James Radcliffe (or Radclyffe), Earl of Derwentwater (1689–1716), was one of the leaders of the Jacobite rebellion of 1715. He was captured after the rout at Preston, confined to the Tower and executed.

222 416 *Condemn'd-hole*: see note 267 above.

225 417 *Mantua*: manteau, a loose upper garment worn by women.

226 418 *Herded*: consorted.

page
226 419 *desire Husks with Swine ... that Supply*: The allusion is to the parable of
the Prodigal Son, who 'would fain have filled his belly with the husks
that the swine did eat: and no man gave unto him' (Luke 15:16).

228 420 *nice*: delicate.

232 421 *Marl-pit*: clay-pit. Marl was a kind of soil consisting principally of clay
mixed with carbonate of lime, valuable as a fertiliser.

234 422 *Maderas*: Jack probably refers to the (Portuguese) Madeira Islands,
originally known as the Madera Islands, located around 575 km off the
west coast of north Africa, north of the Canary Islands.

235 423 *Skreen*: presumably a handscreen of the kind used to protect the face in
front of a fire.

424 *more knows Tom Fool, than Tom Fool knows*: This proverb dates from the
mid-seventeenth century (as 'more know').

425 *Nevis ... Antegoa*: Nevis and Antigua belong to the Leeward Isles, in
the West Indies. Nevis has mineral springs.

236 426 *shagreen'd*: chagrined, upset.

237 427 *Gulph of Florida*: or the Straits of Florida; the waters off the east coast of
Florida.

428 *hint*: give some idea. (Defoe uses the word 'hint' here, as often elsewhere, without any suggestion of secret conveyance of meaning.)

238 429 *Brigantine*: a small vessel equipped both for sailing and rowing,
employed for purposes of piracy, espionage, landing, etc.

430 *crowded*: followed at maximum speed, i.e. with all sails set.

431 *a steern Chase*: The guns mounted on the upper deck of a sailing man-
of-war, fixed to fire directly ahead or astern, were known, respectively,
as the 'bow chase', to fire at a vessel being chased, and the 'stern chase'
to fire, as here, at a vessel chasing.

432 *spooning*: scudding.

433 *Road*: A 'road' is 'a sheltered piece of water near the shore where vessels
may lie at anchor in safety' (*OED*).

240 434 *an Act of Grace*: By an Act of Grace in 1717 three Jacobite lords were
released from the Tower, and about one hundred other rebels also freed.

435 *King GEORGE*: George I, first of the Hanoverian kings of Great Britain, reigning from 1714–27.

436 *given in*: committed.

437 *Gratitude is a Debt ... receiv'd remains*: see note 246 above.

241 438 *beating it up*: see note 297 above.

439 *the Bahama Channel*: the channel of water between the Bahama Islands
and the southern tip of Florida.

440 *Barco Longos*: A *barca-longa* was a large Spanish fishing boat, with two
or three masts.

441 *Goal*: a variant spelling of gaol.

442 *Alcade*: mayor.

page
241   443   *Intendant*: see note 326 above.

     444   *Corregidore*: chief magistrate.

     445   *his Catholick Majesty*: Philip V, the Bourbon king of Spain.

244   446   *Assiento*: assent.

     447   *respectively*: see note 403 above.

245   448   *Specie*: money, coin.

     449   *Commanderie*: ruling, ordinance.

246   450   *Flower*: variant spelling of flour.

     451   *Courser*: coarser.

     452   *Road*: see note 433 above.

     453   *Antient*: colours, pennant.

247   454   *Ells*: see note 182 above.

     455   *Bays*: i.e. baize, a kind of coarse open woollen fabric.

     456   *Grimace*: hypocritical pretence.

248   457   *Aviso*: i.e. advice-boat, a boat employed to bring news or intelligence.

     458   *lick my self whole*: recoup my losses.

249   459   *depending*: pending, still to be resolved.

250   460   *bad*: offered.

     461   *Cargaison, so they call it*: 'Cargaison' is the French, not the Spanish, word for 'cargo'.

252   462   *Drugets*: Druggets were a wool material, originally fine but more recently of coarse make. (But see next note.)

     463   *Says*: a cloth of fine texture, resembling serge.

253   464   *Barco Longos*: see note 440 above.

     465   *the famous Sir William Phipps*: In 1686–7, William Phips (1651–95), a Boston sea captain, led an expedition which located the wreck of the *Concepción*, which had foundered forty-two years earlier, off the Bahamas. Using native divers, he recovered silver worth £250,000, at that time a prodigious sum. He was later knighted by James II.

     466   *running away Trade, as they call it*: sailing before the so-called trade winds that in the southern hemisphere blow obliquely from the southeast towards the Equator.

     467   *St John d'Ulva*: i.e. San Juan de Ulúa, a large fortress on an island off the coast at Veracruz in Mexico.

254   468   *Hucksters*: persons ready to make their profit of anything in a mean or petty way; ones who basely barter their services for gain.

     469   *beating it up to Windward*: see note 297 above.

     470   *keeping the shoar of Florida on Board*: see note 389 above.

255   471   *St. Augustine*: off the Atlantic coast of Florida.

     472   *Tire*: tier.

257   473   *Medium*: compromise, middle course. See *Robinson Crusoe*, where the Portuguese captain who wants to buy Xury 'offer'd me this Medium'

page

(*The Novels*, Vol. 1, p. 81). Defoe's usage in *Robinson Crusoe* is the only one recorded in *OED*.

257   474   *Picaroon*: privateer (from the Spanish *picarón*, pirate).

        475   *the Rio Grand*: the Mississippi was known as the Rio Grand at this time.

258   476   *the Inquisition*: The Inquisition was active throughout Spanish and Portuguese possessions in the Americas in this period. (See Michael Baigent and Richard Leigh, *The Inquisition* (London, 1999), pp. 83–97.)

        477   *Super Cargo*: A supercargo is 'an officer on board a merchant ship whose business is to superintend the cargo and the commercial transaction of the voyage' (*OED*).

259   478   *Indian*: i.e. South American Indian.

260   479   *Cochoneal*: cochineal, a scarlet dye.

261   480   *du Roys*: a kind of coarse woollen cloth.

262   481   *strain'd Courtisies*: see note 255.

264   482   *without God in the World*: see Ephesians 2:12.

        483   *to abhor my self in Dust and Ashes*: Job 42:6.

        484   *whether*: whither.

TEXTUAL NOTES

The textual policy for *The Novels of Daniel Defoe* is described in the General Editors' Preface in Vol. 1, pp. 3–4.

The first edition of *The History and Remarkable Life of the Truly Honourable Col. Jacque* was almost certainly published in late December 1722, though dated 1723 on the title-page. (It was advertised as published 'this day' in the *Post Boy* for 18–20 December, and, also as 'this day', in *Mist's Weekly Journal* for 22 December 1722.) It was 'Printed, and Sold by J. Brotherton, at the Royal-Exchange; T. Payne, near Stationers-Hall; W. Mears, at the Lamb, and A. Dodd, at the Peacock without Temple-Bar; W. Chetwood, in Covent-Garden; J. Graves, in St. James's-Street; S. Chapman, in Pall Mall, and J. Stagg, at Westminster-Hall'. A so-called 'second edition', with the same imprint as the first, appeared in 1723. This had a partially reset and corrected title-page, but was otherwise a reissue of the first edition. A 'third edition' (for Brotherton, Payne, Mears, Graves, Chapman and Stagg) published in 1723 (though dated 1724 on the title-page) was also a reissue of the first edition, but with a cancel title-page which read as follows: 'The History and Remarkable Life of the Truly Honourable Colonel Jaque [*sic*], Vulgarly call'd, Colonel Jack; Who was Born a Gentleman, put 'Prentice to a Pick-Pocket, flourish'd Six and Twenty Years as a Thief, and was then Kidnapp'd to Virginia: Came back a Merchant, was Five Times married to Four Whores, went into the Wars, behav'd Bravely, got Preferment, was made Colonel of a Regiment, return'd again to England, follow'd the Fortunes of the Chevalier de St. George, is now Abroad compleating a Life of Wonders, and resolves to die a General'. A 'fourth edition' published by J. Applebee in 1738 (after Defoe's death) carried the title-page attribution 'by the author of *Robinson Crusoe*', and it continued to be described as such in subsequent editions in the eighteenth century. A Dutch translation, *Zeldzame levens-Beschryving van Kolonel Jack*, was published in 1729, and a

German translation, *Leben und Begebenheiten des Obristen Jacques, Von dem Autore des Englischchen Robinsons*, was published in 1740.

There is no reason to believe that Defoe had any involvement in any edition after the first, and so the copy-text used for the present edition is the first edition. Emendations to the title-page are based on the title-page of the second edition; other emendations are those of the present editor. In general, in line with the overall textual policy of the edition, treatment of the text has been conservative. However it should be noted that the first edition was not a particularly well printed work, and there are numerous obvious errors in punctuation (on average about one a page). These mainly involve the use of a semi-colon for a comma, and vice-versa, and the erroneous insertion or omission of commas. Significant emendations to punctuation are included in the list that follows, but where corrections are straightforward, and involve no question of meaning, they have been carried out silently.

29a Merchant, was Five times married to Four *Whores*] Merchant, married four Wives, and five of them prov'd *Whores*
29b *Chevalier, is still abroad*] *Chevalier, and is now abroad*
46a *Evans*] *Evens*
50a quite] quit
50b one] on
55a too] to
56a *says*] *saye*
60a cold. / But why must you sleep there no more? / They will take away my Money. / Here] cold. / They will take away my Money. / But why must you sleep there no more? / Here
60b that I knew] that knew
61a that it requires] that requires
64a then] than
66a above] aboth
67a him; if] him, if
69a off] of
70a him] me
71a he] I
71b *he*] *I*
95a 22*s.*] 2*s.*
96a was it not, no] was it, no
105a that had they any] that they had any
108a then] than
116a hand in it] hand it
116b then] than
118a that we were] that were

125a   removing,] so] removing, so
126a   [Duplicate] at all.] [Duplicate at all.]
127a   Servants and *Negroes*] Servants *Negroes*
130a   of] off
132a   then] than
146a   then] than
151a   Remedy. I] Remedy, I
158a   farther Discourses about on] farther about Discourses on
166a   to] too
168a   do. I] do, I
172a   what End] what to End
172b   I was drawn] I drawn
175a   too] to
178a   I] *she*
183a   at] as
192a   that the Prince] that Prince
195a   way, was passing] way, passing
195b   over powr'd] over pour'd
198a   tyr'd] try'd
204a   Suspicion. I] Suspicion, I
208a   he ever] he be ever
210a   then. I] then, I
212a   Wife, who was] Wife, was
217a   that] the
222a   up: Really] up, really
223a   cry'd. Mrs.] cry'd, Mrs.
225a   the] that
225b   far. I] far, I
226a   far'd] fair'd
227a   too] to
228a   him he was] him was
228b   admirable in Conversation] admirable Conversation
232a   surpriz'd with Joy] surpriz'd Joy
234a   was Circumstanced] was, Circumstances
244a   I,] he,
247a   piece of 30 Ells fine] piece 30 Ells of fine
253a   to] too
258a   Purveyor] Purvor
260a   Price] Piece